Praise for *The Social Future of Academic Libraries*

'Libraries are a people business and their greatest asset are the relationships they can foster and create. But how do we do this and who do we need to connect with? How do we ensure we truly engage and are able to measure that meaning and impact? This book helps to present not only the theory in which we might think about what we do but provides a wealth of examples of it in practice. Although aimed at academic libraries with a US and UK focus this book transcends geographic and sector boundaries. It is a must read for those looking to ensure their libraries not only stay relevant, but drive a culture of innovation and ensure real and lasting impact.'
Michelle Blake, University Librarian, University of Waikato, New Zealand

'By viewing academic libraries afresh through a social lens, *The Social Future of Academic Libraries* provides a thought-provoking challenge to the conventional "space, collections and services" model. A convincing case is made that a renewed, strategic focus on relationships and networks is required if libraries and librarians are to maintain their future value, especially following the impact of the COVID pandemic. This book successfully balances theory and practice; a rigorously academic and wide-ranging survey of intellectual and social capital theory is then illustrated through a diverse set of case studies.'
Christopher Cipkin, Director of Library, Learning Support and Culture, Royal Holloway, University of London, UK

'An important, timely and challenging book whose contributions combine to make new sense of how the social function of academic libraries has evolved and will need to transform further in the future to deliver a compelling and relevant value proposition in dynamically changing societal and higher education environments. The deep understanding it enables of underpinning concepts such as social capital, shared value and social networks, allied to explorations of specific areas of library practice through a social lens, is invaluable in informing the current and future positioning of academic libraries and the skillsets required of those who work in them.'
John Cox, University Librarian, University of Galway, Ireland

'Engagement is critical to the success and sustainability of academic libraries. This book provides a much needed analysis of the "broader intellectual framework in which libraries endeavour to engage their users" as stated in Tim Schlak's Introduction. This is not a book about the usual debate on the value of libraries per se, it encompasses higher-level, broader and intellectual discussion on social capital, network theory and value and offers in-depth perspectives on the social futures of academic libraries, leading to interesting theoretical insights about their evolving position in different contexts. It is highly readable and would be a valuable resource for both librarians and non-librarians keen to understand various intellectual perspectives about the social capital of libraries.'
Gulcin Cribb, Chair, IFLA Academic and Research Libraries Section 2019– and former University Librarian, Singapore Management University 2012–20

'This book is important and timely as libraries continue to cope with the disruptions of COVID-19 and consider their identity and purpose in a post-pandemic world. It presents multiple perspectives through which libraries can plan their future in responsible, social and sustainable ways. It points forward by presenting theory and practice and reflecting broader social influences and trends within the higher education sector and academic library community.'

Dr Mary Delaney, Head of Library and Information Services, South East Technological University, Carlow, Ireland

'This is an exciting book. Exciting because of the important contribution it makes to the new library story and how it aligns with developments within higher education. Under the general heading of the "social turn", it explores the relational networked role of the library within research and learning institutions, and how this role supports the collaborative, emergent redesign of the library and its scope. Refreshingly, it locates more practical and concrete accounts of library interests within wider organizational and social contexts. In this context, it surveys the literatures of social network theory, organizational development, social capital, management and marketing, among other areas. An especially important contribution is how it raises up the sometimes invisible relational work that libraries and librarians do, and places it very much at the center of library work and value.'

Lorcan Dempsey, independent library adviser and writer

'This is an exciting new edited collection that uses social capital theory as a lens to explore key aspects of academic library work. Grounding librarianship within questions of networks, communities and participation, this approach offers a novel perspective on traditional areas of librarian expertise. It also provides a guiding structure for the development of new and emerging areas of practice as libraries evolve to meet the demands of their local contexts. A must read for anyone interested in the past, present and future of academic library work!'

Dr Alison Hicks, Programme Director, Library and Information Studies, University College London, UK; Editor-in-Chief, *Journal of Information Literacy*

'This strategic assemblage of voices provides a unified and necessary framework for thinking about the future of academic libraries positioned within the broader campus context using social capital, social network and design thinking theory. The book recognizes the importance of libraries turning outward toward their campus communities, working together with college and university colleagues to redefine the evolving and valuable role of libraries within the academy. As academic libraries move from transactional toward a more relational and participatory culture, this book brings together theory with practice to provide useful new approaches to reimagining how the Library 3.0 can engage with the broader campus community to co-create a new vision for the academy's post-pandemic future.'

Nancy Kranich, Teaching Professor, Rutgers University School of Communication and Information; Special Projects Librarian, Rutgers University Libraries, USA; and Past President, American Library Association

'The social future of academic libraries is uncertain. In the uncharted waters of expectations that are disturbed by frequent change in academic library communities, *The Social Future of Academic Libraries* is a valuable lighthouse. Authoritative, stimulating and useful, it is a wonderful resource for academics and practitioners alike, providing timely thoughts on how to reorient academic libraries so that connections are prioritized over collections and space. This is the surest way to turn academic libraries into centers of knowledge for students and faculty in the twenty-first century.'
Tom Kwanya, Professor of Knowledge Management and Director, School of Information and Communication Studies, The Technical University of Kenya

'Recent years have been marked by multiple crises: COVID-19, market recession, and the major war in the centre of Europe that is deepening economic, energy, and ecological problems. The solutions will demand even more intensive collaboration on each level of society than before. This book explores the future role of academic libraries in terms of social engagement and participation through a collection of thoughtful essays and enticing stories with the focus on attracting multiple partners and trust building. It is both useful and necessary in the contemporary context.'
Elena Maceviciute, Professor, Swedish School of Library and Information Science, University of Borås, Sweden; Deputy Editor of *Information Research*; and Professor, the Faculty of Communication, Vilnius University, Lithuania

The
Social Future of
Academic Libraries

Every purchase of a Facet book helps to fund CILIP's advocacy, awareness and accreditation programmes for information professionals.

The
Social Future of
Academic Libraries

New Perspectives on Communities, Networks and Engagement

Edited by
Tim Schlak, Sheila Corrall
and Paul J. Bracke

facet
publishing

Published by Facet Publishing
7 Ridgmount Street, London WC1E 7AE
www.facetpublishing.co.uk

Facet Publishing is wholly owned by CILIP: the Library and Information Association.

British Library Cataloguing in Publication Data
A catalogue record for this book is available from the British Library.

ISBN 978-1-78330-471-4 (paperback)
ISBN 978-1-78330-472-1 (hardback)
ISBN 978-1-78330-473-8 (PDF)
ISBN 978-1-78330-517-9 (EPUB)

First published 2022

Text printed on FSC accredited material.

Typeset from editors' files in 10/13 pt American Garamond and Frutiger
by Flagholme Publishing Services.
Printed and made in Great Britain by CPI Group (UK) Ltd, Croydon, CR0 4YY.

Contents

Figures, Tables and Boxes

A Note on the Online Glossary and Bibliography

Written in response to the dynamic social conditions challenging higher education, *The Social Future of Academic Libraries* charts the trajectory of academic librarianship from a traditional collections–services–space model to the communities–networks–engagement paradigm required for the 21st century. Combining thematic reviews and case studies with thought pieces and conceptual overviews, this multi-authored work offers a wide-ranging introduction to the application of social capital theory to academic library practice.

A key feature of the book is the provision of additional **downloadable resources** designed to help readers navigate the present text and accelerate future practitioner take-up of the perspectives and frameworks introduced in the narrative. The two resources each integrate an **authoritative glossary of key terms and concepts** discussed or referenced in the current volume with a **selective bibliography of classic and contemporary literature** suggested as further reading and thought starters for readers interested in exploring the application of the concepts and theories described to their own institutions and practices.

Each of our two 'biblio-glossaries' explains around 100 concepts and contains more than 125 bibliographical citations. They are designed for use both as an online companion to *The Social Future of Academic Libraries*, to help readers make sense of unfamiliar material as they go through the text, and as stand-alone tools, to support practitioner learning and engagement with vital new ways of thinking about academic library practice and research.

Rather than supplying our own working definitions, we have based our explanations of concepts and terms on the primary literature of the field, using the words and phrases of their originators (authors or translators) to explain meanings and bring out nuances that distinguish alternative interpretations of the same concept. In many cases you will find two or more definitions of terms that reflect different perspectives on a concept or illustrate its evolutionary development. We have also included cross-referencing and notes to highlight related terms and variant terminology. You can use the accompanying lists of references to gain additional insights into the concepts defined and to explore potential applications to your own practice and research.

The first glossary has a more theoretical focus on the terminology of intellectual and social capital scholarship, while the second resource has a more practical orientation on terms related to the social turn in higher education. Together they offer a ready-made conceptual toolkit for colleagues motivated to engage with emergent capital-based frameworks that offer fresh perspectives on the social issues and problems facing contemporary academic libraries. Both resources can be downloaded from the Facet Publishing website at www.facetpublishing.co.uk/socialfuture. To facilitate navigation between the book and these companion resources, we have highlighted terms covered in the glossaries on their first use in each chapter, using **bold text** for terms in the *Intellectual and Social Capital and Networks* glossary and ***bold italics*** for terms in the *Social Development of Higher Education* glossary.

Key concepts in intellectual and social capital and networks

The conceptual landscape of intellectual and social capital is complex, pluralist and dynamic. The academic and professional literature reveals diverse perspectives, eclectic interpretations and continual development of new forms of capital as sub-components, specific combinations or rival versions of existing concepts that have been found wanting, which makes this a challenging and rewarding field of scholarship. Social capital concepts and theories have proven value as frameworks for understanding what is going on in higher education and how things could be done differently to achieve better outcomes, but so far have not been widely adopted in academic libraries. The case studies and supporting literature in *The Social Future of Academic Libraries* demonstrate that capital perspectives have the potential to enhance professional practice across many areas, including collection development, data services, information literacy, liaison librarianship, library fundraising, service design, space utilisation, subject specialties and student success. Our glossary aims to make social capital scholarship more accessible and valuable to academic librarians.

Key concepts in the social development of higher education

The social turn in higher education has been influenced and shaped by government bodies, student movements and university coalitions as well as wider social developments that have forced institutions to rethink their roles and responsibilities in the knowledge economy and participatory society of the 21st century. Commercialisation, digitalisation, massification and globalisation have transformed academic activities, professional practices and institutional relationships, generating new ways of doing things and novel vocabulary for changed modes of working, including the development of specialist terminology and adoption of particular meanings for everyday terms. Social trends are playing out differently around the world, but with common interests centred on community, democracy, engagement, participation, relationships and sustainability. Our second glossary defines the educational and social contexts forming the operational and strategic environment for academic librarians. It concentrates on current issues and concerns, but also includes terms originating in particular countries that are not widely used in other parts of the world.

Contributors

The editors
Paul J. Bracke is the Dean of the Foley Library and Associate Provost for Research and Interdisciplinary Initiatives at Gonzaga University. Prior to joining Gonzaga, he served in leadership roles at Purdue University and the University of Arizona. He holds a Master of Science in Library and Information Science degree from the University of Illinois and a PhD in Higher Education from the University of Arizona. His research interests are in organisational development for academic libraries and community-based infrastructure to support digital scholarship.

Sheila Corrall worked in public libraries and the British Library before moving into higher education where she directed library, information and technology services at three United Kingdom universities. In 2004 she became Professor of Librarianship and Information Management at the University of Sheffield and served as Head of the iSchool before moving in 2012 to the University of Pittsburgh as Chair of the Library and Information Science program. She retired in 2019, but continues to work on strategic issues for libraries, including data literacy, intellectual capital, open movements, professional development and reflective practice.

Tim Schlak is the former Dean of the University Library at Robert Morris University, where he now works as Associate Provost for Academic Alliances. He holds a PhD and Master's in Library and Information Science as well as an MA in Russian Literature. His research interests range from social capital and leadership development to organisational theory.

The contributors
Michael Brenes is Associate Director of the Brady-Johnson Program in Grand Strategy and Lecturer in History at Yale University. From 2017 to 2019, he was the Senior Archivist for American Diplomacy in Manuscripts and Archives at the Yale University Library. His writing has appeared in multiple outlets, including the *New York Times* and the *Chronicle of Higher Education.*

Andrew Dillon is the V. M. Daniel Professor of Information Science and former Dean of the School of Information at the University of Texas at Austin. His research interests focus on our understanding of human behaviours and experiences in an evolving information infrastructure so as to enable designs that augment all lives appropriately. He serves as co-editor of the journal *Information & Culture* and on the board of directors of Patient Privacy Rights, a group committed to enhancing individual privacy in the health domain.

Kathryn Dilworth is Professor of Practice for Philanthropy, John Martinson Honors College, Purdue University. She has worked as a frontline fundraiser in a wide variety of nonprofit sectors, including higher education, libraries, museums, conservation and hospitals. Her consulting practice, GoodRuption, is built upon her social capital-based fundraising model. She holds a PhD in Philanthropy from the Lilly Family School of Philanthropy at Indiana University, where she teaches in the Master's program. Her research is focused on fundraising practice and the role of philanthropy in community well-being.

Amanda L. Folk is assistant professor and Head of Teaching & Learning at the Ohio State University Libraries. Her research interests include the exploration of the development of undergraduate students' information literacy, as well as understanding the library experiences of student populations who have traditionally been marginalised in higher education in the United States. She was the recipient of the 2020 Association of College and Research Libraries Instruction Section's Ilene F. Rockman Instruction Publication of the Year Award and currently serves as editor-in-chief for *The Journal of Academic Librarianship.*

Scott Fralin is the Exhibit Program Manager and Learning Environments Librarian at the Virginia Tech Libraries, where he works directly with faculty and students to create exhibits based on the work students are doing in classes at Virginia Tech. His interests include creative place-making and devising new and interesting ways to share student and faculty works. He received his Master of Information Science from the University of Tennessee, Knoxville.

Alice Kalinowski is the Manager, Public Services, Research & Discovery at the Stanford Graduate School of Business Library. She was previously the Business Librarian at the University of Pittsburgh, where she received a Master of Library and Information Science. Her research interests include knowledge management and user experience in academic libraries.

Matthew Kelly holds a PhD in Library and Information Science from the University of South Australia. His research interests include bibliometric methods to improve public library collection management and the epistemics of librarianship. He is currently a member of the editorial advisory board of the journal *Collection and Curation* and is the CEO of Library Management Australia.

James Kessenides is the Kaplanoff Librarian for American History at the Yale University Library. His research interests include the digitisation of historical materials, and scholarly communication and publishing in the humanities. He currently serves on the editorial board of Association of College and Research Libraries Publications in Librarianship.

Andrea Kosavic is Associate Dean of Libraries, Digital Engagement and Strategy, York University, Canada. Her research interests include scholarly recognition and communication, copyright, political economy, gift economies and social capital. She holds a Master of Information Studies from the University of Toronto and is a PhD candidate with the Department of Communications and Culture at York University.

Rebecca Metzger is Associate University Librarian for Learning & Engagement at UC Santa Barbara. Prior to receiving her Master of Library and Information Science from Simmons College, she was a public relations officer for various art museums, arts organisations and artists in New York City. Metzger has taught continuing education courses on library marketing, held leadership positions in the Library Leadership and Management Association and Association of College and Research Libraries and serves on the advisory board of the open access *Marketing Libraries Journal.*

Alice Rogers is currently manager of the Media Design Studios at Virginia Tech and has previously served as manager of the Active Learning Curation Program. Her interests are centred on bringing academic work to public spaces and creative storytelling through multimedia projects. She holds an MA in Ethnomusicology from University of Maryland, College Park.

Sara Sweeney Bear is the Fusion Studio Manager and Learning Space Assessment Coordinator for the University Libraries at Virginia Tech. She holds an MA Ed. in Higher Education from Virginia Tech. Her interests include developing environments and instruction to support collaboration and exploring the role of play in adult learning.

Minglu Wang is a Research Data Management Librarian at York University, Canada. Before joining York University Libraries, she had been a Data Services Librarian at Rutgers University for eight years with direct experience supporting Research Data Management (RDM) initiatives. She has published a number of book chapters, conference papers and research articles that are closely related to academic libraries and RDM services.

Foreword: Capital, Value and the Becoming Library

A welcome for the book

It is a privilege and a pleasure to write the foreword for this book on *The Social Future of Academic Libraries*, and especially kind to be invited to contribute from this side of the Atlantic to a work largely based on the thought and experience of United States (US) colleagues. Over the last twenty-five years my own practice and theory has been immeasurably enriched, and my life generally made more enjoyable, through association with North American colleagues, partners and friends. Writing the foreword to this volume allows me the indulgence of continuing that dialogue.

This work contributes to a tradition in our field that seeks to understand libraries as part of broader social worlds. Librarians have always been curious about their own world and willing to change it, despite the tropes often attached to the profession. In the earlier parts of the last century, as a result of the broader trend for understanding organisations using scientific methods, librarians also became driven with the idea of librarianship as a science and towards the adoption of what was termed scientific management. This was not unhelpful, but had a tendency to restrict library thinking to processes and systems within its own black box and for measurement of the social dimensions and impacts of library activity to be considered too difficult. Perceptive commentators were able to consider social aspects beyond that black box of internal processes, but these ideas were often, in Blaise Cronin's (2008, p. 466) description, 'inchoate'. Margaret Egan's (1955) contribution of the idea of social epistemology to build on European ideas of documentation recognised that social value is created through behaviour that develops social impact, and that the library could be viewed 'as a social agency . . . ultimately in support of the smooth functioning and continued progress of society' (Furner 2004, p. 802).

Egan records John Dewey's shock of realisation that social concerns were of relevance to the sacred core of information science in indexing, classification and retrieval. I encountered a similar reaction very early in my career when challenging the late Jack Mills on how he could talk about classification for an hour without once mentioning users and their own identities and beliefs as a contribution to knowledge organisation. Much of what interested thinkers in the past in that classical period of documentation research has now been effectively outsourced in the contemporary academic library. Although Cronin rightly suggests that social philosophers whose work was cited in professional discourse indicated a sociological turn in information science, neither information science nor library philosophy theorists have yet constructed an encompassing social theory in which to base library practice or prove social value.

The very names of library science and information science are perhaps no longer as helpful as they were in earlier times. The period since the 1970s has been one of continuous adaptation to new realities for libraries. For those of us whose careers have coincided exactly with this period, a tightly bounded scientific model of libraries has not been sufficient to deal with changes in technology, society and, in particular, our users and their expectations. Our libraries were never merely clockwork, but always 'cloudy' in Popperian terms, however static and solid we may have tried to make them. The material, shape and design of libraries in the academy has always been formed by social pressures and influences, and not always for the better where these forces created injustice in collections, services and the management of people and patrons.

What is needed now are other ways of understanding the library, and one of these ways will be in a library social science. Gathering momentum since the early 1990s has been the need to form a better understanding of libraries through what might be called a social turn. The development and application of social theory and its associated methods of research and analysis to libraries has occurred as much through the enthusiasm and curiosity of individual librarians at all levels as through any concerted movement. To a girl or boy with a hammer, everything looks like a nail, and the fields of library assessment and performance particularly have been driven by practitioners who have found a new hammer from the available range of social theory and techniques with which to address individual local library problems. This admirable drive is well reflected in this book, providing evidence of a dynamic and expanding range of perspectives and experience towards a more developed intellectual framework for our social value. I therefore welcome this volume as an important addition to both the theoretical and practical understanding of libraries.

The editors

Libraries have responded to change much better over this period than many organisations or other parts of their parent institutions. We are by nature both a reflective and a practical profession, and leadership plays a key role in facilitating change through encouraging those at all levels in their libraries to explore, investigate and change libraries for the better. I have always thought it important that library leaders should also write in order to share their perspectives, assumptions, experience and resulting accrued wisdom. A long time ago a predecessor of Sheila Corrall as University Librarian at Reading University wrote about library power (Thompson 1974), decrying his contemporaries' failure to exercise their influence fully, and argued for a more elite corps of candidates for senior posts. Preparation for leadership has improved substantially since the early 1990s and this volume demonstrates an effective partnership across its editors, combining their wise authority, energy and innovative thinking. They are all leaders with experience of success beyond their library within their respective institutions, and each of whom has engaged with study and research into our profession, as well as facilitating the contribution of other professionals to this volume to help them develop their own professional knowledge and understanding, and to share it with others.

My first association with Professor Corrall began in the early 1990s within the quality movement when we were both relatively new to library leadership positions and seeking to draw in contemporary management trends to the benefit of our own libraries and professional understanding generally. Sheila has consistently opened up library thinking to broader management theory, and our approaches since that time have been similarly driven by appreciation of library users and stakeholders. Sheila and I have been involved in some of the movements that have helped underpin this turn either theoretically or pragmatically: quality, information literacy, strategic appreciation and organisational leadership; and now to a broader understanding of library value as constituted by capital. A well-deserved consequence of her intellect and energy has been moves to direct two of the world's highest-rated library schools. Sheila thus occupies a unique position as research library leader, researcher and teacher with experience on both sides of the Atlantic. Her desire for successful libraries continues unabated.

Paul Bracke is the Dean of the Foley Library at Gonzaga University, with additional responsibility for the Office of Sponsored Research and Programs, and is also now Associate Provost of the new Institute for Research and Interdisciplinary Initiatives. He was a member of the Association of College and Research Libraries (ACRL) Leadership Fellows program. I became interested in Paul's work while he was at Purdue through his contribution to the International Performance Measurement conference. I was pleased to include his paper on relationship capital in the conference special edition of *Library Management*. This article pointed up the historic lack of appropriate measurement for library liaison activity and proposed social network theory as a potential model for future assessment. Paul has also been active in research data management, open access publishing, digitisation and scholarly workflows. He brings relevant and important appreciation to this volume as a key player in ACRL's current work on extending the open scholarly publication agenda towards social and ethical issues of diversity, equality and inclusion.

Tim Schlak also fulfils a leadership position at Robert Morris University. In common with the other editors, his role has gone beyond the library into joining the institutional leadership team, with a focus on academic alliances. Important to the ideas in this book have been his reflective thoughts on leadership in the *Journal of Library Administration*. Tim has also provided probably the most extensive and trenchant application of social capital to academic librarianship, via a series of articles in *Library Management*, the *Journal of Academic Librarianship* and the *Journal of Library Administration*. While most other authors have concentrated on developing social capital concepts for one particular constituency or context, Tim has applied the idea to library leadership and management, liaison librarianship and faculty and student engagement. His most recent work on the significance of social capital to library leadership and its connections to trust and values brings an important appreciation to this volume.

All three editors have opened themselves up to learning from beyond the traditional boundaries of the library and information science discipline and have shown themselves not only to be good leaders but also thoughtful and reflexive researchers. In Paul's and Tim's cases it is pleasing to see members of a new generation of leaders coming through to take libraries forward towards the future and giving time to advancing professional knowledge in the process.

Libraries, social capital and value: a personal response

A particular strength of this book is its combination of theory and practice, creating a work of international significance for librarians, teachers and researchers. Kurt Lewin's dictum that there is nothing more practical than a good theory applies here, and in his terms this book can be seen as a compendium of applied action research cases based on a range of social theory. My own interest in this book is in its contribution to the search for a more developed (social) theory of libraries through this approach, and towards the end of demonstrating impact on institutions and communities. In our context it might be said that library theorists and theories have struggled to keep pace with the lived experience of library practice in the academy, suggesting a need for a deeper reflection on the contemporary role and value of libraries. At the same time there is much untapped work in the broader social science and management field that also to me cries out to be applied, or at least considered, as relevant to library practice. This book is important and timely to that process of sense-making of what libraries are, what they do and how they understand themselves.

My personal connection to this work has been through a desire to understand, project and advocate the value of libraries, from an academic library leadership perspective and in my research. This has been a 30-year journey through ideas and applications of quality in the 1990s, to value and impact with the Society of College, National and University Libraries (SCONUL) initiative in the first decade of this century, and ultimately to the broader social value of libraries expressed in a capital scorecard (Town 2018). Capital is a polysemic concept, and one of very long duration, since its origins are in the counting of heads of cattle. The economic term has been used in a material sense for the worth of goods used in the making of other goods at least since the 17th century, implying that a valuation can be made of these assets. Adam Smith extended the idea to the contribution of human agency, and over the last century a plethora of immaterial assets have become candidates for valuation from a broad range of social relations, institutions and human capabilities (Hodgson 2014). The building of social capital through libraries has been recognised at least since Nancy Kranich's term as President of the American Library Association (ALA) in 2000–2001 (Kranich 2020). The authors in this volume have come to ideas of social capital through different routes; some through Robert Putnam, some through Pierre Bourdieu and others through Bruno Latour. This work makes these ideas seem more visible and relevant to libraries through collecting them together. There will be other strands of social science and philosophy in future to draw on to provide a more complete picture. The question of the full assessment of library value remains open, despite the dismissive response at US immigration when I said the purpose of a trip to the country was to speak to the ALA about library value, this being that 'everyone knows libraries are valuable'.

Following James Coleman, capital is inherent in relations between persons and among persons to make it distinct, and it is here where origins of value lie. David Graeber's (2013, p. 219) ethnographic perspective suggests that there is something out there called 'value' and that human beings organise their lives, feelings and desires around its furtherance: 'It is value that brings universes into being'. This suggests that we can see social worlds not just as a collection of persons and things, but as a project of mutual creation of value, as something collectively made and remade, and this is perhaps a good picture for thinking about the future of libraries. Natasha Gerolami (2015) almost uniquely in the library literature draws on Deleuze and Guattari (1988) to recognise the library-as-assemblage in this respect, although libraries have been thought of as assemblages for over a thousand years. The new concept of assemblage as a range of entangled heterogeneous entities in relation, in which each component has its own vibrant dynamic, provides a different set of metaphors for social worlds such as libraries, which might be as a mosaic or patchwork in transitory and exchangeable configurations. I think this volume begins to move the picture of the research library onwards from libraries beyond simply transcending traditional walls and boundaries, to libraries as a spectrum of agentic capabilities involving different people, materials, documents, tools, values and tangible and intangible capital assets, not all necessarily fully owned, tightly controlled or completely organised and managed in a traditional sense (Bennett 2010).

It is gratifying to see one's own work on library capital critically quoted in several of the contributions here, as this is the best way to develop and explain it further. The way I now see my own doctoral work on organisational value (Town 2018), building on Martha Kyrillidou and my original conception of a future-oriented capital scorecard (Town & Kyrillidou 2013), is as a hybrid but porous and enfolded set of dimensions feeding off each other in either a virtuous spiral of becoming, or a vicious spiral of decline. The idea of the library as a creative institution was a fundamental part of recognising momentum (the pace of innovation) within the scorecard. The main dimensions were differentiated to reflect a requirement for proofs of worth across two perspectives; the hybridity here reflecting the practical need for leaders to provide justification within increasingly neoliberal economic and managerial institutional values of tangible capital assets and competitive innovation, while retaining a balance that gives weight and worth to the more intangible but no less real value and impact of the library as a collaborative, virtuous and relational common good.

This book brings out some of the organisational tensions that arise from that hybridity. Most of those tensions have been considerably heightened since I wrote 10 years ago about the variety of cross-pressures on those who manage and seek measures to reflect the contribution to that common good (Town 2011). Alasdair MacIntyre (1981) suggests that practices will always be in ethical debate with the institutions that contain them, and this seems to be increasingly true of libraries and their university institutions in this recent period of economic crisis, pandemic and publishing reformation. While my position is now within a management school, I took that role to try to develop my own understanding of the library as organisation. This is still driven by ideas of excellence, but more importantly now into ethical organisation, and its people being engaged in virtuous practice with that common good in mind. This also involves saying clearly what we do and linking it to society's broader ethical frameworks. The activities and services that form part of the library's total value proposition are well reflected in the chapter contributions here.

A suggestion for reading

The volume has been carefully curated in terms of blending the various contributions together in a logical sequence, and may be read to advantage successively in that way. Tim Schlak's Introduction provides an excellent digest of the content and it will not be my purpose to anticipate it. That contribution sets out the context, key ideas and also the tone and style of the work, which is maintained throughout by careful and sensitive editing.

I provide here a few thoughts from my own perspective as to one alternative way of how to read the contributions. Drawing on S. R. Ranganathan's laws, probably each chapter or group will have its own reader, related to particular precise needs and current concerns. Some readers will want to engage with theory first; others may be more eager to dip into favourite areas of practice.

The book is organised into a contextual and theoretical prelude in Part 1 to the empirical descriptions and analyses of Part 2. I found it fruitful in the first part of the work to follow each individual editor's chain of thought through their respective chapters. Sheila Corrall's contributions in Chapters 1, 3 and 5 provide a thoroughgoing review of the broader social influences and trends that are impacting and influencing libraries in the academy, moving from the broad societal level, through the changeful nature of the academy, to the social purpose of its libraries. Taken together, these position the book selectively in time, space and within trends in social ideology, identifying the potential existential threats we face. Tim Schlak in Chapters 4 and 6 provides the necessary grounding in core concepts of social capital together with a potential program to meet the required transformative challenge, placing organisational learning at its heart. Paul Bracke's Chapter 2 focuses on association, linking social network theory to libraries as both an essential ontological component and a vital epistemological method for analysis and understanding. Paul's Conclusion teases out the various strands of thought and practice provided by the contributors that will help the library's dynamic reconfiguration. The global pandemic's sharpening and accelerating influence on contemporary academic library social positioning and service trends is also covered here. The online BiblioGlossaries of terminology and concepts will be an essential help for those new to this field.

In Part 2 I found it useful to follow the threads of my own historic interests and managerial concerns.

Relationships

Given my own interest in the question of the relationship of academic fields to the library I started my selection on this topic. The organisation and people structures focused on relations with academic fields, disciplines and departments have occupied my mind as a library leader for over 30 years, but with increasing attention required over later periods with the advent of new research-related services and the resulting more direct library involvement in academic processes. The chapters by Metzger, Kalinowski, Kessenides and Brenes, and Kosavic and Wang seemed to me to provide a broad range of helpful thought and practice on those issues.

In Chapter 7 James Kessenides and Michael Brenes provide a useful historical review focused on US professionalism and subject specialism. I think this connects well with Alice Kalinowski's thoughts in Chapter 11 on the intersectionality of liaison relationships and turnover. When mapping is undertaken it is possible to see the vast unrecognised and undervalued hinterland of relationships and activities that libraries provide to underpin the academic enterprise. I was also forcibly reminded of the irritation of academic staff at the constant reorganising of academic liaison roles without consideration of the disruption of loss of knowledge capital. It is pleasing to see the practice of engaging faculty in recruitment of new liaison staff surfaced in print. The issue of loyalty is also raised, and this has become a key virtue in my own consideration of working lives in the academy. There are many stories still to be told here in terms of how these relationships are developed and created, to say nothing of the subcultures involved within and beyond the library, deserving more ethnographic investigation.

This approach figures in Chapter 12, in which Rebecca Metzger describes the experience of her own seven-year formation as an 'outreach and collaboration' manager. This autoethnographic story reveals some of the gaps in understanding and organisation that hamper the achievement of the 'engaged library' and provides an insightful commentary on the absorption of new theories into existing practices. In my experience it is both difficult and frustrating to be obliged to bind the library into institutional programs that are founded on weaker theories and practice than the library's own understanding and historical applications in this field. The lure of what Juris Dilevko (2009, p. 56) called the 'short-term patina of dynamic sexiness' of new terminology for old ideas seems irresistible to administration in the academy. Andrea Kosavic and Minglu Wang in Chapter 10 take a social capital perspective on structural approaches to the extension of the library's role to research data management. Interestingly, using a quantitative symbolic capital approach reveals some key issues and obstacles around rank and status. The unique positionality of the library in the academy, and the key role of the library director, is recognised here, and although I no longer have to make these decisions, I find myself still torn by the question of how much the library should structure itself around its market of academic disciplines, or whether the demands of specialised knowledge for new processes and technologies should override this. The answer will probably be contextual, but having started my career as a medical librarian I still have an enduring sense of what a good subject specialist or liaison librarian can be.

Information literacy

It was also a pleasure to return to thinking about information literacy (IL), provoked by Amanda Folk's Chapter 8. Sheila Corrall and I worked together with others in SCONUL and CILIP two decades ago to champion and define the first national United Kingdom frameworks and models for information literacy, and so I appreciate attempts to sharpen and develop the concept. There is a justifiable critique here of lack of theory, and a concern which I share for the reductionism and commodification of IL programs to tools and skills. The recognition of IL as a component of the Bourdieusian social capital we try to develop in students extends beyond the idea of academic cultural capital into a form of wisdom as a habit of practice for life. The idea of IL as wisdom was central to the origination of the first SCONUL model in 1999. It is an enduring regret that this understanding was then largely submerged amid the political requirement to focus on the skills agenda, and the weakness of subsequent theorising, and pleasing to see it rediscovered in the deeper appreciation developing here.

Space

The current heavy investment in library as place in the academy is especially gratifying to those of us who lived through being told our libraries would become car parks. This is another area in which theory is struggling to keep pace with the creative acceleration of practice, and Andrew Dillon in Chapter 15 mounts a plea for incorporating more design thinking and practice. This provides a supporting theory and justification for the type of innovative and collaborative design activity that is a feature of the more strategically minded libraries in higher education. In my experience it is vital to temper the supposed rationality of architects and designers with a vision to create a variety of affective social spaces of wonder, creativity and enchantment. Alice Rogers, Sarah Sweeney Bear and Scott Fralin's Chapter 9 on the studio creation approach in their institution deploys social network analysis as a success measure in achieving these environments, demonstrating how social theory can be incorporated into the formality of program management.

Community

Social impact on our communities is vital to justifying the library. Kathryn Dilworth in Chapter 14 applies her Social Capital Fundraising Model (SCFM) as intentional leverage for fundraising activities. The lack of outside recognition of the library as an institutional fundraising unit can ring true in some environments. I was fortunate for much of my career to work in an avowedly entrepreneurial university in which all methods of earning additional income were understood as both the method and route to achieving a virtuous spiral of increasing both tangible and intangible assets, as well as building the library's reputational capital.

Last in this brief personal review of the book's content, but by no means least, is Matthew Kelly's Chapter 13 contribution on community reading. This brought the empirical chapters to an end where the ending probably should be, in the library's role in developing the social capital of others. The recognition that libraries create social capital in their users puts them at the heart of forming and providing a mechanism for greater equality in society. Kelly is critical of distinctions between public and academic library collection policies. The boundaries between libraries serving different communities can and should be much more porous, and relationships formed to enhance integration are called for to move 'from clique to community'. A new sense of pride in our fundamental purpose seems an appropriate virtue to aim at here.

The becoming library

Two recent works on library history have pointed up the fragility of libraries (Pettegree & der Weduwen 2021; Ovenden 2020). While I share Richard Ovenden's anger at recent wanton destructions of libraries, there is also hope from the evidence in these stories of the library's long-term survival. The most recent pandemic seems more a story of resilient strength rather than fragility. While the vibrant but transient material nature of libraries is undeniable, outside accidents, it is power and ideology that usually dictates survival. A social world is a universe of presuppositions in which violence is a potential, and the presuppositions about libraries require positive influence through our own charisma and symbolic capital. Ovenden (2020, p. 225) suggests that 'The educational role of libraries and archives is truly powerful' and we need to deploy all our powers to counter current existential threats and violent disruption. Libraries continue to be one of the things that people find important in life, and, to persuade people to invest in our future, we will need a complete sense of our value beyond the economic. This will come from a fuller understanding of our social field (in Bourdieu's terms) as part of an armamentarium to be deployed against the contemporary pressures upon us. There is a continuing need to be able to offer a sense of our value that is not simply defined within our field boundary, but one that resonates and transcends politically and socially beyond, to our parent institutions and to our wider communities as we move into the future.

'Becoming' conveys at least two ideas in English. A library can thus be becoming in the sense of attractively suitable, and also in the ontological sense of prioritising changefulness over organisation as the current reality (Shotter & Chia 2002, drawing on *inter alia* William James and Henri Bergson). Attractive suitability seems a sensible aim for future libraries, and this reinforces the relevance of the positive ideas of social capital highlighted in this book, as well as prompting more consideration of the moral virtues that develop attraction, such as equity, fairness, justice, trustworthiness and wise leadership. In my experience, academic libraries have sometimes been held back from achieving organisational virtue through the academy's traditions of hierarchy, exclusionary behaviours and utilitarian human capital policies, as well as by their own unwise ethical choices. There is a considerable challenge here in achieving the simultaneously virtuous and becoming library, with librarians successfully becoming the *animateurs* sought by James Thompson (1974) in creating the capital necessary to be a positive social force.

I should perhaps finish this preamble where I started, with dialogue. The future library will be an act of mutual creation achieved through dialogue. There will no doubt be much debate about detail, and between those in established practices, traditions and rituals as opposed to iconoclasts, innovators and the impatient; but I would suggest it is possible to be all of these simultaneously, as well as tolerant of others with different perspectives. Other streams of professional thought contributing include the assessment community of practice, and those engaged in the philosophy of librarianship and information. There is a growing role here for critical librarianship, as evidenced by the recognition of its contribution to critiques of existing hegemonies and hierarchies in the academy, in its recognition of the failure of library neutrality, and in the decolonisation of research library assumptions and collections. There is never likely to be a neatly agreed synthesis that interprets successfully the role of libraries in society, but that is no excuse for not seeking a fuller understanding. There is a consensus and unity achieved in this volume in understanding the problems and providing potential theories and practical methods for revealing relevant social truths. The book thus forms an important part of a beginning of the next phase of dialogue and debate, as well as an effective summary of progress so far. I commend it to the attention of all engaged in the present and future creation of libraries.

Stephen Town MA PhD FCMI FCLIP
Honorary Fellow
The University of York Management School
May 2022

References

Bennett, J., (2010). *Vibrant matter: a political ecology of things*. Durham, NC: Duke University Press.

Cronin, B., (2008). The sociological turn in information science. *Journal of Information Science*. 34(4), 465–475. doi:10.1177/0165551508088944

Deleuze, G. and Guattari, F., (1988). *A thousand plateaus: capitalism and schizophrenia*. London: Athlone Press.

Dilevko, J., (2009). *The politics of professionalism: a retro-progressive proposal for librarianship*. Duluth, MN: Library Juice Press.

Egan, M., (1955). The library and social structure. *Library Quarterly*. 25(1), 15–22. doi:10.1086/618147

Furner, J., (2004). "A brilliant mind": Margaret Egan and social epistemology. *Library Trends*. 52(4), 792–809. http://hdl.handle.net/2142/1698

Gerolami, N., (2015). The library assemblage: creative institutions in an information society. *Journal of Documentation*. 71(1), 165–174. doi:10.1108/JD-09-2013-0120

Graeber, D., (2013). It is value that brings universes into being. *HAU: Journal of Ethnographic Theory*. 3(2), 219–243. doi:10.14318/hau3.2.012

Hodgson, G., (2014). What is capital? Economists and sociologists have changed its meaning: should it be changed back? *Cambridge Journal of Economics*. 38(5), 1063–1086. doi:10.1093/cje/beu013

Kranich, N., (2020). Libraries and democracy revisited. *Library Quarterly*. 90(1), 121–153. doi:10.1086/707670

MacIntyre, A., (1981). *After virtue: a study in moral theory*. Notre Dame, IN: University of Notre Dame Press.

Ovenden, R., (2020). *Burning the books: a history of knowledge under attack*. London: John Murray.

Pettegree, A. and der Weduwen, A., (2021). *The library: a fragile history*. London: Profile Books.

Shotter, H. and Chia, R., (2002). On organizational becoming: rethinking organizational change. *Organization Science*. 13(5), 567–582. doi:10.1287/orsc.13.5.567.7810

Thompson, J., (1974). *Library power: a new philosophy of librarianship*. London: Clive Bingley.

Town, J.S., (2011). Value, impact and the transcendent library: progress and pressures in performance measurement and evaluation. *Library Quarterly*. 81(1), 111–125. doi:10.1086/657445

Town, J.S. and Kyrillidou, M., (2013). Developing a values scorecard. *Performance Measurement and Metrics*. 14(1), 7–16. doi:10.1108/14678041311316095

Town, S., (2018). The value scorecard. *Information and Learning Science*. 119(1/2), 25–38. doi:10.1108/ILS-10-2017-0098

Introduction: Charting a Course to the Social Future of Academic Libraries

Tim Schlak

The relationship between the user and the academic library has been the lifeblood of information and library work since the very beginning of libraries. Yet the interaction between users and library workers had long been tacitly accepted as an unchanging assumption about the nature of users' information needs. While previously out of the spotlight in favour of processes and services that emphasised efficient, demonstrable and tactile outcomes, the latest focus on social relations represents a sea change in the value proposition of academic libraries and foregrounds a subtle but fundamental shift in the dynamics between user and library. Where services and resources were previously reliable and predictable functions, they are now evolving and growing organisational outcomes that are driven by user behaviour around information, technology and pedagogy. The timeline of these changes is overwhelming: in just over two decades, libraries have gone from card catalogues to the digital shift, and now to the social transformation of the library and its staff into an interconnected and networked organisation. So important has the connection to users become that libraries as organisations unto themselves have had to grapple with a new kind of organisational learning: the library that fails to evolve may find itself relegated to a peripheral status relative to its peers and partners that it would not otherwise have chosen.

What this all means is that libraries find themselves as dependent on their users as the latter previously found themselves dependent on the former for good information. The very nature of the reciprocal agreement that libraries have maintained in some form with their user community is now almost entirely socially conditioned and interrelational. Libraries have kept up in practice by becoming adept managers of their social content in the context of social media and branding and by reimagining the mechanisms that deliver services and resources, including, for example, liaison programs, embedded librarians and a social media presence, among many others. In the wake of each of these innovations, a literature on best practices and implications has kept up to ensure other library workers have access to the latest information to design their own local responses.

Yet, where practice has kept pace, the broader intellectual framework in which libraries endeavour to engage their users has, regrettably, remained under-developed and lacking in strength and cohesion. The same forces of technological disruption and social connection through digital means that have pushed libraries towards greater social orientations to their communities have also long been at work in society at large. Indeed, entire academic domains have been spawned in trying to cope with and explain the immense upheavals and reorganisations societies worldwide have experienced since the dawn of the Information Era began towards the latter part of the 20th century. Social and intellectual capital as well as Social Network Theory provide the practical *and* theoretical underpinnings of the social changes that have upended and revolutionised the library profession. They also contextualise the social shift that has overtaken almost all aspects of library work and, in so doing, demonstrate how libraries can leverage contemporary social conditions for enhanced success.

A central tenet in the arguments put forth is that academic libraries possess numerous assets in addition to the information resources that have long been the bread and butter of library operations. Foremost among these assets is the social or relational capital that emerges from and in turn fuels the library, successfully supporting the evolving mission of institutions of higher learning as well as the sophisticated systems of interconnection that grow out of and are layered onto the networks of creativity and productivity that academic libraries increasingly serve.

Traditional assets such as print, archival and digital collections find new life as forms of intellectual capital when they are incorporated into the complex social environment of higher education as assets in service to knowledge production and sharing across the scholarly lifecycle and paradigms of student learning and engagement. Add to this emerging forms of intellectual capital and its creation, such as Open Access publishing models and an overwhelming perspective on library agency in the 21st century comes into focus. From this new vantage point, the library worker emerges as a social agent working within ever more complex constellations of connections, while the library itself can transform into a responsive learning organisation that could potentially be the organising force behind large swaths of the academy's pursuits. Within this overall schema, several key trends in academic libraries and higher education can be situated and form the foundation of the *social future of academic libraries* that is advanced in this book. Primary among these are:

- the historic turn to greater social engagement and presence that has transformed libraries from passive information warehouses based on a reactive, on-demand model of use to a transformative presence within institutions of higher education that relies on interpersonal relationships and social networks to fulfil its greatest potential;
- the concurrent broader institutional movement within higher learning towards a more entrepreneurial orientation to its surrounding environs as a way of remaining competitive in a shifting landscape where the perceived relevance and value of the product has diminished;

- the similar shift within academic libraries from an existence based on an assumed and stable value that libraries contribute to the institutional mission to a negotiated comprehension of services and resources where social and intellectual capital provide apt and useful frameworks for conceiving of the exchanges that occur between libraries, librarians, users, communities, institutions and other stakeholders.

The motivation for this volume grew out of a mutual interest in social capital and network theory in the context of academic libraries that the editors had previously expressed in a 2017 Association of College and Research Libraries biennial conference panel. Having spent large parts of our careers as library leaders in the United Kingdom and United States in aiding academic libraries and knowledge workers to embrace aspects of the *social turn* that this volume explores, we realised the potential for the frameworks of social/intellectual capital and social networks to serve as helpful frameworks in which to advocate for change and to undertake with greater foresight and intention the transformation of services and resources that the libraries we have worked in have been required to achieve.

Prior to the COVID-19 pandemic, we had observed the focus in academic libraries shifting in social directions such as partnership culture, student engagement and a burgeoning emphasis on networking. As the COVID-19 pandemic extends into its third year, with hopes of a resumption of some kind of normalcy, however new and negotiated, it would stand to reason that greater emphasis on the social nature of library work can help to balance the unbelievably swift advances towards digital work and collaboration that the pandemic ushered in. Moreover, it is also reasonable to expect a desire for even greater connection, thanks to higher acceptance of virtual work and the productivity gains that higher education will realise through the innovations that were forced upon us during the pandemic. After all, it is the nature of the work that has changed, from in-person to virtual, and not the internal constituents, which remain the same. These include information literacy, open access and educational resources, print and digital collections, readership and relationships with partnering libraries, student learning and engagement, among many examples of library practices that will certainly change but will still be recognisable when the acute portion of the pandemic has concluded.

It is a sure bet that the increasing socially driven dynamics of academic libraries will continue to develop not only in predictable ways such as prior to the pandemic, but in unexpected ways, thanks to new ways of working collaboratively and virtually. In this sense, this volume is even more urgently needed because no one has as yet provided the comprehensive grounding of various practices and theoretical causes that have pushed libraries in this direction, both willingly and at times by necessity. The unified view that emerges from this edited volume demonstrates the degree to which the profession relies on practices no longer rooted in traditional notions of resources and services. The profession is now completely undergirded by both the theories and practices that have emerged over the past 10–15 years and that are aimed at providing enhanced justifications for the existence of and investment in academic libraries as socially responsive institutions that facilitate the scholarly and pedagogical lifecycle of higher education.

The goals of this book are:

1   to investigate the *social turn* that academic libraries have taken in ways that clarify professional practice and advance library theory around collaboration, partnership and engagement;

2   to provide a fuller framework for library practitioners to understand and explain their contributions and impacts in language that resonates forcefully outside of academic library circles;

3   to anticipate future directions and organisational imperatives based on past and current experiences and practices while introducing a new vocabulary for the work we are and will be doing in the reconfigured value propositions that are just around the corner.

Book organisation

This book is divided into three parts, each providing a different perspective on the social nature of library work. Part 1, Contexts and Concepts, presents the editors' contributions across six chapters that set the stage for the subsequent part by introducing key trends, theories and definitions. Social capital, intellectual capital and social network theory are introduced in considerable detail and explored both historically and as future possibilities for the further evolution of academic libraries along social lines.

Part 2, Theory Into Practice, is organised along a productive observation that grew out of this overall project. The social turn in academic libraries and the wider environment that Sheila Corrall explores in three different chapters can be conceptualised along a continuum of relationships separated by the degree of internal versus external focus. At its most inward, increased collaborations within the library to reposition services for greater engagement marks one end of the continuum. On the other end is the social means of engaging at or within networks of scale, such as national, international and global-level interactions within disciplinary and cross-disciplinary collaborations. In the middle of either extreme are initiatives like the development of transformed partnerships with campus faculty or staff. An additional demarcation is the locus of collaboration, which should be somewhat familiar in rough form to any library worker who lived through the phase of extending services beyond the library walls. Looking again at a continuum, we can position on one side collaborations that are fundamentally in a physical and/or virtual environment such as a centre or partnership that blossoms primarily in the context of the library's spaces, including digital. At the other end of the spectrum, we can locate collaborations that exist in a boundaryless context where the library is enmeshed in broader social networks on campus. To return to the opening point, not only have libraries always been an expression of their relationship to their users but the distance between the library/librarian and the user is a functional measurement of the degree of social orientation *and* that the library/librarian's position relative to those users within productivity networks is an overarching consideration in understanding library-user dynamics.

The third part, Glossary and Bibliography, is provided online as a downloadable resource and gives added elaboration of the conceptual and theoretical frameworks introduced in Parts 1 and 2, combining a glossary of key terms and concepts discussed in the book with a bibliography of classic and contemporary literature. Our two 'biblio-glossaries' are intended not only to help readers make sense of unfamiliar material as they go through the chapters and follow up references, but also to stimulate further reading around concepts of interest and support their application to research and practice in academic libraries. We have used bold text to highlight terms covered in the glossaries on their first mention in a chapter to make it easier to navigate between the book and these additional resources.

Part 1

The broader questions this volume grapples with are not only about how we build the capacity to leverage the network position and intangible assets of our libraries but also to explore these reconfigured relations in ways that conceptualise them in productive terms that the layperson can intuitively grasp. In Chapter 1 Sheila Corrall reviews the seminal cultural and technological seismic shifts that began in the 1990s as the fuller implications of electronic communication technologies began to come into their own through mass availability and new habits of consumption and connection. Key themes are traced, beginning with the culture of participation that emerged prior to its consolidation and expansion with Web 2.0 technologies in the early 2000s that ushered in disruptive practices such as mass publishing. Blurred boundaries, role ambiguity and the re-constellation of business–stakeholder participation in the business world anticipate the chapter's presentation of a 'multicapitalist' lens that synthesises and expands existing models of capitalism. Through this holistic lens, social capital is situated in its strategic and operational context and its relation to human and moral capital is clarified, as well as its potential for entrepreneurship and innovation.

Paul Bracke in Chapter 2 adapts these types of interactions into a broader framework of social interconnection that academic libraries participate in and to which they contribute. Through introducing and foregrounding social network theory and social capital, the chapter aligns network thinking alongside academic libraries and situates recent trends in library collaboration that can be understood at a systems level as foundational to the future of academic libraries and the university itself. Trends that evidence the social turn are evolving professional roles where skills and/or expertise are concerned and assessment frameworks that capture intangible assets through an intellectual capital lens, among others. The network-level approach, with emphasis on social connectedness, enables a new look at existing concepts of librarianship and opens vistas onto library work as a reconfigured function in the academy that underpins research and learning networks.

In Chapter 3 Corrall follows up the *multicapitalist* framework with a consideration of how scholarly efforts over the past two decades have laid the foundations for a renewed and revitalised social mission for higher education. In particular, she traces the evolving role that institutions of higher learning have played over the past half century, moving from an elite to a mass system of education that transcends parochial educational interests to encompass broad public concerns at national and international levels. The drivers of this 'social transformation' are vast in their complexity, but a manageable framework is developed that in turn explains the emergence of higher education's 'third mission', which comes to encompass a wide range of locations and commitments. By problematising and locating the tensions inherent in using a capitalist lens in higher education, Corrall explores the utility of both social capital and social networks as established yet evolving frameworks for looking at the factors surrounding student success.

A number of chapters that are included in this volume rely on foundational texts and articles on social and intellectual capital that originate outside of library and information science (LIS) literature in fields such as business and sociology. Over the past decade, these works have begun to permeate the theory, practice and scholarship of academic libraries in ways that help to triangulate library services and library workers with observations about the socially derived assets of the workplace and capital. In Chapter 4 Tim Schlak offers an exegesis on both this outside scholarship as well as its adaptation into library literature. Beginning with the social framework that critical American and French thinkers created in explaining what was previously conceived of as self-interested and rational action, his chapter contextualises how actors in a network of mutually held needs rely on trust, trustworthiness, reciprocity, mutuality and social/network norms to ensure outcomes that no one individual could alone achieve. Useful definitions of terms are offered and an important distinction is drawn between social and intellectual capital that will help the reader approach the many chapters that use these terms. In addition, an in-depth exploration of the implications of these theories is offered in terms of the shift from a transactional approach to librarianship to one that is transformational.

Moving beyond the 'basics', in Chapter 5 Corrall returns to the *social turn* to develop the key trends reviewed in Chapters 1 and 3 as foundational to emerging models of academic librarianship. These trends include: (1) a sharp shift in the library's relationship to its client base in terms of more holistic services around student orientation and career focus; (2) academic entrepreneurship and community engagement where innovation supports the fostering of global citizenship; (3) a transition towards internationalisation and multiculturalism; (4) a reconfigured focus on academic success and student well-being; and (5) new literacies and library pedagogies. Weaving all of these threads together are the intellectual and social capital perspectives that come together to form a conceptual framework around student success, community building and library assessment, among others. The chapter ends with an emphasis on the centrality of developing relationships, sustaining communities and strengthening belonging for marginalised groups, an emerging task for librarians moving forward.

Similar explorations are made in Schlak's Chapter 6 on forecasting a future for academic libraries. Engagement as a baseline activity of academic libraries is posited as a key driver in the dynamic of organisational learning. The chapter brings together various areas of LIS literature to demonstrate how engagement can spark a model for continual improvement and evaluation of library services, thanks to cycles of mutuality and reciprocity. As academic libraries seek to position their work more centrally in the social enterprise of modern academic institutions of higher learning, greater organisational alignment with student engagement as understood outside of libraries as well as with forms of collaboration that continually and organically produce collective learning becomes possible. The skills and capabilities required to embark on organisation-wide changes are reviewed and theories from the business and information science literature are introduced to demonstrate the relevancy of this approach to libraries' strategic activities.

Part 2

As the location for the volume's contributed chapters, Part 2 explores how we can build the capacity to leverage the network position and intangible assets of our libraries through both theoretical and practical lenses. Each chapter relates substantively to the main theories at hand and proceeds to position the academic library in a new orientation to those it serves. By challenging the overly narrow conceptual distinction between functional and subject-specialist librarians, in Chapter 7 James Kessenides and Michael Brenes offer an expanded view of the subject specialist and the different values that they bring to teaching, learning and research at their home institutions. They also question the limitations of the current overly simplified understanding of the subject specialist as a traditional asset of academic libraries and posit that they have enduring and reconfigured value, thanks to a social capital lens that permits a novel analysis of the ways subject specialists and functionalists interact. Three primary values that subject expertise permits include: the development of trust and network expansion in teaching and research environments; the importance of subject knowledge in collection development as an intangible asset; and the enduring benefits that subject expertise represents in a knowledge-sharing capacity

In Chapter 8 Folk returns to the long-standing question of the value and limits of the one-shot instruction session to develop a broader framework for information literacy that includes sociocultural considerations in students making the transition to college-level research. This chapter introduces and synthesises several conceptual constructs to recap prior research by the author on first-generation college students and to extend a framework that incorporates communities of practice, social and cultural capital and academic literacies as foundational to student success. The accumulation of social capital is critical for these students in gauging the expectations for performance and in developing relationships with peers and faculty as they progress through their curricula. Academic literacies comprise one such space, and research assignments represent excellent opportunities for situated learning and developing the social capital to negotiate belonging in a learning community.

In looking at programs and services that have until recently been considered atypical for academic libraries, in Chapter 9 Alice Rogers, Sara Sweeney Bear and Scott Fralin explore non-traditional uses of spaces to leverage engagement opportunities and express new articulations of library value. Social network analysis provides the theoretical lens to demonstrate the value of the three examples they relate in detail: Fusion Studio, the Course Exhibit Initiative and the Active Learning Curation Program. The interdisciplinary nature of the connections made and the way these connections can be leveraged provide fertile soil for a sustained discussion of their successes and lessons learned in the context of a socially expanded library system.

In Chapter 10, Andrea Kosavic and Minglu Wang present functional librarianship in the context of Research Data Management (RDM) as a factor in the creation of an academic library's social capital. The chapter summarises current RDM literature and finds strong evidence for tacit recognitions that greater social orientation on the part of librarians towards researchers will increase engagement of researchers with open science, thus advancing both the impact of RDM from within the library as well as the development of social capital. This last point is traced through various dimensions of the theories of social capital, including symbolic capital, normative ways of bonding and bridging connections, and a network approach that links individual mobilisation of resources in a network and their positionality inside it. In reviewing recent library literature on RDM services informed by a qualitative coding methodology, the authors arrive at several important findings related to symbolic capital, liaison librarianship models and approaches to project management which they discuss in detail.

Pivoting to a different dynamic distant from the previous chapter's expansion, Chapter 11 assembles a novel juxtaposition between liaison relationships and staff turnover. Alice Kalinowski develops a framework for understanding the organisational risks that staff turnover poses in losing the social capital inherent to relationship-based liaison roles and programs. Social capital theory advances the discussion to explore academic librarianship, management and marketing research for the implications of the boundary-spanning nature of liaison activity. This chapter makes clear the practical value that lies in comprehending an increasingly turbulent work environment, marked by turnover, for those leaders and managers looking to bolster supporting processes and procedures.

While new academic library positions around outreach, engagement and student success have proliferated from the early 2000s, organisational structure and matching vision and mission accommodations that are more strategic than reactive have been lacking. In Chapter 12, Rebecca Metzger introduces many of the programmatic steps implemented in a large university library setting in service to developing an Outreach and Academic Collaboration division. What is needed, the chapter argues, is greater leadership commitment to outreach so as to harness previously invisible work and to adapt that social work to new and strategic models of engagement. In listing the program goals and performance competencies, Metzger provides a much-needed skills-based inventory grounded in relational and social capital and subject liaison librarianship from an individual perspective following her professional successes in this area.

In Chapter 13 Matthew Kelly offers a unique and rare linkage of academic and public libraries in terms of social and intellectual capital generation through a conceptual and theoretical treatise on the limitations of selection and collection development practices. The narrative takes up a sociology of knowledge perspective to model a public–academic library partnership that redresses the collection gaps that emerge from the respective institutional-type content-acquisition model for meeting users' information needs. Through a collaborative reorientation to our work driven by a renewed social conscience, librarians are in a position to redirect organisational energy and attention to a joint infrastructure of municipal and educational interests in service to a community development role where cultures of reading intersect. Such partnerships could produce libraries that furnish for readers the materials they wish to read while also making important contributions to the development of a civil society where lifelong access to wide-ranging collections offers readers more than the limits they currently face.

Kathryn Dilworth makes the case in Chapter 14 that an academic library's existing social capital is the foundation that enables successful fundraising. Integrating philanthropy research on giving within academic libraries, the chapter argues that philanthropic funding is a transformative mechanism for academic libraries that often assume they have no natural constituents, as compared to other units on campus such as academic schools. Research suggests, however, that even the largest institutions lack the capacity to reach their entire constituencies, making cultivation of students and faculty a long-term possibility for libraries. Library services become cultivation tools that are brought into the socially informed giving models of the day and result in benefits like information, knowledge and reconceived spaces. Dilworth also argues persuasively that a social capital model of fundraising requires a skilled fundraising practice underpinned by a long-term strategy and a team of dedicated professionals.

Design thinking offers a radically different approach from the service provision framing concepts that underline many of the chapters in this volume. In Chapter 15 Andrew Dillon brings design thinking into sharper focus alongside a framework of social and intellectual capital to question the implications of a sluggish field-wide response to the challenges raised by those in the last decade who implored librarians to more fully absorb the needs and preferences of users to make engagement the fundamental difference in the profession. Design thinking as a problem-solving process is introduced as a way of more deeply integrating the users' world into the practices of libraries and to suggest an alternative approach to change management that permits radical change in accordance with the work context, rather than forcing users into traditional but worn paradigms. When used strategically, this process enables libraries to create and maintain ties with existing partners and to explore relationships with better-resourced collaborators we may have struggled to work with in the past. Such an approach requires questioning existing practices but yields higher and/or different returns than tried and true methods that offer few prospects of a future that is different from the past.

Glossary and bibliography

Consistent with our goal of supplying a fuller framework for practitioners to articulate their contributions and impacts, two specialist biblio-glossaries complement the narrative content of the book with a keyword guide to the central concepts, theories and models referenced in the preceding chapters. The two downloadable resources that constitute the final part of the book provide explanations of both specialist terminology and familiar terms given particular meanings in sociological scholarship documenting the social turn in higher education, professional practice and community development. Our definitions are taken directly from primary, secondary and tertiary literature of the field, which then forms the basis of the supporting bibliographies, intended to serve as suggestions for further reading and thought starters for readers interested in exploring and adopting the perspectives and theories described in their own institutions and practices. The first biblio-glossary has a more theoretical focus on the terminology of intellectual and social capital scholarship, while the second biblio-glossary has a more empirical orientation, covering social developments in higher education and the wider environment. Together these two resources offer a conceptual toolkit for colleagues motivated to engage with intellectual and social capital and related perspectives and contribute to advancing academic library scholarship in exciting new directions. To make it easier to navigate between the book and these resources, we have highlighted terms covered in the glossaries when first used in each chapter, using **bold text** for terms in the *Intellectual and Social Capital and Networks* glossary and ***bold italics*** for terms in the *Social Development of Higher Education* glossary.

Sources of contributions and key themes

Our call for proposals was distributed in Spring 2019 via national and international e-mail listservs targeting academic librarians, educators and technologists. We received 22 abstracts spread across four continents and, following an editorial review process, we accepted 11 proposals. Two authors were not able to submit manuscripts, resulting in nine total submitted manuscripts in addition to the six chapters contributed by the three editors.

In addition to a diverse background of authors from a variety of institutions and locations, the contributions share practices and perspectives from a wide variety of institutional types, from small academic libraries to large research library systems to library and information schools. Whether at teaching or research institutions, our findings are consistent that social and intellectual capital as well as social network theory are powerful tools for investigating trends in librarianship and library work, indicating that a commitment to leveraging more than just the traditional assets libraries possess is an emerging framework held in common in the teaching and learning practices of the profession.

While the range of contributions is varied, we can collectively point to a number of touch points across all the chapters that point to developments in academic librarianship in the 21st century up to the disruptions of COVID-19 and that anticipate the kinds of challenges that await library workers upon return to a post-pandemic world. Most salient of these themes is the social impetus that increasingly informs the response academic libraries make to the shifted dynamics between information need and information service in a world of ubiquitous information access at our fingertips that recognises authoritative institutions like libraries in reconfigured ways. A related theme that emerges is relationship building as a fundamental activity of today's knowledge workers who use this social skillset and their subject expertise to span boundaries across their institutions in pursuit of contributing to a changing value proposition of the academy as a research and teaching infrastructure. From this vantage point, many of the contributions substantiate the invisible work librarians perform as they 'bridge' and 'bond' connections weak and strong to and from the library across and beyond traditional boundaries. A view of the library worker as a form of human capital in possession of cultural and relational capital and working in service to producing intellectual capital that can be harnessed in mutually reinforcing cycles of reciprocity and mutuality emerges when these forms of capital are exchanged across social networks of productivity that constitute the mainstay of knowledge workers across the globe. Some of the primary intersection points of these forms of capital in this asset-based approach are information literacy, collections and research infrastructures, among many others, all of which are explored in the various chapters that follow.

Part 1
Contexts and Concepts

1

The Social Turn in Communities, Professions and the Economy

Sheila Corrall

People participate through and within communities: participatory culture requires us to move beyond a focus on individualized personal expression; it is about an ethos of "doing it together" in addition to "doing it yourself".

(Jenkins, Ito & boyd 2016, p. 181)

Introduction

The social life of academic libraries is the product of a dynamic operating environment and subject to multiple influences, particularly from the higher education sector and institutions where they reside, but also from their local *communities*, professional networks, the global economy and civil society. The argument we advance in this book is that the social changes taking place in universities and colleges in the 21st century demand a radical rethinking of the mission and business philosophy of libraries in higher education to shift the focus of academic librarians from managing collections and delivering services to growing **assets**, building networks, cultivating relationships and developing communities. Forward-looking practitioners have recognised the need for change and have been exploring new roles, experimenting with new practices and examining their value and impact. But such work is often performed at the periphery of library life, it takes a long time to move to centre stage and even longer to become embedded in everyday operations and *organisational culture*.

We argue that the new social context not only requires us to do new things: it requires new thinking at every level, including a future-present strategy mindset and the disposition to consider library–society links simultaneously from outside-in and inside-out perspectives. We need to understand the social influences that are changing the shape of our institutions as well as the social impacts that our activities are having on both our local community and society at large so that we can create shared value through policies and practices that provide meaningful all-round benefits to all our stakeholders. We have a duty of care to the people who work in, with and for libraries, to the people we serve directly every day and also to the whole population now and in the future in the connected global environment. Our central thesis is that the complex pluralist context of the 21st century necessitates the use of multiple perspectives to resolve the social problems facing libraries and librarians today and tomorrow. We contend that **intellectual** and **social capital** concepts and theories offer our profession models and tools that help us to see things differently, gain critical insights and respond to the challenges presented with reflexive engagement and purposeful action.

We therefore begin our inquiry into the social future of academic libraries not with a review of the past and present library landscape, but with a survey of key ideas, concepts and theories shaping the way individuals, groups and organisations are behaving, interacting and relating to others in their personal, social and professional lives, by way of introducing the 'social turn' in the world around us. Informed by an environmental scan and multidisciplinary literature, our focus is the current century, supported by seminal work from the 1990s and earlier as needed, covering both scholarly and practitioner material. While libraries are not at the centre of our survey, we connect the narrative to our own field by showing how the practices described are playing out in libraries and the academy. This chapter is organised around key themes emerging from the literature, representing distinct but overlapping trends in thinking and practice.

We start with the *culture* of participation and 'online sociality' emerging in the 1990s that became a mass movement in the early 2000s with the development of Web 2.0 technologies and social media facilitating disruptive practices such as do-it-yourself (DIY) publishing, *crowdsourcing* and *'working out loud'*. We next look at how participatory practices and power shifts have played out in professional domains such as healthcare and journalism in the 'apomediated' 2.0 environment, resulting in blurry boundaries and role ambiguities as modes of operation evolve and the social responsibilities, obligations and aspirations of professionals are redefined. We then move to the business world, where *corporate social responsibility* has been successively reconceptualised as social responsiveness, societal relationships, social integration and shared values, with ethical obligation, stakeholder participation and cross-boundary collaboration invoked to support pressure for sustainability management.

The final part of the chapter brings together threads from disparate discussions to reconceptualise social roles and responsibilities through a 'multicapitalist' lens, synthesising and extending frameworks developed in recent decades to reform capitalism and promote sustainability. Building particularly on the work of British environmentalists (Forum for the Future) and Spanish organisation theorists (Intellectus Forum), we present a composite relational capital-based model that integrates forward thinking around capitalism, environmentalism, **intangible assets**, business ethics and context-based sustainability. The model encapsulates current arguments for integrating social perspectives into corporate strategy by viewing 'resources in action' through a holistic lens and illuminating the interconnections and interdependencies between different kinds of capital assets. Significantly, it sets the concept of social capital in context and reframes all types of organisations as *social enterprises* united in a broader view of value creation.

Participatory culture and online sociality

The origins of the current culture of participation go back to the 1980s, when home computers became commonplace and social researchers explored issues such as contribution, collaboration and collective knowledge. The concept is generally attributed to American scholar Henry Jenkins, who introduced the term in his 1992 book *Textual poachers*, but its realisation in practice is particularly associated with developments in networking technologies, internet access and online services over the following decade. Other seminal work includes Manuel Castells's (1996) vision of the 'network society' transforming work, learning and play through decentralised participatory networks; Howard Rheingold's (1987; 1993) concept of *The virtual community* as an emergent form of 'online sociality' or 'online socializing', expanding and changing the notion of '*community*' to accommodate 'webs of personal relationships in cyberspace'; and Tim O'Reilly's (2005) conceptualisation of a new generation of interactive collaborative technologies as Web 2.0.

Delwiche and Henderson (2013, pp. 4–7) describe four phases of *participatory culture* from the mid-1980s to 2011, each linked with key socio-technical moves and seminal concepts:

- *Emergence* (1985–93), with the advent of personal computing and the idea of individuals as producers (*active* users) as well as consumers (*passive* users) of content/information, later characterised as '*prosumption*' and '*produsage*' (Bruns 2013);
- *Waking up to the web* (1994–98), with web browsers and internet search engines, invention of the wiki, arrival of online shopping and the evolution of 1960s 'hacker culture' into the Open Source Initiative and collaborative software development (O'Reilly 1999);
- *Push-button publishing* (1999–2004), with user-friendly web authoring/publishing, content hosting via multi-user blogging software and social networking services enabling people to share, annotate, publish and remix digital media, exemplified by *commons-based peer production* models, such as *Wikipedia* (Benkler 2005);
- *Ubiquitous connections* (2005–11), with widespread broadband internet connectivity, the launch of video hosting and streaming sites, and mobile/handheld devices enabling multimedia/cross-media/transmedia publishing, illustrated by Jenkins's (2010) concept of transmedia storytelling and Howe's (2006) notion of 'crowdsourcing' as a creative collaborative low-cost alternative to outsourcing.

Jenkins used the participatory culture label to capture shifts in the contemporary media environment, particularly changes in interactions among consumers of popular culture, between consumers and texts (books, films, etc.) and between consumers and producers, which blurred the boundaries between cultural actors, actions and artefacts, so that 'Consumption becomes production; reading becomes writing; [and] spectator culture becomes participatory culture' (Jenkins 2006b, p. 60). For Jenkins (2006a, p. 290), participatory culture is thus 'Culture in which . . . consumers are invited to actively participate in the creation and circulation of new content', thereby producing new texts, new cultures and new communities. He elaborated the concept in a widely cited study on digital media and learning for the MacArthur Foundation: 'a culture with relatively low barriers to artistic expression and *civic engagement*, strong support for creating and sharing one's creations, and some type of informal mentorship whereby what is known by the most experienced is passed along to novices' and 'in which members believe their contributions matter, and feel some degree of social connection with one another' (Jenkins et al. 2006, p. 3).

An essay originally published in 2000 (Jenkins 2006b) positions the new culture at the intersection of three key developments:

- *new tools and technologies* enabling consumers to archive, annotate, appropriate and recirculate media content faster and farther via global networks;
- *emerging knowledge subcultures* promoting DIY media production and distribution and influencing consumer use of such tools;
- *evolving media economies* encouraging the flow of images, ideas and narratives across multiple channels and demanding more active modes of spectatorship.

Jenkins consistently emphasises that while computer networks and interactive technologies have enabled the new culture to emerge, it is the changing interactive *practices*, and particularly the changed *relations* between consumers and producers, that determine the change in culture, rather than technologies. Media conglomerates continue to be powerful players in the knowledge economy, but 'audiences are gaining greater power and autonomy as they enter into the new knowledge culture. The interactive audience is more than a marketing concept' (Jenkins 2006b, p. 136). Another important dimension is the emphasis on *collective* above individual agency, highlighted in his work on media literacies, which are repeatedly described as '*social* skills and *cultural* competencies' (Jenkins 2014; Jenkins et al. 2006, emphasis added).

Participating through projects

Crowdsourcing is the classic example of participatory culture as a transformative practice, rapidly taken up by all kinds of organisations and individuals, notably in museums and libraries to add value to special collections, reference services and even graphic design (Carletti et al. 2013; Douglas & Becker 2015; Severson & Sauvé 2019; Stonebraker & Zhang 2016). Howe (2008b, p. 47) originally defined the concept as 'the act of taking a job once performed by employees and outsourcing it to a large, undefined group of people via an open call, generally over the Internet', while Brabham (2013, p. xix) promotes a problem-centric conception, defining crowdsourcing as 'an online, distributed problem-solving and production model that leverages the collective intelligence of online communities to serve specific organizational goals'. Brabham (2013, p. xxi) argues that crowdsourcing is essentially a *power-sharing* model: 'the locus of control regarding the creative production of goods and ideas exists *between* the organization and the public, a shared process of bottom-up, open creation by the crowd and top-down management by those charged with serving an organization's strategic interests'.

This differs from open-source software production (such as Linux) and commons-based peer production (like *Wikipedia*), which are both bottom-up, self-organising/self-governing processes, where control is distributed among participants in a third model distinct from firm-based and market-based production. Scholars have categorised crowdsourced projects according to the functions fulfilled, activities undertaken and participant characteristics. Howe (2008a) defines four basic types of crowdsourcing based on what the crowd contributes: crowd wisdom, crowd creation, crowd voting and crowd funding. In contrast, Brabham (2013, pp. 44–45) proposes a four-way typology that relates the types of tasks performed to the kinds of problems to be solved:

- knowledge discovery and management – finding and collecting information;
- broadcast search – solving empirical problems;
- peer-vetted creative production – creating and selecting ideas; and
- distributed-human-intelligence tasking – analysing large-scale data.

In the context of e-learning in academic libraries, Stonebraker and Zhang (2016, p. 163) describe crowdsourcing as 'an instructional technology that is intentionally designed to be disruptive to the status quo of reference service' and suggest four methods for crowdsourcing (open course, closed course, open expert and closed expert), the choice depending on library goals for *community development/capacity building* and user engagement.

Whatever the focus, crowdsourcing represents a radically new way of working participatively by moving existing practices of co-operation, aggregation, teamwork and consensus to an altogether different level. Kelty et al. (2015) used a multidisciplinary literature review and 102 case studies of contemporary participatory projects enabled by the internet and mobile or social media technologies to clarify what 'participation' means in practice. They identified seven distinct aspects of participation, which can be used as a framework for evaluation and design of participatory initiatives. The key message here is that 'participation is not a simple either/or parameter . . . it is not its presence or absence that is important, but the configuration of dimensions which render it "participatory"' (Kelty et al. 2015, p. 485). Box 1.1 on the next page summarises the seven dimensions.

Box 1.1 Seven dimensions of highly participative projects

1 *Educational dividend* – learning gained from participation, particularly learning how to participate effectively.
2 *Decisional involvement* – contributing to decision making and goal setting in addition to undertaking tasks.
3 *Resource control* – participant ownership and use of **resources** resulting from their participation.
4 *Exit conditions* – right to leave a project without penalty and with resources.
5 *Effective voice* – mechanisms for participants to 'speak back' with influence and without retribution.
6 *Visible metrics* – transparent demonstration to participants of their contributions to collective outcomes.
7 *Collective experience* – affective, communicative capacity, including sociability and a sense of belonging.

Adapted from Kelty et al. 2015.

Working out loud

Web 2.0 tools are also shifting the everyday practices of individual workers towards more interaction and collaboration within and beyond their workplace, enabling people to form new personal and professional relationships and (perhaps counterintuitively) to become more productive and innovative as a result of their online socialising. This trend is exemplified by the Working Out Loud (WOL) movement, also known as narrating or showing your work, observable work and making work visible and discoverable (Bozarth 2014; Margaryan et al. 2015; Stepper 2015; Williams 2010). WOL was originally characterised as a dual construct, Observable Work + Narrating Your Work, or 'creating/modifying/storing your work in places that others can see it, follow it and contribute to it IN PROCESS' and 'journaling (blogging, microblogging, etc.) what you are doing in an open way for those interested to find and follow' (Williams 2010, para. 3–4). The practice has subsequently been elaborated and promoted by John Stepper (2016; 2020) via blog posts, free guides, videos and a book; his concept of WOL circles (small, confidential peer-support groups) has been implemented in more than 60 countries.

Stepper's (2016) WOL model has five elements, expanding significantly on the simple formula promoted by Bryce Williams (2010). *Visible work* remains central to the model, but a subtle reordering in 2016 placed it below *Relationships* (building a **social network**) and *Generosity* (framing posts as contributions), shifting the emphasis from sharing work to developing relationships. The fourth and fifth elements have also evolved from making work better and making it purposeful to *Purposeful discovery* and *A growth mindset*. Stepper describes how working in 'a more open, connected way' helps people to feel more empowered, access more opportunities and become more effective, taking advantage of feedback given and received, relationships and collaborations formed, and knowledge and learning gained. He contrasts the self-promotion that often motivates social networking with the *reciprocal altruism* that informs his model.

Both Stepper and Bozarth (2014) promote WOL as a practice that benefits both individuals and organisations. Showing your work (or, more specifically, *showing workflow*) can create dialogue and get feedback and help for individuals, saving time and stopping reinvention; it can improve learning and practice through reflection and explaining to others; establish credibility/expertise through portfolio building; and ultimately strengthen performance and enhance careers (Bozarth 2014, pp. 30–49). For organisations, WOL can enhance communication and break down silos, build **trust** in leaders and raise worker morale, preserve institutional knowledge and locate individual talent, increase operational efficiency and capacity for innovation, improve customer service and public perception, and support organisational learning, particularly learning from mistakes (Bozarth 2014, pp. 12–29).

In one of the few scholarly studies of WOL, Sergi and Bonneau (2016, p. 379) characterise it as 'a communicative practice . . . that blends talk and text in an interesting way'. Despite limiting their focus to microblogging (Twitter), their analysis reveals a rich repertoire of practices, categorised as six distinct multifaceted forms confirming the methods advocated by WOL proponents. Box 1.2 presents their six categories with typical practices.

Box 1.2 Six forms of Working Out Loud

1 *Exposing* – showing work in progress, including problems and feedback received.
2 *Contextualising* – supplying background, such as work setting and worker status.
3 *Documenting* – reporting tasks completed, methods used and plans for projects.
4 *Teaching* – offering solutions to problems, lessons learned and best practices.
5 *Expressing* – sharing positive or negative emotions and feelings about work.
6 *Thinking reflectively* – stepping back and communicating inner reflections-in-action and reflections-on-action.

Adapted from Sergi & Bonneau 2016.

Sergi and Bonneau (2016, pp. 396, 398) demonstrate how even very short posts 'have the potential to open up conversations, foster interactions, and establish relations' and, more significantly, beyond the specific actions produced by WOL tweets, 'they also have the potential to contribute to the performance of two things: the work being accomplished and the professional identity of the person who is working out loud'. Their conclusion again places *relationships* at the centre of emergent work practices, and also highlights the blurring and merging of the personal, professional and organisational in contemporary online social interactions:

starting from the individualised practice of working out loud . . . we suggest that conversations can arise from tweets, that these conversations can create relationships, and that these personal relationships can evolve into professional ties, moving from transient and circumstantial interactions to more formalised collaborative agreements. These agreements can give rise to projects, and at the moment that such a collaboration (what 'we' do together) becomes a common project ('it'), we witness the birth of a temporary or even more permanent organisation.

(Sergi & Bonneau 2016, p. 399)

There are obvious parallels here with the move towards *open pedagogy* (Hegarty 2015) and *open notebook science* (Clinio & Albagli 2017) in higher education, as well as echoes of the computer-supported co-operative work movement of the 1980s, the *community of practice* concept in the 1990s (Brown & Duguid 1991; Wenger 1999) and related concepts of *faculty learning communities* (Cox, 1999) and **personal learning networks** (Cooke 2012; Siemens 2005; Warlick 2009) in education, in addition to the open innovation paradigm of the 2000s (Chesbrough, Vanhaverbeke & West 2006). In academic libraries, WOL and related practices are evident in librarians using blogs, Twitter and other Web 2.0 tools for online interaction with users and peers to update learning, share knowledge, test ideas and get feedback on services and research, and to engage in academic/social networking, professional conversation and political debate (Dalton, Kouker & O'Connor 2016; Jackson-Brown 2013; Mi 2015; Stranack 2012).

Citizen-practitioners 2.0 and social professionals

The original concept of participation has been developed, reinterpreted and relabelled by Jenkins and others in various domains, notably politics (civic engagement, open government, Government 2.0, participatory activism), the arts (collaborative digital poetry, *participatory design*), journalism (*citizen/open-source/participatory journalism*), education (connected learning, participatory pedagogy), science (*citizen/crowd/participatory/open science*, Science 2.0), health (Health/Medicine 2.0, participatory medicine, patient engagement), business (employee involvement, Enterprise 2.0, participative management, worker participation) and also libraries (*Library 2.0, participatory librarianship*). Like Jenkins, other scholars acknowledge the role of Web 2.0 technologies and tools in facilitating and accelerating public/community participation, but consider them less significant than the principles and values they represent, such as collaboration, contribution and co-creation.

Librarians also see *technology* as 'a means to an end and not the end in itself', with *interpersonal attributes* (especially facilitation skills) the key competency requirement for Librarian 2.0 (Lankes, Silverstein & Nicholson 2007; Partridge, Lee & Munro 2010, p. 325). Academic Library 2.0 is essentially *open, interactive, convergent* and *collaborative* in addition to being *participatory* and *dynamic* – not only *user centred*, but distinctively 'user originated, socially rich, multimedia enabled and communally innovative' (Maness 2006; Xu, Ouyang & Chu 2009, p. 328). For example, library services could be originated from users in an environment where library users 'answer reference questions with self-created wiki entries', utilising collective intelligence (Xu, Ouyang & Chu 2009, p. 328). In practice, libraries have deployed a range of locally-built, community-sourced and proprietary systems to facilitate user-friendly crowdsourced reference services, including the CrowdAsk system developed at Purdue University and Q&A sites like Quora and StackExchange, as well as existing institutional systems such as Sharepoint or Piazza, which can be embedded in a course management system/virtual learning environment (Stonebraker & Zhang 2016). Significantly, Maness (2006, Library 2.0, para. 4) argues, 'as communities change, libraries . . . must allow users to change the library'. The participatory library is thus 'much more than a place, [it] is a community of users working together' (Stonebraker & Zhang 2016, p. 163).

Commentators also highlight the different levels of participation (and power) represented by variant uses of the 'participatory' label within and across domains, and the varying meanings given to 'participation' and other terms. As Kelty et al. (2015, pp. 474–475) observe, 'In some cases the concept of participation is confounded with democracy or democratization, and in places it is used interchangeably with cooperation, collaboration, engagement, or access'. Outing (2005) describes 11 'layers' of *citizen journalism*, representing varying levels of editorial control over content, while Ferguson (2007, pp. 8–9) elaborates four levels of empowerment for e-patients (Accepting, Informed, Involved and In-Control) based on patient attitudes towards their physicians and the severity of their condition, with the latter tending to drive networked patients from medical passivity to medical autonomy.

Fumagalli et al. (2015, pp. 384–385) discuss the multiple and overlapping meanings of terminology in participatory medicine, describing the 'explosion of terms' – empowerment, engagement, enablement, involvement and activation, as well as participation – variously treated as synonyms, antonyms or unrelated concepts. Thus patient empowerment can be interpreted as a *process*, an emergent *state* or a participative *behaviour*. Their concept map clarifies distinctions and relationships between terms, which they also summarise in a composite definition of empowerment potentially transferable to other areas:

> Patient *empowerment* is the acquisition of motivation (self-awareness and attitude through *engagement*) and ability (skills and knowledge through enablement) that patients might use to be involved or participate in decision-making, thus creating an opportunity for higher levels of power in their relationship with professionals.
>
> (Fumagalli et al. 2015, p. 390, emphasis added).

Eysenbach (2008) elaborates five major aspects of the Web 2.0 environment in medicine and healthcare generalisable to other domains: social networking, collaboration, participation, **apomediation** and openness (contrasted with traditional 'hierarchical, closed structures'). Apomediation is a key feature, representing a 'third way' between human intermediation and disintermediation that provides guidance for users via 'networked collaborative filtering processes' from agents (people or tools) operating in stand-by mode, rather than gatekeepers/middlemen standing between information and consumer. Specific issues arising include: the autonomy, empowerment and emancipation of information seekers; the shift in information behaviour from consumption to prosumption/co-production, from simple to complex (individual and group) interactions, and from upstream (top-down) to downstream (bottom-up) filtering as quality assurance; also the shift to more informal learning through participation, application and information production, with implications for cognitive load and information literacy.

In the library world, Kwanya, Stilwell and Underwood (2015) identify *apomediation* as a defining characteristic of Library 3.0, an evolution of Library 2.0 that is also characterised as *intelligent*, *organised*, *federated* and *personalised*. Table 1.1 draws selectively on their comprehensive comparison of evolving library service models to illustrate the trajectory of successive generations of web-based library models, showing how conceptions of the participatory library based on the 'wisdom of the crowd' (collective intelligence) are moving towards a more nuanced understanding of user-led service based on the 'wisdom of the expert' (selective intelligence), where experienced/expert users, professional/technical expertise and intelligent systems/agents can be brought into play and 'provide cues and meta-information which enable information users to navigate the infosphere and locate credible information' (Kwanya, Stilwell & Underwood 2015, p. 76).

Table 1.1 *Evolving features of participatory library models*
(adapted from Kwanya, Stilwell & Underwood 2015, p. 81)

Library 0.0	Library 1.0	Library 2.0	Library 3.0
Oral 'web'	Read-only web	Social web	Semantic web
Network of persons	Network of webpages	Network of links	Network of data
Custodian mediation	Intermediation	Disintermediation	Apomediation
Individual intelligence	Professional intelligence	Collective intelligence	Selective intelligence
Sacrosanct environment	Sacred environment	Communal environment	Personalised environment
Just-in-case acquisition	Just-in-case acquisition	Just-in-time acquisition	Just-for-you acquisition
Paper materials	Hybrid libraries	Electronic resources	Digital artefacts
Page thumbing	Web crawling	Dumb searching	Smart searching

Apomediation has potential to empower information users without totally disempowering information professionals: users are in control of their information choices, they can opt to use systems designed by professionals to offer 'expert' guidance at the 'point of failure', but, crucially, apomediaries have no direct power over the information or its use by individuals.

Democratising the professions

Just as the roles of citizens are changing in relation to their health, news gathering, scientific research and other domains, so too are the roles and responsibilities of professionals in domains where members of the public are engaging and participating in their work. Terms such as *civic*, *democratic*, *public* and *social* journalists are used to signal new professional practices associated with the participatory journalism movement (Dzur 2002; Hedman & Djerf-Pierre 2013; Singer 2012a; Voakes 1999). While later discussions emphasise the use of social media, earlier contributions predate Web 2.0 and focus on changing conceptions of journalism's role in society, particularly in relation to their local communities. Voakes (1999, p. 757) characterises civic journalism as 'bound up with the public life of a community' with 'an obligation to engage citizens with their communities', manifest in four emergent practices: reinvigoration of public life, information for public judgement, facilitation of public discourse and attention to citizens' concerns.

Dzur (2002, p. 316) similarly sees a rethinking of 'what counts as news', with a shift to longer-term issues (such as the environment) and the promotion of community dialogue. Observing that 'Public journalism departs from traditional reporting practices by advocating *public listening* in newsgathering, by producing *purposeful news* and by encouraging *public debate*', he also refers to 'joint ownership of the newsmaking, newsgathering and reporting process', with news becoming a 'co-creation of journalists and the people' as citizens engage with members of the press during focus groups or community meetings and also 'make news through interviews and contributions to informational commons pages' (Dzur 2002, pp. 315, 318). Singer (2012a, p. 3) describes *social journalism* as 'a form of the craft that is more self-consciously open and participatory' and as 'work done by journalists within the social network that constitutes the contemporary media universe' – work taking place on and around websites, blogs and social networking platforms such as Facebook and Twitter.

Hedman and Djerf-Pierre (2013) use the term social journalist specifically for one who uses social media, emphasising the increased audience interaction, collaboration and transparency/openness facilitated by the new tools, while also noting their extensive use for traditional tasks of environmental scanning and information gathering. The continuous blurring of boundaries resulting from social media is a key theme, including blurring of professional/public and personal/private lives, and blurring of lines between producers and consumers of media content, generating questions about professional identities and relationships, and 'an increased demand for professional journalism to relate not only to audience participation and citizen journalism but also to publicly justify itself, its norms and its practices relative to the "nonprofessionals" and the general public' (Hedman & Djerf-Pierre 2013, p. 371).

Singer (2012b) characterises the challenges as social pressures coming simultaneously from two directions: 'outside-in' pressures when everyone outside the newsroom is potentially both a source of information and a contributor/producer/publisher of news, views, photos, etc. (user-generated content); and 'inside-out' pressures where journalists are expected to reach out and socialise with the public in a way that is both personally engaging and professionally acceptable. Both types of pressure have resulted in news organisations issuing expanded guidance to deal with ethical and legal concerns surrounding the new ways of working. Significantly, the 'outside-in and inside-out' characterisation of the paradigm shift for professional practice described here is now gaining traction in the library world (Dahl 2018; Dempsey 2012; 2016; Ovenden 2018).

Gruen, Pearson and Brennan (2004) use the term 'physician-citizen' to signal a rethinking of the public roles and professional obligations of medical practitioners beyond their regular practice settings, emphasising their responsibility to raise public awareness about socio-economic issues affecting people's health and work with others to solve problems in their communities, arguing that engagement, advocacy, participation, outreach and collective action must become mainstream activities for physicians. Following an open-ended definition of physicians' public roles as 'advocacy for and participation in improving the aspects of communities that affect the health of individuals' (Gruen, Pearson & Brennan 2004, p. 94), they provide a more nuanced discussion of how such roles could be realised in practice, supported by a conceptual model differentiating professional *obligations* and professional *aspirations* in relation to environmental influences on health. A survey confirmed the importance of three evolving public roles – *community participation*, *collective advocacy* and (to a lesser extent) *political involvement* – with broad consensus on the scope and limits of responsibilities (Gruen, Campbell & Blumenthal, 2006).

The Gruen, Pearson and Brennan (2004, p. 95) model arguably has applicability beyond the medical profession as a way of conceptualising possible boundaries for the social responsibilities of professionals assuming expanded public roles in a modern participatory civil society. Figure 1.1 adapts their model with minor amendments to wording: the shaded areas represent core/central professional *obligations* and the unshaded areas are designated professional *aspirations*, as areas of concern or social goals that form part of a larger public

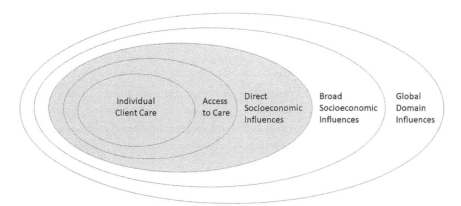

Figure 1.1 *Environmental influences on professional social responsibilities*
Adapted from Gruen, Pearson & Brennan 2004, p. 95.

agenda to be pursued with other citizens. However, realisation of the model depends on promotion of 'the skills and attitudes of good citizenship' in professional education (and practice).

Building on his earlier discussion of public/democratic journalism, Dzur (2004, p. 6) applies the term *democratic professional* to other professions (doctors, lawyers and teachers) that have recognised their civic roles and their 'democratic responsibilities – to enable rather than disable citizen participation within their spheres of professional authority'. His conception of democratic professionalism emphasises the political dividends of a shift from *task-monopoly* to *task-sharing* through lay participation that moves beyond raising public awareness to facilitating citizen engagement, public competence and *political socialisation*. More controversially, Dzur (2004, p. 12) also suggests that the label democratic professional 'might also characterize citizens who participate in previously expert or professionally dominated domains', taking the sharing of knowledge, authority and power to another level and highlighting further blurring of boundaries between citizen practitioners and civic/public professionals. While Gruen et al. (2004; 2006) emphasise collective advocacy/action for public purposes through professional organisations, Dzur's (2004) model involves citizens directly in collective deliberation, decision making and action – professionals working not only *for* citizens, but *with* citizens.

Dzur (2018) argues that in our complex, fast-paced society, the traditional 'social trustee' model of managerial, paternalistic, technocratic professionalism needs to evolve into a more collaborative working relationship with society, which combines and blends the specialist expertise of professionals with the knowledge and agency of citizens to help lay people to manage their personal and collective affairs. He criticises the *anti-professionalism* represented by the 'radical critique' of professional power from the 1960s that challenged technocratic monopolies without advancing viable alternatives, advocating instead a constructive power-sharing model of 'democratic professionalism oriented toward public capability', whereby professionals 'aim to understand the world of the patient, the offender, the client, the student, and the citizen on their terms – and then work collaboratively on common problems' (Dzur 2018, p. 15).

Dzur's (2018) model represents a middle ground between the traditional and radical positions, reinterpreting the social roles and responsibilities of professionals by widening access to specialist knowledge and participation in knowledge creation, but also requiring a radical shift to a co-operation and partnership model predicated on exchange of ideas and co-direction of services. Like Gruen, Pearson and Brennan (2004), Dzur (2018, p. 68) flags the need to reform professional education to incorporate the 'different modes of task-sharing, collaboration, coownership and democratic divisions of labor' that characterise the daily work of innovative practitioners in the field, echoing Singer (2012b) in suggesting the need for 'in-reach' to import ideas and best practices from the community into the university, in contrast to existing 'public outreach' models that assume knowledge flows in the opposite direction.

Dzur (2019) has also discussed how his model could be enacted in universities, by adopting a more participatory culture where administrators share power with faculty and faculty involve students in co-producing their own education as democratic professionals. There are parallels here with the emergent 'students as partners' movement in higher education and academic libraries (see Chapter 3), which advocates the sharing of tasks, knowledge and power with students across multiple domains (Healey, Flint & Harrington 2016; Salisbury, Dollinger & Vanderlelie 2020). Saltmarsh (2017, p. 4) links democratic professionalism in higher education to the renewed outward-looking focus on *community engagement*, which he sees as part of a larger pervasive *collaborative turn* in society, representing a disruptive shift in both practice and thinking that acknowledges the new realities of the 21st century and 'runs counter to the dominant culture of the academy which privileges specialized expertise above all else'. Earlier, in academic librarianship, Shuler (1996, p. 424) uses the emergent principles of public/civic journalism to provide a blueprint for reinventing government information librarians as *civic librarians*, while Kelley (2008) describes how exploring social software gave her a new professional identity as a *social librarian*.

Such language is more often used in public libraries, although the web/Library 2.0/3.0 has arguably moved the whole profession closer to a social democratic model. However, in Kenya, library researchers have adopted the term *citizen librarian* for 'the involvement of ordinary library users to create, review and share library services and content' and 'to perform roles which were conventionally reserved for librarians', facilitated by the use of 'citizen (social) media' (Gikunju, Nyamato-Kwenda & Kwanya 2019, pp. 109, 110, 111). They anchor their concept of *citizen librarianship* in the involvement of non-experts/lay people in *citizen science* and *citizen journalism*, but also link it to the Library 2.0 paradigm, though their survey found limited engagement with these practices among university libraries.

Corporate responsibility and sustainable development

The idea that businesses and other private sector organisations have 'an obligation to be socially responsible' and 'provide "service" beyond profits' or, more specifically, 'to work for social betterment' (Frederick 1994, p. 151) has been accepted for more than 50 years and formally acknowledged in the concept of corporate social responsibility (CSR), although understandings of what that means in practice have expanded in line with changes in social values and priorities. In the second half of the 20th century, thinking and practice around CSR evolved from vague notions of public purpose, good citizenship and the like to more active interpretations of the concept as corporate social *responsiveness* (Ackerman 1973) or 'the capacity of a corporation to respond to social pressures', thus moving from a philosophical ideal to a managerial requirement, in particular 'the ability to *manage* the company's relations with various social groups' (Frederick 1994, p. 156).

Key drivers here included significant social legislation of the 1970s in the USA (and in the UK and other countries) covering areas such as equal employment opportunities, occupational health and safety, and environmental protection, in turn a response to efforts of social activist groups in the 1960s (Carroll 1991). Related movements in management and organisational behaviour include business ethics (De George 1987) and stakeholder analysis/management as the role of stakeholders in decision making shifted from influence towards participation (Freeman & Reed, 1983). Other terms in the literature of the period include corporate social *policy* and corporate social *performance* (CSP). Wood (1991, p. 691) suggests that CSP 'can provide a coherent framework for the field of business and society' by synthesising apparently competing ideas and perspectives into a definition that integrates different dimensions of organisational behaviour and also illustrates how CSR/CSP is essentially about social *relationships*: 'a business organization's configuration of *principles* of social responsibility, *processes* of social responsiveness, and *policies*, *programs*, and observable *outcomes* as they relate to the firm's societal relationships' (Wood 1991, p. 693, emphasis added).

Frederick (2018, p. 9) defines five 'distinct, though overlapping CSR meanings' as evolutionary stages or phases, in which the focus shifted in turn from balancing profits with philanthropy (1950s–1960s) through responding to social demands (1960s–1970s), fostering an ethical culture (1980s–1990s), achieving planetary sustainability (1990s–2000s) and adapting to contemporary global challenges (2000s–). Note that the new focal concerns represent additions, not replacements for managerial attention as the social agenda for organisations of all sizes and types evolved during the late 20th and early 21st centuries. The terms 'corporate citizenship', 'global (corporate) citizenship', 'sustainability' and 'sustainable development' have been used increasingly since the 1990s, along with and in preference to CSR, signalling a strategic shift to longer-term social concerns and community relations/integration (Carroll & Brown, 2018).

A related theme here is recognising the need to make social concerns an integral and central part of business thinking and decisions on both operations and strategy, rather than an optional add-on, a trend exemplified in recent variants of CSR that focus on improving the social conditions in which an organisation operates, such as creating shared value from corporate social *integration* (CSI) (Porter & Kramer 2006; 2011) and corporate sustainability management (CSM) using context-based performance assessment (McElroy & van Engelen 2012; McElroy, Jorna & van Engelen 2008).

Integrating social perspectives

Carroll's (1991, p. 42) layered pyramid model is an early example of the more holistic and inclusive view of social responsibilities that evolved from the 1990s. His pyramid provides a four-part perspective on societal expectations of business that integrates four different but related types of responsibilities or aspects of performance, representing the economic, legal, ethical and philanthropic obligations of business to society. Figure 1.2 presents his model with some elaboration of wording to improve clarity.

Figure 1.2 *Four components of corporate social responsibility*
Adapted from Carroll 1991, p. 42.

Carroll (1991, p. 42) notes overlaps and tensions among these obligations, especially between the basic requirement for business success/economic performance and discretionary options for social initiatives/philanthropic activities, but argues that such are 'organizational realities'; firms should 'focus on the total pyramid as a unified whole' and strive to simultaneously fulfil all their responsibilities. His accompanying Stakeholder/Responsibility Matrix translates this pyramid into a practical decision-support tool for managers to consider their relationships and responsibilities towards key segments of society (individuals and groups), showing how the stakeholder concept 'personalizes social or societal responsibilities by delineating the specific groups or persons business should consider in its CSR orientation' (Carroll 1991, p. 43). With nine rows representing owners, customers, employees, community, competitors, suppliers, social activist groups, public at large and others, and four columns for the specified responsibilities, the matrix has 36 data cells 'to organize a manager's thoughts and ideas about what the firm ought to be doing in an economic, legal, ethical, and philanthropic sense with respect to its identified stakeholder groups' (Carroll 1991, p. 44).

Others argue that concerns around balance and tension between the profit motive and social good arise from a failure to think strategically about the interdependence of business and society, and from the common disconnect between CSR initiatives and company strategies and operations. Porter and Kramer (2006, p. 84) describe how an organisation should 'integrate a social perspective into the core frameworks it already uses to understand competition and guide its business strategy', which will in turn bring a strategic perspective to its social activities. Referencing the familiar inside-out/outside-in dichotomy, they explain the need to consider business–society links from both directions – both the social impact of their business operations (*inside-out linkages*) and the social influences or constraints on their business competitiveness (*outside-in linkages*). Thus, business decisions, social policies and operating practices should all be guided by the principle of creating *shared value* ('a meaningful benefit for society that is also valuable to the business'), by 'making social impact integral to the overall strategy' (Porter & Kramer 2006, pp. 84, 90).

Porter and Kramer (2006, p. 92) contrast traditional *responsive CSR* based on damage control or public relations with their model of *strategic CSR* aimed at creating shared value, concluding that 'NGOs, governments and companies must stop thinking in terms of "corporate social responsibility" and start thinking in terms of "corporate social integration"'. They later argue that 'Creating shared value (CSV) should supersede corporate social responsibility (CSR)': CSR and CSV both assume legal compliance and ethical standards, but CSV presents social agendas as integral and essential to competitiveness and profitability, instead of separate and discretionary (Porter & Kramer 2011, p. 76).

Shared value is defined in business terms as 'policies and operating practices that enhance the competitiveness of a company while simultaneously advancing the economic and social conditions in the communities in which it operates', but Porter and Kramer (2011, pp. 66, 67, 72) emphasise that its principles 'apply equally to governments and nonprofit organizations' and the concept blurs the boundary and distinction between for-profit and non-profit organisations, giving rise to new kinds of 'hybrid enterprises'. Three distinct but mutually reinforcing strategies create the 'virtuous circle' of shared value: reconceiving products and markets to create societal benefits; redefining productivity and costs in an organisation's activities; and building support and capabilities in the local community. However, collaboration among all stakeholders, particularly the ability and willingness to engage in 'new and heightened forms of collaboration' across profit/non-profit boundaries emerges as the key to linking economic development with social progress.

There are parallels here between the social integration model (Porter & Kramer 2006; 2011) and calls for higher education institutions to 'integrate social responsibility principles into their teaching and research activities as well as into their management and community engagement activities' (Larrán Jorge & Andrades Peña 2017, p. 303; Symaco & Tee 2019). *University social responsibility* has taken various forms, ranging from *knowledge transfer*/exchange and collaborative capacity building for socio-economic development to community engagement contributing to civic education and democratic participation, as well as responsible management of environmental impact through sustainability strategies (Barth, 2013; Chile & Black 2015; Davis 2009; Kalar & Antoncic 2015; Shiel et al. 2016). Academic libraries are involved in university knowledge exchange and community building, supporting technology transfer/commercialisation, community research partnerships, *service/community-based learning* and socially inclusive employment (Elliott et al. 2017; Hernandez & Knight 2010; Sidorko & Yang 2011; Wiggins, Derickson & Jenkins 2020).

Libraries are also contributing to institutional economic, social, environmental and cultural sustainability strategies. *Sustainability* is an aspect of social responsibility where they are not just supporting institutional strategies, but proactive partners in advancing campus and community agendas. With 'a moral imperative . . . to become sustainable organizations' (Jankowska & Marcum 2010, p. 167), they aspire to be 'an exemplar of "sustainability in action" for the university' (Brodie 2012, p. 6) and understand that 'environmental stewardship is an expression of community engagement' and 'a social choice with economic ramifications' (Reynolds 2012, pp. 19, 36). Thus, Concordia University Library is a neighbourhood library and meeting place for local residents, as well as providing teaching facilities, reading rooms, private study, collaborative learning and social spaces for students and faculty (Reynolds 2012). The green library movement has evolved from environmental management of buildings and operations, through sustainability strategies for collections and services, towards integrated frameworks for evaluation and assessment that promise a richer picture of their economic, social and other contributions beyond their institutions, for example by using relevant United Nations Sustainable Development Goals to frame a blend of quantitative and qualitative indicators (Missingham 2021).

Prioritising the environment

The World Commission on Environment and Development (WCED, led by Norwegian prime minister, Gro Harlem Brundtland) put *sustainable development* on global agenda in the late 1980s, defining the concept as 'development that meets the needs of the present without compromising the ability of future generations to meet their own needs' (United Nations 1987, p. 43) and advocating the wholesale integration of environmental thinking into social, political and economic activities. British environmental consultant John Elkington turned sustainability into a business issue by formulating the '*triple bottom line*' accounting, auditing and reporting framework, elaborated in his book, *Cannibals with forks*, and characterised as 'focusing on economic prosperity, environmental quality, and – the element which business had preferred to overlook – social justice' (Elkington 1997, p. 70).

While the WCED definition is widely cited, the report and related documentation were criticised for being vague about both the concept of sustainability and policies to accomplish it; triple bottom line (TBL, also known as 3BL) brought focus and structure, as well as using the familiar (financial) bottom line metaphor to encourage managers to extend their measurement systems to non-financial performance. More significantly, as well as extending the scope for strategic performance assessment to the impacts and outcomes of organisational activities on the economy, society and the environment, Elkington (1997; 1998) was an early advocate of what was later described as 'the capitals-based theory of sustainability performance', 'the capital theory approach to sustainability', 'multiple capital theory' and 'multiple capitals-based frameworks' (McElroy, Jorna & van Engelen 2008, p. 223; McElroy & van Engelen 2012, p. 32; McElroy & Thomas 2015, p. 425; UNEP 2015, p. 52): 'sustainable capitalism will need . . . new views of what is meant by social equity, environmental justice and business ethics. This will require a much better understanding not only of financial and physical forms of capital, but also of natural, human, and social capital' (Elkington 1997, p. 72).

Elkington (1997; 1998) here exemplifies the shift from **monocapitalism** (the traditional focus on **economic capital**, historically limited to *financial* and *physical* forms of capital, the latter including machinery and plant) to **multicapitalism**, 'a kind of pluralistic form of capital management instead of the traditional monistic one' (McElroy & van Engelen 2012, p. 52), by specifying *human* or *intellectual* capital, critical and renewable **natural capital** and *social* capital as other key areas for businesses to measure and manage. While the corporate world had begun to view non-tangible entities (such as knowledge, brands and reputation) as business assets, the breakthrough here was including the natural environment as a capital asset. TBL is often referenced as the '3Ps' (people, planet and profits), which has given widespread recognition to the basic idea, but has resulted in superficial interpretation and frequent dilution of the concept by journalists and managers failing to appreciate the third P is about tracking *economic* value added (or destroyed), not just *financial* performance (Elkington 2018).

British environmentalist Jonathon Porritt (2005) followed Elkington's 3Ps/3BL with his **Five Capitals Framework**, elaborated in the book *Capitalism as if the world matters* as a 'hypothetical model of sustainable capitalism'. His five forms basically follow Elkington, but he replaces '**physical capital**' with '**manufactured capital**'. Defining capital as 'a stock of anything that has the capacity to generate a flow of benefits which are valued by humans', Porritt (2005 pp. 112, 113) acknowledges the discomfort of many environmentalists with the 'terminological reduction' of natural resources, human capabilities and social relationships to the language of capitalism as yet more evidence of 'the inexorable commodification of our world', but argues compellingly that adopting (and adapting) some of the insights, tools and drivers of capitalism – a strategy of *reform from within* – is the only viable option: 'any genuinely sustainable variant of capitalism . . . will need to work within the conceptual and linguistic conventions that people are now so familiar with. The concept of capital serves not only to explain the productive power of capitalism; it also provides the clearest means of explaining the conditions for its sustainability.'

There have been several efforts to move sustainability management from concept to implementation by developing tools to improve how organisations report their social, ecological and economic impacts. A review by the United Nations Environment Programme (UNEP 2015) supports the trend towards context-based and multi-capital approaches, best exemplified by the **MultiCapital Scorecard (MCS)** developed by McElroy and Thomas (2015, p. 434; 2016) as 'a capital- and context-based integrated measurement and reporting system' that is a *stakeholder-based multiple capital* system, not *shareholder-based financial-capital-centric*. McElroy and Thomas (2015, p. 426) argue that without integrated measurement and reporting, 'there can be no integrated thinking and management' as advocated by contemporary strategists; their system claims to be the first 'fully operationalized triple bottom line method' (McElroy & Thomas 2016, p. 7).

In the library sector, there are a few examples of multi-capital measurement tools that combine tangible and intangible assets, including a multidimensional framework developed at the Council for Scientific and Industrial Research in South Africa (van Deventer & Snyman 2004) and the more expansive Value Scorecard developed at the University of York in the UK (Town 2018), but neither model explicitly covers library performance across all three dimensions of the environmental agenda (economic, social and environmental/ecological).

Reframing capitalism for social development

Conceptions of the social roles and responsibilities of individuals and organisations have expanded to integrate social stewardship with social activism, social justice, social diversity and *global citizenship*, while striving to balance the economic operations of corporations and the social aspirations of communities. Commentators have recognised the need to rethink established capitalist models in response to the social, economic, environmental and political challenges of the 21st century: Porter and Kramer (2011, p. 77) discuss how to 'reinvent capitalism', calling for 'a more sophisticated form . . . imbued with a social purpose' based on 'a deeper understanding of . . . economic value creation' and strategies that take account of social and environmental concerns in their economic thinking. Other proposals include *conscious capitalism* (O'Toole & Vogel 2011) and *moral capitalism* (Young 2003), in addition to the *sustainable capitalism* advocated by Elkington (1997), Porritt (2005) and Zohar and Marshall (2004).

Sustainable capitalism and CSV/CSI (Porter & Kramer 2006; 2011) start from different premises, speak to different constituencies and propose different frameworks, but both point towards a future path for organisations based on the judicious combination and strategic integration of outside-in and inside-out connections and dependencies. Several authors (Elkington 1997; Porritt 2005; Young 2003) have elaborated their vision for corporate reform in capital-based models or frameworks informed by the **resource-based view (RBV)** of the firm from the 1980s (Grant 1991) and the intellectual capital (IC) perspective of the 1990s (Peppard & Rylander 2001) with its focus on 'resources in action' and the contribution of *intangible assets* such as professional competence, business processes and stakeholder relationships to value creation.

IC models came from the corporate sector, but their holistic view of organisations (typically concentrating on human, structural and relational assets) also supports integrated reporting, performance appraisal and strategy development for start-ups, non-profits and public bodies, particularly as the public sector has become more innovative and IC frameworks have evolved to reflect contemporary management concerns (Mouritsen et al. 2004; Ramírez 2010). Katsikas, Rossi and Orelli (2017, p. 7) argue that 'in public organizations the recognition and communication of intangible assets is pivotal' in the context of new business models based on stakeholder engagement and citizen participation as co-producers in service delivery and co-creators of public value. Conceptions of public value have also evolved in line with integrated thinking and social needs: Benington (2009, p. 237) extends his definition beyond economic value to *ecological value*, *political value* and *social and cultural value* as significant aspects and underlines the vital role of collaborative networks in value creation.

In the early 2000s, the Intellectus Model of IC from Spain introduced an explicit focus on *social capital* by separating the **relational capital** component into business/market relationships and social relationships, the latter including the environment (Bueno, Salmador & Rodríguez 2004). The latest version of their model adds an *entrepreneurship* and **innovation capital** component, combining and integrating the creative capabilities represented by the intangible assets in different capital elements, in order to improve the practical relevance of the model as a strategic management tool (Bueno, Merino & Murcia 2016). Zohar and Marshall (2004, p. 41) take the broadening of capital to another level, advocating reform based on a wider and deeper commitment to society that has both social and *moral* dimensions, represented by **spiritual capital**, which comprises 'our shared meaning, our shared purpose, our shared vision of what most deeply matters in life – and how these are implemented in our lives and in our behavioral strategies' and is 'increased by drawing on the resources of the human spirit'.

To round out and wrap up this discussion, we provide an enriched multi-capital relational model that synthesises theories, concepts and ideas from key thinkers in business, economics, ethics and politics to provide a transdisciplinary perspective on the tangible resources and intangible assets that represent 'vital capitals' (McElroy & Thomas 2015) for mobilisation and deployment to create value for stakeholders (Peppard & Rylander 2001). Figure 1.3 on the next page displays our model, which promotes holistic thinking about the range of internal and external resources organisations and communities draw on, develop, combine, organise, distribute and deploy in their operational activities to support their strategic vision. The model indicates how intellectual and physical resources interact to create value and illustrates the fundamental role of human interactions and social relationships in resource renewal and depletion.

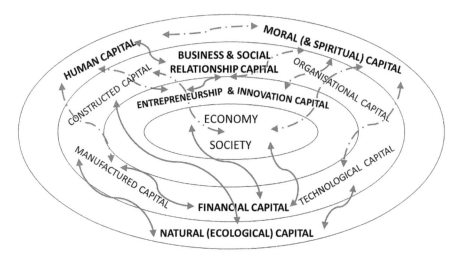

Figure 1.3 *A multi-capital perspective on asset management*

The proposed model also places social capital in its strategic and operational context, showing how it is derived from human and **moral capital**, then in turn feeds forward into entrepreneurship and innovation capital, as well as feeding back to enhance human and moral assets in a system of reciprocal flows. The bidirectional arrows indicate how different forms of capital have the potential to feed off each other to a greater or lesser extent, depending on levels of capital available; so, for example, if an organisation's stated values of social responsibility and sustainability are not shared by all members of the organisation, that will reduce the ability to use its moral capital assets to enhance **human capital** and influence organisational behaviour.

The model combines elements from the Intellectus Model (Bueno, Merino & Murcia 2016) and the Five Capitals Framework (Porritt 2005), adopting the latter's concentric circles design and distinction between primary and derived capitals, but with a modified layout and extended scope bringing in other related capitals to give a fuller picture of salient resources requiring responsible management for sustainable development. In particular, our conception is augmented by critical insights into relationships between social capital, moral capital and physical/manufactured capital provided by scholars like Alejo Sison (2003) and Xiaoxi Wang (2015), who argue that morality is a sufficiently distinct and significant aspect of human capital to justify its own place in any capital-based typology.

Several scholars observe that while emotional, moral and spiritual capacities are vital human qualities, contemporary models of intellectual assets tend to focus on 'harder' measurable dimensions of human capital, such as knowledge, skills and abilities (KSA), often ignoring 'softer' aspects like values, beliefs and attitudes (VBA). Such reductionist thinking fails to appreciate how the spiritual capital of individuals generates social capital for organisations and how moral development contributes to workforce productivity, product quality and economic growth (Stokes, Baker & Lichy 2016; Wódka 2017). Wang (2015, pp. 56–57) presents moral capital as 'a kind of "spiritual capital" or "**knowledge capital**"' that overlaps with both human capital and physical (manufactured) capital as 'the spiritual aspect of human capital and the spiritual element of physical capital' or 'the spiritual factor of production', explaining how the value orientation of workers contributes to human-centred design, manufacture, distribution, sales and consumption of products and services.

Sison (2003, p. viii) concentrates on the contribution of moral capital to social capital, illustrating its crucial role in business transactions by showing how social capital represented by extensive networks of influence and high levels of trust can be exploited for criminal gain as well as social benefit and is thus 'morally ambivalent in its uses and effects', drawing an important distinction here between trust and *trustworthiness*. Arguing that 'business ethics needs to be institutionalized in such a way that it permeates even apparently isolated individual practices' by 'integrating moral value operatively into corporate culture', Sison (2003, p. ix) explains how moral capital elevates business ethics beyond superficial compliance with codes of conduct to a deeper commitment to a set of values. Moral capital thus provides the missing link in capitals-based strategies for sustainable development and is another 'vital capital' for individuals, organisations and communities to cultivate in the participatory collaborative culture of the 21st century.

Conclusion

Participation has become the watchword of the digital world, with participatory principles, processes, policies and programs spreading to all areas of our personal, social, professional and organisational lives as formal procedures or *de facto* practices, enabled by web-based interactive technologies. Participatory culture and the prevalence of related concepts such as access, agency, collaboration, community, engagement and empowerment are the result of both bottom-up pressures from community groups, social networks and activist movements and top-down factors that include global commitments to environmental management, sustainable development and social equity. The online world of the 21st century has given us novel vocabulary such as produsage, crowdsourcing and apomediation; it has made work, learning and everyday tasks more co-operative, open and reflective and is blurring private–public, personal–professional, patient–practitioner and lay person–expert boundaries.

The creative potential and productive capacity represented by social interactions and collaborative networks is universally acknowledged, with the result that building and nurturing positive relationships is now recognised as a critical factor for business and professional success. Scholars and practitioners are accordingly incorporating social perspectives and relational strategies into their business models and reporting templates, notably by expanding capital-based frameworks to include environmental and social issues. The changes outlined here are impacting every aspect of our individual and collective lives, and have significant implications for education, professions and organisations of all kinds.

We have already noted how some of the practices discussed here are being adopted in or adapted for higher education and academic libraries, evident in the use of blogging, crowdsourcing and learning communities/networks, and are also generating new conceptions of practitioners as civic, democratic or social professionals who exchange knowledge and share tasks with others via more open and collaborative ways of working. The following chapters provide a closer look at how the environmental developments and social trends presented here are playing out in the higher education sector and academic library community.

References

Ackerman, R. W., (1973). How companies respond to social demands. *Harvard Business Review.* 51(4), 88–98.

Barth, M., (2013). Many roads lead to sustainability: a process oriented analysis of change in higher education. *International Journal of Sustainability in Higher Education.* 14(2), 160–175. doi:10.1108/14676371311312879

Benington, J., (2009). Creating the public in order to create public value? *International Journal of Public Administration.* 32(3–4), 232–249. doi:10.1080/01900690902749578

Benkler, Y., (2005). *Common wisdom: peer production of educational materials.* Logan, UT: COSL Press. http://www.benkler.org/Common_Wisdom.pdf

Bozarth, J., (2014). *Show your work: the payoffs and how-to's of working out loud.* San Francisco, CA: Wiley.

Brabham, D. C., (2013). *Crowdsourcing.* Cambridge, MA: MIT Press.

Brodie, M., (2012). Building the sustainable library at Macquarie University. *Australian Academic & Research Libraries.* 43(1), 4–16. doi:10.1080/00048623.2012.10722250

Brown, J. S. and Duguid, P., (1991). Organizational learning and communities-of-practice: toward a unified view of working, learning, and innovation. *Organization Science.* 2(1), 40–57. doi:10.1287/orsc.2.1.40

Bruns, A., (2013). From prosumption to produsage. In: R. Towse and C. Handke, eds. *Handbook on the digital creative economy.* Cheltenham, UK: Edward Elgar. pp. 67–78. https://pdfs.semanticscholar.org/05db/154e87113915d0d6475e42ba31c1dda31259.pdf

Bueno, E., Merino, C. and Murcia, C., (2016). Intellectual capital as a strategic model to create innovation in new technology based firms. In: K. North and G. Varvakis, eds. *Competitive strategies for small and medium enterprises: increasing crisis resilience, agility and innovation in turbulent times.* Cham, Switzerland: Springer. pp. 93–105. doi:10.1007/978-3-319-27303-7_6

Bueno, E., Salmador, M. P. and Rodríguez, Ó., (2004). The role of social capital in today's economy: empirical evidence and proposal of a new model of intellectual capital. *Journal of Intellectual Capital.* 5(4), 556–574. doi:10.1108/14691930410567013

Carletti, L., Giannachi, G., Price, D., McAuley, D. and Benford, S., (2013). Digital humanities and crowdsourcing: an exploration. In: *MW2013: Museums and the web, April 17–20, Portland, OR.* https://mw2013.museumsandtheweb.com/paper/digital-humanities-and-crowdsourcing-an-exploration-4

Carroll, A. B., (1991). The pyramid of corporate social responsibility: toward the moral management of organizational stakeholders. *Business Horizons*. **34**(4), 39–48. doi:10.1016/0007-6813(91)90005-G

Carroll, A. B. and Brown, J. A., (2018). Corporate social responsibility: a review of current concepts, research, and issues. In: J. Weber and D. M. Wasieleski, eds. *Corporate social responsibility*. Bingley, UK: Emerald. pp. 39–69. doi:10.1108/S2514-175920180000002002

Castells, M., (1996). *The rise of the network society*. Oxford: Blackwell.

Chesbrough, H., Vanhaverbeke, W. and West, J. eds., (2006). *Open innovation: researching a new paradigm*. Oxford: Oxford University Press.

Chile, L. M. and Black, X. M., (2015). University–community engagement: case study of university social responsibility. *Education, Citizenship and Social Justice*. **10**(3), 234–253. doi:10.1177/1746197915607278

Clinio, A. and Albagli, S., (2017). Open notebook science as an emerging epistemic culture within the open science movement. *Revue Française des Sciences de l'information et de la communication*. **11**. doi:10.4000/rfsic.3186

Cooke, N. A., (2012). Professional development 2.0 for librarians: developing an online personal learning network (PLN). *Library Hi Tech News*. **29**(3), 1–9. doi:10.1108/07419051211241840

Cox, M. D., (1999). Peer consultation and faculty learning communities. *New Directions for Teaching and Learning*. **79**, 39–49. doi:10.1002/tl.7905

Dahl, M., (2018). Inside-out library services. In: G. J. Fowler and S. S. Hines, eds. Challenging the "Jacks of all trades but masters of none" librarian syndrome. *Advances in Library Administration and Organization*. **39**. Bingley, UK: Emerald. pp. 15–34. doi:10.1108/S0732-067120180000039003

Dalton, M., Kouker, A. and O'Connor, M., (2016). Many voices: building a biblioblogosphere in Ireland. *New Review of Academic Librarianship*. **22**(2–3), 148–159. doi:10.1080/13614533.2016.1155998

Davis, S. F., (2009). Knowledge exchange: capacity building in a small university. *Education + Training*. **51**(8/9), 682–695. doi:10.1108/00400910911005235

De George, R. T., (1987). The status of business ethics: past and future. *Journal of Business Ethics*. **6**(3), 201–211. doi:10.1007/BF00382865

Delwiche, A. and Henderson, J. J., (2013). Introduction: what is participatory culture? In: A. Delwiche and J. J. Henderson, eds. *The participatory cultures handbook*. New York: Routledge. pp. 3–9. doi:10.4324/9780203117927

Dempsey, L., (2012). Libraries and the informational future: some notes. *Information Services & Use*. **32**(3–4), 203–214. doi:10.3233/ISU-2012-0670

Dempsey, L., (2016). Library collections in the life of the user: two directions. *LIBER Quarterly*. **26**(4), 338–359. doi:10.18352/lq.10170

Douglas, V. A. and Becker, A. A., (2015). Encouraging better graphic design in libraries: a creative commons crowdsourcing approach. *Journal of Library Administration*. **55**(6), 459–472. doi:10.1080/01930826.2015.1054765

Dzur, A. W., (2002). Public journalism and deliberative democracy. *Polity.* **34**(3), 313–336. doi:10.1086/POLv34n3ms3235394

Dzur, A. W., (2004). Democratic professionalism: sharing authority in civic life. *The Good Society.* **13**(1), 6–14. doi:10.1353/gso.2004.0026

Dzur, A. W., (2018). *Rebuilding public institutions together: professionals and citizens in a participatory democracy.* Ithaca, NY: Cornell University Press. doi:10.7591/j.ctt20d89c6

Dzur, A., (2019). Conclusion: sources of democratic professionalism in the university. In: N. V. Longo and T. J. Shaffer, eds. *Creating space for democracy: a primer on dialogue and deliberation in higher education.* Sterling, VA: Stylus. pp. 285–294.

Elkington, J., (1997). *Cannibals with forks: the triple bottom line of 21st century business.* Oxford: Capstone.

Elkington, J., (1998). Accounting for the triple bottom line. *Measuring Business Excellence.* **2**(3), 18–22. doi:10.1108/eb025539

Elkington, J., (2018). 25 years ago I coined the phrase "triple bottom line." Here's why it's time to rethink it. *Harvard Business Review.* 25 June 2018. https://hbr.org/2018/06/25-years-ago-i-coined-the-phrase-triple-bottom-line-heres-why-im-giving-up-on-it

Elliott, C., Dewland, J., Martin, J. R., Kramer, S. and Jackson, J. J., (2017). Collaborate and innovate: the impact of academic librarians on the commercialization of university technology. *Journal of Library Administration.* **57**(1), 36–48. doi:10.1080/01930826.2016.1215674

Eysenbach, G., (2008). Medicine 2.0: social networking, collaboration, participation, apomediation, and openness. *Journal of Medical Internet Research.* **10**(3), e22. doi:10.2196/jmir.1030

Ferguson, T., (2007). *e-Patients: how they can help us heal health care.* White paper. Nutting Lake, MA: Society of Participatory Medicine. https://participatorymedicine.org/e-Patient_White_Paper_with_Afterword.pdf

Frederick, W. C., (1994). From CSR_1 to CSR_2: the maturing of business-and-society thought. *Business & Society.* **33**(2), 150–164. doi:10.1177/000765039403300202

Frederick, W. C., (2018). Corporate social responsibility: from founders to millennials. In: J. Weber and D. M. Wasieleski, eds. *Corporate social responsibility.* Bingley, UK: Emerald. pp. 3–38. doi:10.1108/S2514-175920180000002001

Freeman, R. E. and Reed, D. L., (1983). Stockholders and stakeholders: a new perspective on corporate governance. *California Management Review.* **25**(3), 88–106. doi:10.2307/41165018

Fumagalli, L. P., Radaelli, G., Lettieri, E. and Masella, C., (2015). Patient empowerment and its neighbours: clarifying the boundaries and their mutual relationships. *Health Policy.* **119**(3), 384–394. doi:10.1016/j.healthpol.2014.10.017

Gikunju, M., Nyamato-Kwenda, R. and Kwanya, T., (2019). A review of citizen librarianship in academic libraries in Kenya. In: T. Kwanya, J. Kiplang'at, J. Wamukoya and D. Njiraine, eds. *Digital technologies for information and knowledge management.* Nairobi, Kenya: Technical University of Kenya. pp. 109–117. http://repository.tukenya.ac.ke/handle/123456789/1757

Grant, R. M., (1991). The resource-based theory of competitive advantage: implications for strategy formulation. *California Management Review.* **33**(3), 114–135. doi:10.2307/41166664

Gruen, R. L., Campbell, E. G. and Blumenthal, D., (2006). Public roles of US physicians: community participation, political involvement, and collective advocacy. *Journal of the American Medical Association.* **296**(20), 2467–2475. doi:10.1001/jama.296.20.2467

Gruen, R. L., Pearson, S. D. and Brennan, T. A., (2004). Physician-citizens – public roles and professional obligations. *Journal of the American Medical Association.* **291**(1), 94–98. doi:10.1001/jama.291.1.94

Healey, M., Flint, A. and Harrington, K., (2016). Students as partners: reflections on a conceptual model. *Teaching & Learning Inquiry.* **4**(2), 8–20. doi:10.20343/teachlearninqu.4.2.3

Hedman, U. and Djerf-Pierre, M., (2013). The social journalist: embracing the social media life or creating a new digital divide? *Digital Journalism.* **1**(3), 368–385. doi:10.1080/21670811.2013.776804

Hegarty, B., (2015). Attributes of open pedagogy: a model for using open educational resources. *Educational Technology.* **55**(4), 3–13.

Hernandez, M. and Knight, L. A., (2010). Reinventing the box: faculty–librarian collaborative efforts to foster service learning for political engagement. *Journal for Civic Commitment.* 14(Special issue). https://scholarlycommons.pacific.edu/cop-facarticles/825

Howe, J., (2006). The rise of crowdsourcing. *Wired.* **14**(6). https://www.wired.com/2006/06/crowds/

Howe, J., (2008a). *Crowdsourcing: how the power of the crowd is driving the future of business.* New York: Crown Business.

Howe, J., (2008b). The wisdom of the crowd resides in how the crowd is used. *Nieman Report.* **62**(4), 47–50. https://niemanreports.org/articles/the-wisdom-of-the-crowd-resides-in-how-the-crowd-is-used

Jackson-Brown, G. M., (2013). Content analysis study of librarian blogs: professional development and other uses. *First Monday.* **18**(2). doi:10.5210/fm.v18i2.4343

Jankowska, M. A. and Marcum, J. W., (2010). Sustainability challenge for academic libraries: planning for the future. *College & Research Libraries.* **71**(2), 160–170. doi:10.5860/0710160

Jenkins, H., (1992). *Textual poachers: television fans and participatory culture.* New York: Routledge.

Jenkins, H., (2006a). *Convergence culture: where old and new media collide.* New York: New York University Press.

Jenkins, H., (2006b). Interactive audiences? The collective intelligence of media fans. In: H. Jenkins, *Fans, bloggers, and gamers: exploring participatory culture.* New York: New York University Press. pp. 134–151.

Jenkins, H., (2010). Transmedia storytelling and entertainment: an annotated syllabus. *Continuum.* **24**(6), 943–958. doi:10.1080/10304312.2010.510599

Jenkins, H., (2014). Rethinking 'rethinking convergence/culture'. *Cultural Studies.* **28**(2), 267–297. doi:10.1080/09502386.2013.801579

Jenkins, H., Clinton, K., Purushotma, R., Robison, A. J. and Weigel, M., (2006). *Confronting the challenges of participatory culture: media education for the 21st century.* White paper.

Chicago, IL: MacArthur Foundation.
https://www.macfound.org/media/article_pdfs/jenkins_white_paper.pdf

Jenkins, H., Ito, M. and boyd, d., (2016). *Participatory culture in a networked era: a conversation on youth, learning, commerce, and politics.* Cambridge, UK: Polity Press.

Kalar, B. and Antoncic, B., (2015). The entrepreneurial university, academic activities and technology and knowledge transfer in four European countries. *Technovation.* 36–37, 1–11. doi:10.1016/j.technovation.2014.11.002

Katsikas, E., Rossi, F. M. and Orelli, R. L., (2017). *Towards integrated reporting: accounting change in the public sector.* Cham, Switzerland: Springer.

Kelley, J., (2008). The making of a social librarian: how blogs, wikis and Facebook have changed one librarian and her job. In: *PCA/ACA 2008: Joint conference of the National Popular Culture and American Culture Associations, March 19–22, San Francisco, CA.* https://dc.cod.edu/librarypub/2

Kelty, C. et al., (2015). Seven dimensions of contemporary participation disentangled. *Journal of the Association for Information Science and Technology.* 66(3), 474–488. doi:10.1002/asi.23202

Kwanya, T., Stilwell, C. and Underwood, P., (2015). *Library 3.0: intelligent libraries and apomediation.* Waltham, MA: Chandos.

Lankes, R. D., Silverstein, J. and Nicholson, S., (2007). Participatory networks: the library as conversation. *Information Technology and Libraries.* 26(4), 17–33. doi:10.6017/ital.v26i4.3267

Larrán Jorge, M. and Andrades Peña, F. J., (2017). Analysing the literature on university social responsibility: a review of selected higher education journals. *Higher Education Quarterly.* 71(4), 302–319. doi:10.1111/hequ.12122

Maness, J. M., (2006). Library 2.0 theory: Web 2.0 and its implications for libraries. *Webology.* 3(2). https://www.webology.org/data-cms/articles/20200515033842pma25.pdf

Margaryan, A., Boursinou, E., Lukic, D. and de Zwart, H., (2015). Narrating your work: an approach to supporting knowledge sharing in virtual teams. *Knowledge Management Research and Practice.* 13(4), 391–400. doi:10.1057/kmrp.2013.58

McElroy, M. W. and Thomas, M. P., (2015). The multicapital scorecard. *Sustainability Accounting, Management and Policy Journal.* 6(3), 425–438. doi:10.1108/SAMPJ-04-2015-0025

McElroy, M. W. and Thomas, M. P., (2016). *The multicapital scorecard: rethinking organizational performance.* White River Junction, VT: Chelsea Green Publishing.

McElroy, M. W. and van Engelen, J. M. L., (2012). *Corporate sustainability management: the art and science of managing non-financial performance.* Abingdon, UK: Earthscan

McElroy, M. W., Jorna, R. J. and van Engelen, J. M. L., (2008). Sustainability quotients and the social footprint. *Corporate Social Responsibility and Environmental Management.* 15(4), 223–234. doi:10.1002/csr.164

Mi, M., (2015). Expanding librarian roles through a librarian initiated and facilitated faculty learning community. *Journal of Library Administration.* 55(1), 24–40. doi:10.1080/01930826.2014.978683

Missingham, R., (2021). A new lens for evaluation – assessing academic libraries using the UN Sustainable Development Goals. *Journal of Library Administration.* 61(3), 386–401. doi:10.1080/01930826.2021.1883376

Mouritsen, J., Thorbjørnsen, S., Bukh, P. N. and Johansen, M. R., (2004). Intellectual capital and new public management: reintroducing enterprise. *The Learning Organization*. **11**(4/5), 380–392. doi:10.1108/09696470410538279

O'Reilly, T., (1999). Lessons from open-source software development. *Communications of the ACM*. **42**(4), 32–37. doi:10.1145/299157.299164

O'Reilly, T., (2005). *What is Web 2.0? Design patterns and business models for the next generation of software*. Sebastopol, CA: O'Reilly Media. https://www.oreilly.com/pub/a//web2/archive/what-is-web-20.html

O'Toole, J. and Vogel, D., (2011). Two and a half cheers for conscious capitalism. *California Management Review*. **53**(3), 60–76. doi:10.1525/cmr.2011.53.3.60

Outing, S., (2005). The 11 layers of citizen journalism. *Poynter Online*. 31 May 2005. https://www.poynter.org/archive/2005/the-11-layers-of-citizen-journalism

Ovenden, R., (2018). Outside in: the role of the university library in open science. *Wonkhe*. 12 June 2018. https://wonkhe.com/blogs/outside-in-the-role-of-the-university-library-in-open-science

Partridge, H., Lee, J. and Munro, C., (2010). Becoming "Librarian 2.0": the skills, knowledge, and attributes required by library and information science professionals in a Web 2.0 world (and beyond). *Library Trends*. **59**(1–2), 315–335. http://hdl.handle.net/2142/18735

Peppard, J. and Rylander, A., (2001). Using an intellectual capital perspective to design and implement a growth strategy: the case of APiON. *European Management Journal*. **19**(5), 510–525. doi:10.1016/S0263-2373(01)00065-2

Porritt, J., (2005). *Capitalism as if the world matters*. London: Earthscan.

Porter, M. and Kramer, M., (2006). Strategy and society: the link between competitive advantage and corporate social responsibility. *Harvard Business Review*. **84**(12), 78–92.

Porter, M. E. and Kramer, M. R., (2011). Creating shared value: how to reinvent capitalism – and unleash a wave of innovation and growth. *Harvard Business Review*. **89**(1–2), 62–77.

Ramírez, Y., (2010). Intellectual capital models in Spanish public sector. *Journal of Intellectual Capital*. **11**(2), 248–264. doi:10.1108/14691931011039705

Reynolds, K. M., (2012). Building a green community at Concordia University Library. In: M. Antonelli and M. McCullough, eds. *Greening libraries*. Sacramento, CA: Library Juice Press. pp. 17–40.

Rheingold, H., (1987). Virtual communities – exchanging ideas through computer bulletin boards. *Whole Earth Review*. **57**(Winter). [Reprinted *Journal for Virtual Worlds Research*. **1**(1).] doi:10.4101/jvwr.v1i1.293

Rheingold, H., (1993). *The virtual community: homesteading on the electronic frontier*. Reading, MA: Addison-Wesley. https://www.rheingold.com/vc/book

Salisbury, F., Dollinger, M. and Vanderlelie, J., (2020). Students as partners in the academic library: co-designing for transformation. *New Review of Academic Librarianship*. **26**(2–4), 304–321. doi:10.1080/13614533.2020.1780275

Saltmarsh J., (2017). A collaborative turn: trends and directions in community engagement. In: J. Sachs and L. Clark, eds. *Learning through community engagement*. Singapore: Springer. pp. 3–15. doi:10.1007/978-981-10-0999-0_1

Sergi, V. and Bonneau, C., (2016). Making mundane work visible on social media: a CCO investigation of working out loud on Twitter. *Communication Research and Practice*. 2(3), 378–406. doi:10.1080/22041451.2016.1217384

Severson, S. and Sauvé, J.-S., (2019). Crowding the library: how and why libraries are using crowdsourcing to engage the public. *Partnership: The Canadian Journal of Library and Information Practice and Research*. 14(1). doi:10.21083/partnership.v14i1.4632

Shiel, C., Leal Filho, W., do Paço, A. and Brandli, L., (2016). Evaluating the engagement of universities in capacity building for sustainable development in local communities. *Evaluation and Program Planning*. 54, 123–134. doi:10.1016/j.evalprogplan.2015.07.006

Shuler, J. A., (1996). Civic librarianship: possible new role for depository libraries in the next century? *Journal of Government Information*. 23(4), 419–425. doi:10.1016/1352-0237(96)00022-6

Sidorko, P. E. and Yang, T. T., (2011). Knowledge exchange and community engagement: an academic library perspective. *Library Management*. 32(6–7), 385–397. doi:10.1108/01435121111158538

Siemens, G., (2005). Connectivism: a learning theory for the digital age. *International Journal of Instructional Technology & Distance Learning*. 2(1), article 1. http://itdl.org/Journal/Jan_05/article01.htm

Singer, J. B., (2012a). The ethics of social journalism. *Australian Journalism Review*. 34(1), 3–16.

Singer, J. B., (2012b). Social journalism: outside-in and inside-out. *Rhodes Journalism Review*. 32, 36–39. http://www.rjr.ru.ac.za/no32.html

Sison, A. J. G., (2003). *The moral capital of leaders: why virtue matters*. Cheltenham, UK: Edward Elgar.

Stepper, J., (2015). *Working out loud: for a better career and life*. New York: Ikigai Press.

Stepper, J., (2016). The 5 elements of working out loud (revisited). *Working Out Loud*. 2 March 2016. https://workingoutloud.com/blog/the-5-elements-of-working-out-loud-revisited

Stepper, J., (2020). *Working out loud: a 12-week method to build new connections, a better career, and a more fulfilling life*. Rev. ed. Vancouver, Canada: Page Two Books.

Stokes, P., Baker, C. and Lichy, J., (2016). The role of embedded individual values, belief and attitudes and spiritual capital in shaping everyday postsecular organizational culture. *European Management Review*. 13(1), 37–51. doi:10.1111/emre.12065

Stonebraker, I. and Zhang, T., (2016). Participatory culture and e-learning: using crowdsourcing as a catalyst for online student engagement. In: S. Rice and M. N. Gregor, eds. *E-learning and the academic library: essays on innovative initiatives*. Jefferson, NC: McFarland. pp. 159–173.

Stranack, K., (2012). The connected librarian: using social media for "do it yourself" professional development. *Partnership: The Canadian Journal of Library and Information Practice and Research*. 7(1). doi:10.21083/partnership.v7i1.1924

Symaco, L. P. and Tee, M. Y., (2019). Social responsibility and engagement in higher education: case of the ASEAN. *International Journal of Educational Development*. 66, 184–192. doi:10.1016/j.ijedudev.2018.10.001

Town, S., (2018). The value scorecard. *Information and Learning Science*. 119(1/2), 25–38. doi:10.1108/ILS-10-2017-0098

UNEP., (2015). *Raising the bar – advancing environmental disclosure in sustainability reporting*. Paris, France: United Nations Environment Programme, Division of Technology, Industry and Economics. https://www.unenvironment.org/resources/report/raising-bar-advancing-environmental-disclosure-sustainability-reporting

United Nations., (1987). *Our common future: World Commission on Environment and Development (Brundtland report)*. Oxford: Oxford University Press.

van Deventer, M. J. and Snyman, R. (M. M. M.) (2004). Measuring for sustainability: a multi-dimensional measurement framework for library and information services. *Libri,* 54(1), 1–8. doi:10.1515/LIBR.2004.1

Voakes, P. S., (1999). Civic duties: newspaper journalists' views on public journalism. *Journalism & Mass Communication Quarterly*. 76(4), 756–774.

Wang, X., (2015). *On moral capital*. Heidelberg, Germany: Springer. doi:10.1007/978-3-662-45544-9

Warlick, D., (2009). Grow your personal learning network: new technologies can keep you connected and help you manage information overload. *Learning & Leading with Technology*. 36(6), 12–16. https://files.eric.ed.gov/fulltext/EJ831435.pdf

Wenger, E., (1999). *Communities of practice: learning, meaning, and identity*. Cambridge, UK: Cambridge University Press.

Wiggins, B., Derickson, K. D. and Jenkins, G. S., (2020). Resourcing community partnerships through academic libraries. *Journal of Higher Education Outreach and Engagement*. 24(3), 115–124. https://openjournals.libs.uga.edu/jheoe/article/view/2063

Williams, B., (2010). When will we work out loud? Soon! *TheBrycesWrite*. 29 November 2010. https://thebryceswrite.com/2010/11/29/when-will-we-work-out-loud-soon

Wódka, M., (2017). Social and economic significance of moral capital. *Annales: Etyka w Etyka w życiu Gospodarczym*. 20(4), 65–75. doi:10.18778/1899-2226.20.4.05

Wood, D. J., (1991). Corporate social performance revisited. *Academy of Management Review*. 16(4), 691–718. doi:10.2307/258977

Xu, C., Ouyang, F. and Chu, H., (2009). The academic library meets Web 2.0: applications and implications. *Journal of Academic Librarianship*. 35(4), 324–331. doi:10.1016/j.acalib.2009.04.003

Young, S., (2003). *Moral capitalism: reconciling private interest with the public good*. San Francisco, CA: Berrett-Kohler.

Zohar, D. and Marshall, I., (2004). *Spiritual capital: wealth we can live by*. London: Bloomsbury.

2
Networks, Higher Education and the Social Future of Libraries

Paul J. Bracke

Networks constitute the new social morphology of our societies, and the diffusion of networking logic substantially modifies the operation and outcomes in processes of production, experience, power, and culture.

(Castells 1996, p. 469)

Introduction

Networks are everywhere. Interconnection defines many, if not most, aspects of life. Transport, economic and communication networks, for example, shape how we collectively engage with the world around us, and social networks structure how we interact with those around us. The connections, and the nature of the connections, in which we are all deeply enmeshed can be viewed as foundational to understanding social life. As Castells (1996, p. 469) wrote, networks are the primary social morphology of our time. Rainie and Wellman (2012, pp. 21–57) describe the emergence of networked individualism, facilitated by online technologies, as a revolution in how people relate to one another. Others have gone so far as to hypothesise that virtually every aspect of our lives is driven by our social networks, ranging from our health to our emotions to our political choices (Christakis & Fowler 2011).

Libraries are no stranger to networks, connecting both libraries and librarians and other library employees. For decades, libraries have engaged in organisational networks to enhance services to users. Library consortia and resource-sharing networks are key examples of how libraries have worked together to achieve efficiencies, better leverage collective resources and foster innovation. Librarians and other employees of academic libraries have also, of course, long been part of social networks with each other and with other members of their campus *communities*. As we consider the social future of academic libraries, however, it is important to consider the ways in which position within social networks may enable or constrain new roles at organisational and individual levels. The interlocking networks of academic librarians, with other librarians, faculty and other professionals, and of academic libraries, represent a complex social environment that can be challenging, if not impossible, to conceptualise without doing so in the relational framework of social networks.

Social network theory and social capital: a brief introduction

Before discussing the relationship between **social network** theory, **social capital** and the future of libraries, it is helpful to outline some basic conceptual underpinning of the theory. A natural place to start is by defining a *social network* and outlining some of its properties. A basic definition of a social network is as 'a set of socially relevant nodes connected by one or more relations' (Marin and Wellman 2011, p. 11). In other words, it consists of individuals or organisations (*nodes*) that are connected to one another, potentially in a variety of ways (*relations*). These relations may include similarities, friendships, information flows, **resource** exchanges, collaborations or other sorts of connections (Wasserman and Faust 1994). **Social network analysis** (SNA) allows one to describe networks based on a variety of characteristics, which are often visualised using graphs. Characteristics that are often of interest may focus on the nodes and their relationships (e.g., how connected is a node, how distantly connected are two nodes), social structure (e.g., what cliques or subgroups exist) and social roles (e.g., how does an actor function to connect different networks). These structures can then be used to gain insight into social phenomena of interest. For example, Haythornthwaite (1996) discussed SNA as an approach to understanding information exchange, an approach that has gained in popularity in understanding the social contexts of information, information technologies and information behaviours (Sheble, Brennan & Wildemuth 2017).

There are many ways of viewing social networks, but one common view is that networks can be characterised by understanding transactional content of network *ties* (e.g., influence, services), the nature of ties between actors (e.g., intensity, **reciprocity**) and structural characteristics of the network including its size, the *density* of connections within it, the connectedness of network members and the presence of holes (Tichy, Tushman & Fombrun 1979). Considering these network characteristics in the context of academic libraries, a useful starting point is the transactional content of *social relationships*, or what is exchanged, in the networks in which libraries and librarians are part. There has been considerable research, for example, on the formation of networks to facilitate different types of exchanges such as information, influence, service or friendship. Ibarra's (1995; Ibarra & Andrews 1993) classification of transactional content into *instrumental* and *expressive* ties has been widely used for analysing such networks. Instrumental ties tend to be task related and are based on the exchange of services, advice, ideas or other resources. Expressive ties are affect based. There are other characteristics of social networks, however, that are also useful in understanding social structures and phenomena. For example, the reciprocity, directionality, complexity, formality, intensity and frequency of connections may reveal other aspects of social structure. These might include power relationships, centrality in networks and core–periphery structures, and small-world phenomena (Pescosolido 2006).

Going beyond the types of relationships and structures that might be quantified and otherwise characterised from a methodological perspective in SNA, social network theory provides a framework for drawing meaning from such characterisations and leveraging SNA to gain insight into social phenomena. Social network theory and SNA build from the notion that individuals are *embedded* within webs of social interactions, and provide insight into the pattern of relations within networks and seek to explain the myriad functions and phenomena of society (Borgatti et al. 2009). Social network theory provides the conceptual framework in which social context as described by network properties is used to describe and understand social structure and phenomena from a relational perspective.

There are a few basic assumptions and concepts in social network theory that are helpful in understanding the perspective. Marin and Wellman (2011, pp. 13–14) outline the basic assumptions as:

1 *Relations, not attributes*. Social outcomes are caused by position in a social network, rather than attributes of the individual in the network, although individuals in similar network positions may have common attributes.
2 *Networks, not groups*. It is not assumed that individuals are parts of cohesively, neatly bounded groups. Rather, they are part of networks that may be participated in and benefited from differently by different individuals and that potentially have dynamic characteristics.
3 *Relations in a relational context*. Networks must be understood in a broader relational context. For example, the mentoring networks within an academic library may also be reflective of the administrator–librarian networks within that same organisation, which in turn may be reflective of other macro-level networks at the institutional or professional level.

Given the focus on the relationships in understanding social networks, it should be unsurprising that some of the most fundamental concepts in social network theory help us to understand the nature of ties. Ties may be of many types – formal or informal, affective or utilitarian, frequent or infrequent, among others. One significant line of inquiry in network theory is based upon strength of tie. Granovetter (1973) defined the strength of ties as a combination of the time, affective intensity, intensity and reciprocity shared between two actors. The more of these factors that two actors share, the stronger the ties. In this seminal article, Granovetter argues for the *strength* of **weak ties**. His argument is that network structures characterised by weak ties play an important role in sharing novel information between groups and are thus important for developing *social capital*, at both an individual and group level. Similarly, Burt (1992) argues that individuals with more non-redundant connections in a network, referred to as '**structural holes**', have access to sources of novel information. In this view, social capital is defined by the information and control advantage of network **brokerage** – being the *broker* in relations between otherwise disconnected parts of a social structure. Social capital is thus the opportunity based on *positioning* within a social network, the value of which is contingent on the number of people with similar positions in the network (Burt 1997).

Strong ties are often connected with **homophily,** or the notion that similarity between individuals leads to connection. Homophily, which may be based on many personal identities, results in homogeneous personal networks, which in turn may have an impact on the information available to them, the experiences they have in life and the attitudes that are formed as a result (Lazarsfeld & Merton 1954; McPherson, Smith-Lovin & Cook 2001). While some argue that this is the source of many of the greatest divides in society writ large, others argue that strong ties engender social cohesion and **trust,** and are thus important in organisational change (Krackhardt & Hanson 1993) and conflict resolution (Nelson 1989). Coleman (1988; 1990) argues that social capital investments are more likely in the presence of strong social ties based on trust. Others have described frequent communication between collaborators, one characteristic of strong ties, as leading to enhanced innovation (Moran 2005; Reagans & Zuckerman 2001).

Networks in higher education

As Marin and Wellman (2011) pointed out, from a network perspective, social relations can be understood only within the context of ever-larger sets of social relations in which they are embedded. Academic libraries are embedded within parent institutions. These colleges and universities, in turn, are simultaneously constituted by overlapping sets of social networks and embedded within even larger networks that connect professionals, institutions and other external organisations. These broader institutional networks not only connect whole institutions but also connect libraries to one another. As we consider emerging and future roles for academic libraries and librarians within higher education, it is thus imperative to have a sophisticated understanding of these networks that constitute the social structure of higher education at both a system and an institutional level. It is through understanding the nature of these networks and the opportunities for leveraging them that academic librarians will be able to develop effective strategies for communicating with campus constituents, developing deeper integration into the social fabric of their campuses and fostering research and instructional collaboration. Social networks play an important part in the functioning of any organisation, both internally and in its inter-organisational relationships. Higher education is no exception to this. The literature studying colleges and universities as organisations has covered many aspects of the ways in which networks shape the social structures and practices of institutions, the shaping of disciplines, the relationships among higher education institutions and the relationships between higher education institutions and external stakeholders such as governments or businesses. This section will highlight some of the ways in which networks play critical roles in shaping the work of higher education institutions.

One central set of questions that have been addressed through network perspectives is centred on the conditions of work within higher education and the role of *professional* and *disciplinary* networks in shaping universities and colleges. Studies of these networks allow us to gain insight into basic functions of these institutions such as: how does recruiting work and how do individuals end up working where they do? How do individuals collaborate and publish with one another? In what contexts do collaborations across professions or disciplines occur, and how might we understand them in a larger organisational context? Much of the literature on these topics understandably focuses on tenure-track faculty, treating them as the central profession in higher education. It is the faculty, after all, who bear the primary responsibility for educating students and creating knowledge. There is some interest, however, in non-tenure track instructors, who make up over 75% of instructional staff in American universities (American Association of University Professors 2018) and other non-faculty professionals.

The starting point of academic labour is the recruiting and hiring process. Network analysis has been used frequently to understand various aspects of this process, such as the role of prestige (the '**prestige effect**') in the hiring process and the social stratification among institutions that results. Clauset, Arbesman and Larremore (2015) found a clear pattern of hiring practices following prestige hierarchies and being reflective of deep inequalities among higher education institutions in their study of 19,000 faculty placements in three disparate fields. Similar results have been found in other studies looking at disciplinary hiring networks (Wiggins, Adamic & McQuaid 2006; DiRamio, Theroux & Guarino 2009). These findings correlating programmatic prestige with the structure of hiring networks have even been used as a means for analysing the quality of doctoral programs as an alternative to traditional program rankings (Barnett et al. 2010). Others have suggested that prestige hierarchies are of less importance than personal ties within hiring networks. For example, connections developed through conference attendance create advantages for individuals in the recruiting process that quickly expand as individuals gain connections in their personal networks (Mai, Liu & González-Bailón 2015). Zuo, Zhao and Ni (2019) studied the relationship between tie-strength among research collaborators and hiring practices at information schools, finding weak tie networks, manifested by rich sets of collaborators not including a doctoral dissertation advisor, to be particularly beneficial to individuals who were hired by the most attractive programs.

Another area in which SNA has been used to understand the structure of the academic workforce is in relation to *diversity*. There have been many studies that demonstrate the principle of homophily in hiring networks, and the ways in which historic hiring practices have led to homogeneous faculties (Clauset, Arbesman & Larremore 2015; Fowler, Grofman & Masuoka 2007; Hartlep et al. 2017). O'Meara, Culpepper and Templeton (2020) suggest that many historic practices leveraging social networks operate with implicit and cognitive bias that marginalises potential candidates who may not be well positioned in disciplinary networks. Women from marginalised racial or ethnic groups, for example, are more likely to be in a position where they do not have the same level of network access as candidates with other characteristics (Kachchaf et al. 2015; Weeden, Thébaud & Gelbgiser 2017). Similarly, differential opportunities to participate in mentoring or peer networks have been cited as an issue in retention of faculty from underrepresented or marginalised backgrounds (Cawyer, Simonds & Davis 2002; Zambrana et al. 2015). Some have found that cluster or cohort hiring can improve the social networks of newly hired faculty from diverse backgrounds (Smith et al. 2004; Sgoutas-Emch et al. 2016; Writer & Watson 2019). It is also important to note that social network theory has been used to understand diversity among students as well, such as in Clarke and Antonio's (2012) proposal for a network-centric research agenda for understanding the complexities of diverse student bodies. This agenda would examine 'the embeddedness of student interaction in the larger social structure, account directly for the effects of peers, and allow for variation within social categories and campus environments' (Clarke & Antonio 2012, p. 46).

Network perspectives may also be used to understand the changing division of labour within higher education, its implications for collaborative work within universities, and even the implications for faculty development programs and support services. Many colleges and universities, for example, have been seeing significant changes in their models of instruction and instructional design. An argument might be made that some of these changes are driven by the rise of online education, particularly the unbundling of faculty roles (Kinser 2002). The basic concept of *unbundling* was described by Paulson (2002) as the disaggregation of faculty instructional roles and their assignment to distinct professional groups. In her description, the five roles associated with delivering instruction by a faculty member are moved from an integrated set of activities carried out by a single faculty member to a co-ordinated set of activities which may, or may not, be enacted by a faculty member. Tucker and Neely (2010) describe the ways in which the unbundling of instructional functions has required new administrative structures and practices, resulting from the need to co-ordinate new sorts of collaborative networks. Macfarlane (2011) describes these new professions as 'para-academics', who constitute what Whitchurch (2008) describes as a *'third space'*, in between academics and other types of support employees. These descriptions of new roles could easily be framed in network terms as the emergence of new nodes that function as weak ties in intra-institutional professional networks.

While networks define the formal roles of faculty and other professionals in the university, other networks, some informal, are also critical to faculty learning and development even if they are not always obvious even to those enmeshed within them. As Neumann (2009, p. 188) wrote: 'First, colleagues can, and occasionally do, learn their subjects of study and teaching from one another . . . And second, despite this reality, colleague-based teaching and learning are quite invisible, even to the professors who are drawn to and involved in them'.

Mentoring networks and *communities of practice* have emerged as popular models for faculty development, building on the recognition that assistant professors may be more successful in research and scholarly productivity when they receive mentoring from multiple sources (Peluchette & Jeanquart 2000). Zellers, Howard and Barcic (2008) elaborate on the value of having multiple mentors to help develop different aspects of the mentee, as well as the potential benefit of reciprocal mentoring relationships. Communities of practice, representing long-term, institutionalised mentoring networks built upon reciprocity, have gained favour (Calderwood & Klaf 2014; Smith et al. 2016; Bottoms et al. 2020).

The work of the faculty is not, however, limited to instruction. At many institutions, research is a primary area of endeavour, and the patterns of collaboration as well as organisational reconfigurations related to research that have emerged in a network have had a profound impact on universities. Although some might trace the history of scientific and research periods to the formation of early societies and journals, the focus here will be on network dynamics that are uniquely impactful on our present environment. Science is a collaborative activity, and increasingly an activity that draws upon networks of peers. This is an area that should be familiar to scholars in library and information science (LIS), as the bibliometric and informetric networks that can be used to understand these patterns of collaboration have been well studied. These techniques have been used to develop typologies of scientific collaboration (Subramanyam 1983), describe collaboration in specific geographic areas (Anuradha & Urs 2007; Abramo et al. 2009a; Toivanen & Ponomariov 2011) and patterns of international research collaboration (Han et al. 2013; Tang & Shapira 2011), evaluate research quality and productivity (Lawani 1986; Seglen & Aksnes 2000; Abramo, D'Angelo & Di Costa 2009b; Shari, Haddow & Genoni 2012) and uncover disparities and inequities in science (Aksnes, et al. 2011; Larivière et al. 2013). As Börner et al. (2010, p. 1) wrote in introducing a framework for the study of *team science*:

> A study of more than 21 million papers published worldwide from 1945 to the present reveals a fundamental and nearly universal shift in all branches of science: Teams increasingly dominate solo scientists in the production of high-impact, highly cited science; teams are growing in size; and teams are increasingly located across university boundaries rather than within them. Similar patterns were found for all the patents published worldwide.

This has been described as being driven by increased interest in large, complex questions that cut across disciplinary areas and that can be answered only by diverse teams composed of individuals representing many areas of knowledge (Rosenfield 1992). This team-based approach, sometimes referred to as Mode 2 research (Gibbons et al. 1994), is also often focused on short-lived teams brought together to seek applied approaches to solving real-world problems. Although much of this research focuses on scientific and technical fields, interdisciplinarity and collaborative approaches have also emerged in fields that are often perceived as more solitary endeavours, such as those in the humanities (Burdick et al. 2012, p. vii).

A particularly important aspect of this increased interest in multidisciplinary, interdisciplinary and transdisciplinary research is its connection to the rise of entrepreneurial, market-driven approaches to managing universities. According to Shrum, Genuth and Chompalov (2007, cited in Börner et al. 2010, Table 1), 'Structural elements of collaboration (among them the team formation, size and duration, organization, technological practices, and participant experiences) are interrelated and connected to a complex external environment (including the sector, organizational, and funding contexts)'.

Models have been developed describing the ways in which universities, industry and government are interrelated. In the ***triple helix*** model of innovation, the interrelationships are seen as creating the conditions for the formation of new organisational forms that drive innovation (Etzkowitz & Leydesdorff 1995). This model and its explanation of economic growth is cited by Arizona State University President Michael Crow in his description of new interdisciplinary research structures in his model of the 'New American University' (Crow & Dabars 2015, pp. 187–188).

Other models describe the same phenomenon, but in more critical terms. **Academic capitalism**, for example, describes the market and market-like strategies of universities and colleges in response to external pressures such as the emergence of a global knowledge economy and the decline of public funding for higher education (Slaughter & Leslie 1997; Slaughter & Rhoades 2004). In this view, the intellectual property that is created at universities is an increasingly valuable **asset** in a knowledge economy that can be capitalised to spur growth at the institutional level despite declining direct public investment in the institutions. This requires new networks at every level of higher education. At the *system* level, it requires the development of networks and relationships with government to develop the regulatory environment necessary to allow universities to engage in market-like behaviours. At the *institutional* level, it requires the development of networks and relationships that allow a university to influence its local policy environment and develop partnerships with industry. And at the *researcher* level, it is facilitated by incentivising engagement with research that attracts external funding. This often means the team-based approaches described earlier in the section and the development of robust research networks.

While this is not an exhaustive treatment of the types of networks one could find in higher education, it does provide an overview of the broader context of social organisation and collaborative work that forms the current and future professional and organisational contexts for academic libraries. When one examines almost any aspect of academic life at colleges and universities, they are increasingly defined by work in relation to others. From recruitment to teaching and research, work is co-ordinated and delivered through social networks. Furthermore, the network environment of higher education works at multiple levels. At one level, individual networks are important. Faculty and professional recruitment often occurs through personal networks; faculty and other professionals may work through intra-institutional networks in the design and delivery of instruction; and research in many fields is largely conducted through collaborative networks that extend well beyond the boundaries of any given campus. At an institutional level, many universities are seeking to form organisational-level networks that go beyond consortial models, seeking closer relationships with industry and government. This is the network context that academic libraries must consider while developing strategies for their own futures.

Networks and libraries

Just as networks are shaping higher education, they are also core to the future of academic libraries. The Council on Library and Information Resources (CLIR) made a number of recommendations to higher education leaders regarding the future of research libraries in the report *No brief candle: reconceiving research libraries for the 21st century* (CLIR 2008). Collaboration, and networks, are present throughout. These include exhortations for libraries to align their functions to the research and instructional agendas of the institution and the need to form new alliances and networks of practice with faculty and information technology specialists. Perhaps most intriguingly, the report proposes a redefinition of the research library as a multi-institutional endeavour, federating collections, services and expertise through collaboration networks. Although these recommendations were made for research libraries specifically, they continue to resonate for academic libraries more generally.

This section will build upon such thinking to discuss network concepts and the future of academic libraries in the context of *transitions* that have been put forward in the literature. The first is the shift from the collection-centric library to the engagement-centric library, in which librarian roles and library services are repositioned in the context of the broader teaching and research workflows of their institutions. The second is focused on the institutional networks that are leading to new forms of inter-institutional collaboration as well as the changing models of collection provision in a connected library environment.

The engagement-centric library

Several years ago, Lynn Silipigni Connaway (2013, p. 83) opened a chapter with the proclamation that 'The library in 2020 will be engagement centered', describing it as follows:

> The library of 2020 will provide user-centered services and systems that will meet the expectations of the *community*. The library staff will need to develop relationships with their users and partner with other organizations in order to produce, store, and preserve content and data sets and to provide personalized services. Recruiting and retaining innovative, creative individuals who are willing to engage with users and to embrace new technologies and modes of communication will be imperative for the success of the library of 2020. Access to the library and its resources when and where users need them (which may involve being accessible in multiple physical and virtual locations), will be essential since convenient access to resources, whether human, print, or electronic, is the most critical factor for users.
>
> (Connaway 2013, p. 86).

Librarians have long been interested in user-centred practices and the development of collections and services to meet the needs of user populations. Connaway's provocation, however, builds upon an influential blog post by Lorcan Dempsey (2005) that reframed the notion of library engagement in its call to 'be in the flow'. In this view, libraries need to be integrated into *digital workflows* to fit into the lives of their users in a networked information environment. Furthermore, 'the library needs to be in the user environment and not expect the user to find their way to the library environment', and 'integration of library resources should not be seen as an end in itself but as a means to better integration with the user environment, with workflow'. Coupled with evolving views of professional roles, this set the stage for an outward-facing, engagement-centred view of libraries in which relationship building and the development of engaged roles for librarians have become central. Although the use of the term 'engagement' is somewhat varied in the literature (Schlak 2018), it generally refers to meaningful and deep *participation* of the library in the life of its academic community.

Work at the University of Minnesota inspired by Dempsey resulted in a redefinition of librarian roles that was described as moving 'from a collection-centered model to an engagement-centered one' and was characterised by intentionality about the ways in which emerging services for meeting user needs such as scholarly communication, digital curation, online learning and other functions might be built upon traditional liaison roles (Williams 2009, p. 3). These roles, in aggregate, result in engaged liaisons who seek 'to enhance scholar productivity, to empower learners, and to participate in the entire lifecycle of the research, teaching, and learning process' (Jaguszewski & Williams 2013, p. 4). To achieve this, however, it is also important to realise that liaison roles, representing connections to discipline, must be complemented with the functional expertise that facilitate services and partnerships that contribute to the success of faculty and students. Such a leveraging of the historic liaison model would allow for the claim 'that the library is more than a purveyor of content and that its expertise is an essential component of the academic knowledge infrastructure on and off campus' (Kenney 2014, p. 11).

Within this approach, there has been considerable work in defining the evolving librarian roles that are based upon *embeddedness* within research, teaching and learning processes (Malenfant 2010; Kenney 2015; Miller and Pressley 2015; Pasek 2015; Schoonover, Kinsley, and Colvin 2018). This has been particularly the case with roles related to research support, where emerging roles reflecting changes in network relationships between librarians and their colleagues on campus are apparent. A spectrum of new roles such as digital scholarship librarians, digital humanities librarians and research data management librarians reflects new forms of embeddedness and attempts to form new types of partnerships within the context of disciplinary work. For example, a range of roles have emerged around research data management (RDM) services in academic libraries (Tenopir et al. 2014; Pinfield, Cox & Smith 2014; Cox et al. 2017). From a network perspective, the embedding of librarians in research networks is a particularly notable feature of these developments. RDM specialists have worked to position themselves 'upstream' in the research process (Witt et al. 2009), engaging in data management planning early in research projects (Mischo, Schlembach & O'Donnell 2014; Bishoff & Johnston 2015; Smale et al. 2020), and as members of research teams (Federer 2016; García-Milian et al. 2013; Janke & Rush 2014). Similar developments can be seen with library roles in digital humanities, resulting in embeddedness within research networks in humanistic fields (Vandegrift & Varner 2013; Wong 2016; Cassella 2017). One can also find parallels in initiatives to embed librarians within the formal curriculum (Stanger 2009; Farrell and Badke 2015; Ranger 2019), or course design and redesign initiatives (Maybee 2018, pp. 49–60; Flierl & Hamer 2019; Flierl & Maybee 2020) that result in the connection of libraries to other networks on campus.

There has also been literature on library value and assessment that provides a lens into the specific contributions that the engagement-centred academic libraries are seen as bringing to their campuses. Corrall (2014, p. 28) proposed an **intellectual capital** perspective to this issue, which 'can enable library practitioners to evaluate their human, structural, and relational assets, and recognize their IAs [intangible assets] as distinctive competencies with current relevance and enduring value'. Town and Kyrillidou (2013, p. 12) suggest **relational capital** as a dimension of library value in their 'values scorecard', noting that libraries are 'fundamentally relationship organisations', but that the lack of consideration of the value of these relationships is a problem when considering the overall value of the library.

Evaluating these **intangible assets** of libraries and their value has proven to be a challenge, however. Shumaker (2012, pp. 123–142), for example, developed an 'embedded librarian maturity questionnaire'. The questionnaire provides a tool for self-assessment against a set of indicators that describe how ready for embedded engagement a librarian might be. This questionnaire is paired with a 'readiness assessment questionnaire', which provides a similar assessment of readiness at the organisational level. Broughton (2016) describes the development of a rubric at Ohio University to assist subject librarians in developing more engagement-centred roles and to measure progress. In this rubric, examples of various aspects of subject librarian responsibility (e.g., teaching and learning, collection development and data management) are provided along a continuum from emergent through generative to productive. While fundamentally developmental in its orientation, this matrix did allow the library to identify quantitative and qualitative examples of its development of partnerships on campus. Rinio (2019) described an approach in a school library context for using SNA to help librarians better identify collaborative opportunities within their schools.

Bracke (2016) proposed using SNA as a conceptual framework for addressing the issue laid out by Town and Kyrillidou (2013), arguing that assessment techniques that are more focused on counting library activities in a transactional manner fail to adequately describe the engagement-focused, expertise-based service models emerging in research and other academic libraries, and that the failure of library assessment models to account for the relational value of librarian activities is problematic in justifying and incentivising new strategic activities and understanding the importance of libraries' relationships with users and other stakeholders. This is particularly problematic in that the observable outcomes of some of these relational activities (e.g., digital scholarship collaborations, informed learning strategies for information literacy) can be complex and difficult to describe or measure. It is thus argued that the social network perspectives now commonplace in organisational studies to provide relational and contextual understandings of organisational behaviour could be applied to library performance measurement and evaluation so as to provide a fuller picture of library impact. Ujwary-Gil (2019) uses a broader form of network analysis, *organisational network analysis*, to study the broader sets of relationships between social actors and technological assets within an academic library to study the efficiency of resources within an academic library from an economic perspective.

Discourse on the future roles of librarians has often focused on the transition to the digital environment. While technology and concomitant changes in scholarly communication and information resources are certainly important components of the trends introduced above, emerging roles can also be seen as efforts on the part of librarians to change the nature of their social networks. These roles, building upon historic liaison models, are intended to connect librarians to disciplinary and other networks on their campuses, and beyond, that are the locus of much of the research and teaching work. They also provide opportunities for librarians to play a role in the new forms of inter-institutional networks described in the previous section on networks in higher education. For example, emerging librarian roles in research data management and e-science services not only facilitate roles for providing information management partnerships and skills at the point of need (i.e., embedded within research networks), but also allow them to connect to the interdisciplinary research centres that are valued at the institutional level at many universities.

Collaboration at scale, the inside-out library and the facilitated collection

Just as individual librarians find themselves in new network relations with colleagues as they develop new responses to a changing socio-technical environment, so do academic libraries find themselves forming new *inter-institutional networks* as they navigate a changing context. Identifying means for achieving operational scale, promoting local content at a global scale and connecting local users to a universe of information resources all have implications for the relations of academic libraries and the structure and nature of their networks.

In 2008, the libraries of the Committee on Institutional Cooperation (CIC), now known as the Big Ten Academic Alliance, were in the process of discussing the creation of a shared digital repository for collectively managing digitised books. Members of the consortium were accustomed to sharing resources in a distributed fashion, but developing a centralised platform for sharing and achieving economies of scale was proving to be a challenge. Two members of the consortium who felt a particular urgency around this need lost patience with the process and acted on their own, later bringing in the other CIC members and other partners in the newly created HathiTrust (Centivany 2017). This partnership has developed its services over the past decade, including developing shared preservation (York 2009; York 2010) and a computational research environment (Plale et al. 2013; Downie et al. 2016). It also provided essential infrastructure for libraries responding to COVID-19 through its Emergency Temporary Access Service (HathiTrust 2020). While HathiTrust is often viewed as a success as a digital library, it is also an interesting example of the ways in which institutional networks are shaping the future of libraries. This example is a particularly important illustration of a number of features of networks and the ways in which reconfigurations of inter-institutional networks may shape the future of academic libraries. The ability of two closely allied libraries to shape the decisions of an entire network are illustrations of the properties of *tie strength* (Marsden & Campbell 1984) in a network and the power of *centrality* (Freeman 1978) in inter-institutional networks. It also illustrates the ways in which new forms of inter-institutional networks, in this case moving from the *loosely coupled* systems typical of educational institutions to a *tightly coupled* model (Weick 1976) based on strengthening ties between libraries and increased interdependence, are changing the ways academic libraries are reconfiguring their strategies for content and service provision.

There has been increasing interest in developing institutional networks to achieve scale in a networked environment and promote innovation for libraries in a broader socio-technical environment in which user needs, expectations and possibilities are shifting. Neal (2012) foresees a future in which libraries move toward '*radical collaboration*' by moving towards models of mass production in backroom functions, creating centres for sharing specialised expertise, developing shared infrastructure and developing shared initiatives based on these shared investments. Shore (2014) describes efforts by CLIR to promote a holistic redefinition of the library in a manner that is inter-institutional by deconstructing library functions and understanding them as interrelated and interdependent across institutional boundaries. As Wheeler (2014) described in writing about collaboration in technology and libraries more broadly, this leads libraries from the modest interdependence of consortial participation to a state of intentional interdependence in which libraries and universities are fundamentally reliant on one another to provide infrastructure and basic services.

Others have focused more on the changing nature of collections and information resources in a digital networked environment and, in turn, the ways in which these reflect changes in the roles of libraries both at the institutional level and in terms of inter-institutional networks. Some view digital networks as allowing libraries to *unbundle* and *rebundle* content and services in a manner that allows for greater efficiencies and scale in providing resources, while also changing user behaviours and expectations for how they access these resources, and changing contexts for research, teaching and learning. In the process, this creates the possibility of network-level change as libraries are able to achieve more of their ends with, or in relation to, other libraries (Dempsey, Malpas & Lavoie 2014). The remainder of this section will present the twinned concepts of the 'inside-out library' and the 'facilitated collection' as examples of changing library practice that are changing the nature of inter-institutional networks among academic libraries.

The first aspect of this is the notion of the *inside-out library*. First described by Dempsey (2010) in the context of resource discovery, inside-out resources refer to the resources that are unique to a particular institution but with potential users on a more global basis. This implies a more *global role* for libraries in the provision of collections, but also requires that libraries consider the sorts of collaborations in supporting research and creative processes described in the previous section to be effective in facilitating external sharing (Dempsey 2016). Lewis (2016, pp. xv–xvi) speculates that the primary role of the academic library will flip from an organisation that brings external knowledge resources into a university for use by its faculty and students to one that becomes 'a means for providing access to and preserving the knowledge created in and by the university so that this knowledge is available to everyone else in the world'. It could be argued that, in Lewis's notion of the library collecting functions, the library becomes a *primary network linkage* between the university and its faculty and students and the global network of information providers and seekers. This role of the library as a tie to external networks is more than a technical role, requiring them to participate in inter-institutional organisational networks with whom interdependencies are built. For example, the Association of Research Libraries (ARL) has developed a series of initiatives under its SHared Access Research Ecosystem (SHARE) initiative to build tools for encouraging innovation in digital scholarship, particularly around promoting and leveraging institutional repositories (Hudson-Vitale et al. 2017). As was mentioned earlier, HathiTrust was formed as a regional network to collaboratively manage the challenges of preserving and managing access to digitised book content. This network has since become global in scope as universities beyond the United States have participated in the organisation.

The second aspect is the shift from the 'owned collection' to the 'facilitated collection' in which resources provided by a library for its campus community do not need to be physically owned by that campus community. As Dempsey (2016, p. 339) describes: 'Increasingly, the library does not assemble collections for local use, but facilitates access to a coordinated mix of local, external and collaborative services assembled around user needs and available on the network.' This model incorporates a variety of concepts related to meeting user needs in a distributed information environment, such as an expanded view of what might be included in discovery environments and changes in acquisitions practices to centre on user preferences. A particularly interesting aspect from a network perspective is the notion of 'collective collections' as a primary component of the facilitated collection. The notion of the *collective collection* has its roots in multiple threads of historic library collaboration: loosely coupled resource-sharing networks, consortia, remote print storage, co-operative collection development initiatives and more recent projects on shared *digitisation* such as HathiTrust. These all represent moves to manage and provide access to resources within inter-institutional networks.

While these networks have existed, in some cases, for decades, there do appear to be trends toward more strongly co-ordinated networks that represent a transformation in the social structure of academic libraries. For example, the Big Ten Academic Alliance has a long history of co-operation on library initiatives, ranging from interlibrary loans and resource sharing to joint licensing. Recently, however, the leaders of these 15 major research libraries have committed to 'managing the separate collections of the Big Ten university libraries as if they were a single collection' (Big Ten Academic Alliance 2020). While the Big Ten might be unique in their explicit statement of intentionality in developing shared collections, it is not difficult to find numerous examples on a global level that point in similar directions. From a network perspective, this suggests reconfigurations of academic libraries and their collaboration networks. At one level, shifts towards collaborations that result in institutional interdependencies can be viewed as changing the nature of inter-institutional networks in a manner characterised by strong rather than weak ties. Looking at the issue of social structure among academic libraries, such networks could, even as they propagate practical benefit throughout the system, reinforce stratification among academic libraries. At a system level, libraries that are rich in the collection or human resources necessary to collaboration may find themselves in positions of great centrality in such networks and thus in a position of power and influence over smaller or resource-poor libraries on the network periphery.

Conclusion

Social networks, whether explicitly mentioned or not, are central to much of the thinking about the contemporary and future academic library, and the university itself. Libraries and librarians have sought to develop new approaches to contextualising their work within the academic life of their institutions and to collaborating to develop innovative services at scale.

Approaching these efforts through a network lens affords an understanding of their positioning within the social structures of the university, of higher education and of the information environment. In turn, this provides the opportunity to understand the networks that shape academic life and to develop strategies for deepening integrations and engagement between libraries and their institutions – socially. Similarly, academic libraries are finding themselves in a position in which they are developing collaborative approaches to resources and service provision in a broader information environment characterised by information behemoths such as Google and Amazon, by the sharing of scholarly resources directly by scholars on platforms outside of the library's control, and by challenges of scale in digital preservation and the management of born-digital collections such as research data. In this environment, understanding the networks among libraries and adjacent organisations (e.g., publishers and data centres) can help with the development of strategies that will ensure central roles for libraries in an increasingly decentralised environment.

Social networks are also a topic that warrant further investigation in the LIS literature. There is a need for usage of social network analysis in the assessment of library services, particularly related to liaison services and library engagement, building upon the conceptual foundation already outlined in the literature. Similarly, there is opportunity for work in analysing networks at the institutional, or even inter-institutional, level to understand faculty and student networks as a means for identifying opportunities for the integration of library services and resources within them, and perhaps as a means for assessing opportunities for library programming to connect disparate segments of academic networks. Finally, social networks could be a useful framework for understanding changed institutions, collaborative networks and professional networks in the wake of the COVID-19 pandemic. It is difficult at this point to clearly foresee the changes to academic libraries and higher education as a result of the global pandemic, but it seems reasonable to assume that the changes to instruction, research and the practice of librarianship necessitated by the current experiences will continue to have impacts into the future. Remote work, the increased use of teleconferencing for professional meetings and the technology-mediated approaches to education that have become pervasive, for example, have changed not only the ways in which the work of universities and academic libraries happen, but also the ways in which social relationships are developed and maintained. As academic libraries grapple with their future, both in the long term and near, the conceptual lens of social networks provides perspective that can empower an evidence-based approach to the construction and positioning of contextualised approaches to library practice in an evolving environment.

References

Abramo, G., D'Angelo, C. A. and Di Costa, F., (2009b). Research collaboration and productivity: is there correlation? *Higher Education.* 57(2), 155–171. doi:10.1007/s10734-008-9139-z

Abramo, G., D'Angelo, C. A., Di Costa, F. and Solazi, M., (2009a). University–industry collaboration in Italy: a bibliometric examination. *Technovation.* 29(6–7), 498–507. doi:10.1016/j.technovation.2008.11.003

Aksnes, D. W., Rørstad, K., Piro, F. and Sivertsen, G., (2011). Are female researchers less cited? A large-scale study of Norwegian scientists. *Journal of the American Society for Information Science and Technology.* 62(4), 628–636. doi:10.1002/asi.21486

American Association of University Professors., (2018). *Data snapshot: contingent faculty in US higher education.* Washington, DC: American Association of University Professors. https://www.aaup.org/news/data-snapshot-contingent-faculty-us-higher-ed

Anuradha, K. T. and Urs, S., (2007). Bibliometric indicators of Indian research collaboration patterns: a correspondence analysis. *Scientometrics.* 71(2), 179–189. doi:10.1007/s11192-007-1657-4

Barnett, G. A., Danowski, J. A., Feeley, T. H. and Stalker, J., (2010). Measuring quality in communication doctoral education using network analysis of faculty-hiring patterns. *Journal of Communication.* 60(2), 388–411. doi:10.1111/j.1460-2466.2010.01487.x

Big Ten Academic Alliance., (2020). The BIG collection. *Big Ten Academic Alliance.* https://www.btaa.org/library/the-big-collection

Bishoff, C. and Johnston, L., (2015). Approaches to data sharing: an analysis of NSF data management plans from a large research university. *Journal of Librarianship and Scholarly Communication*. 3(2), eP1231. doi:10.7710/2162-3309.1231

Borgatti, S. P., Mehra A., Brass, D. J. and Labianca, G., (2009). Network analysis in the social sciences. *Science*. 323(5916), 892–895. doi:10.1126/science.1165821

Börner, K. et al., (2010). A multi-level systems perspective for the science of team science. *Science Translational Medicine*. 49, 49cm24. doi:10.1126/scitranslmed.3001399

Bottoms, S. I., Pegg, J., Adams, A., Risser, H. S. and Wu, K., (2020). Mentoring within communities of practice. In: B. J. Irby, J. N. Boswell, L. J. Searby, F. Kochan, R. Garza and N. Abdelrahman, eds. *The Wiley international handbook of mentoring: paradigms, practices, programs, and possibilities*. Hoboken, NJ: John Wiley & Sons. pp. 141–166.

Bracke, P. J., (2016). Social networks and relational capital in library service assessment. *Performance Measurement and Metrics*. 17(2), 131–141. doi:10.1108/PMM-04-2016-0019

Broughton, K., (2016). Developing a matrix and using self-reported scoring to measure librarian engagement on campus. *Performance Measurement and Metrics*. 17(2), 142–149. doi:10.1108/PMM-04-2016-0018

Burdick, A., Drucker, J., Lunenfield, P., Presner, T. S. and Schnapp, J. T., (2012). *Digital humanities*. Cambridge, MA: MIT Press.
https://www.dropbox.com/s/dl/1vj4usz3v5p8rgl/9248.pdf

Burt, R. S., (1992). *Structural holes: the social structure of competition*. Cambridge, MA: Harvard University Press.

Burt, R. S., (1997). The contingent value of social capital. *Administrative Science Quarterly*. 42(2), 339–365. doi:10.2307/2393923

Calderwood, P. E. and Klaf, S., (2014). Facilitating mentoring across three models of faculty work: mentoring within a community of practice for faculty development. *Journal on Centers for Teaching and Learning*. 6, 59–91.
https://openjournal.lib.miamioh.edu/index.php/jctl/article/view/141

Cassella, M., (2017). New trends in academic library partnerships: academic libraries and digital humanities. In: *38th IATUL Conference, 18–22 June, Bolzano, Italy*.
https://docs.lib.purdue.edu/iatul/2017/partnership/2

Castells, M., (1996). *The rise of the network society*. Malden, MA: Blackwell.

Cawyer, C. S., Simonds, C. and Davis, S., (2002). Mentoring to facilitate socialization: the case of the new faculty member. *International Journal of Qualitative Studies in Education*. 15(2), 225–242. doi:10.1080/09518390110111938

Centivany, A., (2017). The dark history of HathiTrust. In: *50th Hawaii International Conference on system sciences, 4–7 January, Waikoloa Village, HI*. pp. 2357–2366.
http://hdl.handle.net/10125/41440

Christakis, N. A. and Fowler, J. H., (2011). *Connected: the amazing power of social networks and how they shape our lives*. London: Harper Press.

Clarke, C. G. and Antonio, A. L., (2012). Rethinking research on the impact of racial diversity in higher education. *The Review of Higher Education*. 36(1), 25–50. doi:10.1353/rhe.2012.0060

Clauset, A., Arbesman, S. and Larremore, D. B., (2015). Systematic inequality and hierarchy in faculty hiring networks. *Science Advances*. 1(1), c1400005. doi:10.1126/sciadv.1400005

CLIR., (2008). *No brief candle: reconceiving research libraries for the 21st century*. Washington, DC: Council on Library and Information Resources. https://www.clir.org/pubs/reports/pub142

Coleman, J. S., (1988). Social capital in the creation of human capital. *American Journal of Sociology*. 94, S95–S120. doi:10.1086/228943

Coleman, J. S., (1990). *Foundations of social theory*. Cambridge, MA: Harvard University Press.

Connaway, L. S., (2013). The library in 2020 will be engagement centered. In: J. Janes, ed. *Library 2020: today's leading visionaries describe tomorrow's library*. Lanham, MD: Scarecrow Press. pp. 83–87.

Corrall, S., (2014). Library service capital: the case for measuring and managing intangible assets. In: *Assessing libraries and library users and use: 13th International Conference Libraries in the Digital Age (LIDA), 16–20 June, Zadar, Croatia*. pp. 21–32. http://lida.ffos.hr/files/LIDA_2014_Proceedings.pdf

Cox, A. M., Kennan, M. A., Lyon, L. and Pinfield, S., (2017). Developments in research data management in academic libraries: towards an understanding of research data service maturity. *Journal of the Association for Information Science and Technology*. 68(9), 2182–2200. doi:10.1002/asi.23781

Crow, M. M. and Dabars, W. B., (2015). *Designing the new American university*. Baltimore, MD: Johns Hopkins University Press.

Dempsey, L., (2005). In the flow. *Lorcan Dempsey's weblog: on libraries, services, and networks*. 24 June 2005. https://www.lorcandempsey.net/orweblog/in-the-flow

Dempsey, L., (2010). Outside-in and inside-out. *Lorcan Dempsey's weblog: on libraries, services, and networks*. 11 January 2010. https://www.lorcandempsey.net/orweblog/outside-in-and-inside-out

Dempsey, L., (2016). Library collections in the life of the user: two directions. *LIBER Quarterly*. 26(4), 338–59. doi:10.18352/lq.10170

Dempsey, L., Malpas, C. and Lavoie, B., (2014). Collection directions: the evolution of library collections and collecting. *portal: Libraries and the Academy*. 14(3), 393–423. doi:10.1353/pla.2014.0013

DiRamio, D., Theroux, R. and Guarino, A. J., (2009). Faculty hiring at top-ranked higher education administration programs: an examination using social network analysis. *Innovative Higher Education*. 34(3), 145–159. doi:10.1007/s10755-009-9104-5

Downie, J. S., Furlough, M., McDonald, R. H., Namachchivaya, B., Plale, B. A. and Unsworth, J., (2016). The HathiTrust Research Center: exploring the full-text frontier. *EDUCAUSE Review*. 51(3), 50–51. https://er.educause.edu/-/media/files/articles/2016/5/erm1638.pdf

Etzkowitz, H. and Leydesdorff, L., (1995). The triple helix – university–industry–government relations: a laboratory for knowledge based economic development. *EASST Review*. 14(1), 14–19.

Farrell, R. and Badke, W., (2015). Situating information literacy in the disciplines: a practical and systematic approach for academic librarians. *Reference Services Review*. 43(2), 319–340. doi:10.1108/RSR-11-2014-0052

Federer, L., (2016). Research data management in the age of big data: roles and opportunities for librarians. *Information Services & Use*. **36**(1–2), 35–43. doi:10.3233/ISU-160797

Flierl, M. and Hamer, R., (2019) Designing student reflections to enable transformative learning experiences. *Teaching Philosophy*. **42**(2), 87–106. doi:10.5840/teachphil201952104

Flierl, M. and Maybee, C., (2020). Refining information literacy practice: examining the foundations of information literacy theory. *IFLA Journal*. **46**(2). doi:10.1177/0340035219886615

Fowler, J. H., Grofman, B. and Masuoka, N., (2007). Social networks in political science: hiring and placement of Ph.D.s, 1960–2002. *PS: Political Science & Politics*. **40**(4), 729–739. doi:10.1017/S104909650707117X

Freeman, L. C., (1978). Centrality in social networks: conceptual clarification. *Social Networks*. **1**(3), 215–239. doi:10.1016/0378-8733(78)90021-7

García-Milian, R., Norton, H. F., Autren, B., Davis, V. I., Holmes, K. L., Johnson, M. and Tennant, M. R., (2013). Librarians as part of cross-disciplinary, multi-institutional team projects: experiences from the VIVO collaboration. *Science & Technology Libraries*. **32**(2), 160–175. doi:10.1080/0194262X.2013.791183

Gibbons, M., Limoges, C., Nowotny, H., Schwartzman, S., Scott, P. and Trow, M., (1994). *The new production of knowledge: the dynamics of science and research in contemporary societies*. London: SAGE.

Granovetter, M., (1973). The strength of weak ties. *American Journal of Sociology*. **78**(6), 1360–1380. doi:10.1086/225469

Han, P., Shi, J., Li, X., Wang, D., Shen, S. and Su, X., (2014). International collaboration in LIS: global trends and networks at the country and institution level. *Scientometrics*. **98**(1), 53–72. doi:10.1007/s11192-013-1146-x

Hartlep, N. D., Hensley, B. O., Wells, K. E., Brewer, T. J., Ball, D. and McLaren, P., (2017). Homophily in higher education: historicizing the AERA member-to-fellow pipeline using theories of social reproduction and social networks. *Policy Futures in Education*. **15**(6), 670–694. doi:10.1177/1478210317715815

HathiTrust., (2020). Emergency temporary access service. *HathiTrust*. https://www.hathitrust.org/ETAS-Description

Haythornthwaite, C., (1996). Social network analysis: an approach and technique for the study of information exchange. *Library & Information Science Research*. **18**(4), 323–342. doi:10.1016/S0740-8188(96)90003-1

Hudson-Vitale, C. R., Johnson, R. P., Ruttenberg, J. and Spies, J. R., (2017). SHARE: community-focused infrastructure and a public goods, scholarly database to advance access to research. *D-Lib Magazine*. **23**(5/6). doi:10.1045/may2017-vitale

Ibarra, H., (1995). Race, opportunity, and diversity of social circles in managerial networks. *Academy of Management Journal*. **38**(3), 673–703. doi:10.2307/256742

Ibarra, H. and Andrews, S. B., (1993). Power, social influence, and sense making: effects of network centrality and proximity on employee perceptions. *Administrative Science Quarterly*. **38**(2), 277–303. doi:10.2307/2393414

Jaguszewski, J. M. and Williams, K., (2013). *New roles for new times: transforming liaison library roles in research libraries*. Washington, DC: Association of Research Libraries. https://www.arl.org/wp-content/uploads/2015/12/nrnt-liaison-roles-revised.pdf

Janke, R. and Rush, K. L., (2014). The academic librarian as co-investigator on an interprofessional primary research team: a case study. *Health Information and Libraries Journal*. 31(2), 116–122. doi:10.1111/hir.12063

Kachchaf, R., Ko, L., Hodari, A. and Ong, M., (2015). Career–life balance for women of color: experience in science and engineering academia. *Journal of Diversity in Higher Education*. 8(3), 175–191. doi:10.1037/a0039068

Kenney, A. R., (2014). *Leveraging the liaison model: from defining 21st century research libraries to implementing 21st century research libraries*. New York: ITHAKA S+R. https://sr.ithaka.org/wp-content/uploads/2014/03/SR_BriefingPaper_Kenney_20140322.pdf

Kenney, A. R., (2015). From engaging liaison librarians to engaging communities. *College & Research Libraries*. 76(3), 386–391. doi:10.5860/crl.76.3.386

Kinser, K., (2002). Faculty at private for-profit universities: the University of Phoenix as a new model? *International Higher Education*. 28(Summer), 13–14. doi:10.6017/ihe.2002.28.6662

Krackhardt, D. and Hanson, J. R., (1993). Informal networks: the company behind the chart. *Harvard Business Review*. 71(4), 104–111.

Larivière, V., Ni, C., Gingras, Y., Cronin, B. and Sugimoto, C. R., (2013). Bibliometrics: global gender disparities in science. *Nature*. 504(7479), 211–213. doi:10.1038/504211a

Lawani, S. M., (1986). Some bibliometric correlates of quality in scientific research. *Scientometrics*. 9(1–2), 13–25. doi:10.1007/bf02016604

Lazarsfeld, P. F. and Merton R. K., (1954). Friendship as a social process: a substantive and methodological analysis. In: M. Berger, T. Abel and C. H. Page, eds. *Freedom and control in modern society*. New York: Van Nostrand. pp. 18–66.

Lewis, D. W., (2016). *Reimagining the academic library*. Lanham, MD: Rowman & Littlefield.

Macfarlane, B., (2011). The morphing of academic practice: unbundling and the rise of the para-academic. *Higher Education Quarterly*. 65(1), 59–73. doi:10.1111/j.1468-2273.2010.00467.x

Mai, B., Liu, J. and González-Bailón, S., (2015). Network effects in the academic market: mechanisms for hiring and placing PhDs in communication (2007–2014). *Journal of Communication*. 65(3), 558–583. doi:10.1111/jcom.12158

Malenfant, K. J., (2010). Leading change in the system of scholarly communication: a case study of engaging liaison librarians for outreach to faculty. *College & Research Libraries*. 71(1), 63–76. doi:10.5860/0710063

Marin, A. and Wellman, B., (2011). Social network analysis: an introduction. In: J. Scott and P. J. Carrington, eds. *The SAGE handbook of social network analysis*. London: Sage. pp. 11–25.

Marsden, P. V. and Campbell, K. E., (1984). Measuring tie strength. *Social Forces*. 63(2), 482–501. doi:10.1093/sf/63.2.482

Maybee, C., (2018). *IMPACT learning: librarians at the forefront of change in higher education*. Cambridge, MA: Chandos.

McPherson, M., Smith-Lovin, L. and Cook, J. M., (2001). Birds of a feather: homophily in social networks. *Annual Review of Sociology*. **27**, 415–444. doi:10.1146/annurev.soc.27.1.415

Miller, R. K. and Pressley, L., (2015). *Evolution of library liaisons*. SPEC Kit 349. Washington, DC: Association of Research Libraries.

Mischo, W. H., Schlembach, M. C. and O'Donnell, M. N., (2014). An analysis of data management plans in University of Illinois National Science Foundation grant proposals. *Journal of eScience Librarianship*. **3**(1), 31–43. doi:10.7191/jeslib.2014.1060

Moran, P., (2005). Structural vs. relational embeddedness: social capital and managerial performance. *Strategic Management Journal*. **26**(12), 1129–1151. doi:10.1002/smj.486

Neal, J. G., (2012). Advancing from kumbaya to radical collaboration: redefining the future research library. *Journal of Library Administration*. **51**(1), 66–76. doi:10.1080/01930826.2011.531642

Nelson, R. E., (1989). The strength of strong ties: social networks and intergroup conflict in organizations. *Academy of Management Review*. **32**(2), 327–401. doi:10.2307/256367

Neumann, A., (2009). *Professing to learn: creating tenured lives and careers in the American research university*. Baltimore, MD: Johns Hopkins University Press.

O'Meara, K., Culpepper, D. and Templeton, L. L., (2020). Nudging toward diversity: applying behavioral design to faculty hiring. *Review of Education Research*. **90**(3), 311–348 doi:10.3102/0034654320914742

Pasek, J. E., (2015). Organizing the liaison role: a concept map. *College & Research Libraries News*. **76**(4), 202–205. doi:10.5860/crln.76.4.9295

Paulson, K., (2002). Reconfiguring faculty roles for virtual settings. *The Journal of Higher Education*. **73**(1), 123–140. doi:10.1080/00221546.2002.11777133

Peluchette, J. V. E. and Jeanquart, S., (2000). Professionals' use of different mentor sources at various career stages: implications for career success. *The Journal of Social Psychology*. **140**(5), 549–564. doi:10.1080/00224540009600495

Pescosolido, B. A., (2006). The sociology of social networks. In: C. D. Bryant and D. L. Peck, eds. *21st century sociology: a reference handbook*. Detroit, MI: Thousand Oaks, CA: SAGE. pp. 208–217.

Pinfield, S., Cox, A. M. and Smith, J., (2014). Research data management and libraries: relationships, activities, drivers, and influences. *PLoS ONE*. **9**(12), e114734. doi:10.1371/journal.pone.0114734

Plale, B. et al., (2013). HathiTrust Research Center: computational access for digital humanities and beyond. In: *13th ACM/IEEE-CS Joint Conference on digital libraries, 22–26 July, Indianapolis, IN*. New York: Association for Computing Machinery. pp. 395–396. doi:10.1145/2467696.2467767

Rainie, L. and Wellman, B., (2012). *Networked: the new social operating system*. Cambridge, MA: MIT Press.

Ranger, K. L., (2019). Introduction. In: K. L. Ranger, ed. *Informed learning applications: insights from research and practice*. Bingley, UK: Emerald. pp. 1–3. doi:10.1108/S0065-283020190000046002

Reagans, R. and Zuckerman, E. W., (2001). Networks, diversity, and productivity: the social capital of corporate R&D teams. *Organization Science*. 12(4), 502–517. doi:10.1287/orsc.12.4.502.10637

Rinio, D., (2019). Social network analysis for school librarians to evaluate and improve teacher collaboration. *School Libraries Worldwide*. 25(1), 57–79. https://journals.library.ualberta.ca/slw/index.php/slw/article/view/8235

Rosenfield, P. L., (1992). The potential of transdisciplinary research for sustaining and extending linkages between the health and social sciences. *Social Science & Medicine*. 35(11), 1343–1357. doi:10.1016/0277-9536(92)90038-R

Schlak, T., (2018). Academic libraries and engagement: a critical contextualization of the library discourse on engagement. *Journal of Academic Librarianship*. 44(1), 133–139. doi:10.1016/j.acalib.2017.09.005

Schoonover, D., Kinsley, K. and Colvin, G., (2018). Reconceptualizing liaisons: a model for assessing and developing liaison competencies to guide professional development. *Library Leadership & Management*. 32(4). doi:10.5860/llm.v32i4.7275

Seglen, P. O. and Aksnes, D. W., (2000). Scientific productivity and group size: a bibliometric analysis of Norwegian microbiological research. *Scientometrics*. 49(1), 125–143. doi:10.1023/a:1005665309719

Sgoutas-Emch, S., Baird, L., Myers, P., Camacho, M. and Lord, S., (2016). We're not all white men: using a cohort/cluster approach to diversify faculty hiring in STEM. *Thought & Action*. 32(1), 91–107. http://qa16.nea.org/home/68489.htm

Shari, S., Haddow, G. and Genoni, P., (2012). Bibliometric and webometric methods for assessing research collaboration. *Library Review*. 61(8/9), 592–607. doi:10.1108/00242531211292097

Sheble, L., Brennan, K. and Wildemuth, B. M., (2017). Social network analysis. In: B. M. Wildemuth, ed. *Application of social research methods to questions in information and library science*. 2nd ed. Santa Barbara, CA: Libraries Unlimited. pp. 339–350.

Shore, E., (2014). Coherence at scale and the research library of the future. *EDUCAUSE Review*. 49(1), 44–45. https://er.educause.edu/-/media/files/article-downloads/erm1416.pdf

Shrum, W., Genuth, J. and Chompalov, I., (2007). *Structures of scientific collaboration*. Cambridge, MA: MIT Press.

Shumaker, D., (2012). *The embedded librarian: innovative strategies for taking knowledge where it's needed*. Medford, NJ: Information Today.

Slaughter, S. A. and Leslie, L. L., (1997). *Academic capitalism: politics, policies, and the entrepreneurial university*. Baltimore, MD: Johns Hopkins University Press.

Slaughter, S. A. and Rhoades, G. D., (2004). *Academic capitalism and the new economy: markets, state, and higher education*. Baltimore, MD: Johns Hopkins University Press.

Smale, N., Unsworth, K., Denyer, G., Magatova, E. and Barr, D., (2020). A review of the history, advocacy and efficacy of data management plans. *International Journal of Digital Curation*. 15. doi:10.2218/ijdc.v15i1.525

Smith, D. G., Turner, C. S. V., Osei-Kofi, N. and Richards, S., (2004). Interrupting the usual: successful strategies for hiring diverse faculty. *The Journal of Higher Education*. 75(2), 133–160. doi:10.1080/00221546.2004.11778900

Smith, E. R., Calderwood, P. E., Storms, S. B., Lopez, P. G. and Colwell, R. P., (2016). Institutionalizing faculty mentoring within a community of practice model. *To Improve the Academy: A Journal of Educational Development*. 35(1), 35–71. doi:10.1002/tia2.20033

Stanger, K., (2009). Implementing information literacy in higher education: a perspective on the roles of librarians and disciplinary faculty. *LIBRES: Library and Information Sciences Research e-journal*. 19(1). https://www.libres-ejournal.info/553

Subramanyam, K., (1983). Bibliometric studies of research collaboration: a review. *Journal of Information Science*. 6(1), 33–38. doi:10.1177/016555158300600105

Tang, L. and Shapira, P., (2011). China–US scientific collaboration in nanotechnology: patterns and dynamics. *Scientometrics*. 88(1), 1–16. doi:10.1007/s11192-011-0376-z

Tenopir, C., Sandusky, R. J., Allard, S. and Birch, B., (2014). Research data management services in academic libraries and perceptions of librarians. *Library & Information Science Research*. 36(2), 84–90. doi:10.1016/j.lisr.2013.11.003

Tichy, N. M., Tushman, M. L. and Fombrun, C., (1979). Social network analysis for organizations. *Academy of Management Review*. 4(4), 507–520. doi:10.5465/AMR.1979.4498309

Toivanen, H. and Ponomariov, B., (2011). African regional innovation systems: bibliometric analysis of research collaboration patterns 2005–2009. *Scientometrics*. 88(2), 471–493. doi:10.1007/s11192-011-0390-1

Town, J. S. and Kyrillidou, M., (2013). Developing a values scorecard. *Performance Measurement and Metrics*. 14(1), 7–16. doi:10.1108/14678041311316095

Tucker, J. and Neely, P., (2010). Unbundling faculty roles in online distance education programs. *International Review of Research in Open and Distributed Learning*. 11(2), 20–32. doi:10.19173/irrodl.v11i2.798

Ujwary-Gil, A., (2019). Organizational network analysis: a study of a university library from a network efficiency perspective. *Library & Information Science Research*. 41(1), 48–57. doi:10.1016/j.lisr.2019.02.007

Vandegrift, M. and Varner, S., (2013). Evolving in common: creating mutually supportive relationships between libraries and the digital humanities. *Journal of Library Administration*. 53(1), 67–78. doi:10.1080/01930826.2013.756699

Wasserman, S. and Faust, K., (1994). *Social network analysis: methods and applications*. Cambridge, UK: Cambridge University Press.

Weeden, K. A., Thébaud, S. and Gelbgiser, D., (2017). Degrees of difference: gender segregation of U. S. doctorates by field and program prestige. *Sociological Science*. 4(6), 123–150. doi:10.15195/v4.a6

Weick, K. E., (1976). Educational organizations as loosely coupled systems. *Administrative Science Quarterly*. 21(1), 1–19. doi:10.2307/2391875

Wheeler, B., (2014). Speeding up on curves. *EDUCAUSE Review*. 49(1), 10–20. https://er.educause.edu/articles/2014/1/speeding-up-on-curves

Whitchurch, C., (2008). Shifting identities and blurring boundaries: the emergence of third space professionals in UK higher education. *Higher Education Quarterly*. 62(4), 377–396. doi:10.1111/j.1468-2273.2008.00387.x

Wiggins, A., Adamic, L. and McQuaid, M., (2006). The small worlds of academic hiring networks. In: *ASNA 2006: 3rd conference on applications of social network analysis, 5–6 October, Zürich, Switzerland.*
https://web.archive.org/web/20070221083452/http://www.andreawiggins.com/research/WigginsAdamicMcQuaid.pdf

Williams, K., (2009). A framework for articulating new library roles. *Research Library Issues*. **265**, 3–8. doi:10.29242/rli.265.2

Witt, M., Carlson, J., Brandt, D. S. and Cragin, M., (2009). Constructing data curation profiles. *International Journal of Digital Curation*. 4(3), 93–103. doi:10.2218/ijdc.v4i3.117

Wong, S. H. R., (2016). Digital humanities: what can libraries offer? *portal: Libraries and the Academy*. **16**(4), 669–690. doi:10.1353/pla.2016.0046

Writer, J. H. and Watson, D. C., (2019). Recruitment and retention: an institutional imperative told through the storied lenses of faculty of color. *Journal of the Professoriate*. **10**(2), 23–46. https://caarpweb.org/wp-content/uploads/2019/11/Haynes-Writer-Watson-Recruitment-and-Retention.pdf

York, J., (2009). This library never forgets: preservation, cooperation, and the making of the HathiTrust digital library. In: W. G. LeFurgy, ed. *Archiving 2009: preservation strategies and imaging technologies for cultural heritage institutions and memory organizations, final program and proceedings, 4–7 May, Arlington, VA.* Springfield, VA: Society for Imaging Science and Technology, pp. 5–10.

York, J., (2010). Building a future by preserving our past: the preservation infrastructure of HathiTrust digital library. In: *Open access to knowledge – promoting sustainable progress: 76th IFLA General Conference and Assembly, 10–15 August, Gothenburg, Sweden.*
https://www.ifla.org/past-wlic/2010/157-york-en.pdf

Zambrana, R.E, Ray, R., Espino, M. M., Castro, C., Cohen, B. D. and Eliason, J., (2015). 'Don't leave us behind': the importance of mentoring for underrepresented minority faculty. *American Educational Research Journal*. **52**(1), 40–72. doi:10.3102/0002831214563063

Zellers, D. F., Howard, V. M. and Barcic, M. A., (2008). Faculty mentoring programs: Reenvisioning rather than reinventing the wheel. *Review of Educational Research*. **78**(3), 552–88. doi:10.3102/0034654308320966

Zuo, Z., Zhao, K. and Ni, C., (2019). Standing on the shoulders of giants? Faculty hiring in information schools. *Journal of Informetrics*. **13**(1), 341–353. doi:10.1016/j.joi.2019.01.007.

3
Renewing and Revitalising the Social Mission of Higher Education

Sheila Corrall

Universities, like other sectors that perform public tasks are transforming into something similar to social enterprises, linking their production of goods and services to a social mission.

(Benneworth & Jongbloed 2010, p. 669)

Introduction

Following on from the opening chapter, the present chapter continues our review of trends and developments shaping the social future of academic libraries with a particular focus on the evolving social roles of higher education institutions (HEIs) in the 21st century. The key trend over the past 50 years is the evolution from an *elite higher education* system serving a small minority of young people to a *mass higher education* model open, in principle, to a majority of the population at a time when the world has also experienced major demographic changes and unprecedented technological advances. The social purpose of higher education (HE) has thus become a matter of wider public concern that has come under renewed scrutiny as a result of the economic downturn, political challenges and social inequalities that have defined the period since the turn of the century. Governments in many countries expect universities to contribute to both economic recovery and social inclusion, to support their local *communities* and to compete in global markets by producing world-leading research and recruiting international students.

Expansion of the HE sector is a worldwide trend manifested in larger and more diverse student and faculty populations across the globe, increasingly recruited from other countries and resulting in the development and diversification of campus infrastructure and professional services. At the same time, HEIs have expanded their portfolios of activities beyond the campus and academy in response to economic and political challenges by engaging more actively with the commercial world of business and industry, on the one hand, and non-profit community organisations and the general public, on the other. Research and teaching activities have both been affected by both business and public agendas, with undergraduate curricula expected to incorporate both business acumen and civic education to prepare students for *global citizenship*, while research funding schemes push academics towards work with demonstrable social and economic benefits, such as the design of new products or services to improve health and well-being that have commercial potential. Academic activities and responsibilities have become more complex, making conflicts of interests, commitments and values more common in the HE workplace.

The chapter is organised thematically and concentrates on areas where the social transformation of HE is having a significant impact. We begin with a short overview of the key drivers of change in the sector, followed by an elaboration of the '*third mission*' concept in universities, which is often seen as the HE equivalent of *corporate social responsibility* and is associated with the emergence of '*third space professionals*', whose work spans both the academic–professional and commercial–public arenas. We next look at the evolution of thinking and practice around student support – another area of significant expansion – and curriculum content, before considering the hot topic of *decolonisation* in HE, which illustrates the power of the emergent 'students as partners' model as an alternative to traditional hierarchical or consumerist relationships. Our final section provides a selective review of the growing body of work using social capital and related concepts to study the changing HE environment, with a particular focus on graduate *employability* and student use of support networks and social technologies.

Change drivers in higher education

Over the past several decades (from the late 1940s in the USA and mid-1960s in the UK/Europe) HE has expanded and diversified in response to political, economic, social and technological changes and challenges, with many institutions now operating at regional and global levels, as well as serving national and local purposes. HEIs in the early 2020s differ significantly from those of the 1970s in both social composition and social interactions. The student (and faculty) population contains many more members drawn from groups previously under-represented in HE and is much more diverse in respect of race, ethnicity and national origin; age, ability and health status; sexual and gender identity; and educational and socio-economic background (Morgan 2013). Institutions have accordingly reviewed, renewed and reformed their roles, responsibilities and relationships with stakeholders (individuals, groups and organisations) to fit the changing social conditions and demands of HE in the 21st century.

The key trends driving the transformation of HE can be summatively captured in the concepts of *massification, widening participation*, privatisation/commercialisation and *internationalisation* (de Wit & Altbach 2021; Guri-Rosenblit, Šebková & Teichler 2007; Shah, Bennett & Southgate 2016; Tight 2019a), representing four critical moves:

- expansion of the sector, intended to increase the proportion of young people entering tertiary education and progressing to highly skilled employment;
- democratisation of educational opportunity, recognising the need to make universities more accessible, inclusive and representative of the diversity of the population;

- marketisation of the system, with reduced public funding forcing institutions to generate additional income from other sources, such as student fees;
- *globalisation* of the economy, driven by *digitalisation*, empowering institutions to grow and recruit internationally and to prepare students for global careers.

These trends are well documented in the education literature as worldwide phenomena, although they are playing out at different speeds in different parts of the world (Osborne 2003). Moreover, the intersection of different environmental forces has generated complexity and tensions: HE has evolved from an elite – essentially *national* – system to a mass market operating on a *global* level, but continuing to reflect national policies and practices that are in turn pushing institutions to reconnect with *local* communities and concerns at the same time as they are being pulled towards *international* markets to maintain competitive positioning and mitigate funding shortfalls. Scholars have devised the *glonacal paradigm* to point up the 'three intersecting planes of existence, emphasizing the simultaneous significance of global, national, and local dimensions and forces' (Marginson & Rhoades 2002, p. 282).

Development of the third mission

The function of HE in society and the economy came under particular scrutiny during the run-up to the 21st century, with institutions in many countries challenged by the state and the public to articulate the social relevance of their activities and programs. Universities have traditionally claimed a third responsibility of service to society alongside their education and research missions, but often presented this role only in general terms. This changed around the turn of the century when commentators began to use the term 'third mission' to describe university contributions to economic development through the commercialisation of academic research via technology transfer, patenting, incubators, spin-off firms and similar (Etzkowitz & Leydesdorff 2000). Since the early 2000s scholars have been revisiting, rethinking and even reinventing the third mission concept to embody both economic/business and societal/community contributions and interactions, and also to encompass education/teaching alongside research (Berghaeuser & Hoelscher 2020; Laredo 2007; Lebeau & Cochrane 2015).

Development of the socio-economic mission of universities reflects two distinct streams of thinking around roles in the knowledge society: first, ideas related to innovation and entrepreneurship, encapsulated as the *entrepreneurial university* (Clark 1998; Etzkowitz 1983), and the related concepts of the *triple helix* of university–industry–government relations (Etzkowitz & Leydesdorff 2000) and **academic capitalism**, which repositions public/non-profit institutions as commercial, profit-making organisations in a global market (Rhoades & Slaughter 1997); second, ideas related to participation and citizenship, variously expressed as *civic engagement* (O'Connor 2006), *community engagement* (Fitzgerald & Peterman 2003), *public engagement* (Furco 2010), engaged scholarship/*scholarship of engagement* (Boyer 1996), the engaged campus (Furco 2010) and *engaged university*

(Hollander & Saltmarsh 2000). Other terms used include third constituent, third stream, third task, third leg, third revolution, university engagement, social and business engagement and social responsibility (Ćulum, Rončević & Ledić 2013; Frondizi et al. 2019).

University social responsibility (USR) is a related concept stressing an ethical commitment to environmental protection and sustainable development (Vasilescu et al. 2010), a key theme in recent literature that has been promoted as an emergent alternative (or fourth) mission of 'co-creation for sustainability', combining the triple-helix and community-engagement models to mobilise academia, government, industry and civil society in 'cross-sector partnerships for sustainability transformations' (Trencher et al. 2014, p. 152). While this alternative model looks like a natural evolution of the university socio-economic mission (in line with the ***triple bottom line*** and sustainable capitalism models of the corporate sector) and Trencher et al. (2014, pp. 157, 159) cite 39 exemplar institutions in Europe, Asia and North America, they also acknowledge that it requires 'a fundamental difference in focus' and will 'encounter tensions with the incumbent values and practices of the third mission regime', which they broadly equate with the entrepreneurial, technocratic model.

Others point to similar tensions *within* the civic engagement movement, which has 'struggled to find conceptual and operational coherence' – with the 'expert model' of knowledge application/***knowledge transfer*** largely continuing to prevail over democratic values of task-sharing and knowledge co-creation (Saltmarsh & Hartley 2011, p. 14). Table 3.1 opposite adapts and synthesises the tabulations of Trencher et al. (2014, p. 158) and Saltmarsh and Hartley (2011, p. 22) with elaboration from other sources (Dzur 2018; Frondizi et al. 2019) to compare and contrast established and emergent thinking around the third (or fourth) mission, community/civic engagement and the social responsibilities of university actors as expert professionals. The table format brings out the serious extent of the tensions between the competitive, technocratic and co-operative, democratic models.

Irrespective of these tensions, the breadth and volume of activities now forming the societal mission is generating more pervasive institutional engagement, with growing reference to mainstreaming, integrating and embedding third-mission activities as central responsibilities rather than peripheral projects (Ćulum, Rončević & Ledić 2013; Nelles & Vorley 2010; Wedgwood 2006), so that 'community involvement is not viewed as a public service project or a supplement to core academic work . . . [but] as an important, legitimate and valued strategy for conducting high quality education and scholarly research' (Furco 2010, p. 387).

Figure 3.1 on page 64 provides a visual summary of the range of activities now associated with the socio-economic (third) mission of HE, drawing on several sources (e.g., Glass & Fitzgerald 2010; Duncan & Manners 2012). As third-stream work becomes institutionalised, business and community interactions are becoming integrated into academic and administrative/professional work on and off campus, with the boundaries between different areas increasingly blurred.

Table 3.1 *Salient characteristics of university socio-economic missions*

	Established third mission (technocratic, expert-based)	Emergent alternative/fourth mission (social, democratic-centred)
Model	Entrepreneurial university: centre of scientific expertise (scholarly work done for the client as consumer; deficit-based view of the community/region)	Transformative university: part of knowledge ecosystem (scholarly work done with the public as co-producer; asset-based view of the community)
Objective	Economic development	Social transformation
Function	Technology transfer for industry (unidirectional flow, applied research and technical training)	Knowledge co-creation for sustainability (multidirectional flow, participatory action research and community learning)
Timeframe	Short- to mid-term	Mid- to long-term
Logic	Competitive market	Co-operative commons
Disciplines	Specific fields (particularly natural sciences and engineering)	Full spectrum (including humanities and social sciences)
Assumptions	• Primacy of academic knowledge • Intellectual property rights • Task monopoly	• Parity of community knowledge • Communal ownership rules • Task sharing
Approach	In-house R&D Selective ad-hoc response to isolated problems	Open innovation Comprehensive systematic response to interwoven problems
Relationships	Project-based collaboration Triple helix (university, industry and government specialists)	Large-scale coalition Quintuple helix (university, business, government, civil society and natural environment specialists and non-specialists)
Setting	Laboratory/controlled environments	Community/real-world locations
Catalyst	Scientific, technical or industrial problem	Societal challenge, issue or need
Channels	• Patents/licences • Science/technology parks • Spin-off firms/start-up companies • Conferences, publications • Consultation, graduates	• Cultural venues • Community centres • Social enterprises • Meetings, public events • Participation, students
Politics	Leverage government policy, incentives and funding	Facilitate inclusive, collaborative, and deliberative democracy
Values	Academic capitalism (privatisation, income generation, profit taking)	Social capital (public good, community building, non profit)

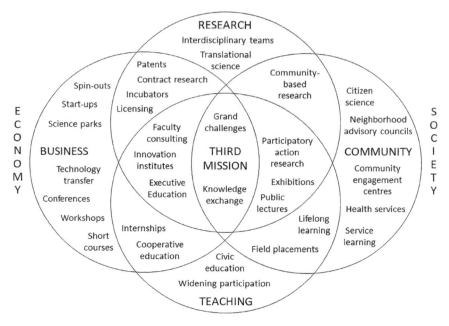

Figure 3.1 *Third-mission activities in higher education*

Whitchurch (2010, pp. 627, 628) reports that 'a new cadre of *"blended professionals"* has emerged', whose work occupies 'a "Third Space" . . . between academic and professional domains' and together spans both publicly oriented activity (e.g., widening participation, schools liaison and bridging activity) and privately oriented (e.g., enterprise, technology transfer and patenting), pointing to recent convergence of these strands of activity as enabling public and private elements to reinforce and enrich each other. As government agendas link widening access to skills development, graduate employability and economic recovery, universities are developing partnerships with 'a range of regional, national and international agencies' that 'bring together the extension of educational opportunity with the regeneration of local communities', in which 'specialist [blended, third-space] professionals . . . work alongside academic colleagues to perform translational functions between academic agendas and the interests of external agencies' (Whitchurch, 2010, pp. 629, 630).

Foregrounding student employability

As we move through the 21st century, we find that both the populations and transactions of HEIs have expanded and diversified as universities and colleges reach out to business and the community to conform with national policies, sectoral guidelines and local aspirations. The focus on *graduate employability* encapsulates the tensions arising from the convergence of the economic and social missions of HE, with continuing debate around the scope of the concept and its place in the academy. Careers advice in the 1970s was a peripheral service, and few universities systematically tracked graduate destinations; first destination graduate employment is now a key performance indicator, with many HEIs delivering enterprise education, *employability learning* and career management skills as part of the 21st-century curriculum. Indeed, graduate employability 'has become a core element of universities' educative, social, and economic missions', and the need for more careers and employability support has generated new specialist roles related to campus employment, entrepreneurship hubs, industry liaison, student development and work-integrated learning as additional examples of emergent boundary-crossing third-space professionals (Healy, Brown & Ho 2022).

The sector has developed frameworks such as graduate attributes and skills awards to help students acquire and document accomplishments and competencies relevant to employment, although embedding employability into the core curriculum for all students obviously ensures more penetration than elective methods and can be done in several ways (Yorke & Knight 2006). Employability is a broad, complex construct that experts stress is 'not just about preparing students for employment' but, rather, about 'supporting students to develop a range of knowledge, skills, behaviours, attributes and attitudes which will enable them to be successful not just in employment but in life' (Cole & Tibby 2013, pp. 5, 6). Cole and Tibby's (2013, p. 9) review of seven definitions/models illustrates a shift since the 1990s 'from demand-led skills sets towards a more holistic view of "graduate attributes" that include 'softer' transferable skills and person-centred qualities, developed in conjunction with subject specific knowledge, skills and competencies'. Bennett et al. (2017, p. 52) agree that 'employability has shifted from a focus on "job-getting" towards the metacognitive capacity to adapt, lead and learn' as a result of 'enormous pressure to develop graduates who can negotiate a crowded, volatile and globally competitive labour market'.

Yet employability continues to be a controversial topic beset by contested assumptions and intersecting tensions, with scholars disparaging the knowledge–skills–attributes models promoted by governments and adopted by universities as instrumentalist, simplistic and insensitive to contextual realities (Walker & Fongwa 2017, pp. 36–39). Critics argue that the human-capital thinking that has dominated the HE policy discourse since the rise of ***neoliberalism*** in the 1980s represents only the baseline requirement and fails to understand other factors critical for graduate success. Higdon (2016, p. 189) uses evidence from current students and recent graduates to show that students need **cultural capital**, **social capital** and **financial capital** ('confidence, contacts and money') in order to develop personal networks in their profession and access the gatekeepers of work opportunities. Students and graduates want connections with practitioners through a curriculum linking theory and practice and bringing academics and professionals together, with courses and projects aligned to industry work; they want work experience, placements and internships organised by the university (not by students) and specialist, discipline-based careers advice, in preference to generic, centralised services (Higdon 2016).

Diversification of student support activities

The boundaries between formerly separate functions of HEIs are blurring as so-called third-mission activities become assimilated into research and education activities that have also evolved to reflect the complex-pluralist context of the contemporary learning economy, notably by rethinking the links between teaching and research, with elite research-intensive institutions committing to research-led teaching and inclusive teaching-oriented universities promoting research-based learning (Healey 2005; Scott 2005). Similarly, the boundaries between academic activities and student services are blurring as institutions move beyond reforming the undergraduate curriculum to improving 'the total life experience of students', realising that students require support 'through every stage of their academic and personal journey at university' and that support needs to provide 'a holistic student experience' and to be 'integrated with . . . academic support' (Sandeen 2004, p. 33; Morgan 2012, pp. 79, 81, 82).

The student services/student affairs function 'has become more complex as . . . students have become more diverse' (Sandeen 2004, p. 30). Services have expanded and diversified beyond traditional 'safety net' functions (such as finance, housing and health) to general well-being services (including careers, counselling and recreation), in addition to special support for disabled, international, mature and part-time students, as well as social, cultural and educational programs (Morgan 2012; Sandeen 2004). Student affairs professionals 'reject any suggestion that they are just "service providers"', seeing themselves 'as an integral part of the academic programs of their campuses and as active contributors to student learning' with involvement in education outside the classroom via *living-learning communities*, *service learning*, leadership-development programs and peer-related education (Sandeen 2004, p. 28), and teaching study skills, employability skills and other key skills as part of the curriculum (Morgan 2012).

Student support is now more co-operative, proactive, student centred and stage based, with many institutions (both teaching-intensive and research-intensive) adopting the concept of the student lifecycle as a tool for designing targeted academic, personal and social interventions both to facilitate progress and success, and to mitigate the risk of drop-out, which increased substantially with massification and diversification, particularly among low-socio-economic, disabled and mature students, especially during or around the end of the first year (Matheson 2018). Lifecycle models typically have four to six phases or stages, representing a series of 'pivotal transition points' in the student journey (Morgan 2013, p. 1447). Lifecycle thinking has advanced prior work foregrounding the first-year experience by including key upstream and downstream phases of higher learning to present the learner journey as a continuum with critical staging points, while also promoting 'a holistic view of the university experience' by involving student peers, professionals, academics and administrators in supporting new student transitions (Krause 2006, p. 2).

Ultimately, as Krause (2006, p. 8) concludes, 'The goal is to build student independence and support networks as part of an integrated academic and social transition' that extends beyond the first year, through the middle and final years to life after university. Table 3.2 shows the transitions defined in four frequently referenced models, replacing the cycle format with a table for comparative purposes.

Table 3.2 *Modelling student lifecycles in higher education*

HEFCE (2001)	Burnett (2007)	Lizzio (2011)	Morgan (2013)
Aspiration raising	**Pre-transition** Beginning to think about university	**Transition towards** FUTURE STUDENTS	**First contact and admissions**
Pre-entry	**Transition** Preparing for university	1. Applying and exploring 2. Clarifying and choosing	**Pre-arrival**
		Transition in COMMENCING STUDENTS	
Admission **First term/semester**	**Orientation week** First year student induction programs	3. Committing and preparing 4. Joining and engaging	**Arrival and orientation** **Introduction to study**
		Transition through CONTINUING STUDENTS	**Re-orientation and reinduction**
Moving through the course	**The middle years** The capstone or final year experience	5. Working for early success 6. Building on success	
Employment		**Transitions up, out & back** GRADUATES & ALUMNI	**Outduction**
	Engagement with lifelong learning Post-graduate student experience	7. Focusing future success 8. Partnering and continuing	Time out/career/future study

The Higher Education Funding Council for England (HEFCE 2001, p. 35) defines six 'mutually dependent' elements that determine successful recruitment, retention and progression. Morgan's (2013) Student Experience Practitioner Model also has six stages, but specifically identifies returning to study (after a vacation, work placement or study abroad) and leaving the university as difficult transitions that may need as much thought and support as first-year induction, hence the term 'outduction'. While the literature on transitions largely concentrates on the undergraduate experience, there is a growing body of research showing that students returning for postgraduate study 'often re-enter the student lifecycle from the beginning, bringing with them new academic and social concerns' (Matheson 2018, p. 8), and consequently need support in adjusting to and developing their changing academic and social, professional and personal identities. Burnett (2007, p. 24) notes that some phases of the University of Queensland Student Experience Model 'occur outside the immediate university environment and . . . require, and depend upon, the fostering of strong and authentic community links'.

Lizzio's (2011) four-part model was developed in Australia, but is cited in studies from other countries. Lizzio (2011, p. 1) defines the student lifecycle as 'the *constellation of evolving identities, needs and purposes* as students enter into, move through and graduate from universities'. His seminal paper argues for the lifecycle-informed design of coherent academic programs, based on a *partnership culture* in which academic teachers, professionals, students and other stakeholders (disciplines, professions, employers) actively explore different ways to collaborate in 'a suite of *next generation partnerships or working relationships*', asserting that '*the stage-responsive organisation of relationships and learning task activities* will encourage better engagement and learning, stronger social and academic links between students and students and staff [professionals and academics], and produce more satisfied and effective graduates and loyal alumni' (Lizzio 2011, p. 4). Significantly, lifecycle-informed academic programs here involve '*coordinated integration of both curricular and co-curricular activities*' (Lizzio 2011, p. 7), confirming the holistic model of university education that is now being promoted in many countries.

Reform of the academic curriculum

Barnett (2000) recounts the many diverse influences (disciplines, professions, students, employers, governments, markets, pedagogies, strategies, etc.) shaping institutional curricula in a mass HE system and concludes that in the contemporary *supercomplex* world, a curriculum must somehow combine the domains of knowledge (understanding), action (performativity) and being (self-identity). There is an emerging consensus that HE curricula must reform to counter the complex mega-problems of contemporary economic and social life, with growing support for cross-disciplinary teamwork, multi-literacy development, creative capacity building, person-centred education and holistic frameworks that integrate cognitive, affective and spiritual dimensions to 'emphasize personal integration, as well as sociocultural, and ecological awareness' (Baxter Magolda & Taylor 2017; Brown 2006; Hutchison & Bosacki 2000, p 182; McWilliam 2010; UNESCO 1996).

McWilliam (2010, p. 293) argues for 'cultural and epistemological agility', represented by 'the ability to move seamlessly across multiple disciplinary, social and cultural terrains'. Such thinking takes down disciplinary silos, cuts across organisational boundaries and calls for closer connection of academic, professional and personal development in ways that signal the growing *academic* importance of student *service* provision in 'educating the whole student' and promoting student well-being (Sandeen 2004; Jayawickreme & Dahill-Brown 2016; Weaver 2008). Hutchison and Bosacki (2000, pp. 181, 182) argue for a 'balanced curriculum [that] alternates between action and reflection, communal and personal, social and solitary' and gives parity to 'the "state of being" alongside "acts of doing" . . . treating both as complementary processes of meaning-making', concluding that 'experiential education can enrich its pedagogy to include guided fantasy, narrative, and contemplative practices among its teaching and learning strategies'. Synthesising ideas from Barnett, Baxter Magolda and others, Jackson (2011) makes the case for a 'lifewide curriculum' based on the knowing–acting–being paradigm, which integrates experiences and learning from different contexts, such as academic study, work placements and extra-curricular activities.

A common theme across the student services, service learning and learning development literature of the 21st century is the focus on partnerships, variously manifest as learning partnerships, community partnerships and, most recently, 'students as partners' and 'partnership learning communities' (Baxter Magolda & King 2004; Healey, Flint & Harrington 2016; Jacoby 2003; Mercer-Mapstone et al. 2017). Proponents conceive students as partners (SaP) as a more active, more authentic and more collaborative form of *student engagement* involving students in multiple roles, including institutional governance, quality assurance, research strategies, community engagement and extra-curricular activities, as well as curriculum design, pedagogic consultancy, peer mentoring, subject-based research and change agents (Healey, Flint & Harrington 2016). Academic librarians have defined additional domains for partnering with students as co-designers, including space transformation, service excellence, resource design and collection renewal (Salisbury, Dollinger & Vanderlelie 2020). SaP has also been characterised as 'a process of renegotiating traditional positions, power arrangements, and ways of working' and an alternative to both traditional hierarchical approaches and neoliberal/consumerist models in HE (Healey, Flint & Harrington 2016, p. 8; Matthews et al. 2018, pp. 958, 968).

Decolonisation of higher education institutions

The current global movement to decolonise the curriculum (Abu Moghli & Kadiwal 2021; Bullen & Flavell 2021; Harvey & Russell-Mundine 2019) provides a large-scale example of students working as partners at an institutional and national level, with contemporary institutional initiatives largely inspired by numerous student-led protests and campaigns over the past decade, notably Rhodes Must Fall, Leopold Must Fall, Galton Must Fall and Gladstone Must Fall; Liberate My Degree, Why Isn't My Professor Black? and Why Is My Curriculum White? The decolonisation debate has a much longer history and wider remit, with surges in the 1960s, 1980s and 2000s, but has been reignited by student action in the 2010s, generating renewed calls to decolonise not just the curriculum but the university, higher education, the academy, open science, established (Western/Eurocentric) knowledge and even *the academic self* 'in a process of forever becoming' (Bhambra, Gebrial & Nişancıoğlu 2018; Dutta et al. 2021; Heleta 2016; Nagdee & Shafi 2021; Naude 2019; Wimpenny et al. 2021, p. 13).

The conceptualisation and terminology of the field are contested, particularly the respective uses of decolonisation, **Eurocentrism**, **Indigenisation** and Africanisation, and related terms such as internationalisation, globalisation and **cosmopolitanism** (Bhambra, Gebrial & Nişancıoğlu 2018; Bullen & Flavell 2021; Crilly & Everitt 2022; le Grange 2018). Much of the literature has a conceptual or theoretical focus, but there is an emerging body of empirical work that offers insight into practical steps being taken towards diversity, equity and inclusion in academic curricula, including case studies of academic librarians collaborating with students and faculty to *decolonise*, *liberate* and *indigenise* their libraries, using *critical race theory*, *historical trauma theory* and other frameworks to audit, review and reconstitute course collections, reading lists, classification systems, library education and information literacy in work that aligns with the *critical*, *progressive* and *radical* librarianship movements (Crilly & Everitt 2022; Nicholson & Seale 2018). Reading lists have emerged as a popular focus for initial work, enabling students, faculty and librarians to work through issues together as a **community of practice**.

Two UK studies explore the diversity of reading lists as a key step towards decolonisation by analysing the gender, ethnicity and location of authors represented, and comparing the distribution with the diversity of their student body and scholarly community. Schucan Bird and Pitman (2020) audited authorship in two examples from social science and science, while Taylor et al. (2021) used the same methodology for a much larger sample across nine life science disciplines. While the percentages varied across disciplines, both studies found their lists were dominated by White, male authors from countries in the Global North, and resolved to diversify their reading lists (through co-creation with students) and to educate students and colleagues about racism and colonialism in science, but noted several unresolved problems in moving forward, such as defining representativeness, determining ethnicities and selecting terminology.

Several scholars use the articulation provided by Andreotti et al. (2015, p. 31) to position decolonising efforts on a spectrum from 'soft-reform' through 'radical-reform' to 'beyond-reform'. Abu Moghli and Kadiwal (2021, pp. 12, 13) found that most of the UK curriculum initiatives analysed were in the soft-reform space and 'although supported and pushed by many students and academics of colour and their allies, the DtC [Decolonise the Curriculum] movement and the available initiatives remain piecemeal and short-lived, and have limited impact on the colonial education approach embodied in HEIs'. They concluded that decolonising the curriculum cannot be accomplished effectively without more fundamental restructuring of the institution and, specifically, 'a deconstruction of asymmetrical power relationships within academic spaces to allow for meaningful decolonisation in practice, and a recognition of plurality of histories, knowledge and epistemic traditions and experiences'.

Two case studies from Australia reinforce this argument. The first example shows an institution moving from soft-reform to radical-reform, progressing from selective embedding of indigenous perspectives in curricula of particular subjects to a whole-of-university approach to *cultural competence* development for students, academics and professional staff by making 'cultural competence' one of six interconnected qualities in their set of graduate attributes (Harvey & Russell-Mundine 2019). Using Martin Nakata's (2002; 2007) concept of the *'cultural interface'*, the authors explain the reciprocal relationships that enable other qualities (critical thinking, problem solving, interdisciplinarity, reflection, ethics) to facilitate development of cultural competence: although 'firmly grounded in Western epistemologies . . . they can nonetheless be used to challenge the dominance of Western ways of knowing, being and doing in our curricula', while 'engagement with Indigenous knowledges . . . can allow all students to more fully engage with those graduate qualities not primarily concerned with disciplinary content' (Harvey & Russell-Mundine 2019, pp. 793, 794).

In contrast, Bullen and Flavell (2021) exemplify a 'beyond-reform' stance (Andreotti et al. 2015), criticising the whole notion of graduate attributes and, particularly, the ubiquitous concept of 'global citizenship' for reinforcing homogeneity, whiteness and a Western worldview of employability. Although they agree that the cultural interface is 'a highly productive learning context for students to engage in', they argue that wholehearted engagement requires more fundamental 'place-based decolonising processes', led by Aboriginal peoples, and needs to expose graduates to indigenous knowledge and 'learning processes . . . grounded in relationships, obligation and connection to country' (Bullen & Flavell 2021, pp. 10–11).

Capital perspectives on higher education

While there has been a substantial increase in the participation of under-represented groups in HE since the turn of the century, despite efforts to support their transition and progression, there is a well-documented persistent 'achievement gap' (also known as an 'attainment' or 'awarding' gap) between students from high and low economic backgrounds, giving rise to numerous studies investigating the causes of disparities and the effects of targeted interventions, such as financial aid, pre-college outreach and social support (Brown 2018; Herbaut & Geven 2019; Marginson 2016; Mishra 2020). Theories and concepts of social capital are increasingly being used to explore student experiences at various stages of the HE lifecycle, with a focus on their **social networks** and relationships, often with the intent of improving support and access to **resources** for disadvantaged groups. Mishra (2020) and Tight (2019b) point to significant growth in social capital-based studies in HE since 2012, following the dramatic surge of interest in social capital across the social sciences from the early 2000s.

Although social capital has long been a contested concept in social science, subject to multiple definitions and interpretations, it has become one of the most widely used theoretical frameworks in social research and has been adopted in diverse contexts, notably economic development, public health, organisational behaviour, democratic governance, civic participation and family studies, as well as primary, secondary and, later, tertiary education. Tight (2019b, pp. 209–210) estimates that around one-tenth of published articles on social capital focus on HE, currently 200–300 per year, supplementing similar quantities using **human capital** theory in HE, which he describes as 'the most influential theory relating to higher education policy (and educational policy in general) – nationally and internationally – over the last 50 years or more', on the basis that public investment in education, training and learning leads to increased productivity and economic growth and benefits both individuals and society. The move towards social capital theory reflects policy concerns around participation and social integration, while the ongoing focus on human capital acknowledges that HE participation is motivated by both economic and social agendas of individuals, communities and society.

Despite ongoing debate on its meaning and significance, the massive growth of social capital as a paradigm for studying social problems has resulted in it acquiring a taken-for-granted status among scholars (in education and other fields), to the extent that the concept is often invoked without formally defining it and the term has become routinised into mainstream discourse and everyday conversation (Fine 2010; Fulkerson & Thompson 2008; Woolcock 2010). Setting aside the debate over whether social capital is primarily an individual or collective attribute and variations among different areas of social research, Fulkerson and Thompson's (2008) comprehensive analysis of two decades of journal articles reveals remarkable consistency in the concepts most frequently used across all areas, with networks, resources, relationships, **trust**, norms and **reciprocity** emerging as key terms.

The main social capital theorists cited in HE research are Pierre Bourdieu (1986), James Coleman (1988), Nan Lin (1999) and Robert Putnam (1995; 2000); other scholars referenced include Granovetter (1973), Burt (1992), Borgatti and Foster (2003), Nahapiet and Ghoshal (1998) and Portes (1998; 2000). Bourdieu's conceptualisation of the relationship between economic, cultural and social capital is the dominant framework used, though often in tandem with Colemanesque theories linking the social capital in social relationships to human capital represented by educational attainment, or with Lin's network theory of social capital. However, recent scholarship argues that overreliance on Bourdieusian theories of **social and cultural reproduction** perpetuates deficit thinking by concentrating on a narrow range of cultural and social resources and ignoring other abundant and significant **assets** that minority groups can deploy and develop to succeed in education and elsewhere. Early examples of social capital research favoured quantitative methods, but the use of qualitative and mixed methods has grown significantly (Mishra 2020).

Exploring student networks

The bulk of the literature concentrates on the experiences of students after enrolment. Mishra (2020) synthesises findings from more than 100 studies from the USA and beyond to provide a model showing how **bonding** and **bridging social capital** represented by close and weak ties in their personal and institutional networks provide social support and information resources for students from under-represented groups that can help them to succeed academically; their 'bonding ties' include family members, ethnic/religious communities and same-race peers, while 'bridging ties' include same-race faculty, successful community members and institutional learning communities. However, a significant strand of research explores formation of social capital at the pre-entry stage, often in the context of college preparation programs. Early studies used US education survey data to analyse the impact of parental involvement and school structures on college enrolment (Perna & Titus 2005; Sandefur, Meier & Campbell 2006). Later research from Ireland synthesises Bourdieusian theories with the **capability (human development) approach** of Amartya Sen (1985) and Martha Nussbaum (2011) as a broader, alternative lens on activities building social capital in an aspiration-raising program for second-year secondary school students (Hannon, Faas & O'Sullivan 2017). Others have used Tara Yosso's (2005) **Community Cultural Wealth** (CCW) framework to analyse resources used by minority students to assist their transition to university.

CCW shifts the focus from the assumed deficits of *non-traditional students* to their distinctive strengths by recognising the 'array of knowledge, skills, abilities and contacts possessed and utilized' as alternative forms of overlapping capital (**aspirational capital**, **navigational capital**, social capital, **linguistic capital**, **familial capital** and **resistant capital**) that build on one another as accumulated (but underutilised) assets which they bring from their homes and communities to the classroom (Yosso 2005, p. 77). O'Shea (2016) found that '**experiential capital**' (derived from life and professional experiences) was another factor in the academic success of mature first-in-family students in Australia, alongside their aspirational, familial, social and other assets. Macqueen (2018, p. 47) similarly found that non-traditional cultural and social capital helped low socio-economic students to succeed, including 'in the moment' emotional and practical support from families, supplemented by social networks based on student friends and peers in similar situations. White (2019) also challenges the assumption that such students have low social capital, finding that they are more active help-seekers than their higher-status peers, using networks of support based on family, peers, administrative staff and teachers/tutors, selected as available, familiar, credible and trustworthy connections, with student services used as secondary sources referred to by their primary networks.

Several scholars have conducted cross-national and/or cross-institutional studies to compare minority student experiences in different settings. Friend's (2021) comparison of experiences at elite universities in the UK and USA describes how institutional practices that promote bridging and bonding networks help and hinder social integration. Rienties, Johan & Jindal-Snape (2015) used **social network analysis** to compare the friendship, work and learning networks of third-year international and UK students in terms of their co-national, multinational and host-national relationships before and after being put into mixed work groups by teachers, and found that the group work resulted in some broadening of networks for Chinese students, who tended to have fewer intercultural interactions. A longitudinal comparison at two contrasting UK universities in the same city shows how middle-class students used the economic and social capital of their parents by exploiting family networks to access top professions, gain competitive internships and improve their employability, while their working-class peers often took low-level jobs to fund their studies and participated less in structured work experience or other extra-curricular activities, which affected their career prospects and positioned university as 'another site for the middle classes to compound and exploit their advantages', rather than the source of social levelling that it was assumed to be (Bathmaker, Ingram & Waller 2013, p. 739).

A small stream of research explores the role of *community-based learning,* service learning and community education in generating social capital for individuals and communities. Dilworth (2006) includes two case studies showing the 'social multiplier effect' created by community education that bridges connections by extending university social networks into disadvantaged communities and widening the social networks of low-income youth. Coleman and Danks (2016) refer to a 'positive spillover effect' from a multi-agency service-learning partnership where 'the establishment of norms and . . . expectations of reciprocity . . . led to an increase in trust and networks' facilitating collaborative action in a community-based forestry initiative. Other studies have investigated the impact of community-based learning on the social capital of individual students by measuring participation in networks and levels of trust (D'Agostino 2010), and perceptions of connectedness and reductions in ethnocentrism (Hoffman 2011).

Elaborating graduate employability

Capital perspectives have generated a rich body of work unpacking and repackaging the contentious concept of graduate employability. Williams et al. (2016, pp. 887–892) present capital as a unifying theme and 'superordinate dimension' of literature on employability from the 1990s onwards, showing how elements of social, cultural and **psychological capital** have been evident in elaborations of the concept from the outset, though often not made explicit, with human capital theory dominating the early agenda, followed by social capital as the focus shifted from individuals to their relationships with others. Different capital theories of employability have gained prominence in HE globally in the form of both capital subcomponents and overarching concepts, including **academic capital** (Hu & Cairns 2017; Lavender 2020), **personal capital** (Brown, Hesketh & Williams 2003; Lehmann 2019), **ethnic capital** (Abrahamsen & Drange 2015; Shah, Dwyer & Modood 2010; Sin 2016), **identity capital** (Côté 2005; Naseem 2019), **mobility capital** (Hu & Cairns 2017; Wiers-Jenssen 2011), **career capital** (D'Amico et al. 2019; Reichenberger & Raymond 2021), *graduate capital* (Tomlinson 2017; Wijayanama, Ranjani

& Mohan, 2021) and *employability capital* (Caballero, Álvarez-González & López-Miguens 2020; Nghia, Giang & Quyen 2019).

Employability researchers have turned to the Bourdieusian multifaceted conceptualisation of embodied, objectified and institutionalised *cultural capital* and related concepts (not only social capital, but also **symbolic capital**, *linguistic capital* and **educational capital** or *academic capital*) to gain a more nuanced understanding of both employer expectations and graduate aspirations, particularly among minority groups, such as mature students and international graduates. Scholarship covers students at a further education college and the Open University in the UK (Lavender 2020; Pegg & Carr 2010), students from China and Malaysia recently graduated from Australia and the UK (Blackmore, Gribble & Rahimi 2017; Sin 2016) and employer practices of 'cultural matching' in advanced manufacturing companies in the USA and financial services firms in Australia (Hora 2020; Parry & Jackling 2015). Bourdieusian theory clarifies relationships between different forms of **capital**, but offers limited insight into contemporary sociocultural influences on employment outcomes, notably for different ethnic groups, but also for similar groups experiencing different issues, hence the use of ethnic capital and personal capital to explain counter-intuitive outcomes.

Another emerging stream of work uses the four-dimensional *psychological capital* framework developed by Fred Luthans (Luthans, Luthans & Luthans 2004) to explore the influence of positive personal qualities on employability (namely, confidence/Efficacy, goal-setting/Hope, Optimism and Resilience, also known as PsyCap and later, in a reordered form, as 'the HERO within'). PsyCap ('who you are' and 'what you can become') draws on the positive organisational behaviour movement in psychology and was developed to expand conceptions of **intangible assets** in organisations beyond human capital ('what you know') and social capital ('who you know'). The concept has been used with students in Asia (Bakari & Khoso 2017; Xu & Yu 2019), Africa (Baluku et al. 2021; Ngoma & Ntale 2016) and Europe (Ayala Calvo & Manzano García 2021; Fabbris & Fornea 2019). Based on interview data, Xu and Yu (2019) replaced self-efficacy with self-acceptance in their survey of disabled college students in China and confirmed the latter as the best predictor of employability for students with disabilities.

A significant trend here is the use and development of holistic multi-capital frameworks to inform employability research and careers education. A growing body of scholarship uses the *career capital* model of Michael Arthur (DeFillippi & Arthur 1994; Inkson & Arthur 2001) that presents career management as three interdependent *ways of knowing* (know-why, know-how and know-whom; broadly equivalent to identity, human and social capital). Researchers have used the model to explore connections between the academic experiences and career trajectories of MBA graduates in Canada and Italy (Sturges, Simpson & Altman 2003; Felker & Gianecchini 2015), HE graduates enrolled in vocational institutions in Australia and Singapore (Harris & Ramos 2013) and community college students across the USA (D'Amico et al. 2019; Xing & Gordon 2021). D'Amico et al. have refined their College and Career Capital Survey over seven years and constructed an index to measure alignment between college and careers. In contrast, Reichenberger and Raymond (2021) chose a Bourdieusian career capital framework to examine how tourism students in New Zealand were adapting their career strategies to a 'career shock' context.

Examples of UK frameworks include the 2013 'Solent Capital Compass' from Southampton Solent University, which comprises 16 elements categorised as Capabilities/Human Capital, Confidence/Psychological Capital and Connections/Social Capital (Whistance & Campbell 2018) and the widely cited '**Graduate Capital Model**' from the nearby University of Southampton, which conceptualises employability as 'constituting a range of dynamic, interactive forms of capital which are acquired through graduates' lived experiences', namely Human Capital, Social Capital, Cultural Capital, Identity Capital and Psychological Capital (Tomlinson 2017, p. 340). Tomlinson's model has been used with a range of student and graduate populations in the UK, USA, Australia and China, including socio-economically diverse undergraduates, minority doctoral students, industry internship candidates and international graduate migrants and returnees (Parutis & Howson 2020; Thomas et al. 2021; Benati & Fischer 2021; Pham, Tomlinson & Thompson 2019; Singh & Fan 2021).

Other tools include a four-capital/seven-factor measurement scale developed in Spain, covering human, social, cultural and psychological capital (Caballero, Álvarez-González & López-Miguens 2020). Capital perspectives have thus enabled scholars to develop more nuanced understandings and reliable assessments of the factors opening up or holding back graduate careers; for example, which forms of capital are most relevant in a competitive job market (Brown, Hesketh & Williams 2003; Caballero, Álvarez-González & López-Miguens 2020; Hora 2020), or how capital shortfalls may force graduates to downshift or modify their occupational goals (Blackmore, Gribble & Rahimi 2017; Lehmann, 2019; Reichenberger & Raymond 2021; Sin 2016). Capital models of graduate employability promote a **resource-based view** (RBV) of career management that extends the rationale of students (and their families) investing in a university education to graduates investing in their career success, viewing their careers as 'repositories of knowledge' and playing their part as a 'career capitalist' (Inkson & Arthur 2001).

Exploiting social media

A large body of work explores the role of social media in developing the social networks and social capital of students. Benson, Morgan and Tennakoon (2015) identify six types of social technologies (collective projects, (micro)blogging, content communities, networking sites, role-playing games and virtual worlds) and provide a model showing nine places in the student journey as sites for developing networking skills and building social capital (from student admission and transitional support via learning activities, leadership development, employability skills, entrepreneurship education and industry links to alumni relations and lifelong learning). However, institutions have been slow to deploy such tools effectively across the lifecycle and 'need to develop [an] appropriate curriculum to foster proactive networking investment for and by students' (Benson,

Morgan & Tennakoon 2015, p. 348). Related research suggests that undergraduate and Master's students need education on using sites such as LinkedIn to build and exploit social capital for social career management and enhanced employability (Benson, Morgan & Filippaios 2014).

Most scholars focus on undergraduate use of Facebook to form and keep relationships, including multiple studies by Ellison et al. (2011), who add the concept of 'maintained social capital' to *bonding* and *bridging capital*, and Kim et al. (2020), who examine the influence of network heterogeneity on social capital and social self-efficacy. Some studies explore the impact of social media on civic (and political) *participation* in different settings (Valenzuela, Park & Kee, 2009; Zhong, 2014). A few studies focus on first-generation students and suggest that social media can have a significant role in widening access to HE, as such students rely more on social network contacts to support their aspirations and applications than do continuing-generation students with college-going friends and parents (Wohn et al. 2013), and they also rely more on close (bonding) ties and new (bridging) ties for emotional and academic support during college (Deng, Fernández & Zhao 2022).

Holtell, Martinez-Alemán and Rowan-Kenyon (2014) use the concept of **college/campus capital** (access to social and cultural capital on campus) to discuss how *summer bridge programs* can deploy social media to broaden the social and academic networks of students whose lifestyles may make traditional engagement activities problematic and to maintain vital connections with home that help them to persist at the institution. Rowan-Kenyon, Martinez Alemán and Savitz-Romer (2018, p. 27) define *campus capital* as 'the various forms of social capital that enhance students' on-campus experiences that . . . affect their persistence to graduation . . . through relational networks', specific to a particular campus. They introduce the term **transitional capital** to describe how first-generation students create new (weak) ties with people of similar background (student peers, peer mentors, faculty and staff) that develop strong-tie characteristics as sources of bonding capital, thus becoming 'a synthesis of bridging and bonding capital' and forming 'an essential and critical type of capital' enabled by social media technology (Rowan-Kenyon, Martinez Alemán & Savitz-Romer 2018, pp. 154–155). Social networking tools are thus critical to improving the social integration, persistence rates and academic outcomes of first-generation students and should be a central element of institutional strategies for non-traditional students (Deng, Fernández & Zhao 2021; Rowan-Kenyon, Martinez Alemán & Savitz-Romer 2018).

Conclusion

This chapter has shown how many of the ideas, concepts and theories identified in the opening chapter are playing out in contemporary HE, notably in the drive to widen access and participation, the adoption of working practices based on collaboration and partnership and the focus on community and engagement. In addition, the blurring of boundaries and cross-boundary collaborations that were a pervasive feature in Chapter 1 are a recurring theme here too, evident in the blurred boundaries between different areas and roles in HE (between third-stream and mainstream functions, private and public sector elements, education and research, academic activities and student services, professors and professionals), along with an interest in holism (including the provision of holistic student support, educating the whole student through holistic curriculum models and adopting a whole-of-university approach). Our review has also confirmed the vital role of personal and institutional networks and relationships in providing the social support and information resources that are critical factors for student success in HE and professional employment.

Notably, it highlights the importance of social networks for students from minority groups, pointing to a need for strategic deployment of social technologies across the whole student lifecycle, a concept that emerged as an important framework for developing interventions to facilitate the personal, academic and professional success of students. We have also confirmed the value of capital perspectives as asset-based or resource-based views of communities and individuals that can help us to gain deeper understanding of problems and their contexts. In particular, just as the opening chapter pointed to a broadening of the intellectual capital frameworks used in the corporate sector to reflect a renewed commitment to social responsibility and sustainable development, our review of social capital research in HE has identified a similar need to broaden the conceptual frameworks used in our field to reflect the move from elitist to pluralist systems. Concepts such as aspirational, campus, career, ethnic, experiential, familial, identity, linguistic, maintained, mobility, navigational, personal, psychological, resistant and transitional capital may be useful additions to our lexicon, particularly as our research and practice increasingly place social justice and fair access at the centre of our agenda. Chapters 4 and 5 continue the narrative by exploring how the concepts, trends and developments described here are playing out in academic library practice and research.

References

Abrahamsen, B. and Drange, I., (2015). Ethnic minority students' career expectations in prospective professions: navigating between ambitions and discrimination. *Sociology*. 49(2), 252–269. doi:10.1177/0038038514542494

Abu Moghli, M. and Kadiwal, L., (2021). Decolonising the curriculum beyond the surge: conceptualisation, positionality and conduct. *London Review of Education*. 19(1), 23. doi:10.14324/LRE.19.1.23

Andreotti, V. de O., Stein, S., Ahenakew, C. and Hunt, D., (2015). Mapping interpretations of decolonization in the context of higher education. *Decolonization: Indigeneity, Education & Society*. 4(1), 21–40. https://jps.library.utoronto.ca/index.php/des/article/view/22168

Ayala Calvo, J. C. and Manzano García, G., (2021). The influence of psychological capital on graduates perception of employability: the mediating role of employability skills. *Higher Education Research & Development*. 40(2), 293–308. doi:10.1080/07294360.2020.1738350

Bakari, H. and Khoso, I., (2017). Psychological determinants of graduate employability: a comparative study of business and agriculture students across Pakistan. *Business & Economic Review*. 9(4), 111–138. doi:10.22547/BER/9.4.6

Baluku, M. M., Mugabi, E. N., Nansamba, J., Matagi, L., Onderi, P. and Otto, K., (2021). Psychological capital and career outcomes among final year university students: the mediating role of career engagement and perceived employability. *International Journal of Applied Positive Psychology*. 6(1), 55–80. doi:10.1007/s41042-020-00040-w

Barnett, R., (2000). Supercomplexity and the curriculum. *Studies in Higher Education*. 25(3), 255–265. doi:10.1080/713696156

Bathmaker, A.-M., Ingram, N. and Waller, R., (2013). Higher education, social class and the mobilisation of capitals: recognising and playing the game. *British Journal of Sociology of Education*. 34(5–6), 723–743. doi:10.1080/01425692.2013.816041

Baxter Magolda, M. and Taylor, K. B., (2017). Holistic development. In: J. H. Schuh, S. R. Jones and V. Torres, eds. *Student services: a handbook for the profession*. San Francisco, CA: Jossey-Bass. pp. 153–168.

Baxter Magolda, M. B. and King, P. M. eds., (2004). *Learning partnerships: theory and models of practice to educate for self-authorship*. Sterling, VA: Stylus.

Benati, K. and Fischer, J., (2021). Beyond human capital: student preparation for graduate life. *Education + Training*. 63(1), 151–163. doi:10.1108/ET-10-2019-0244

Bennett, D., Knight, E., Divan, A., Kuchel, L., Horn, J., van Reyk, D. and Burke da Silva, K., (2017). How do research-intensive universities portray employability strategies? A review of their websites. *Australian Journal of Career Development*. 26(2), 52–61. doi:10.1177/1038416217714475

Benneworth, P. and Jongbloed, B. W., (2010). Who matters to universities? A stakeholder perspective on humanities, arts and social sciences valorisation. *Higher Education*. 59(5), 567–588. doi:10.1007/s10734-009-9265-2

Benson, V., Morgan, S. and Filippaios, F., (2014). Social career management: social media and employability skills gap. *Computers in Human Behavior*. 30, 519–525. doi:10.1016/j.chb.2013.06.015

Benson, V., Morgan, S. and Tennakoon, H., (2015). Developing pragmatic skills of social capital investment: review of the role of social technologies in the student lifecycle. In: *ICEL 2015, 25–26 June, Nassau, Bahamas*. Reading, UK: Academic Conferences International. pp. 343–350.

Berghaeuser, H. and Hoelscher, M., (2020). Reinventing the third mission of higher education in Germany: political frameworks and universities' reactions. *Tertiary Education and Management*. 26(1), 57–76. doi:10.1007/s11233-019-09030-3

Bhambra, G. K., Gebrial, D. and Nişancıoğlu, K. eds., (2018). *Decolonising the university*. London: Pluto Press. https://library.oapen.org/handle/20.500.12657/25936

Blackmore, J., Gribble, C. and Rahimi, M., (2017). International education, the formation of capital and graduate employment: Chinese accounting graduates' experiences of the

Australian labour market. *Critical Studies in Education.* **58**(1), 69–88. doi:10.1080/17508487.2015.1117505

Borgatti, S. P. and Foster, P. C., (2003). The network paradigm in organizational research: a review and typology. *Journal of Management.* **29**(6), 991–1013. doi:10.1016/S0149-2063(03)00087-4

Bourdieu, P., (1986). The forms of capital. In: J. Richardson, ed. *Handbook of theory and research for the sociology of education.* Westport, CT: Greenwood Press. pp. 241–258.

Boyer, E. L., (1996). The scholarship of engagement. *Bulletin of the American Academy of Arts and Sciences.* **49**(7), 18–33. doi.org/10.2307/3824459

Brown, J. S., (2006). New learning environments for the 21st century: exploring the edge. *Change: The Magazine of Higher Learning.* **38**(5), 18–24. doi:10.3200/CHNG.38.5.18–24

Brown, P., Hesketh, A. and Williams, S., (2003). Employability in a knowledge-driven economy. *Journal of Education and Work.* **16**(2), 107–126. doi:10.1080/1363908032000070648

Brown, R., (2018). Higher education and inequality. *Perspectives: Policy and Practice in Higher Education.* **22**(2), 27–43. doi:10.1080/13603108.2017.1375442

Bullen, J. and Flavell, H., (2021). [Forthcoming]. Decolonising the indigenised curricula: preparing Australian graduates for a workplace and world in flux. *Higher Education Research & Development.* doi:10.1080/07294360.2021.1927998

Burnett, L., (2007). Juggling first year student experience and institutional change: an Australian experience. In: *20th international conference on first year experience, 9–12 July, Hawaii.* http://hdl.handle.net/10072/32622

Burt, R. S., (1992). *Structural holes: the social structure of competition.* Cambridge, MA: Harvard University Press.

Caballero, G., Álvarez-González, P. and López-Miguens, M. J., (2020). How to promote the employability capital of university students? Developing and validating scales. *Studies in Higher Education.* **45**(12), 2634–2652. doi:10.1080/03075079.2020.1807494

Clark, B. R., (1998). The entrepreneurial university: demand and response. *Tertiary Education and Management.* **4**(1), 5–16. doi:10.1007/BF02679392

Cole, D. and Tibby, M., (2013). *Defining and developing your approach to employability: a framework for higher education institutions.* York, UK: Higher Education Academy. https://www.heacademy.ac.uk/sites/default/files/resources/Employability_framework.pdf

Coleman, J. S., (1988). Social capital in the creation of human capital. *American Journal of Sociology.* **94**(supplement), S95–S120. doi:10.1086/228943

Coleman, K. and Danks, C., (2016). Service-learning: a tool to create social capital for collaborative natural resource management. *Journal of Environmental Studies and Sciences.* **6**(3), 470–478. doi:10.1007/s13412-015-0239-7

Côté, J. E., (2005). Identity capital, social capital and the wider benefits of learning: generating resources facilitative of social cohesion. *London Review of Education.* **3**(3), 221–237. doi:10.1080/14748460500372382

Crilly, J. and Everitt, R., eds., (2022). *Narrative expansions: interpreting decolonisation in academic libraries.* London: Facet Publishing.

Ćulum, B., Rončević, N. and Ledić, J., (2013). Facing new expectations – integrating third mission activities into the university. In: B. M. Kehm and U. Teichler, eds. *The academic profession in Europe: new tasks and new challenges.* Dordrecht, Netherlands: Springer. pp. 163–195. doi:10.1007/978-94-007-4614-5_9

D'Agostino, M. J., (2010). Measuring social capital as an outcome of service learning. *Innovative Higher Education.* 35(5), 313–328. doi:10.1007/s10755-010-9149-5

D'Amico, M. M., González Canché, M. S., Rios-Aguilar, C. and Salas, S., (2019). An exploration of college and career alignment for community college students. *The Review of Higher Education.* 43(1), 53–83. doi:10.1353/rhe.2019.0090

de Wit, H. and Altbach, P. G., (2021). Internationalization in higher education: global trends and recommendations for its future. *Policy Reviews in Higher Education.* 5(1), 28–46. doi:10.1080/23322969.2020.1820898

DeFillippi, R. J. and Arthur, M. B., (1994). The boundaryless career: a competency based perspective. *Journal of Organizational Behavior.* 15(4), 307–324. doi:10.1002/job.4030150403

Deng, X. (N.), Fernández, Y. and Zhao, M., (2022). Social media use by first-generation college students and two forms of social capital: a revealed causal mapping approach. 35(1), 344–366. *Information Technology & People.* doi:10.1108/ITP-01-2018-0002

Dilworth, R. ed., (2006). *Social capital in the city: community and civic life in Philadelphia.* Philadelphia, PA: Temple University Press.

Duncan, S. and Manners, P., (2012). Embedding public engagement within higher education: lessons from the Beacons for Public Engagement in the United Kingdom. In: L. McIlrath, A. Lyons and R. Munck, eds. *Higher education and civic engagement: comparative perspectives.* New York: Palgrave Macmillan. pp. 221–240.

Dutta, M., et al., (2021). Decolonizing open science: Southern interventions. *Journal of Communication.* 71(5), 803–826. doi:10.1093/joc/jqab027

Dzur, A. W., (2018). *Rebuilding public institutions together: professionals and citizens in a participatory democracy.* Ithaca, NY: Cornell University Press. doi:10.7591/j.ctt20d89c6

Ellison, N. B., Lampe, C., Steinfield, C. and Vitak, J., (2011). With a little help from my friends: how social network sites affect social capital processes. In: Z. Papacharissi, ed., *A networked self: identity, community, and culture on social network sites.* New York: Routledge. pp. 132–153. doi:10.4324/9780203876527-13

Etzkowitz, H., (1983). Entrepreneurial scientists and entrepreneurial universities in American academic science. *Minerva.* 21(2–3), 198–233. doi:10.1007/BF01097964

Etzkowitz, H. and Leydesdorff, L., (2000). The dynamics of innovation: from national systems and "Mode 2" to a triple helix of university–industry–government relations. *Research Policy.* 29(2), 109–123. doi:10.1016/S0048-7333(99)00055-4

Fabbris, L. and Fornea, M., (2019). Psychological capital and locus of control as determinants of graduate employability beyond human and social capital. *Statistica Applicata – Italian Journal of Applied Statistics.* 31(1), 29–52. doi:10.26398/IJAS.0031-003

Felker, J. and Gianecchini, M., (2015). Influence of pre-graduation international experiences on early career internationalization: the mediation effect of career capital. *European Management Journal*. 33(1), 60–70. doi:10.1016/j.emj.2014.07.001

Fine, B., (2010). *Theories of social capital: researchers behaving badly*. London: Pluto Press. https://library.oapen.org/handle/20.500.12657/30775

Fitzgerald, K. and Peterman, W., (2003). *UK research universities and community engagement: developing a practical framework for community partnerships*. Bristol, UK: University of Bristol. https://www.researchgate.net/publication/228912621_UK_Research_Universities_and_Community_Engagement_Developing_A_Practical_Framework_for_Community_Partnerships

Friend, K. L., (2021). The creation of social networks: social capital and the experiences of widening participation students at three elite institutions in the US, England, and Scotland. *Pedagogy, Culture & Society*. 29(3), 359–377. doi:10.1080/14681366.2020.1735496

Frondizi, R., Fantauzzi, C., Colasanti, N. and Fiorani, G., (2019). The evaluation of universities' third mission and intellectual capital: theoretical analysis and application to Italy. *Sustainability*. 11(12), 3455. doi:10.3390/su11123455

Fulkerson, G. M. and Thompson, G. H., (2008). The evolution of a contested concept: a meta-analysis of social capital definitions and trends (1988–2006). *Sociological Inquiry*. 78(4), 536–557. doi:10.1111/j.1475-682X.2008.00260.x

Furco, A., (2010). The engaged campus: toward a comprehensive approach to public engagement. *British Journal of Educational Studies*. 58(4), 375–390. doi:10.1080/00071005.2010.527656 [US]

Glass, C. R. and Fitzgerald, H. E., (2010). Engaged scholarship: historical roots, contemporary challenges. In: H. E. Fitzgerald, C. Burack and S. D. Seifer, eds. *Handbook of engaged scholarship: contemporary landscapes, future directions, Volume 1: Institutional change*. East Lansing, MI: Michigan State University Press. pp. 9–24.

Granovetter, M. S., (1973). The strength of weak ties. *American Journal of Sociology*. 78(6), 1360–1380. doi:10.1086/225469

Guri-Rosenblit, S., Šebková, H. and Teichler, U., (2007). Massification and diversity of higher education systems: interplay of complex dimensions. *Higher Education Policy*. 20(4), 373–389. doi:10.1057/palgrave.hep.8300158

Hannon, C., Faas, D. and O'Sullivan, K., (2017). Widening the educational capabilities of socio economically disadvantaged students through a model of social and cultural capital development. *British Educational Research Journal*. 43(6), 1225–1245. doi:10.1002/berj.3309

Harris, R. and Ramos, C., (2013). Building career capital through further study in Australia and Singapore. *International Journal of Lifelong Education*. 32(5), 620–638. doi:10.1080/02601370.2012.753124

Harvey, A. and Russell-Mundine, G., (2019). Decolonising the curriculum: using graduate qualities to embed indigenous knowledges at the academic cultural interface. *Teaching in Higher Education*. 24(6), 789–808. doi:10.1080/13562517.2018.1508131

Healey, M., (2005). Linking research and teaching: exploring disciplinary spaces and the role of inquiry-based learning. In: R. Barnett, ed. *Reshaping the university: new relationships between research, scholarship and teaching.* Maidenhead, UK: Society for Research into Higher Education & Open University Press. pp. 30–42.

Healey, M., Flint, A. and Harrington, K., (2016). Students as partners: reflections on a conceptual model. *Teaching & Learning Inquiry.* 4(2), 8–20. doi:10.20343/teachlearninqu.4.2.3

Healy, M., Brown, J. L. and Ho, C., (2022). Graduate employability as a professional proto-jurisdiction in higher education. *Higher Education.* 83(5), 1125–1142. doi:10.1007/s10734-021-00733-4

HEFCE., (2001, June). *Strategies for widening participation in higher education: a guide to good practice.* Bristol, UK: Higher Education Funding Council for England. https://webarchive.nationalarchives.gov.uk/ukgwa/20120118164822/http://www.hefce.ac.uk

Heleta, S., (2016). Decolonisation of higher education: dismantling epistemic violence and Eurocentrism in South Africa. *Transformation in Higher Education.* 1(1), a9. https://files.eric.ed.gov/fulltext/EJ1187109.pdf

Herbaut, E. and Geven, K., (2019, April). *What works to reduce inequalities in higher education? A systematic review of the (quasi-)experimental literature on outreach and financial aid.* Washington, DC: World Bank. https://hal.archives-ouvertes.fr/hal-02095249

Higdon, R. D., (2016). Employability: the missing voice: how student and graduate views could be used to develop future higher education policy and inform curricula. *Power & Education.* 8(2), 176–195. doi:10.1177/1757743816653151

Hoffman, A. J., (2011). Community-based learning and social capital: exploring student attitudes and perceptions of connectedness to campus and diverse communities. *Journal of Community Engagement and Higher Education.* 3(1). https://discovery.indstate.edu/jcehe/index.php/joce/article/view/79

Hollander, E. L. and Saltmarsh, J., (2000). The engaged university. *Academe.* 86(4), 29–32. doi:10.2307/40251894

Holtell, D. L., Martinez-Alemán, A. M. and Rowan-Kenyon, H. T., (2014). Summer bridge program 2.0: using social media to develop students' campus capital. *Change: The Magazine of Higher Learning.* 46(5), 34–38. doi:10.1080/00091383.2014.941769

Hora, M. T., (2020). Hiring as cultural gatekeeping into occupational communities: implications for higher education and student employability. *Higher Education.* 79(2), 307–324. doi:10.1007/s10734-019-00411-6

Hu, A. and Cairns, D., (2017). Hai Gui or Hai Dai? Chinese student migrants and the role of Norwegian mobility capital in career success. *YOUNG: Nordic Journal of Youth Research.* 25(2), 174–189. doi:10.1177/1103308816670821

Hutchison, D. and Bosacki, S., (2000). Over the edge: can holistic education contribute to experiential education? *Journal of Experiential Education.* 23(3), 177–182. doi:10.1177/105382590002300310

Inkson, K. and Arthur, M. B., (2001). How to be a successful career capitalist. *Organizational Dynamics.* 30(1), 48–62. doi: 10.1016/S0090-2616(01)00040-7

Jackson, N., (2011). An imaginative lifewide curriculum. In: N. J. Jackson, ed. *Learning for a complex world: a lifewide concept of learning, education and personal development*. Bloomington, IN: AuthorHouse. pp. 100–121. https://www.lifewideeducation.uk/learning-for-a-complex-world.html

Jacoby, B. ed., (2003). *Building partnerships for service-learning*. San Francisco, CA: Jossey-Bass.

Jayawickreme, E. and Dahill-Brown, S. E., (2016). Developing well-being and capabilities as a goal of higher education: a thought-piece on educating the whole student. In: J. Vittersø, ed. *Handbook of eudaimonic well-being*. Cham, Switzerland: Springer. pp. 473–484. doi:10.1007/978-3-319-42445-3_31

Kim, Y., Kim, B., Hwang, H.-S. and Lee, D., (2020). Social media and life satisfaction among college students: a moderated mediation model of SNS communication network heterogeneity and social self-efficacy on satisfaction with campus life. *The Social Science Journal*. 57(1), 85–100. doi:10.1016/j.soscij.2018.12.001

Krause, K.-L., (2006). Transition to and through the first year: strategies to enhance the student experience. *Inaugural Vice-Chancellor's learning and teaching colloquium, University of the Sunshine Coast, 31 May, Sippy Downs, Australia*. https://www.researchgate.net/publication/248771621_Transition_to_and_through_the_first_year_Strategies_to_enhance_the_student_experience

Laredo, P., (2007). Revisiting the third mission of universities: toward a renewed categorization of university activities? *Higher Education Policy*. 20(4), 441–456. doi:10.1057/palgrave.hep.8300169

Lavender, K., (2020). Mature students' experiences of undertaking higher education in English vocational institutions: employability and academic capital. *International Journal of Training Research*. 18(2), 141–154. doi:10.1080/14480220.2020.1830836

le Grange, L., (2018). Decolonising, Africanising, indigenising, and internationalising curriculum studies: opportunities to (re)imagine the field. *Journal of Education (South African Education Research Association)*. 74, 4–18. doi:10.17159/2520–9868/i74a01

Lebeau, Y. and Cochrane, A., (2015). Rethinking the 'third mission': UK universities and regional engagement in challenging times. *European Journal of Higher Education*. 5(3), 250–263. doi:10.1080/21568235.2015.1044545

Lehmann, W., (2019). Forms of capital in working-class students' transition from university to employment. *Journal of Education and Work*. 32(4), 347–359. doi:10.1080/13639080.2019.1617841

Lin, N., (1999). Building a network theory of social capital. *Connections*. 22(1), 28–51. https://assets.noviams.com/novi-file-uploads/insna/Connections_Archive/1999_Volume_22__Issue_1_2.pdf

Lizzio, A., (2011). The student lifecycle: an integrative framework for guiding practice. Brisbane, Australia: Griffith University. https://pdfslide.net/documents/student-lifecycle-framework-griffith-university-teaching-strategy-so-.html

Luthans, F., Luthans, K. W. and Luthans, B. C., (2004). Positive psychological capital: beyond human and social capital. *Business Horizons*. 47(1), 45–50. doi:10.1016/j.bushor.2003.11.007

Macqueen, S., (2018). Family and social capital for the success of non-traditional students in higher education. *International Studies in Widening Participation*. 5(1), 37–50. https://novaojs.newcastle.edu.au/ceehe/index.php/iswp/article/view/91

Marginson, S., (2016). The worldwide trend to high participation higher education: dynamics of social stratification in inclusive systems. *Higher Education*. 72(4), 413–434. doi:10.1007/s10734-016-0016-x

Marginson, S. and Rhoades, G., (2002). Beyond national states, markets, and systems of higher education: a glonacal agency heuristic. *Higher Education*. 43(3), 281–309. doi:10.1023/A:1014699605875

Matheson, R., (2018). Transition through the student lifecycle. In: R. Matheson, S. Tangney and M. Sutcliffe, eds. *Transition in, through and out of higher education: international case studies and best practice*. Abingdon, UK: Routledge. pp. 5–16.

Matthews, K. E., Dwyer, A., Hine, L. and Turner, J., (2018). Conceptions of students as partners. *Higher Education*. 76(6), 957–971. doi:10.1007/s10734-018-0257-y

McWilliam, E., (2010). Learning culture, teaching economy. *Pedagogies: An International Journal*. 5(4), 286–297. doi:10.1080/1554480X.2010.509471

Mercer-Mapstone, L. et al., (2017). A systematic literature review of students as partners in higher education. *International Journal for Students as Partners*. 1(1). doi:10.15173/ijsap.v1i1.3119

Mishra, S., (2020). Social networks, social capital, social support and academic success in higher education: a systematic review with a special focus on "underrepresented" students. *Educational Research Review*. 29, 100307. doi:10.1016/j.edurev.2019.100307

Morgan, M., (2012). The evolution of student services in the UK. *Perspectives: Policy and Practice in Higher Education*. 16(3), 77–84. doi:10.1080/13603108.2011.652990

Morgan, M., (2013). Student diversity in higher education. In: M. Morgan, ed. *Supporting student diversity in higher education: a practical guide*. Abingdon, UK: Routledge. pp. 11–22.

Nagdee, I. and Shafi, A., (2021). Decolonising the academy: a look at student-led interventions in the UK. In: D. S. P. Thomas and J. Arday, eds. *Doing equity and diversity for success in higher education: redressing structural inequalities in the academy*. Cham, Switzerland: Palgrave Macmillan. pp. 139–149. doi:10.1007/978-3-030-65668-3_11

Nahapiet, J. and Ghoshal, S., (1998). Social capital, intellectual capital, and the organizational advantage. *Academy of Management Review*. 23(2), 242–266. doi:10.2307/259373

Nakata, M., (2002). Indigenous knowledge and the cultural interface: underlying issues at the intersection of knowledge and information systems. In: *Libraries for life: democracy, diversity, delivery, 68th IFLA Council and General Conference, 18–24 August, Glasgow, UK*. http://archive.ifla.org/IV/ifla68/papers/149–138e.pdf

Nakata, M., (2007). The cultural interface. In: M. Nakata, *Disciplining the savages: savaging the disciplines*. Canberra, Australia: Aboriginal Studies Press. pp. 195–212.

Naseem, J., (2019). "I didn't have the luxury to wait": understanding the university-to-work transition among second-generations in Britain. *Social Inclusion*. 7(3), 270–281. doi:10.17645/si.v7i3.2033

Naude, P., (2019). Decolonising knowledge: can Ubuntu ethics save us from coloniality? *Journal of Business Ethics*. 159(1), 23–37. doi:10.1007/s10551-017-3663-4

Nelles, J. and Vorley, T., (2010). From policy to practice: engaging and embedding the third mission in contemporary universities. *International Journal of Sociology and Social Policy*. 30(7/8), 341–353. doi:10.1108/01443331011060706

Nghia, T. L. H., Giang, H. T. and Quyen, V. P., (2019). At-home international education in Vietnamese universities: impact on graduates' employability and career prospects. *Higher Education*. 78(5), 817–834. doi:10.1007/s10734-019-00372-w

Ngoma, M. and Ntale, P. D., (2016). Psychological capital, career identity and graduate employability in Uganda: the mediating role of social capital. *International Journal of Training and Development*. 20(2), 124–139. doi:10.1111/ijtd.12073

Nicholson, K. P. and Seale, M. eds., (2018). *The politics of theory and the practice of critical librarianship*. Sacramento, CA: Library Juice Press.

Nussbaum, M. C., (2011). *Creating capabilities: the human development approach*. Cambridge, MA: Belknap Press.

O'Connor, J. S., (2006). Civic engagement in higher education. *Change: The Magazine of Higher Learning*. 38(5), 52–58. doi:10.3200/CHNG.38.5.52-58

O'Shea, S., (2016). Navigating the knowledge sets of older learners: exploring the capitals of first-in-family mature age students. *Widening Participation and Lifelong Learning*. 18(3), 34–54. doi: 10.5456/WPLL.18.3.34

Osborne, M., (2003). Increasing or widening participation in higher education? *European Journal of Education*. 38(1), 5–24. doi:10.1111/1467-3435.00125

Parry, N. and Jackling, B., (2015). How do professional financial services firms understand their skill needs and organise their recruitment practices? *Accounting Education*. 24(6), 514–538. doi:10.1080/09639284.2015.1109528

Parutis, V. and Howson, C. K., (2020). Failing to level the playing field: student discourses on graduate employability. *Research in Post-Compulsory Education*. 25(4), 373–393. doi:10.1080/13596748.2020.1846312

Pegg, A. and Carr, J., (2010). Articulating learning and supporting student employability: using the concept of 'illusio' to make sense of the issues raised by distance learners. *Widening Participation and Lifelong Learning*. 12(Special issue), 78–90. doi:10.5456/WPLL.12.S.78

Perna, L. W. and Titus, M. A., (2005). The relationship between parental involvement as social capital and college enrollment: an examination of racial/ethnic group differences. *Journal of Higher Education*. 76(5), 485–518. doi:10.1080/00221546.2005.11772296

Pham, T., Tomlinson, M. and Thompson, C., (2019). Forms of capital and agency as mediations in negotiating employability of international graduate migrants. *Globalisation, Societies and Education*. 17(3), 394–405. doi:10.1080/14767724.2019.1583091

Portes, A., (1998). Social capital: its origins and applications in modern sociology. *Annual Review of Sociology*. 24, 1–24. doi:10.1146/annurev.soc.24.1.1

Portes, A., (2000). The two meanings of social capital. *Sociological Forum*. 15(1), 1–12. doi:10.1023/A:1007537902813

Putnam, R. D., (1995). Bowling alone: America's declining social capital. *Journal of Democracy*. 6(1), 65–78. doi:10.1353/jod.1995.0002

Putnam, R. D., (2000). *Bowling alone: the collapse and revival of American community*. New York: Simon & Schuster.

Reichenberger, I. and Raymond, E. M., (2021). Tourism students' career strategies in times of disruption. *Journal of Hospitality and Tourism Management*. 48, 220–229. doi:10.1016/j.jhtm.2021.06.011

Rhoades, G. and Slaughter, S., (1997). Academic capitalism, managed professionals, and supply-side higher education. *Social Text*. 51(2), 9–38. doi:10.2307/466645

Rienties, B., Johan, N. and Jindal-Snape, D., (2015). A dynamic analysis of social capital-building of international and UK students. *British Journal of Sociology of Education*. 36(8), 1212–1235. doi:10.1080/01425692.2014.886941

Rowan-Kenyon, H. T., Martinez Alemán, A. M. and Savitz-Romer, M., (2018). *Technology and engagement: making technology work for first generation college students*. New Brunswick, NJ: Rutgers University Press.

Salisbury, F., Dollinger, M. and Vanderlelie, J., (2020). Students as partners in the academic library: co-designing for transformation. *New Review of Academic Librarianship*. 26(2–4), 304–321. doi:10.1080/13614533.2020.1780275

Saltmarsh, J. and Hartley, M., (2011). Democratic engagement. In: J. Saltmarsh and M. Hartley, eds. *"To serve a larger purpose": engagement for democracy and the transformation of higher education*. Philadelphia, PA: Temple University Press. pp. 14–26.

Sandeen, A., (2004). Educating the whole student: the growing academic importance of student affairs. *Change: The Magazine of Higher Learning*. 36(3), 28–33. doi:10.1080/00091380409605577

Sandefur, G. D., Meier, A. M. and Campbell, M. E., (2006). Family resources, social capital, and college attendance. *Social Science Research*. 35(2), 525–553. doi:10.1016/j.ssresearch.2004.11.003

Schucan Bird, K. and Pitman, L., (2020). How diverse is your reading list? Exploring issues of representation and decolonisation in the UK. *Higher Education*. 79(5), 903–920. doi:10.1007/s10734-019-00446-9

Scott, P., (2005). Divergence or convergence? The links between teaching and research in mass higher education. In: R. Barnett, ed. *Reshaping the university: new relationships between research, scholarship and teaching*. Maidenhead, UK: Society for Research into Higher Education and Open University Press. pp. 30–42.

Sen, A., (1985). *Commodities and capabilities*. Amsterdam, Netherlands: North-Holland.

Shah, B., Dwyer, C. and Modood, T., (2010). Explaining educational achievement and career aspirations among young British Pakistanis: mobilizing 'ethnic capital'? *Sociology*. 44(6), 1109–1127. doi:10.1177/0038038510381606

Shah, M., Bennett, A. and Southgate, E. eds., (2016). *Widening higher education participation: a global perspective*. Waltham, MA: Chandos.

Sin, I. L., (2016). Ethnicity and (dis)advantage: exchanging cultural capital in UK international education and graduate employment. *Sociological Research Online*. 21(4), 57–69. doi:10.5153/sro.4070

Singh, J. K. N. and Fan, S. X., (2021). International education and graduate employability: Australian Chinese graduates' experiences. *Journal of Education and Work*. 34(5–6), 663–675. doi:10.1080/13639080.2021.1965970

Sturges, J., Simpson, R. and Altman, Y., (2003). Capitalising on learning: an exploration of the MBA as a vehicle for developing career competencies. *International Journal of Training and Development*. 7(1), 53–66. doi:10.1111/1468-2419.00170

Taylor, M., Hung, J., Che, T. E., Akinbosede, D., Petherick, K. J. and Pranjol, M. Z. I., (2021). Laying the groundwork to investigate diversity of life sciences reading lists in higher education and its link to awarding gaps. *Education Sciences*. 11(7), 359. doi:10.3390/educsci11070359

Thomas, S. D., Ali, A., Alcover, K., Augustin, D. and Wilson, N., (2021). Social and professional impact of learning communities within the Alliance for Graduate Education and the Professoriate Program at Michigan State University. *Frontiers in Psychology*. 12, 734414. doi:10.3389/fpsyg.2021.734414

Tight, M., (2019a). Mass higher education and massification. *Higher Education Policy*. 32(1), 93–108. doi:10.1057/s41307-017-0075-3

Tight, M., (2019b). Human and social capital and their application in higher education research. In: J. Huisman and M. Tight, eds. *Theory and method in higher education research, Volume 4*. Bingley, UK: Emerald. pp. 209–223. doi:10.1108/S2056-375220180000004013

Tomlinson, M., (2017). Forms of graduate capital and their relationship to graduate employability. *Education + Training*. 59(4), 338–352. doi:10.1108/ET-05-2016-0090

Trencher, G., Yarime, M., McCormick, K. B., Doll, C. N. H. and Kraines, S. B., (2014). Beyond the third mission: exploring the emerging university function of co-creation for sustainability. *Science & Public Policy*. 41(2), 151–179. doi:10.1093/scipol/sct044

UNESCO., (1996). *Learning, the treasure within: report to UNESCO of the International Commission on Education for the Twenty-first Century*. Paris: UNESCO Publishing.

Valenzuela, S., Park, N. and Kee, K. F., (2009). Is there social capital in a social network site? Facebook use and college students' life satisfaction, trust, and participation. *Journal of Computer-Mediated Communication*. 14(4), 875–901. doi:10.1111/j.1083–6101.2009.01474.x

Vasilescu, R., Barna, C., Epure, M. and Baicu, C., (2010). Developing university social responsibility: a model for the challenges of the new civil society. *Procedia, Social and Behavioral Sciences*. 2(2), 4177–4182. doi:10.1016/j.sbspro.2010.03.660

Walker, M. and Fongwa, S.., (2017). *Universities, employability and human development*. London: Palgrave Macmillan. doi:10.1057/978-1-137-58452-6

Weaver, M. ed., (2008). *Transformative learning support models in higher education: educating the whole student*. London: Facet Publishing.

Wedgwood, M., (2006). Mainstreaming the third stream. In: I. McNay, ed. *Beyond mass higher education: building on experience*. Maidenhead, UK: Society for Research into Higher Education and Open University Press. pp. 134–157.

Whistance, D. and Campbell, S., (2018). *Seven ESE factors for career-ready students: validation of the Employability Self Evaluation measure and proposal of a readiness/competence career development model.* Southampton, UK: Solent University. https://pure.solent.ac.uk/ws/portalfiles/portal/16819793/hecsu_research_seven_ese_factors_for_career_ready_students.pdf

Whitchurch, C., (2010). Some implications of 'public/private' space for professional identities in higher education. *Higher Education.* 60(6), 627–640. doi:10.1007/s10734-010-9320-z

White, C., (2019). The social capital of LSES students: using student stories to mobilise student success. *Journal of the Australian and New Zealand Student Services Association.* 27(2), 216–223. doi:10.30688/janzssa.2019.10

Wiers-Jenssen, J., (2011). Background and employability of mobile vs. non-mobile students. *Tertiary Education and Management.* 17(2), 79–100. doi:10.1080/13583883.2011.562524

Wijayanama, C., Ranjani, R. P. C. and Mohan, D. U., (2021). Can service learning enhance graduate capital? Evidence from Sri Lankan state universities. *Kelaniya Journal of Management.* 10(1), 1–11. doi:10.4038/kjm.v10i1.7629

Williams, S., Dodd, L. J., Steele, C. and Randall, R., (2016). A systematic review of current understandings of employability. *Journal of Education and Work.* 29(8), 877–901. doi:10.1080/13639080.2015.1102210

Wimpenny, K., Beelen, J., Hindrix, K., King, V. and Sjoer, E., (2021). [Forthcoming]. Curriculum internationalization and the 'decolonizing academic'. *Higher Education Research & Development.* doi:10.1080/07294360.2021.2014406

Wohn, D. Y., Ellison, N. B., Khan, M. L., Fewins-Bliss, R. and Gray, R., (2013). The role of social media in shaping first-generation high school students' college aspirations: a social capital lens. *Computers and Education.* 63, 424–436. doi:10.1016/j.compedu.2013.01.004

Woolcock, M., (2010). The rise and routinization of social capital, 1988–2008. *Annual Review of Political Science.* 13, 469–487. doi:10.1146/annurev.polisci.031108.094151

Xing, X. and Gordon, H. R., (2021) [Forthcoming]. Understanding traditional and non-traditional students' job skill preparation from a career capital perspective. *Community College Journal of Research and Practice.* doi:10.1080/10668926.2021.1991856

Xu, C. and Yu, H., (2019). The relationship between disabled college students' psychological capital and employability. In: *AESSR 2019: international conference on advanced education and social science research, 14–15 September, Dalian, China.* Dordrecht, Netherlands: Atlantis Press. pp. 129–132. doi:10.2991/icaessr-19.2019.31

Yorke, M. and Knight, P. T., (2006). *Embedding employability into the curriculum.* York, UK: Higher Education Academy. https://www.advance-he.ac.uk/knowledge-hub/embedding-employability-curriculum

Yosso, T., (2005). Whose culture has capital? A critical race theory discussion of community cultural wealth. *Race Ethnicity and Education.* 8(1), 69–91. doi:10.1080/1361332052000341006

Zhong, Z.-J., (2014). Civic engagement among educated Chinese youth: the role of SNS (social networking services), bonding and bridging social capital. *Computers and Education*. 75, 263–273. doi:10.1016/j.compedu.2014.03.005

4

Social Capital and Academic Libraries: The Basics

Tim Schlak

Recognizing key people, the types of connections involved in our networks and how we can position ourselves to enable bridging and bonding social capital for our stakeholders, helps us demonstrate the flow of knowledge in our context.

(Dunne 2020, p. 5)

Introduction

Until the mid-2000s, **social capital** was often seen as too materialistic or transactional an encapsulation of the valuable work academic libraries do. The term, however, is increasingly being accepted by the library community as a useful description of a resource which academic libraries possess in abundance. The inclusion of the term **capital** signals the possibility of higher returns from future efforts and conjures up measurements of gain and loss that can be applied to human behaviour and activities. The work of academic libraries has often been removed from the language of the marketplace, with preference instead given to the broader good that we contribute without explicit consideration given to the costs associated with that service. Social capital and academic libraries, nonetheless, share a common root in that both are predicated on enhancing co-operation to advance the interests of a larger unit that relies on various types of bonds to sustain activity.

As academic libraries seek to transition their value proposition to greater engagement and inclusion amid the shifting scholarly and pedagogical practices that constitute higher education, social capital offers a robust framework for exploring the nature of the exchanges we make as part of broader productivity networks that serve faculty research and teaching, student learning, information access and scholarly production. As this chapter argues, social capital can be understood in a more expansive way than merely as a rational economic choice that would alter our behaviour and purpose. Social capital can instead be seen as an intrinsic human characteristic that accords with people's natural preferences and is thus a way of making explicit those activities and behaviours that organically inform academic librarianship.

Social capital first intersected libraries in its more proper, historical context where scholars such as Bourdieu, Putnam and Coleman sought to explain how cultural privileges and societal strengths are preserved through the social workings of a *community* that allow the perpetuation of important, valuable characteristics. Where Bourdieu (1986) traces a story about social reproduction by theorising the ways social (and cultural) capital accrues in order to ensure these forms of capital are enacted and preserved by those who control financial capital, Coleman (1988) reconciles an individual's actions in service to self-interest with the broader societal norms that govern our actions. Putnam (1993) expands the concept to community health and posits that it is the social web of **trust**, mutuality and **reciprocity** that grows out of a social sense of belonging in community. Trust, mutuality and reciprocity are therefore a form of social capital that allows *communities* to thrive; those that lack it struggle with common problems such as social isolation, regressive infrastructure and a host of issues associated with the 'tragedy of the commons' (Hardin 1968), where costs for negative behaviour are shared communally but individuals experience minimal consequences for their (over)use of a common resource. Scholars such as Vårheim (2009) have asked questions that naturally grow out of a public library's role in building a community's social capital. Yet where academic libraries are concerned, similar concerns apply, but must be considered in different contexts, given that a burgeoning literature has explored both intellectual capital and social capital in their own rights.

This chapter summarises social capital's role as a lens for examining and explaining the important shifts that academic libraries are undergoing worldwide in becoming more socially oriented and responsive organisations. As traditional forms of service provision transition, trust, trustworthiness, mutuality and reciprocity will continue to emerge as important levers that can provide new forms of value as academic libraries continue to seek to build and find belonging in scholarly, teaching and learning communities through engagement, partnership and relationship building (Phelps & Campbell 2012). Social capital provides a nuanced lens for viewing how academic libraries can continue to solve problems of collective action by identifying and prioritising the exchange points that help to form the functioning of a productive academic and scholarly enterprise.

The transactional nature of academic libraries

There may have been a time when the exchanges that occurred within an academic library were seen as the central piece of the scholarly cycle. In addition to the services scholars and students needed, the repository of knowledge represented by an academic library's collections was unsurpassed in providing the hard-to-find **resources** so critical to expanding educational and research horizons. Given the changes from the 1990s onwards stemming from information communication technologies and the student, teacher and research experience, however, the academic library has become one more point of service in student success and one more stop in the researcher's increasingly complicated workflows where behaviours and expectations are changing with the shifting scholarly communications landscape (Conrad 2019) as well as with accelerating technologies like on-demand access (Haglund & Olsson 2008). This model of academic librarianship has been under threat for some time as the turn towards a more socially oriented value proposition (Schlak 2018, p. 138) has emerged as a viable alternative that offers a vision for academic libraries and librarians as collaborators in a future which we are creating in partnership with faculty, staff and students. For all the talk about building relevance in a search world dominated by Google, and soon by machines in the next wave of disruption brought by artificial intelligence (Selingo 2017, p. 5), the focus has too often been on the demise of librarianship rather than on the transformation of the librarian's role made possible by the democratisation of discovery and access.

In order to effect such a transition, library commentators and practitioners have focused on the possibility of future roles where librarians build relationships, embed in courses and research practices and infuse their values and expertise into the critical processes that are driving innovation at universities across the globe. In doing this, however, the significant **assets** that academic libraries already possess, thanks in large measure to a transactional legacy, are often ignored as no longer relevant. The very skills and capacities librarians first cultivated during the previous paradigm are critically important and can be deliberately fostered through renewed focus on our access mission. Indeed, this *zeitgeist* is informing the pioneering of new liaison models (Jaguszewski & Williams 2013, p. 7). Chief among these assets is the social capital that academic libraries have accrued over the years in building, supporting and sustaining research and learning processes that are as vital and important as ever.

In applying the concept of social capital, academic libraries will continue to enrich the academic and scholarly experience with resources, services and programs, but the focus expands from the value that a library might bring to its community of users to include the ways in which firms and organisations provide value to their stakeholders. In bringing a more practical business orientation that expounds social capital's relevance to 21st-century work, the building blocks of success that are now critical to business development become the domain of a set of practices that librarians have increasingly engaged in as we grapple with profound changes brought on by the digital age. These include mutuality, trust, trustworthiness, relationship building, shared meaning and network engagement. These social building blocks allow people in a given network doing different work to seemingly different ends to choose a mutually beneficial association. As a product of rational choice theory (i.e., that individuals make rational calculations to guide their behaviour towards outcomes that benefit them), social capital is the result of the exchange of two or more actors in a network who invest in relationships based on their calculation that the rewards will outweigh the risks. This associational impetus relies on a belief that each actor is trustworthy and likely to uphold the commitments they make at the outset of any association (Cook 2005, p. 7). The fulfilment of these commitments is mutually beneficial and establishes mutuality and reciprocity that can now be said to exist as a credit in the relationship as a form of capital that can later be tapped by either party at some future point (Evans & Syrett 2007, p. 68). The interdependence that makes social capital necessary in organisational life also lies at the heart of the library profession (Abu Bakar

2009, p. 107), where libraries are sites and sets of practices driven by an exchange of information and, in return, relevancy and return on investment (ROI) are accrued.

Social capital: a primer

Box 4.1 introduces the two most widely circulated definitions of social capital, which both stress the ability or potential to leverage relationships to some other end.

Box 4.1 Widely cited definitions of social capital

Putnam (2000, p. 67) defines social capital as
  'features of a social organization such as networks, norms, and social trust that facilitate coordination and cooperation for mutual benefit'.

Nahapiet and Ghoshal (1998, p. 243) posit that social capital is
  'the sum of the actual and potential resources embedded within, available through, and derived from the network of relationships possessed by an individual or social unit'.

Each definition outlines the utility of social capital as confined to an exclusive group, membership in which 'provides each of its members with the backing of the collectively-owned capital, a "credential" which entitles them to credit' (Bourdieu 1986, pp. 248–249). The importance of relationships within such a network means that the dynamics of those relationships take centre stage. Trust and trustworthiness are not themselves a form of social capital but, rather, the critical link between social capital and possible outcomes, ranging from exploitation (failure) to exchange (success) (Ahn & Ostrom 2008). These foundational concepts are introduced, each in turn, before the intersection of social capital concepts and academic libraries is more fully introduced.

Trust and trustworthiness

Social capital research takes seriously the motivations that individuals have for collective action, and considerable ink has been spilled on clarifying the intrinsic role that trust and trustworthiness play as organising principles of human behaviour (Ahn & Ostrom 2008).

Box 4.2 opposite shows how trust has several dimensions and can take diverse forms. Uslaner (2008; 2017) categorises trust into distinct types related to the motivation to trust. His first two types of trust (strategic and moralistic) are social and are a form of personal knowledge about how to operate wisely in a world of uncertainty. The last type, institutional trust, is a political calculation of credibility made between citizens and political institutions (Newton 2008, p. 242) and that can be applied to organisations and those they serve. Giddens (1991) similarly distinguishes between the embodied expertise an individual could possess and confidence in higher-level systems. In line with more holistic views of social capital (Ahn & Ostrom 2008, p. 77), Giddens (1991) posits that trust is a 'leap of faith', where the one trusting the other becomes vulnerable to the gap in their information by acknowledging that the needed expertise lies outside of their domain knowledge and that the needed information can be accepted until evidence to the contrary arises.

Box 4.2 Definitions of different forms of trust

Trust is often expressed as having 'faith' or having 'confidence' in people or institutions. Uslaner (2017, pp. 855–858) categorises trust into four distinct forms that have different foundations and different consequences:

Knowledge-based or strategic trust 'rests upon experience . . . is based upon reciprocity' and 'is essential in everyday life. It helps us decide who our friends will be and what types of decisions we make'.

Moralistic or generalised trust (also known as *out-group trust*) 'is a moral command to believe that "most people can be trusted"' and 'is a value learned early in life – from one's parents – and is stable in time and across generations'.

Particularised trust 'is trust *only* in people from your own in-group . . . that depends upon your own sense of identity' and 'is based upon negative stereotypes of out-groups' and 'a lack of faith in people who are different from yourself'.

Institutional trust 'largely reflects performance, especially the state of the economy. When the economy is strong, people have greater faith in governmental, economic, and even social institutions'.

Giddens (1991, p. 244) includes both words, *confidence* and *faith*, in his definition of trust: 'the vesting of confidence in persons or in abstract systems, made on the basis of a "leap into faith" which brackets ignorance or lack of information'.

Trust and trustworthiness are often conflated, but scholars have made important conceptual distinctions between these constructs and have interpreted trustworthiness in various ways. Box 4.3 displays a selection of definitions from highly cited authors.

Box 4.3 Definitions and descriptions of trustworthiness

According to Coleman (1988, p. S102), the trustworthiness of a social environment is the degree to which obligations have been or will be repaid.

Similarly, Glaeser et al. (1999, p. 3) define trustworthiness as 'behavior that increases the returns to people who trust you'.

Mayer, Davis and Schoorman (1995, pp. 716–720) equate trustworthiness with 'factors that lead to trust', specifically 'three characteristics of a trustee [that] appear to explain a major portion of trustworthiness':

Ability 'is that group of skills, competencies, and characteristics that enable a party to have influence within some specific domain'.

Benevolence 'is the extent to which a trustee is believed to want to do good to the trustor, aside from an egocentric profit motive'.

Integrity 'involves the trustor's perception that the trustee adheres to a set of principles that the trustor finds acceptable'.

Coleman (1988, p. S103) explains *trustworthiness* by way of example where friendly rotating-credit agencies among friends depend solely on the goodwill of everyone to remain and contribute in the agency until all actors have received a payout and not to seek self-gain by quitting immediately upon payout. In this light, Uslaner (2008) further differentiates strategic and moralistic trust: strategic trust is an acceptance of a calculated risk of another's trustworthiness while moralistic trust is a desire to believe that individuals inherently merit trust and confidence. With strategic trust, 'We trust others *only* if we perceive them as trustworthy'; with moralistic trust, 'we have a moral obligation to treat them *as if* they were trustworthy' (Uslaner, 2017, p. 855). The Coleman example demonstrates the principle of **network closure** as a form of social capital (Burt 2001), since acts of dishonesty or distrust face steep penalties in the form of exclusion, excommunication and social shame, thereby giving strong incentives to reciprocal, upstanding behaviour. Institutional trustworthiness is a prediction based on past or current behaviour that an institution warrants confidence in its ability to fulfil its expressed obligations.

When trust and trustworthiness are present, a relationship is characterised by *reciprocity* and *mutuality* in that participants in the social arena can be reasonably assured that obligations will be fulfilled with regard to what they owe others and what will be repaid to them. These social factors stem from voluntary participation and are governed by both internal motivations and self-beliefs as well as by the 'power of community' or the common social structure that governs behaviour (Portes 1998, p. 9). The arising goodwill that participants receive from this exchange is a form of mutuality and interdependence that increasingly defines the common social structure as one of mutual need fulfilment rather than of exploitation and unwarranted risk (Schlak 2015, p. 400).

Networks, norms and institutions

Where the building blocks of trust and trustworthiness imply individual and micro-level interactions, the broader view incorporates a group's capacity to achieve collectively held goals through collaboration and associational life. Here it is useful to introduce the network-based theory of social capital, which can be applied at micro or macro level and is outlined in Box 4.4.

Box 4.4 The network theory of social capital

Lin, Fu and Hsung (2001, p. 58) define social capital as 'resources embedded in a social structure which are accessed and/or mobilized in purposive actions', which has been described as the 'network-resources approach' or a *network theory* of social capital.

Of particular relevance to academic libraries, they argue that social capital consists of three ingredients:

1 the resources embedded in a given social structure;
2 access to those resources by agents in the structure; and
3 the use of those resources by those engaged in collective action.

In this analysis, it becomes a question of identifying which resources are held in the social structure that academic libraries increasingly model. Likewise it is a question of how access to those resources is structured and what is the appropriate use of those resources. Prior to addressing these questions by reviewing the academic library literature on social capital, we must introduce several additional concepts and clarifications. Box 4.5 provides definitions of some important terms that have specific meanings in social capital theory.

Box 4.5 Definitions of key terms in social capital

A **social network** is 'a set of socially relevant nodes connected by one or more relations' (Marin & Wellman 2011, p. 11).

As explained in Chapter 2, the *nodes* (network members) can be individuals or organisations, and the *relations* may include similarities, friendships, information flows, resource exchanges, collaborations or other connections.

Social norms 'specify what actions are regarded by a set of persons as proper or correct, or improper or incorrect' (Coleman 1990, p. 242).

More formally, *norms* are 'macro-level constructs, based on purposive actions at the micro level' and 'a social construction which is part of a feedback process' (Coleman 1990, p. 244) as people are rewarded or penalised for their social behaviour.

Institutions are 'formal or informal rules' or 'prescriptions that specify what actions (or outcomes) are required, prohibited or permitted, and the sanctions authorized if the rules are not followed' and 'the results of human beings' efforts to establish order and increase predictability of social outcomes' (Ostrom & Ahn 2009, p. 28).

This social sciences use of *institution* to mean an established practice (or law) thus interprets the term at a more abstract level than its everyday usage as a synonym for organisation (as in *higher education institution*) and is similar to the definition of *norm* quoted above. However, institution is a broader term, which can be used to cover formal laws and social conventions as well as informal norms and shared beliefs.

When many interactions occur within a confined social structure such as a network, individuals find themselves embedded in social *networks* of ongoing trust where they recognise that it is in their best interest not to exploit but, rather, to reciprocate in order to keep the relationships going. The flow of reciprocal actions generates a stream of benefits in the future that are perceived as greater than the gains from exploitation. In addition, these calculations become *norms* so that 'habits and values' inform societal and social behaviour where individual preferences broadly shared become aggregated at a societal level (Fukuyama 1995, pp. 33–35). The norms function as a behavioural code that underpins trust because they must be upheld as expected by members of the community for individuals to continue to benefit from association with the social structure.

Institutions are higher-level expressions of 'working rules', a set of diverse rules governing collective-action scenarios as mutually agreed upon and enforced prescriptions, which inform individuals how to behave in reciprocal ways that further the organisation's social capital and simultaneously benefit the individual agent (Ahn & Ostrom 2008). In this sense, institutions and social structures that build social capital become channels for information and knowledge communication and transfer. Research has shown, for example, that organisations capable of transferring knowledge effectively within the organisation are more effective than those that struggle (Kostova & Roth 2003; Hansen 2002).

Social capital theorists have distinguished between different types of connections, interactions and relations in social networks and explained their functions in preserving, accessing and mobilising resources. Box 4.6 provides definitions of concepts that define seminal theories in the field, including the 'strength of **weak ties**' (Granovetter 1973) and **structural holes** (Burt 1992), as well as Putnam's (2000) distinction between **bonding and bridging social capital** and Lin's (2001, p. 55) resource-based theory of social capital as 'actions that are taken for the purpose of either maintaining or gaining valued resources' embedded in social networks.

Box 4.6 Definitions of key concepts in social networks

Homophily: 'a tendency for friendships to form between those who are alike in some designated respect' (Lazarsfeld & Merton 1954, p. 23), or 'the degree to which two or more individuals who interact are similar with respect to certain attributes, such as beliefs, education, social status, and the like' (Rogers 2003, p. 19).

Heterophily: 'a tendency for friendships to form between those who differ in some designated respect' (Lazarsfeld & Merton 1954, p. 23), or 'the degree to which two or more individuals who interact are different in certain attributes' (Rogers 2003, p. 19).

Strong ties ('friends'): 'tend to move in the same circles that we do, the information they receive overlaps considerably with what we already know . . . may be more interested than acquaintances in helping us'. 'If each person's close friends know each other, they form a closely knit clique' (Granovetter 2005, p. 34).

Weak ties ('acquaintances'): 'know people that we do not and, thus, receive more novel information . . . typically less similar to us than close friends . . . they connect us to a wider world. They may therefore be better sources when we need to go beyond what our own group knows' (Granovetter 2005, p. 34).

Network closure (cohesive groups): 'networks in which everyone is connected such that no one can escape the notice of others, which . . . usually means a dense network'. 'Closure describes how dense or hierarchical networks lower the risk associated with transaction and trust' (Burt 2001, pp. 37, 52).

Structural holes (network **brokerage**): 'an opportunity to broker the flow of *information* between people, and *control* the projects that bring together people from opposite sides of the hole. Structural holes separate nonredundant sources of information, sources that are more additive than overlapping' (Burt 2001, p. 35).

Bonding social capital ('exclusive', within groups): 'inward-looking and tend[s] to reinforce exclusive identities and homogenous groups', 'good for "getting by" . . . bolsters our narrower selves . . . constitutes a kind of sociological superglue' [works like an adhesive] (Putnam 2000, pp. 22, 23).

Bridging social capital ('inclusive', across or between groups): 'outward-looking and encompass[es] people across diverse social cleavages', 'crucial for "getting ahead" . . . can generate broader identities and reciprocity . . . provides a sociological WD-40' [works like a lubricant] (Putnam 2000, pp. 22, 23).

Lin (2001, p. 39) applies the principle of *homophily* (also known as the *like-me hypothesis*) that '*social interactions tend to take place among individuals with similar lifestyles and socioeconomic characteristics*' to show how investing in relationships outside your immediate circle (weak ties, heterophilous/bridging relations) requires more effort than connecting with those closer to you, but provides better returns in terms of obtaining additional resources and/or attaining higher status. For example, an impoverished academic library may enter into a heterophilous relationship with a campus fundraising unit, but must present a persuasive case as to how the sharing of resources benefits the giving party and not merely the receiving end. In this model for social capital creation, those who have early and broad access to information and entrepreneurial control over information benefit most. However, the close relationships of cohesive groups also have value, for example in promoting mental health and enhancing life satisfaction (Lin 2001). Scholars argue that the different forms of network can be utilised together to complement and augment each other (Burt 2000).

Social capital and academic libraries

It is important to note that the terms social and intellectual capital are often used interchangeably in the library and information science (LIS) literature, but an important distinction exists between the two. While they are both **intangible assets** that are critical to the work librarians do, *social capital* is increasingly coming to be considered a subset of **intellectual capital** in LIS literature. It is occasionally reduced to **relational capital** within a number of frameworks that explain how organisations are more than just a summary of the credits, debts and various assets on their ledgers. Relational capital differs from social capital, however, in that relationship capital is regarded as an actor's personal resource whereas social capital refers to both the individual's relationship investments as well as the network processes that permit the exchange of relational value in order to produce outcomes neither party could more easily arrive at individually (Esser 2008).

Social capital matters to academic libraries and the broader sphere of higher education because it is a measure of an organisation's worth that transcends the purely financial (Kostagiolas & Tsoubrakakou 2014). With the mission-centrality of information access to academic libraries and the vital role that social structures play in a university's scholarly and pedagogical productivity cycles, academic librarians continue to find themselves 'uniquely qualified to take on knowledge management responsibilities because of their proficiency with information technology and their ability to identify, collect, and disseminate information to members of their organizations' (Snyder & Pierce 2002, p. 479). In this analysis, which is typical of the intellectual capital approach in LIS and library practitioner literature, social capital is both a practice of librarianship at the nexus of information dissemination throughout learning and research networks as well as an asset that can be developed intentionally to further a library organisation's reach and impact on the lives of researchers, teachers and students (Ramsey 2016).

The importance of the *social assets* that are possessed and held in common by academic library professionals is greater than ever amid the ongoing database, journal and budgetary pressures academic libraries of all sizes are experiencing. The access we provide to scholarly articles, information products and certain e-book packages ends the moment we cease to be able to afford it, making painfully clear that this form of **structural capital** (Kostagiolas & Tsoubrakakou 2014) is not actually our own but, rather, belongs to the copyright holders with whom we have entered into finite and often costly agreements to rent their content. In bringing new approaches to our work, it is important that we recognise that, in coming to terms with an increasingly tenuous value proposition based on someone else's tangible assets, academic '[l]ibraries are fundamentally relationship organizations' (Town & Kyrillidou 2013, p. 12).

This trend portends significant disruption for the transactional model of librarianship where (near) infinite resources are offered through collection building with increasing emphasis on a partnership model (Harvell 2018). For this shift to happen, it will be crucial for a broader recognition that our intellectual capital and intangible assets, including value and information creation, are only useful as the social structures in place to harness them take hold (Koenig 1997, p. 113). Academic libraries are increasingly moving towards mission reorientations and ROI strategies that prioritise the functional role libraries play in learning and research processes, as well as recasting the librarian role as that of a social agent capable of embedding more deeply and purposely into the lives of teachers and researchers (Jaguszewski & Williams 2013). As they do so, they are increasingly aware of the need to measure, assess and report on these nebulous dimensions of their impact where social and intellectual capital are concerned. The promise that these frameworks hold is for a more prosperous and connected university with a social academic library actively creating and/or supporting *communities of practice* and knowledge in a virtuous cycle. This cycle comes about when the academic library system leverages the social and intellectual resources it continues to build for itself while the community it serves continues to gain through broader and more robust networks that fill structural and individual information gaps in the organisation.

The majority of scholarship in this area focuses on intellectual capital with particular emphasis on identifying the intangible assets that academic libraries possess. Kostagiolas and Asonitis (2009, p. 421) identify three broad types of intellectual capital: (1) human capital; (2) structural or **organisational capital**; and (3) relational capital. Social capital in academic libraries would be an amalgam of these three types where the human capital individually possesses relational capital, which is expressed as a form of structural capital embedded in the organisation and leveraged across the organisation's boundaries. While useful, what must not be forgotten in this type of analysis are the benefits to the community as expressed in trust, trustworthiness, shared norms and values, all of which constitute bonding capital (Johnson 2015) and are core to the types of intangible assets (i.e., human, structural, relationship and *service capital*) that exist in academic libraries (Corrall & Sriborisutsakul 2010.

The forms of social capital that an academic library can possess would include: existing and emerging liaison programs (Schlak 2016), embedded librarianship, the trust and trustworthiness we rely on to do our jobs (Leith 2013), the networks we rely on and the networks in which we provide support for faculty and students (Bracke 2016), and service capital in operation (Corrall 2014). Additional forms would include the values that we, as a long-standing institutional presence in higher education, support and reinforce on behalf of the academic community as a form of virtue (Town 2018, p. 31), including academic integrity, information access and deliberative democracy (Kranich 2010). These core attributes are difficult to measure, but a number of findings have emerged since the late 1990s demonstrating their centrality to academic librarianship. Koenig (1998, p. 227) contextualised trust's importance to the information profession in social capital as the perfect instrument to 'enhance communications, transactions, and cooperation'. Where Leith (2013) posits that greater trust in an information professional's relationships can be engendered through a more intentional situation of the information provider in the context of the recipient's information practices, Schlak (2016) found a virtuous cycle of social capital generation in strong liaison relationships between librarians and faculty members. Zimmer and Henry (2017) found that the social context in which individuals are located has an impact on the quality and accessibility of their interpersonal sources.

A number of publications, moreover, have called for greater awareness and integration of social and intellectual capital theories and principles into the management of academic libraries (Anglada 2007; White 2007; Dakers 1998), as well as broader assessment measures that more fully capture the range of interactions and activities required for *deep collaboration* (Bracke 2016; Town 2015). Information professionals ultimately depend on their **reputational capital** when they wish to endeavour in new areas in partnership with others who would rely on their informational support capacity, as Bracke (2011, p. 67) describes in the sphere of research data management. These are examples of strategic trust that is influenced by institutional trust, but there are also elements of moralistic trust implicit in these frameworks. Underlying these theories and propositions is the recognition that human capital is a primary resource that underpins all the work academic libraries do because it is both a measurement of an individual's information, knowledge and skills, and in aggregate, the sum total of what an organisation can accomplish when arranged in various organisational forms (Wright & McMahan 2011, p. 94). Assessment of the *goodwill* of community users in an academic library (Dole & Hill 2012, p. 270) is a consideration of institutional trust and a fine example of how academic libraries can leverage their resources and reputations to expand their social reach and efforts and therefore social capital, however difficult to measure.

As the profession completes its transition of extending beyond traditional models of service provision, assessment and measurement of new engagement models such as the functional model of library liaisonship (Jaguszewski & Williams 2013) or the hybrid model of specialisation (Covert-Vail & Collard 2012) will provide opportunities to expand traditional assessment approaches that focus on more tangible outcomes and assets. The goal will be to capture 'higher-order effects or impacts of libraries, from the perspective of service users, in relation to the missions and goals of their parent organizations' (Corrall

2014, p. 22). To this end, the **Balanced Scorecard**, initially conceived by Kaplan and Norton (1992), has been put forward in an extended capacity by Town and Kyrillidou (2013) as a comprehensive library performance measurement centred on organisational values, strengths and contributions. Capable of multivariate input ranging from hard economic and operational data to softer forms of feedback such as narrative, the scorecard represents an attempt at a comprehensive ontology (Town 2018) of the 'overall health of the organization' (Reid 2011, p. 86) that gives management a complete picture of the library's success and struggles in order to determine overall strategy.

As White (2007) points out prior to the Balanced Scorecard's introduction in a fuller extended version to library audiences several years later by Town, measuring human capital is an imperfect exercise replete with challenges. The principal cause of these challenges is that the work libraries do in generating social capital is invisible, as Bracke (2016, p. 135) reminds us, and who points out: 'Work that is viewed as critical to the future of academic libraries and higher education, such as developing collaboration and contextual knowledge through liaisons, is thus essentially rendered invisible to decision makers, stakeholders, and practitioners themselves.' One possible reason for this work being rendered so is that the organisational returns academic libraries seek are not ends in themselves but, rather, the means to generating additional benefits for the communities they serve (Town 2018, p. 30). This may explain why intellectual capital has predominated in usage in academic libraries where the softer term social capital has warranted secondary consideration. In addition, these fundamental building blocks are some of the most basic qualities of associational life and are therefore assumed as fundamental in discussions of human and relational capital.

What is lost, however, is not only the ways these dynamics contribute to the relational future academic libraries are pioneering. Also lost is a sustained discussion of the ways human and relational capital function at the highest level to fashion functional bonds within the library that can be leveraged to bond with external constituents and bridge structural gaps within the institutional setting. Regardless, the latter part of this virtuous cycle, namely where an academic library's successes in serving its community are leveraged as learning opportunities to further calibrate services and practices, allows the interpolation of social capital into the service and program development cycle as an additional and worthwhile output because it is a real-time assessment technique that allows for the incorporation of the 'changing needs of their institutions and of the individual clients', as Wien and Dorch (2018, p. 12) remark in a similar scholarly context. In one sense, this analysis recognises the fundamental social constitution of academic libraries, as with any organisation (Torbert et al. 2004), but also posits that social capital is the necessary bridge between human/relational capital and **social network analysis** that is increasingly *en vogue* (Bracke 2016). It is a question not only of measuring relational capital, which is difficult to do (Cooke et al. 2011), but also of understanding more fully and capturing the virtuous cycles of social capital generation that transcend the sum total of human, relational and structural capital. Chapter 6 explores these questions in fuller detail by introducing theories on the *organisational development* of academic libraries.

Conclusion

Social capital's relevance to academic libraries resides primarily in the promise it makes for librarians to realise a virtuous cycle where each party that engages in a given venture would receive a distinct beneficial outcome and would create a credit of goodwill and trustworthiness that can be tapped in subsequent collaborations. The reverse is true as well where those libraries that do not engage in ways seen by others as meaningful might find their relevance diminished, and likewise their capacity for subsequent engagement reduced. Additional benefits of social capital exploration by libraries include understanding the way in which academic libraries function as reinforcers of norms and virtues. This influence can be profound in shifting a user group's preferences and behaviours, as well as in creating organisational capacity to pursue alternative decisions and explore new directions that would otherwise have been ill-advised (University of California 2019). In so doing, academic libraries can seek to leverage further those relationships that have been built and the intangible assets they have generated. Incentives to co-operate and collaborate within our internal systems, and broadly at pan-institutional and consortial levels, have never been higher, and altruism is in the DNA of libraries (Aabø & Audunson 2002).

Altruistic groups have even been shown to outcompete selfish groups (Wilson 2019). For example, the California Digital Library's (CDL) cultivation of shared values around open research communications among the University of California's ten universities' faculties was instrumental in securing a viable transformative agreement with Cambridge University Press following the termination of negotiations with Elsevier. But it is the consultation services CDL now offers other research libraries and their systems that continue to sustain and generate their social capital as they leverage their knowledge and expertise to partner with other large libraries and library systems to pursue beneficial and productive terms with publishers that more accurately reflect their faculties' needs. This example would be one of many in the world of academic libraries where the possibility exists for collaborative action to result in greater 'community building' (Morris & Hammer, 2019, p. 83) and where the surplus relational capital we possess is intended to enhance our organisational level of development to prosper in ways that our communities have not up to this point (Putnam 1993).

In both the social capital and intellectual capital literature, there are few calls for doing things radically different. Rather, emphasis is on understanding how these dynamics function, how we can start measuring them and how we can do more of what we are already doing. The situation we find ourselves in accords perfectly with Putnam's (1993) observation that social capital need not be an intentional undertaking or the result of an action undertaken to generate social capital. Rather, it is a by-product of something that we do because we are mission driven to do those things that put us into an information-spanning context within the associational life of our institutions as they pursue teaching, research and scholarly production. Social capital is thus offered as an implicit recognition that we value our interdependence and wish to harness a greater sense of belonging (Block 2018, p. 7). A more expansive view of social capital is ours for the taking where we eschew the view that our behaviour is purely strategic or self-serving. Rather, the work we do results in past investments that we can draw on in the future as this mode is people's natural preferences (Ostrom & Ahn 2009 pp. 18–19) and the way that healthy organisations and associations have always functioned.

References

Aabø, S. and Audunson, R., (2002). Rational choice and valuation of public libraries: can economic models for evaluating non-market goods be applied to public libraries? *Journal of Librarianship and Information Science*. 34(1), 5–15. doi:10.1177/096100060203400102

Abu Bakar, A. B., (2009). Perceived value of satisfaction with services provided to faculties among liaison librarians. *Malaysian Journal of Library & Information Science*. 14(1), 105–111. https://mjlis.um.edu.my/index.php/MJLIS/article/view/6954

Ahn, T. K. and Ostrom, E., (2008). Social capital and collective action. In: D. Castiglione, J. W. Van Deth and G. Wolleb, eds. *The handbook of social capital*. New York: Oxford University Press. pp. 70–100.

Anglada, L. M., (2007). Collaborations and alliances: social intelligence applied to academic libraries. *Library Management*. 28(6/7), 406–415. doi:10.1108/01435120710774530

Block, P., (2018). *Community: the structure of belonging*. 2nd ed. Oakland, CA: Berrett-Koehler.

Bourdieu, P., (1986). The forms of capital. In: J. G. Richardson, ed. *Handbook of theory and research for the sociology of education*. Westport, CT: Greenwood Press. pp. 241–258.

Bracke, M. S., (2011). Emerging data curation roles for librarians: a case study of agricultural data. *Journal of Agricultural & Food Information*. 12(1), 65–74. doi:10.1080/10496505.2011.539158

Bracke, P., (2016). Social networks and relational capital in library service assessment. *Performance Measurement and Metrics*. 17(2). 134–141. doi:10.1108/PMM-04-2016-0019

Burt, R. S., (1992). *Structural holes: the social structure of competition*. Cambridge, MA: Harvard University Press.

Burt, R. S., (2001). Structural holes versus network closure as social capital. In: N. Lin, K. Cook and R. S. Burt, eds. *Social capital: theory and research*. Hawthorne, NY: Aldine de Gruyter. pp. 31–56.

Coleman, J., (1988). Social capital in the creation of human capital. *American Journal of Sociology*. 94(Supplement), S95–S120. doi:10.1086/228943

Coleman, J. S., (1990). *Foundations of social theory*. Cambridge, MA: Belknap Press.

Conrad, L. Y., (2019). Investing in the researcher experience. *The Scholarly Kitchen*. 18 April 2019. https://scholarlykitchen.sspnet.org/2019/04/18/investing-in-the-researcher-experience

Cook, K. S., (2005). Networks, norms, and trust: the social psychology of social capital. *Social Psychology Quarterly*. 68(1), 4–14. doi:10.1177/019027250506800102

Cooke, L., Norris, M., Busby, N., Page, T., Franklin, G., Gadd, E. and Young, H., (2011). Evaluating the impact of academic liaison librarians on their community: a review and case study. *New Review of Academic Librarianship*. 17(1), 5–30. doi:10.1080/13614533.2011.539096

Corrall, S., (2014). Library service capital: the case for measuring and managing intangible assets. In: S. Faletar Tanacković and B. Bosančić, eds. *Assessing libraries and library users and use: proceedings of the 13th international conference Libraries in the Digital Age (LIDA), 16–20 June, Zadar, Croatia*. pp. 21–32. http://ozk.unizd.hr/lida/files/LIDA_2014_Proceedings.pdf

Corrall, S. and Sriborisutsakul, S., (2010). Evaluating intellectual assets in university libraries: a multi-site case study from Thailand. *Journal of Information and Knowledge Management*. 9(3), 277–290. doi:10.1142/S021964921000267X

Covert-Vail, L. and Collard, S., (2012). *New roles for new times: research library services for graduate students*. Washington, DC: Association of Research Libraries. https://www.arl.org/resources/nrnt-graduate-roles

Dakers, H., (1998). Intellectual capital: auditing the people assets. *INSPEL*. 32(4), 234–242. http://archive.ifla.org/VII/d2/inspel/98-4dakh.pdf

Dole, W. V. and Hill, J. B., (2012). Assessing the good will of community users in an academic library. *New Library World*. 113(5/6), 270–280. doi:10.1108/03074801211226355

Dunne, M., (2020). Enhancing social capital in our stakeholder networks. *Insights*. 33, 27. doi:10.1629/uksg.530

Esser, H., (2008). The two meanings of social capital. In: D. Castiglione, J. W. Van Deth and G. Wolleb, eds. *The handbook of social capital*. New York: Oxford University Press. pp. 22–49.

Evans, M. and Syrett, S., (2007). Generating social capital? The social economy and local economic development. *European Urban and Regional Studies*. 14(1), 55–74. doi:10.1177/0969776407072664

Fukuyama, F., (1995). *Trust: the social virtues and the creation of prosperity*. New York: Free Press.

Giddens, A., (1991). *Modernity and self-identity: self and society in the late modern age*. Cambridge, UK: Polity.

Glaeser, E. L., Laibson, D., Scheinkman, J. A. and Soutter, C. L., (1999). *What is social capital? The determinants of trust and trustworthiness*. NBER Working Paper No. 7216. Cambridge, MA: National Bureau of Economic Research. doi:10.3386/w7216

Granovetter, M. S., (1973). The strength of weak ties. *American Journal of Sociology*. 78(6), 1360–1380. doi:10.1086/225469

Granovetter, M., (2005). The impact of social structure on economic outcomes. *Journal of Economic Perspectives*. 19(1), 33–50. doi:10.1257/0895330053147958

Haglund, L. and Olsson, P., (2008). The impact on university libraries of changes in information behavior among academic researchers: a multiple case study. *Journal of Academic Librarianship*. 34(1), 52–59. doi:10.1016/j.acalib.2007.11.010

Hansen, M. T., (2002). Knowledge networks: explaining effective knowledge sharing in multiunit companies. *Organization Science*. 13(3), 232–248. doi:10.1287/orsc.13.3.232.2771

Hardin, G., (1968). The tragedy of the commons. *Science*. 162(3859), 1243–1248. doi:10.1126/science.162.3859.1243

Harvell, J., (2018). Disrupting the transactional library model: the challenges and opportunities of being a partner in digital humanities research [presentation]. In: *The changing role for libraries in the context of the research university: JISC and CNI Leaders conference 2018, 2 July, Oxford, UK.* https://www.slideshare.net/JISC/disrupting-the-transactional-library-model-the-challenges-and-opportunities-of-being-a-partner-in-digital-humanities-research

Jaguszewski, J. M. and Williams, K., (2013). *New roles for new times: transforming liaison roles in research libraries.* Washington, DC: Association of Research Libraries. https://www.arl.org/wp-content/uploads/2015/12/nrnt-liaison-roles-revised.pdf

Johnson, C. A., (2015). Social capital and library and information science research: definitional chaos or coherent research enterprise. *Information Research.* 20(4), 690. http://InformationR.net/ir/20-4/paper690.html

Kaplan, R. S. and Norton, D. P., (1992). The balanced scorecard – measures that drive performance. *Harvard Business Review.* 70(1), 71–79. https://hbr.org/1992/01/the-balanced-scorecard-measures-that-drive-performance-2

Koenig, M. E. D., (1997). Intellectual capital and how to leverage it. *The Bottom Line.* 10(3), 112–118. doi:10.1108/08880459710175368

Koenig, M. E. D., (1998). From intellectual capital to knowledge management: what are they talking about? *INSPEL.* 32(4), 222–233. https://archive.ifla.org/VII/d2/inspel/98-4koem.pdf

Kostagiolas, P. and Asonitis, S., (2009). Intangible assets for academic libraries: definitions, categorization, and an exploration of management issues. *Library Management.* 30(6/7), 419–429. doi:10.1108/01435120910982113

Kostagiolas, P. and Tsoubrakakou, A., (2014). An analysis of library's intellectual capital resources for library networks. *Qualitative and Quantitative Methods in Libraries.* 3(3), 627–636. http://www.qqml.net/index.php/qqml/article/view/170

Kostova, T. and Roth, K., (2003). Social capital in multinational corporations and a micro-macro model of its formation. *Academy of Management Review.* 28(2), 297–313. doi:10.2307/30040714

Kranich, N., (2010). Academic libraries as hubs for deliberative democracy. *Journal of Public Deliberation.* 6(1), 374. doi:10.16997/jdd.102

Lazarsfeld, P. F. and Merton R. K., (1954). Friendship as a social process: a substantive and methodological analysis. In: M. Berger, T. Abel and C. H. Page, eds. *Freedom and control in modern society.* New York: Van Nostrand. pp. 18–66.

Leith, D., (2013). Representations of the concept of trust in the literature of library and information science. *Cosmopolitan Civil Societies: An Interdisciplinary Journal.* 5(3), 54–74. doi:10.5130/ccs.v5i3.3430

Lin, N., (2001). *Social capital: a theory of social structure and action.* Cambridge, UK: Cambridge University Press.

Lin, N., Fu, Y. and Hsung, R., (2001). The position generator: measurement techniques for investigations of social capital. In: N. Lin, K. Cook and R. S. Burt, eds. *Social capital: theory and research.* Hawthorne, NY: Aldine de Gruyter. pp. 57–81.

Marin, A. and Wellman, B., (2011). Social network analysis: an introduction. In: J. Scott and P. J. Carrington, eds. *The SAGE handbook of social network analysis*. London: Sage. pp. 11–25.

Mayer, R. C., Davis, J. H. and Schoorman, F. D., (1995). An integrative model of organizational trust. *Academy of Management Review*. **20**(3), 709–734. doi:10.2307/258792

Morris, J. and Hammer, S., (2019). Consortia taking responsibility for their technology ecosystem: cultivating agency with emerging community owned solutions. *Journal of Library Administration*. **59**(1), 74–85. doi:10.1080/01930826.2018.1549411

Nahapiet, J. and Ghoshal, S., (1998). Social capital, intellectual capital, and the organizational advantage. *Academy of Management Review*. **23**(2), 242–266. doi:10.2307/259373

Newton, K., (2008). Trust and politics. In: D. Castiglione, J. W. Van Deth and G. Wolleb, eds. *The handbook of social capital*. New York: Oxford University Press. pp. 241–272.

Ostrom, E. and Ahn, T. K., (2009). The meaning of social capital and its link to collective action. In: G. T. Svendsen and G. L. H. Svendsen, eds. *Handbook of social capital: the troika of sociology, political science and economics*. Cheltenham, UK: Edward Elgar. pp. 17–35.

Phelps, S. F. and Campbell, N., (2012). Commitment and trust in librarian–faculty relationships: a systematic review of the literature. *Journal of Academic Librarianship*. **38**(1), 13–19. doi:10.1016/j.acalib.2011.11.003

Portes, A., (1998). Social capital: its origins and applications in modern sociology. *Annual Review of Sociology*. **24**, 1–24. doi:10.1146/annurev.soc.24.1.1

Putnam, R., (1993). The prosperous community: social capital and public life. *The American Prospect*. **13**(4), 35–42. https://prospect.org/infrastructure/prosperous-community-social-capital-public-life

Putnam, R., (2000). *Bowling alone: the collapse and revival of American community*. New York: Simon & Schuster.

Ramsey, E., (2016). It's not just what you know but who you know: social capital theory and academic library outreach. *College & Undergraduate Libraries*. **23**(3), 328–334. doi:10.1080/10691316.2016.1206317

Reid, M. M., (2011). Is the balanced scorecard right for academic libraries. *The Bottom Line*. **24**(2), 85–95. doi:10.1108/08880451111169106

Rogers, E. M., (2003). *Diffusion of innovations*. 5th ed. New York: Free Press.

Schlak, T., (2015). Social capital and leadership in academic libraries: the broader exchange around 'buy-in'. *Library Management*. **36**(6/7), 394–407. doi:10.1108/LM-11/2014-0133

Schlak, T., (2016). Social capital as operative in liaison librarianship: librarian participants' experiences of faculty engagement as academic library liaisons. *Journal of Academic Librarianship*. **42**(4), 411–422. doi:10.1016/j.acalib.2017.09.005

Schlak, T., (2018). Academic libraries and engagement: a critical contextualization of the library discourse on engagement. *Journal of Academic Librarianship*. 2018, **44**(1), 133–139. doi:10.1016/j.acalib.2017.09.005

Selingo, J. J., (2017). *The future of work and what it means for higher education, part 1: the changing workplace and the dual threats of automation and a gig economy* [White paper]. Pleasanton, CA:

Workday. https://forms.workday.com/content/dam/web/en-us/documents/reports/future-of-work-part-1.pdf

Snyder, H. W. and Pierce, J. B., (2002). Intellectual capital. *Annual Review of Information Science and Technology*. 36, 467–500. doi:10.1002/aris.1440360112

Torbert, B. et al., (2004). *Action inquiry: the secret of timely and transforming leadership*. Oakland, CA: Berrett-Koehler.

Town, S., (2015). Implementing the value scorecard. *Performance Measurement and Metrics*. 16(3), 234–251. doi:10.1108/PMM-10-2015-0033

Town, S., (2018). The value scorecard. *Information and Learning Science*. 119(1/2), 25–38. doi:10.1108/ILS-10-2017-0098

Town, S. and Kyrillidou, M., (2013). Developing a values scorecard. *Performance Measurement and Metrics*. 14(1), 7–16. doi:10.1108/14678041311316095

University of California., (2019). Open statement: why UC terminated journal negotiations with Elsevier. University of California, Office of Scholarly Communication. https://osc.universityofcalifornia.edu/2019/03/open-statement-why-uc-terminated-journal-negotiations-with-elsevier

Uslaner, E. M., (2008). Trust as a moral value. In: D. Castiglione, J. W. Van Deth and G. Wolleb, eds. *The handbook of social capital*. New York: Oxford University Press. pp. 101–121.

Uslaner, E. M., (2017). Trust. In: F. M. Moghaddam, ed. *SAGE encyclopedia of political behavior*. Thousand Oaks, CA: Sage. pp. 855–858.

Vårheim, A., (2009). Public libraries: places creating social capital? *Library Hi Tech*. 27(3), 372–381. doi:10.1108/07378830910988504

White, L. N., (2007). Imperfect reflections: the challenges in implementing human capital assessment in libraries. *The Bottom Line*. 20(4), 141–147. doi:10.1108/08880450710843969

Wien, C. N. and Dorch, B. F., (2018). Applying Bourdieu's field theory to analyze the changing status of the research librarian. *LIBER Quarterly*. 28(1), 1–17. doi:10.18352/lq.10236

Wilson, E. O., (2019). *Genesis: the deep origin of societies*. New York: Liveright.

Wright, P. M. and McMahan, G. C., (2011). Exploring social capital: putting human back into strategic human resource management. *Human Resource Management Journal*. 21(2), 93–104. doi:10.1111/j.1748-8583.2010.00165.x

Zimmer, J. C. and Henry, R. M., (2017). The role of social capital in selecting interpersonal information sources. *Journal of the Association for Information Science and Technology*. 68(1), 5–21. doi:10.1002/asi.23577

5

The Social Mission of Academic Libraries in Higher Education

Sheila Corrall

When libraries served more as warehouse utilities, data-driven decision-making was crucial. Now as more of our work increasingly revolves around forming complex relationships and ongoing interactions, a more humanistic approach is required for growth and improvement.

(Mathews 2014, p. 461)

Introduction

Our review of social developments in higher education (HE) showed how key trends such as the shift from an elite to a mass system coupled with the drive for social inclusion and reductions in public funding against a backdrop of *digitalisation* and *globalisation* are shaping policies, pedagogies and professions for the 21st century. Significant developments include the expansion and diversification of student services to support larger heterogeneous populations through educational and social transitions, including the adoption of lifecycle models and a commitment to *educating the whole student*; a renewed focus on the so-called *third mission* of universities, which puts their responsibilities to the economy and society on a par with their roles in learning, teaching and research; and the resurgence of a global student-led movement to *decolonise* the academic curriculum, the HE sector and the whole scholarly knowledge system, which has foregrounded difficult questions for institutions around colonialism, *Eurocentrism* and racism, and also forced a step-change in evolving relationships with *students as partners*.

The present chapter returns to the narrative on the social turn in HE, with a closer look at the service responses of academic libraries to the many complex challenges of the 21st century. The chapter adopts a topical structure and concentrates on areas where the social transformation of HE is having a major impact on library work. We start with a classic business dilemma, the challenge of serving very large diverse populations with different needs at different times in ways that are affordable, equitable and inclusive. We next review library participation in university strategies for socio-economic development based on reaching out to business and the local community, and then switch to the global arena with library strategies for international students. The following sections deal with two other areas where librarians have assumed broader responsibilities, namely student well-being and literacy development, while our final section provides a selective review of the growing body of work using **intellectual and social capital** and related concepts to provide insights into academic library **resources**, roles and relationships.

The topical arrangement enables us to pull out significant developments, such as the strengthened commitment of libraries to helping students manage their learning journeys from before they enter HE to after they leave the academy; and the broader interpretation of their educational responsibilities that librarians have now assumed, which extends beyond the academic development of students to their personal and social needs. Together, such developments suggest significant job enlargement, with librarians facilitating both lifelong and lifewide learning for larger student populations. Many of the service enhancements identified have been accomplished by extending or adapting existing jobs, notably via the well-established role of academic liaison librarian and its variants (such as personal and first-year librarians, international and student-service liaisons). Finally, the role of librarians in literacy development is an important recurring theme: library teaching has expanded substantially since the 1990s, which is evident in the many references to literacy occurring throughout the chapter, the array of different literacies that librarians are promoting and the range of pedagogies they have adopted for diverse contexts.

Mass customisation and lifecycle thinking

A key theme of 21st-century work in HE and beyond is the blurred boundaries between different areas and roles, notably between 'third-stream' and mainstream functions and between academic activities and student services, manifest in cross-boundary collaborations, multi-professional teams, the integration of service interventions in academic curricula and vice versa. Weaver (2013, p. 103) describes 'the seismic shift' in relationships 'between libraries and their client base, libraries and their counterpart support services, and libraries and their institutions', noting the UK trend of universities physically co-locating and/or structurally merging library and other professional services into new organisational units, known as 'super-convergence' to distinguish them from prior models combining libraries with technology and/or learning support. Such units are designed to provide 'seamless, integrated services' and may include 'careers, welfare and counselling, student administration, chaplaincy support, student finance, learning development, study skills and programme administration' in addition to library, IT and media (Heseltine et al. 2009; Weaver 2013, p. 104).

Setting aside organisational arrangements, the general trend is towards holistic services in HE delivering lifewide support for the personal and social development of students, with libraries assuming an 'extended role in the retention and progression of students across the multiple transition points' of the student journey and, indeed, 'in the life of students', instead of concentrating on their academic needs while 'on course' (Weaver 2013, pp. 103, 114). The concept of *lifewide* learning originated in adult education and literacy as an outgrowth of the *lifelong* learning movement as a broader three-way conception of learning that acknowledges the potential benefits of *informal* learning on the job, in everyday life and civic participation, alongside *formal* learning through educational institutions and *non-formal* learning via workplace training or professional networks (Clark 2005, p. 52; Desjardins 2003, p. 15; OECD 2001, p. 18). It is also associated with broader conceptions of how learning represented by human (and social) capital contributes to personal, psychological and social well-being.

In HE, Norman Jackson (2008, p. 3; 2011) has promoted the concept via a pioneering lifewide experiential learning award 'for commitment to Professional, Personal and Social Development' at the University of Surrey in line with a vision of *'whole life' learning* that links lifelong and lifewide learning with personal well-being. Similar thinking informs the American Association of Colleges and Universities (AACU) *integrative learning* initiative in the USA, which is about 'Fostering students' abilities to integrate learning – across courses, over time, and between campus and community life' (Huber & Hutchings 2004, p. 13), and the *connected curriculum* at University College London, through which students 'make connections across subjects and out to the world', 'connect academic learning with workplace learning' and 'connect with each other, across phases and with alumni', where 'curriculum' includes 'not only planned teaching and learning activities and curricular content but also the students' lived experiences of learning while they study' (Fung 2016, pp. 31, 32). In turn, academic libraries are facilitating 'whole life' learning by reviving recreational reading collections 'to help students create connections between what they learn inside and outside of the classroom' (Hallyburton, Buchanan & Carstens 2011, p. 110) and teaching information literacy from 'multiple life perspectives' to support the personal, professional and academic needs of students (Ruleman et al. 2017).

Weaver (2013) uses a four-stage model of the student journey lifecycle (pre-entry, first-year, on-course, employment or further study) to review library contributions to student transitions and success. Student lifecycle models rarely feature in the library literature, but it is evident that academic librarians are now designing services that are not just tailored to disciplinary needs but customised to different lifecycle stages (and life-style requirements). Figure 5.1 on the next page draws on multiple sources to provide an overview of the much fuller range of support now provided by academic libraries, contextualised by the change drivers previously elaborated.

Pre-arrival and orientation

Library outreach to school students prior to university entry is a long-established strategy in the USA, but has evolved from talks and tours into multifaceted interventions in schools, on campus and via websites to develop information literacy (IL) and support educational transition (Adeyemon 2009; Burhanna & Jensen 2006; Collins 2009; Martin, Garcia & McPhee 2012). Such programs serve multiple purposes, such as building community relations, bridging digital divides and promoting HE, as well as introducing academic resources, reducing library anxiety and helping student recruitment, and have gained momentum from technology developments and continuing efforts to improve access to HE for under-represented groups. Libraries in the UK have similarly contributed to

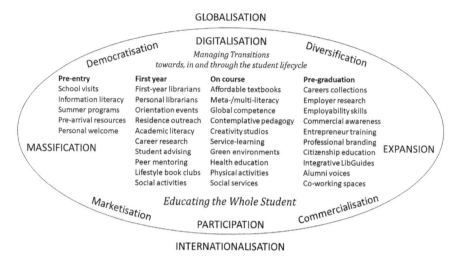

Figure 5.1 *Library services across the student lifecycle*

institutional strategies for ***widening participation*** through pre-entry interactions with schools, often enlisting current students to serve as ambassadors for workshops and visits (Ackerley & Wilson 2012; Stewart 2005).

University libraries in Australia have used Higher Education Participation and Partnerships (HEPP) program funding awarded to their parent institutions to recruit staff specifically to enhance transitional support for students with low socio-economic status (LSES) and promote social inclusion. Both Western Sydney and Monash University Libraries rejected the deficit model of support that treats LSES students differently and instead created and delivered skills programs to all first-year students (Dewi & Manuell 2014; Reading 2016). UK librarians have recognised the need to support transition to study and 'learning before arriving' for students entering Master's programs; Murphy and Tilley (2019) describe an open educational resource developed at Cambridge as a pre-arrival intervention for a heterogeneous home and international student population to help students with academic practices and identity formation in their discipline.

US librarians have responded to the first-year experience (FYE) movement in the sector both by participating in institutional activities (such as orientation, first-year seminars and learning communities) and by developing their own customised programs, including provision for early-college high-school students, first-generation students, English for speakers of other languages (ESOL)/international students and leisure book clubs. They have formed FYE interest groups within professional associations (Association of College and Research Libraries, Reference and User Services Association) and created specialist roles in libraries such as first-year and personal librarians to extend and strengthen their contributions (Moniz & Moats 2014; Pun & Houlihan 2017). Burhanna and Jensen (2006, p. 510) note that such positions have strategic significance in 'making a strong institutional commitment to the first-year success of students and the library's role in this success'.

First-year librarian positions emerged in the 1990s with growth in institutional initiatives to improve support for incoming students and reduce drop-outs before year two; other titles include first-year engagement librarian, first-year experience librarian and first-year success librarian (Angell 2018; Peacock 2013; Todorinova 2018). Coordinating IL instruction for first-years is generally a core responsibility, along with other activities (centrally managed and library-organised) providing a full spectrum of student support from academic advising to social well-being. Examples include *summer bridge programs* (high school to college transition), new student orientations, student organisation fairs, first-year writing programs, career research workshops, *common reading programs* and residence hall outreach, in addition to handling general queries and hosting social events (Angell 2018; Peacock 2013). Liaising and collaborating with student services and academic units emerges as critical to providing coherent support; service partners include admissions, advising, careers, counselling, health, residences and tutoring, as well as academic departments, writing centres and student organisations (Angell 2018; Todorinova 2018).

Personal librarian programs also go back to the 1990s and earlier, but were not widely adopted until the 2000s and later, when libraries began to step up efforts to connect with incoming students in a more proactive way and at a more personal level, recognising the need to support new students both academically and socially. Personal librarian programs may cover all students, but generally concentrate on first-years or target groups such as first-generation, indigenous, transfer or international students (Lafrance & Kealey 2017; Moniz & Moats 2014). Both general and targeted programs are essentially about giving *personal* attention to the *individual* needs of a heterogeneous group, on the basis that one-size-fits-all models of orientation and outreach are no longer adequate for the diverse student population of the 21st century (Lafrance & Kealey 2017). The model assigns each student a named librarian (typically existing reference or liaison librarians) as their personal contact for help to make the library more accessible. Librarians typically introduce themselves and the program via a customised video, welcome e-mail, pre-or post-arrival letter, or postcard handed out at a required event (MacDonald & Mohanty 2017).

Personal librarian programs are less about providing special or extra services and more about new ways of communicating and connecting with students. However, in practice they significantly augment what the library offers by building *relationships* with students, forming *community* for students and prioritising *engagement* of students to support their academic and social integration and success (MacDonald & Mohanty 2017). As Resnis and Natale (2017, p. 144) explain 'Personal Librarianship aims to foster relationships beyond the point-of-need with a focus on sustained communication between the librarian and students', and the personal connection and individual relationship then enables enhanced, personalised service.

Employability and careers

Libraries have responded to the *employability* agenda by contributing to institutional and departmental programs and aligning their reference and instruction services to jobsearch and workplace requirements, often collaborating with other services, such as career centres (Hollister 2005; Pun & Kubo 2017; Tyrer, Ives & Corke 2013). Librarians have highlighted important contextual and functional differences between academic and workplace IL and across different employment sectors, compounded by misunderstandings among stakeholders about the scope and applicability of IL (Crawford & Irving 2011; Quinn & Leligdon 2014). In the UK, the Society of College, National and University Libraries (SCONUL) has produced a 'graduate employability lens' on its Seven Pillars model of IL, as part of an Employability Toolkit that includes case studies and a review on 'how graduate employability relates to information 'know-how' (Goldstein 2015a). Library interventions here are expanding from IL to information and digital literacy, with a particular focus on the role of social media in job seeking, personal branding and professional networking as 'e-professionalism' (Mawson & Haworth 2018; Skoyles, Bullock & Neville 2019).

The University of Sheffield case illustrates the value of cross-university multi-partner collaborations in developing student-centred employability interventions aligned with institutional strategies and disciplinary needs. Supported by a holistic Information and Digital Literacy Framework 'for education, employment and citizenship', the Library has partnered with the careers service, enterprise unit and skills centre on workshops leading to an Academic Skills Certificate; collaborated with careers and enterprise staff on a commercial awareness workshop that has been integrated into a careers course for biologists as well as being delivered via the information skills program and the career management skills course; and created an Employability LibGuide that features video clips and case studies of students and alumni discussing workplace IL, commercial awareness and employability (Mawson & Haworth 2018). Similarly, at Macquarie University, the Library, Biological Sciences, and Careers and Employment combined discipline-based knowledge, transferable skills and career management skills to incorporate 'career information literacy' and employability into a final-year capstone course (Lin-Stephens et al. 2019).

Academic entrepreneurship and community engagement

Figure 5.2 opposite draws on library literature from the 1980s to the 2010s to show the many different areas where academic librarians are contributing to so-called '*third mission*' activities that involve engagement with business and the community beyond the campus.

Innovation and enterprise

Library support for university work with industry goes back to the 1980s, with services for science parks and corporate users that ranged from basic access to books, journals and reference resources to preferential use of specialist databases and information consultancy, the latter often for a subscription or fee (Luther 1989; McDonald 1985). Libraries in

Figure 5.2 *Library contributions to third mission agendas*

America, Europe, Asia and Africa continue to support both incubated and mature companies located on science and technology parks associated with their parent institutions, with some parks using the benefits of specialised library and information resources to attract new tenants (Aportela-Rodríguez & Pacios 2019). University of Toronto Libraries provides a market intelligence service to science and technology entrepreneurs in partnership with an urban innovation hub adjacent to campus supporting the institutional research commercialisation strategy; embedded librarians work alongside business advisors to deliver free value-added services (Fitzgerald, Anderson & Kula 2010).

The growth of tech transfer and entrepreneurship programs on campuses has expanded the role of business librarians beyond managing collections and instruction for business faculty and students to involvement in campus-wide initiatives, such as entrepreneurship cross-training, interdisciplinary education and technology commercialisation programs. They now promote business information competency to a broader audience, supporting faculty and students from diverse disciplines in multiple venues (including university spin-offs and business start-ups), providing market research and business planning resources to sci-tech entrepreneurs, and contributing to institutional economic development strategies by using their resources and expertise to raise their university's profile with local businesses (MacDonald, 2010). Business librarians collaborate with diverse university organisations and community agencies, including business school entrepreneurship centres, university career centres, alumni groups, technology incubators, small business development centres, chambers of commerce, economic development offices, statewide initiatives and multi-agency associations that include public libraries (Feldmann 2014).

They also collaborate with library colleagues (notably engineering librarians and data-visualisation specialists) to deliver 'entrepreneurial information literacy' for innovation hubs or institution-wide entrepreneurship education (Klotzbach-Russell, Rowley & Starry 2022). The 21st-century *makerspace* movement has stimulated university–industry–community collaborations for innovation and entrepreneurship, creating opportunities for libraries to have a more prominent role in incubation facilities. Ohio University established CoLab in the Library as a central unifying resource to 'bridge' entrepreneurship on campus and in the surrounding region, and 'leverage siloed resources and expertise' to facilitate cross-pollination of ideas and projects (Mathuews & Harper 2019). Similarly, at California State University, Northridge, the Library collaborated with the Colleges of Business, Engineering and Arts on an expanded makerspace in an evolving 'innovation ecosystem . . . a continuum of services and spaces distributed across campus', with the library location providing both practical tools and 'readily available assistance with researching and writing business plans as well as intellectual property issues such as copyright, patents, and trademarks' (Stover, Jefferson & Santos 2019, pp. 144, 146).

Other libraries have experimented with co-working spaces as alternative workspaces for independent entrepreneurs, contract workers and other self-employed professionals in an effort to build real-world networking/learning communities on campus that contribute to entrepreneurship education and demonstrate the economic value of the library (Lumley 2014; Schopfel, Roche & Hubert 2015). The ability to create and sustain relationships across campus and community emerges as a challenging but critical issue for successful library engagement with *academic entrepreneurship*.

Communities and citizens

Civic engagement became an issue for academic librarians around the turn of the century, though many had long served their local *communities* by offering access to collections (via exhibitions and borrowing) and teaching information skills to school students to support their transition to HE. John Shuler (1996) was an early advocate of *civic librarianship* on campus, using a multi-capital perspective to redefine the role of government document librarians facing the shift from print collections to electronic information. Invoking the model of civic (or public) journalism, he argues that 'to reclaim their traditional rhetoric "documents to the people," [government information librarians] have to reformulate a new relationship among their physical, human, and social capital' by moving 'from passive collection development practices . . . into a more active program of citizen outreach and education [as] community information organizations' (Shuler 1996, pp. 422, 423). Thus, as *civic librarians*, 'government information librarians must explore the idea of participatory community involvement' and 'create a form of social capital that supports active citizen participation, public problem solving, and deliberative dialogue' (Shuler 1996, p. 424).

Academic librarian Nancy Kranich (2001, p. 41) assumed intellectual leadership of the library *community engagement* and civic education movement, using her American Library Association presidency to promote the responsibility of 'all types of libraries and librarians' to build *social capital* 'for the whole community and society', by preparing citizens for civic participation and providing 'real and virtual community commons . . . where citizens can work together on personal and community problems . . . in cyberspace as well as in public buildings'. Walter and Goetsch (2009, p. 11) differentiate current understandings of university **public engagement** from its public *service* predecessors of *extension* and *outreach* by its 'focus on collaboration between campus and community to address common concerns and the mutual benefit that accrues to partners on both sides as the result of engagement activities', following academic scholarship, which generally contrasts the *one-way transactions* that position outreach as doing things *for* people with the *two-way interactions* that characterise engagement as doing things *with* people, usually in the context of a continuing relationship.

Engagement is thus more purposeful and more ambitious than outreach, concerned 'to address real-world problems and improve local communities' and 'to address the needs and opportunities of society' (Walter & Goetsch 2009, p. 11). Librarians have been urged to move beyond reactive ad hoc individual efforts and to institutionalise external relations work as central to their mission, and to 'look beyond traditional services to deliver innovative programs and services that enhance their institutions' abilities as engaged institutions' (Courtney 2009, p. 5). Surveys of community/public engagement in academic libraries worldwide reveal a mix of library-managed and institution-led provision that can be broadly categorised as extending access to collections, promoting literacy/lifelong learning and providing civic/community spaces (Dunne 2009; Leong 2013; Walter & Goetsch 2009). Practitioner case studies from the period since 2000 confirm that library spaces, librarian expertise and institutional collections all have 'a vital role to play in civic engagement efforts on campus' (Ryan & Swindells 2018, p. 623), especially when creatively combined to advance community agendas. Table 5.1 synthesises a range of sources to illustrate the wide variety of activities and programs initiated by libraries in Asia, Europe and North America.

Table 5.1 *Library responses to community engagement agenda*

Collections/information	Learning/research support	Space/events
Civic information centres	Civic literacy education	***Deliberative forums***
Linked open data	Digital preservation advice	Lecture series
Online heritage exhibitions	Co-created learning packages	Reading clubs
Collaborative digitisation	High school visits/workshops	Bilingual poetry readings
Community history portals	Digitisation workshops	Film screenings
Crowdsourced metadata	Offsite technology training	Research cafes
Volunteer-based transcription	Health literacy collaborations	SciPop talks
Community-created collections	Community teaching	Science-themed exhibits
User-led classification schemes	partnerships	Co-produced exhibitions
University partnership archives	Service-learning mediation	Wikipedia edit-a-thons
Community-centred repositories	Community research support	Open Access Week events
Citizen science LibGuides	Citizen science facilitation	NaNoWriMo* activities
	GIS Day programs	

* National Novel Writing Month (https://nanowrimo.org)

Engaged libraries have moved beyond partnering with other cultural heritage institutions on *digitisation* programs, to working with local organisations and individuals on knowledge-exchange projects to preserve and 'publish' both historical and contemporary hidden materials, using public scanning events and oral history interviews to collect both analogue and born-digital items, and thereby create, document and contextualise community and family histories as resources to support academic and community research and learning (Cho 2011; Gwynn, Henry & Craft 2019; McIntosh, Mangum & Phillips 2017). Libraries are also repurposing their institutional repositories as expertise locators (expert finders) to support institutional knowledge-exchange endeavours (Sidorko & Yang 2011) and as public archives for digital artefacts (project documentation and final outputs) from community-centred work, such as campus events and community-based teaching and learning (Makula 2019; Miller & Billings 2012; Moore, Collins & Johnston 2020).

The overall picture is impressive, yet committed practitioners express disappointment at the varying levels of civic participation across the profession, with some academic librarians preferring a campus focus for community building and others operating in outreach mode rather than real engagement. Kranich (2010) provides some examples of college and university libraries serving as public fora and working with civic partners, but notes limited involvement in the widespread *community-based service-learning* movement. A decade later, she reiterated the call to serve as 'civic agents' and a 'practice ground for democracy', but acknowledged many were only starting to move up the Public Participation Spectrum (https://www.iap2.org/page/pillars), operating at the 'informing' level (as depositories for government and community information and creators of civic engagement LibGuides and archives), with only a few 'involving, collaborating with and empowering future citizens on the issues of the day' (Kranich 2019, p. 199). She called for a more interactive role in public problem solving and urged librarians to strengthen civic literacy by extending IL teaching beyond college and career to the 'third *c*' of citizenship.

Library engagement in *service learning* lags behind participation at institutional level, with many early examples limited to learning experiences on campus for librarianship students. Later literature shows librarians collaborating with faculty on SL courses in other disciplines and also initiating stand-alone library/literacy courses in collaboration with community partners (Blodgett 2017; Marrall 2014; Sweet 2013; Nutefall 2016). Proponents of service learning point to evident synergies with both traditional library values (democracy, diversity, lifelong learning, public good, service, social responsibility) and current professional concerns, such as critical thinking and social justice education; but they also acknowledge the impact of service learning on library practice in IL, collection development, reference work, institutional repositories, exhibition content and collaboration spaces, in facilitating access to a wider range of resources and facilities for students, faculty and community partners (Branch, Nutefall & Gruber 2020; Nutefall et al. 2021; Yates 2014). Yates (2014) describes a more strategic role where her university library hosts and partners the campus service learning centre.

A similar situation emerges with *citizen science*, where librarians seem surprisingly reluctant to get involved, despite the obvious synergies between citizen science goals and library roles in science literacy, open access, scholarly communication, data and media labs, visualisation studios and co-creation/makerspaces, and also the natural alignment of citizen science with library commitments to widening access, empowering people (particularly under-represented groups) and building community on and beyond campus (Cohen et al. 2015; Harrington 2019). Most volunteer-based research in libraries still has a humanities focus and is more accurately described as 'citizen humanities' or *crowdsourcing* cultural heritage, but a group of European research libraries are now actively involved in citizen science and have documented a set of roles for libraries as well as producing initial guidance on library support for citizen science projects, which draws on emerging practice in Europe and the USA (Hansen 2021; Ignat et al. 2018).

Internationalisation, multiculturalism and global citizenship

Literature on the *internationalisation* of academic libraries started to emerge in the 1990s and now includes surveys, case studies, review articles and books. It concentrates on services and support for international students (previously referred to as 'foreign' or 'overseas' students), but also covers other areas that feature in institutional internationalisation strategies, notably study/education abroad (overseas programs for 'home' students in institutional and now community settings), the development of international branch campuses and the restructuring of academic curricula to promote *global competence* and global readiness for *global citizenship* (Click, Wiley & Houlihan 2017; Green 2013; Hughes 2001; Kutner 2019; Kutner & Armstrong 2012; Lindell 2008; Pun, Collard & Parrott 2016; Stevens & Campbell 2006; Whitehurst 2010).

The literature largely reflects US library experiences and perspectives, but contributions from Australia, Canada and the UK indicate that issues and responses have been remarkably consistent across time and place. Many reported challenges relate to the prior experience of international students with different education and library systems, often combined with language/communication issues (verbal and non-verbal) and other cultural/societal differences (Click, Wiley & Houlihan 2017). Hughes (2001) uses the terms 'culture shock', 'study shock' and 'library shock' to signal the severity of problems for many incoming students, which extend to racism (overt or perceived) and health issues (physical and emotional). She argues that the 'international-friendly library' facilitates the *social adjustment* of students as well as their *academic progress* and serves 'an important role as a contact, information and referral centre' with campus-wide and community links, ideally with a designated physical space for internationals in addition to an information point and dedicated web pages.

Libraries have responded by customising and augmenting services to ease the transition to new systems and procedures for students and their families, with relationship building and partnership working emerging as a key theme here. Box 5.1 on the next page shows the range of strategies documented over the past two decades (Amsberry & Snavely 2011;

Box 5.1 Library strategies for supporting international students

- Customised services – tailored versions of standard services (e.g., induction/orientation programs, web/social media pages, course/study guides, information/academic skills sessions and international reference/liaison librarians).
- Augmented services – enhanced services for particular groups (e.g., welcome messages, audio tours, library guides and newspaper collections in alternative languages; special/annual social events for international students).
- Global learning – rethinking the content, depth and breadth of information literacy education in response to institution-wide initiatives to infuse global understanding across disciplinary curricula.
- Student ambassadors – multilingual peer support and knowledge sharing (e.g., in-person/online assistance, native-language tours and social media outreach).
- Blended teams – combining disciplinary expertise with language proficiency/cultural knowledge at point of need (e.g., pairing a subject librarian and area studies librarian).
- Library glossaries – English-language or multilingual explanations of terminology.
- Service partnerships – library collaborations with other units (e.g., international offices, admissions offices, orientation programs, language centres, counselling services, health services, student unions, multicultural centres and international student associations)
- Cross-cultural/*intercultural competence* – culturally competent staff and practices (e.g., cultural awareness training, *culturally responsive teaching* and sociocultural literacy).

Kenney & Li 2016; Kutner & Armstrong 2012; Mawhinney & Zhao 2017; Senior et al. 2008; Sheu & Panchyshyn 2017; Stevens & Campbell 2006; Toner 2019; Whitehurst 2010). Introducing case studies of *The globalized library*, Luckert and Carpenter (2019, p. x) observe 'academic librarians are approaching their international students as whole people with a host of emotional, social, and intellectual concerns that intersect to inform students' experiences on American campuses', which is evident in 'efforts to make these students feel welcome and included' throughout their time on campus. The annual reception for international students and their families at Kent State University exemplifies such enhanced levels of social engagement (Sheu & Panchyshyn 2017).

Many authors stress the need for interventions that develop cultural awareness, understanding and sensitivity among library staff to improve intercultural communication and cross-cultural capability. Scholars also advocate a sociocultural perspective on IL to develop culturally inclusive and responsive library teaching (Blas 2014; Foster 2018; Hicks 2019; Hughes et al. 2016). Libraries evidently need a policy/strategy for internationalisation to identify services that may need highlighting, adjustment or development for both incoming international students and outgoing study-abroad students. Senior et al. (2008) urge libraries to formulate their own international strategy, based on their institution's strategy/policy and reflecting institutional missions and objectives. Witt, Kutner and Cooper (2015) found that US libraries actively contributed to campus internationalisation, but lagged behind institutional efforts in levels of activity and priority, with a perceived lack of focus and few references to internationalisation in their missions.

Kenney and Li (2016, pp. 8, 14) similarly argue that libraries need to shift from a passive *supporting* position to a proactive *participating* role and become more deeply *engaged*, *integrated* and *embedded* in the planning and management of international work at their institutions; they need to realign 'towards an engagement-centered structure', enabling teamwork that blends disciplinary expertise with language/cultural knowledge at the point of need, and must develop the mindset that international students are integral to their efforts (rather than exceptional) and internationalisation is everyone's business and 'a whole library responsibility'. Senior et al. (2008, p. 23) note that good customer care, jargon-free library publications and accommodating different learning styles are 'equally relevant to both home and international students', but 'it is also important that international students realise that their needs are recognised and addressed' and 'helpful to badge certain services and facilities which help international students adapt to the host country's libraries'.

The 'debate over exclusivity versus inclusivity' (Senior et al. 2008) is a significant strategic issue applicable to other minority groups in higher education, which captures the library version of the wider educational challenge 'to affirm cultural diversity and advance world unity' (Rawlings-Sanaei 2017, p. 66), namely, how to balance personalised help, social inclusion, targeted support and universal service in the contemporary academic library.

Academic success and student well-being

The development of libraries as learning centres and information commons offering a wider range of services to meet the academic, personal and social needs of students through co-located, collaborative and integrated multi-professional teams prepared the ground for major involvement in campus-wide efforts to protect student mental health and promote students' overall well-being. New and remodelled libraries emphasise an integrated learning environment and integrated student support, with facilities such as multi-faith prayer and contemplation rooms, cafes with vending machines open 24/7 and one-stop information and referral to counselling services, disability support, careers advice and academic tutoring (Lewis 2010; Orgeron 2001). The literature shows an upsurge in library initiatives related to student well-being as institutions acknowledge its contribution to academic success and commit to mental health and well-being as a strategic priority. Student well-being is now a top trend in libraries, which are 'well-positioned to help, due to their central locations, longer operating hours, and perception as a safe space' (ACRL 2020, p. 275).

ACRL (2020) highlights mental and spiritual well-being and development of neurodiversity support, particularly for autistic students, as featured in recent literature (Anderson 2021; Cho 2018; Shea & Derry 2019). Hinchliffe and Wong (2010) proposed a 'wellness wheel' model (based on Hettler 1980) for planning and design of integrative student-centred services to facilitate holistic development in the learning commons environment, using six dimensions of wellness as a strategy framework to deploy collections, displays, events, workshops and spaces to support the emotional, physical, social, occupational and spiritual growth of students in conjunction with their intellectual development, partnering with other campus units to educate the whole student. The social dimension emphasises formal and informal social interaction and awareness in the context of community membership and social responsibility. Ramsey and Aagard (2018) also reference Hettler in their case study, while Brewerton and Woolley (2017, pp. 16, 24) use Maslow's (1943) 'hierarchy of basic needs' (physiological, safety, love, esteem, self-actualisation) to frame their efforts 'to support the "whole student"' and help the student to 'go from stressful to successful', along with the 'five ways to wellbeing' (connect, be active, take notice, keep learning, give) currently promoted as public (mental) health messages in the UK (Aked & Thompson 2011).

The various well-being models adopted are all based on the principle of holism. While Maslow's hierarchy is a theory of human motivation, his characterisation of healthy people is referenced in the literature on wellness interventions in educational settings and on mental healthcare and recovery. In the academic library context it has the advantage of giving more prominence to critical issues threatening student success in the current environment (such as food insecurity, housing problems and money worries), and encouraging libraries to consider how they can help. Bladek (2021, p. 5) describes two basic strategies adopted by library well-being programs: inserting the library into institution-wide initiatives or joining with other campus units; and incorporating wellness into existing library functions, such as providing access to information, the latter including 'modifying, extending and adding services' in response to institutional priorities and student needs.

Joining, collaborating and partnering with other campus units is a recurring theme in the literature that covers a spectrum of co-operative relationships, ranging from *signposting* library users to relevant campus services (a traditional referral service), through *hosting* well-being activities delivered by other units (as a convenient comfortable space), to *partnering* at the level of ***deep collaboration*** (Horton 2013, p. 66), where effective delivery is dependent on expertise or other significant inputs from two or more parties. Examples include librarians asking counselling and health staff to assist with materials selection for collections and displays on mental health topics, and librarians contributing modules ranging from researching employers to courses on career management (Bladek 2021; Cox & Brewster 2020; Hinchliffe & Wong 2010). Some libraries formalise their relationships with student services through liaison programs, assigning librarians to units such as student success, disability services, careers centre, counselling, international office, multicultural centres and residential life (Miller & Pressley 2015).

Table 5.2 opposite shows the widening array of library-led and campus-collaborative well-being initiatives in Canada, the USA and UK, including developments based on collections, services (often events) and space (see, for example, Bladek 2021; Cox & Brewster 2020; Henrich 2020; Hines 2017; Rourke 2020; Terrile 2021; Walton 2018).

Table 5.2 *Library interventions to promote student well-being*

Collections/information	Services/events	Space/equipment
Affordable textbooks	Extended opening	Universal design
Contemporary bestsellers	Stress busters	Balance chairs
Graphic novels	Therapy animals	Therapy lamps
Hobby books	Board games	Meditation mats
Travel guides	Colouring tables	Standing workstations
Self-help titles	Craft making	Treadmill desks
Audio books	Mindfulness workshops	Brain-sensing headbands
Kindle readers	Yoga classes	Digital-detox teams
Reading groups	Pop-up gyms	Reflection spaces
Popular magazines	Nutrition advice	Napping stations
Consumer health information	Late-night snacks	Relaxation areas
Leaflet displays	Food banks	Maker spaces
Resource guides	Vaccination clinics	Wellness rooms

Libraries also use their websites, Facebook pages and other social media channels to provide information for students with disabilities and to promote health and well-being by highlighting relevant resources, services and events offered by the library, university or others, with links for appointments with campus services (such as accessibility, counselling and financial aid). Librarians are using LibGuides to provide information, advice and guidance on healthy living and wellness topics, including spiritual care and social issues. Some libraries have a Q&A section where users send questions and concerns via an anonymous online form, with responses posted on the website.

Library literature on supporting autistic students advocates applying ***universal design*** (UD) principles to physical spaces and pedagogical strategies for formal instruction and individual learning support (Anderson 2021; Braumberger 2021; Cho 2018; Shea & Derry 2019). UD originated in architecture during the 1970s, but has been adopted and adapted for multiple settings, particularly in education with the development of ***Universal Design for Learning*** (UDL) and ***Universal Design for Instruction*** in the 1990s and early 2000s. UD take-up in libraries is growing, both for physical spaces and for websites, help desks, learning resources and instructional activities (Chodock & Dolinger 2009; Vautier 2014; Zhong 2012). Instead of designing things for the 'average' user and making adjustments for different needs, UD recognises diversity as the norm and plans accordingly, which results in better experiences for everyone, as well as enhancing accessibility and inclusivity for people experiencing difficulties in interacting with resources and facilities.

While the surge in library support for mental health and well-being evidently reflects developments at institutional and national levels, it is also consistent with prior trends in the profession towards person-centred services and community building reflected in the growth of personal librarian programs (Moniz & Moats 2014; Nann 2010) and partnering with student services to educate the whole student and support student success (Swartz, Carlisle & Uyeki 2007; Weaver 2008).

Expanding literacies and library pedagogies

ACRL (2021) highlights 'additional literacies being taught by librarians across all spheres' (such as data, digital, financial, maker, privacy and science literacy) as a significant contemporary development. In practice, academic libraries have been engaging with a continually expanding array of literacies for more than three decades – long before the establishment of IL standards for the sector – but the pace of change has evidently quickened in the decade since 2010, as a result of changing student demographics, continually advancing technologies, repositioning of subject-specific literacies as general education requirements and innovative thinking within the academic library community. Table 5.3 opposite traces the history of library engagement with such multiple literacies, showing how library thinking and practice has followed and occasionally led the development of literacy thinking and practice in education, the professions and society.

The development of formal IL models and standards around the turn of the century (e.g., ACRL 2000; SCONUL 1999) was quickly followed by heated debate on their scope and conceptualisation, in view of theories of related/competing literacies emerging in the participatory Web 2.0 environment and repeated calls for the profession to revise, rethink, reframe, reconceptualise and reclaim IL for the 21st century (Marcum 2002; Ward 2006; Buschman 2009; Markless & Streatfield 2009; Mackey & Jacobson 2011; Kutner & Armstrong 2012; Secker & Coonan 2013; Whitworth 2014; Hicks 2016). Critics variously referenced New Literacy Studies (Street 1993); the New London Group's (1996) pedagogy of multiliteracies, including multilingual/multicultural and multimodal literacies (Cope & Kalantzis 2009); Tyner's (1998) model of tool and representational literacies; and Lankshear and Knobel's (2000; 2007) concept of new/postmodern literacies, among others. The consistent message was that library frameworks lagged behind the current thinking and practices of literacy scholars, teaching librarians and student learners.

Existing models were criticised as skills based, linear sequenced and library centric. They were also denounced for Eurocentric and Anglo-American biases that ignored the cultural diversity and social practices of contemporary HE. SCONUL's (2011) revised *Seven Pillars* model and the new ACRL *Framework* (2016) offer broader, more holistic conceptions, taking account of related multiple literacies and moving towards the practice-based focus adopted by literacy theorists. The *Seven Pillars* revision resulted in a core model supplemented by 'lenses' facilitating application in specific real-world learning contexts that reflect current sector concerns, namely digital literacy, open content, research, graduate employability and evidence-based practice in healthcare (Dalton 2013; Goldstein 2015b). The *Framework* was informed by both the emergent reframing of IL as an overarching *metaliteracy* emphasising critical agency (Mackey & Jacobson 2011) and the pedagogical frameworks of *threshold concepts* (Meyer & Land 2003) and *backward design* (Wiggins & McTighe 2005).

Yet, the search for more holistic and inclusive information literacy conceptions and pedagogies continues, with additional impetus coming from the movement for *decolonisation* and *indigenisation* of academic libraries; notably in Canada, where

Table 5.3 Library engagement with multiple literacy developments

Multiliteracies (Tools & Modes)		Infoliteracies (Breadth & Depth)		21C literacies (Lifelong & Lifewide)	
Computer literacy (Piele et al. 1986; Wood 1988)	Information literacy (McCrank 1992; Isbell & Hammond 1993)	Computer & information literacy (Shapiro & Hughes 1996; Sreenivasulu 1998)	Data (information) literacy (Carlson et al. 2011; Stephenson & Caravello 2007)	Career information literacy (Hollister 2005; Lin-Stephens et al. 2019)	Science literacy (Holden 2010; Kearns & Hybl 2005)
Network literacy (Devlin 1997; Hu 1996)	Media literacy (Dilevko & Grewal 1998; Robinson & Nelson 2002)	Critical literacies (Stonebraker et al. 2017; Swanson 2004)	Archival/primary source literacy (Archer et al. 2009; Morris et al. 2014)	Academic literacies (Bent 2013; Peacock 2008)	Health literacy (Keane 2009; Lantzy 2016)
Technology literacy (Sharkey & Brandt 2005; Warnken 2004)	Spatial literacy (Krygier & Peoples 2005; Nicholson 2007)	Metaliteracy (Mackey & Jacobson 2011; Witek & Grettano 2014)	Privacy literacy (Wissinger 2017; Hartman-Caverly & Chisholm 2020)	Mobile information literacy (Havelka 2013; Walsh 2012)	Sustainability literacy (Carter & Schmidt 2014; Stark 2011)
e-Literacy (Beatty & Mountifield 2006; Martin 2006)	Visual literacy (Harris 2005; Rockenbach & Fabian 2008)	Transliteracy (McBride 2012; Wilkinson 2011)	Copyright literacy (Repanovici et al. 2018; Joseph et al. 2020)	Entrepreneurial literacy (Kirkwood & Evans 2012; Klotzbach-Russell et al. 2021)	Financial literacy (Li 2012; Reiter 2015)
Digital literacy (Sheppard & Nephin 2014; Feerrar 2019)	Multimodal literacy (Carlito 2018; Cordes 2009)	Digital & information literacy (Hallam et al. 2018; Reedy & Goodfellow 2014)	Algorithmic literacy (Kampa & Balzer 2021; Ridley & Pawlick-Potts 2021)	Maker literacies (Radniecki & Klenke 2017; Wallace et al. 2017)	Civic literacy (Cope 2017; Shuyler & Chenevey 2018)

librarians have been exploring the development of *indigenous information literacy* (Chong & Edwards 2022; Loyer 2018). Loyer (2018, p. 145) introduces her discussion with the now familiar call for educators to attend to the whole student experience, reminding us that 'librarians need to address the student's whole self – mental, emotional, spiritual, and physical – in information literacy instruction'. Practitioners accordingly stress the vital importance of *building relationship* between students and instructors, leaning towards experience-centred models of information literacy that recognise the emotional challenges of student research and the need for reciprocal relationships.

In tandem with the expanding literacy agenda, librarians have evolved their pedagogies, exploring different learning theories and experimenting with alternative teaching practices to fit the changing environment. Along with factors referenced above, influences include development of institutional teaching strategies, creation of new learning spaces and activist movements within the sector and society. The turn of the century brought a shift from behaviourist to *constructivist learning* models as practitioners began moving from teacher-centred methods (lectures, demonstrations, workbooks, tutorials) to more interactive learner-centred experiences exploiting the capabilities of the web to facilitate active, creative online learning (Dewald 1999; Woodard 2003). The shift towards teacher as guide/facilitator/co-learner continued with the adoption of social constructivist and *sociocultural learning* theories, emphasising social and cultural aspects of learning, conceptualised as an interactive, collaborative *social process* (Bowles-Terry, Davis & Holliday 2010; Wang 2007). Participatory Web 2.0 technologies then led towards *connectivism* as a theory based in the digital world that views learning as a *continual process* based on *social networks* connecting people, technology and information (Farkas 2012; Guder 2010).

Librarians have also responded to social and cultural diversity in a student population including people with diverse linguistic and educational backgrounds and different learning styles and preferences, by following *universal design* principles to make IL accessible and inclusive (Chodock & Dolinger 2009; Zhong 2012) and adopting *asset-based* **culturally relevant pedagogies** in response to **multicultural education** needs (Foster 2018; Morrison 2017). With many US colleges and universities incorporating the AACU **high-impact practices** (HIPs) into their educational strategies, libraries are contributing to *learning communities* and other effective educational practices both through instruction and via their collections and facilities (Crowe 2015; Murray 2015). Examples of emergent space-based pedagogies include *constructionist learning*, which is associated with makerspaces and other settings where learners solve problems by constructing a physical or digital artefact (Carnagey, May & Weaver 2014; Beatty 2016), and *studio pedagogies* adopted by librarians supporting interdisciplinary design courses or hosting writing centres in collaborative spaces (Nichols, Williams & Ervin 2020; Zaugg & Warr 2018).

Critical pedagogy (or the related concept of *critical library instruction*) is another key theme as part of the critical librarianship movement that includes *critical information literacy* (Doherty & Ketchner 2005; Swanson 2004; 2005). *Hip-hop pedagogy* is an example of culturally relevant, *reflective pedagogical praxis* adopted by critical library instructors (Arthur

2015; Ellenwood 2013; Jacobs 2008). Critlib proponents argue the profession must take a stronger stance on issues such as social justice, anti-racism and decolonisation by embedding such values into every area of academic libraries, including instruction and IL. Critics of the 2000 IL *Standards* acknowledge that the 2016 *Framework* incorporates more critical perspectives, but some argue that it is still not fit for purpose and have called for explicit integration of *information social justice* and *anti-racist information literacy* into the *Framework* (Rapchak 2019; Saunders 2016). Librarians have also responded to the global movement to decolonise HE by using *critical race theory* to audit and review academic reading lists (Crilly, Panesar & Suka-Bill 2020) and to develop academic skills and IL workshops on Decolonising Research Methods and Open Access for Resistance Researching (Clarke 2020). **Contemplative pedagogy** is a nascent practice among US librarians stressing reflection and critical thinking, which has been linked to both sustainable development and critical librarianship movements (Charney & Colvin 2018; Duffy, Rose-Wiles & Loesch 2021).

Capital perspectives in academic librarianship

There are two distinct strands of capital-based work in academic librarianship: one exploring the potential of **intangible assets** (IA) as *intellectual capital* (IC), largely derived from business management and economics literature that deals with strategy and accounting; and another concerned with *social capital*, drawing primarily on theories from sociology and political science, but also on management and economics literature spanning intellectual and social capital. A few library scholars, notably Tim Schlak (2015) and Stephen Town (2018), draw on both perspectives.

Library interest in IA/IC goes back to the 1990s, when the subject gained prominence in relation to knowledge management and practitioners began considering the potential of IC frameworks for auditing intangible knowledge resources on behalf of their institutions (Corrall 1998; Dakers 1998). The focus shifted in the 2000s as librarians started exploring the incorporation of performance measures/indicators for IAs into library assessment frameworks to demonstrate value to their institutions. Table 5.4 on the next page provides examples of IC frameworks developed for academic libraries in Australia, Finland, Greece, Thailand and the UK, showing how library scholars have adopted, adapted and augmented the established tripartite framework of **human capital**, **relational** (or **customer/market**) **capital** and **structural** (or **organisational/infrastructural**) **capital**.

Three of the five studies reference the Kaplan and Norton (1992; 2004) **Balanced Scorecard** as a direct or indirect influence on their work, confirming its wide appeal as a strategic management tool in the private and public sectors. Iivonen and Huotari (2007) use classic IC scholarship to define the different sub-components of their framework. Corrall and Sriborisutsakul (2010, p. 283) augment the tripartite model with a library-specific fourth category of *collection and service assets* as 'the end-products of core knowledge-based processes in libraries . . . derived from a combination of human, structural and relationship assets'. Cribb (2005) follows Kaplan and Norton (2004) in incorporating their three types of **asset** (with minor modification) into the Learning and Growth

Table 5.4 *Intellectual capital frameworks for academic libraries*

Cribb (2005)	Iivonen & Huotari (2007)	Kostagiolas & Asonitis (2009)	Corrall & Sriborisutsakul (2010)	Town (2015; 2018)
Human capital	Human capital	Human capital	Human assets	Library capital Tangible capital Intangible assets Human capital
Information/ technology capital	Structural capital Organisational Innovation Systemic Process	Organisational/ structural capital	Structural assets	Library momentum Innovation Momentum Strategy progress
Organisational capital	Relational capital Customer Market Network	Relational capital	Relationship assets	Library relationships (Relational capital) Consciousness and congruence Communities and communications Causality and comeback
			Collection and service assets	Library virtue Quality Impact

perspective of the Bond University Library Balanced Scorecard (a 'sub-scorecard' of the University scorecard).

In contrast, Town (2015, p. 239) describes an overarching Value Scorecard for the University of York Library that supplements measures from an existing Balanced Scorecard to provide 'a fuller, richer picture' and document achievement of *value*, not just vision and strategy. Indeed, their novel scorecard intentionally is (or can be) both *unbalanced* and *complex* to fit the real-world context of academic libraries. Though not formally part of his framework, Town (2018, p. 30) evidently sees social capital as a component of relational capital, using the term 'relational social capital' in his preamble, where he cites key social capital theorists (Bourdieu, Fukuyama, Putnam, Lin) and explains how 'the research library invests in social relations to gain access to resources to enhance expected returns [as] a means to generate further benefits for its community'.

The social capital literature on academic libraries is more varied in focus and theoretical framing. Librarians have used the concept to gain insight into library and information use, to develop and enhance IL interventions and to articulate library contributions to campus life and the wider community. Stevens and Campbell (2006) use human and social capital theories to contrast economic and humanistic conceptions of lifelong learning and discuss how IL can (and should) prepare students for civic engagement. More recently, librarians have used a Bourdieusian **cultural capital** perspective to consider how the design and delivery of reference services and instruction can help first-generation students succeed at university by developing their 'library cultural capital' and repositioning information literacy as 'academic cultural capital' (Borrelli et al. 2019; Folk 2019).

Ramsey (2016) argues that librarians need to move beyond connecting users with conventional information resources and focus on building connections between people to build social capital that will support their academic and professional success and personal well-being; suggested strategies include prioritising group activities in IL classes and engaging students through social networking sites, as well as providing meeting spaces for student groups and partnering or hosting other student services. Others have a more ambitious vision of academic libraries as '*third spaces*' building social capital for the campus and surrounding communities by partnering external organisations, and hosting gaming tournaments, lecture series and other social gatherings, thus enacting community engagement as their campus and library missions (Frey & Codispoti 2010; Lehto, Toivonen & Iivonen 2012).

Several librarians discuss the role of social media in building social capital for libraries. Solomon (2013) argues that social media work is essentially about long-term relationship management and uses a banking analogy to argue that librarians need to balance their social capital deposits and withdrawals to add value, build trust and promote reciprocity. Garofalo (2013) also emphasises roles in developing relationships, building communities and demonstrating value to the academy, arguing that libraries can use social capital accumulated through curriculum support and research assistance to make additional connections via social networking. Other research uses a social/relational capital perspective to examine networks and relationships of individual librarians and gain critical insights into factors affecting performance of key roles in libraries, including engagement/liaison librarianship (Bracke 2016; McBurney et al. 2020; Schlak 2016) and management/library leadership (Schlak 2015; Lombard 2018). O'Bryan (2018) uniquely looks at the development and use of **political capital** by library leaders.

Conclusion

Our review of library service developments in response to the challenges represented by social trends and changes in higher education and society is a story of continuing efforts by librarians to rethink, redefine and reposition their offerings for a more diverse, more remote and often conflicted student community. While library literature documents myriad initiatives at a micro level, from a macro perspective we detect the overarching trends that largely characterise contemporary academic librarianship. First, librarians have extended their interactions with students upstream and downstream, acknowledging that most students will benefit from informed help with managing their transitions towards, within and through their higher education journey, which is manifest in offering tailored support prior to entry, in the first year and for life after graduation. Second, along with life-course support, libraries have expanded the scope of their offer, recognising that their central place in the habits, minds and lives of students makes them ideally positioned to become a lifewide resource that complements academic guidance with personal support and social facilities, thus enacting the emergent student service philosophy of educating the whole person.

Lifewide support for cognitive, behavioural and emotional well-being now permeates all areas of library work, from collection building and space planning to facilities management and literacy development. Key strategies adopted for the coherent delivery of stage-based, holistic support to diverse, heterogeneous populations include the creation of additional library liaison and co-ordinating roles to build relationships with individual students, student groups and other student-facing services, in addition to the formation of collaborations and partnerships with campus units, external agencies and community groups; the latter are becoming more prevalent as libraries step up their involvement in third-mission activities with convergence of the knowledge exchange and open access/open science agendas. Developing and managing relationships, building and sustaining communities and strengthening identity and belonging (especially for minority groups) will be central tasks for librarians moving forward, suggesting social skills and cultural competence as priority areas for professional development. Intellectual and social capital concepts and theories can help to build critical understanding of social networks and relationships in academic libraries, but we need more empirical work to test and validate library conceptual frameworks.

References

Ackerley, C. and Wilson, T., (2012). Increasing the engagement: widening participation at York. *SCONUL Focus*. 56, 18–21.
https://www.sconul.ac.uk/sites/default/files/documents/8_7.pdf

ACRL., (2000). *Information literacy competency standards for higher education*. Chicago, IL: Association of College and Research Libraries. https://alair.ala.org/handle/11213/7668

ACRL., (2016). *Framework for information literacy for higher education*. Chicago, IL: Association of College and Research Libraries. https://www.ala.org/acrl/standards/ilframework

ACRL Research Planning and Review Committee., (2020). 2020 top trends in academic libraries: a review of the trends and issues affecting academic libraries in higher education. *College & Research Libraries News*. 81(6), 270–278. doi:10.5860/crln.81.6.270

ACRL Research Planning and Review Committee., (2021). *2021 environmental scan*. Chicago, IL: Association of College & Research Libraries. https://www.ala.org/acrl/issues/whitepapers

Adeyemon, E., (2009). Integrating digital literacies into outreach services for underserved youth populations. *The Reference Librarian*. 50(1), 85–98. doi:10.1080/02763870802546423

Amsberry, D. and Snavely, L., (2011). Engaging international students in academic library initiatives for their peers. In: P. A. Jackson and P. Sullivan, eds. *International students and academic libraries: initiatives for success*. Chicago. IL: Association of College and Research Libraries. pp. 69–81.

Angell, K., (2018). An exploration of academic librarian positions dedicated to serving first year college students. *Collaborative Librarianship*. 10(1), 18–29.
https://digitalcommons.du.edu/collaborativelibrarianship/vol10/iss1/5

Aked, J. and Thompson, S., (2011, 5 July). *Five ways to wellbeing: new applications, new ways of thinking*. London: New Economics Foundation.
https://neweconomics.org/2011/07/five-ways-well-new-applications-new-ways-thinking

Anderson, A., (2021). From mutual awareness to collaboration: academic libraries and autism support programs. *Journal of Librarianship and Information Science*. 53(1), 103–115. doi:10.1177/0961000620918628

Aportela-Rodríguez, I. M. and Pacios, A. R., (2019). Science and technology parks and their relationships with university libraries. *Information Research*. 24(4), 845.
http://informationr.net/ir/24-4/paper845.html

Archer, J., Hanlon, A. M. and Levine, J. A., (2009). Investigating primary source literacy. *Journal of Academic Librarianship*. 35(5), 410–420. doi:10.1016/j.acalib.2009.06.017

Arthur, C., (2015). Kool Aid, frozen pizza, and academic integrity: learning from MacMiller's mixtape missteps. *Internet Reference Services Quarterly*. 20(3/4), 127–134.
doi:10.1080/10875301.2015.1109572

Beatty, J. F., (2016). Zotero: a tool for constructionist learning in critical information literacy. In: K. McElroy and N. Pagowsky, eds. *Critical library pedagogy handbook, volume two: lesson plans*. Chicago, IL: Association of College and Research Libraries. pp. 215–221.
http://hdl.handle.net/1951/70045

Beatty, S. and Mountifield, H., (2006). Collaboration in an information commons: key elements for successful support of e-literacy. *ITALICS: Innovation in Teaching and Learning in Information and Computer Sciences*. 5(4), 232–248. doi:10.11120/ital.2006.05040232

Bent, M., (2013). Developing academic literacies. In: J. Secker and E. Coonan, eds. *Rethinking information literacy: a practical framework for supporting learning*. London: Facet Publishing. pp. 27–40.

Bladek, M., (2021). Student well-being matters: academic library support for the whole student. *Journal of Academic Librarianship*. 47(3), 102349. doi:10.1016/j.acalib.2021.102349

Blas, E. A., (2014). Information literacy in the 21st century multicultural classroom: using sociocultural literacy. *Education Libraries*. 37(1–2), 33–41.
https://files.eric.ed.gov/fulltext/EJ1054008.pdf

Blodgett, J., (2017). Taking the class out of the classroom: libraries, literacy, and service learning. In: P. McDonnell, ed. *The experiential library: transforming academic and research libraries through the power of experiential learning*. Cambridge, MA: Chandos. pp. 43–52.
doi:10.1016/B978-0-08-100775-4.00004-2

Borrelli, S., Su, C., Selden, S. and Munip, L., (2019). Investigating first-generation students' perceptions of library personnel. *Performance Measurement and Metrics*. 20(1), 27–36.
doi:10.1108/PMM-07-2018–0018

Bowles-Terry, M., Davis, E. and Holliday, W., (2010). "Writing information literacy" revisited: application of theory to practice in the classroom. *Reference & User Services Quarterly*. 49(3), 225–230. doi:10.5860/rusq.49n3.225

Bracke, P., (2016). Social networks and relational capital in library service assessment. *Performance Measurement and Metrics*. 17(2), 134–141. doi:10.1108/PMM-04-2016-0019

Branch, N. A., Nutefall, J. E. and Gruber, A. M., (2020). Service learning, community-based learning. In: J. D. Ruelle, ed. *The engaged library: high-impact educational practices in academic libraries*. Chicago, IL: Association of College and Research Libraries. pp. 121–137.

Braumberger, E., (2021). Library services for autistic students in academic libraries: a literature review. *Pathfinder: A Canadian Journal for Information Science Students and Early Career Professionals*. 2(2), 86–99. doi:10.29173/pathfinder39

Brewerton, A. and Woolley, B., (2017). Study happy: library wellbeing initiatives from the University of Warwick. *SCONUL Focus*. 68, 15–25. https://www.sconul.ac.uk/sites/default/files/documents/4_18.pdf

Burhanna, K. J. and Jensen, M. L., (2006). Collaborations for success: high school to college transitions. *Reference Services Review*. 34(4), 509–519. doi:10.1108/00907320610716413

Buschman, J., (2009). Information literacy, 'new' literacies, and literacy. *Library Quarterly*. 79(1), 95–118. doi:10.1086/593375

Carlito, M. D., (2018). Supporting multimodal literacy in library instruction. *Reference Services Review*. 46(2), 164–177. doi:10.1108/rsr-02-2018–0015

Carlson, J., Fosmire, M., Miller, C. and Nelson, M. S., (2011). Determining data information literacy needs: a study of students and research faculty. *portal: Libraries and the Academy*. 11(2), 629–657. doi:10.1353/pla.2011.0022

Carnagey, A., May, M. D. and Weaver, J. B., (2014). What would Jesus hack? Libraries, makerspaces, and constructionist learning: the Maker Lab at Abilene Christian University. In: *ATLA 2014 proceedings: 68th annual conference of the American Theological Library Association, 18–21 June, New Orleans, LA*. pp. 126–131. https://serials.atla.com/proceedings/issue/view/42/23

Carter, T. M. and Schmidt, G. J., (2014). Sustainability literacy and information literacy: leveraging librarian expertise. In: M. A. Jankowska, ed. *Focus on educating for sustainability: toolkit for academic libraries*. Sacramento, CA: Library Juice Press. pp. 45–59.

Charney, M. and Colvin, J., (2018). Contemplative pedagogy: building resilience in academic libraries. In: P. Hauke, M. Charney and H. Savahirta, eds. *Going green: implementing sustainable strategies in libraries around the world, buildings, management, programmes and services*. Berlin: de Gruyter Saur. pp. 32–45.

Cho, A., (2011). Bringing history to the library: university–community engagement in the academic library. *Computers in Libraries*. 31(4), 15–18

Cho, J., (2018). Building bridges: librarians and autism spectrum disorder. *Reference Services Review*. 46(3), 325–339. doi:10.1108/RSR-04-2018-0045

Chodock, T. and Dolinger, E., (2009). Applying universal design to information literacy: teaching students who learn differently at Landmark College. *Reference & User Services Quarterly*. 49(1), 24–32. doi:10.5860/rusq.49n1.24

Chong, R. and Edwards, A., (2022). Indigenising Canadian academic libraries: two librarians' experiences. In: J. Crilly and R. Everitt, eds. *Narrative expansions: interpreting decolonisation in academic libraries*. London: Facet Publishing. pp. 105–126.

Clark, T., (2005). Lifelong, life-wide or life sentence? *Australian Journal of Adult Learning*. 45(1), 47–62. doi:10.2572/1443-1394.45.1.2993. https://files.eric.ed.gov/fulltext/EJ797638.pdf

Clarke, M., (2020). Liberate our library: doing decolonisation work at Goldsmiths Library. *Art Libraries Journal*. 45(4), 148–154. doi:10.1017/alj.2020.23

Click, A. B., Wiley, C. W. and Houlihan, M., (2017). The internationalization of the academic library: a systematic review of 25 years of literature on international students. *College & Research Libraries*. 78(3), 328–358. doi:10.5860/crl.v78i3.1659

Cohen, C. M., Cheney, L., Duong, K., Lea, B. and Pettway Unno, Z., (2015). Identifying opportunities in citizen science for academic libraries. *Issues in Science and Technology Librarianship*. 79(Winter). https://doi:org/10.5062/F4BR8Q66

Collins, B. L., (2009). Integrating information literacy skills into academic summer programs for precollege students. *Reference Services Review*. 37(2), 143–154. doi:10.1108/00907320910957189.

Cope, B. and Kalantzis, M., (2009). "Multiliteracies": new literacies, new learning. *Pedagogies: An International Journal*. 4(3), 164–195. doi:10.1080/15544800903076044

Cope, J. T., (2017). The Reconquista student: critical information literacy, civics, and confronting student intolerance. *Communications in Information Literacy*. 11(2), 264–282. https://doi.org/10.15760/20comminfolit.2017.11.2.2

Cordes, S., (2009). 'New school' literacy: concepts, context, and the self. *Synergy*. 7(2), 7220098. https://slav.vic.edu.au/index.php/Synergy/article/view/v7220098

Corrall, S., (1998). Are we in the knowledge management business? *Ariadne*. **18**. http://www.ariadne.ac.uk/issue/18/knowledge-mgt

Corrall, S. and Sriborisutsakul, S., (2010). Evaluating intellectual assets in university libraries: a multi-site case study from Thailand. *Journal of Information and Knowledge Management*. 9(3), 277–290. doi: 10.1142/S021964921000267X

Courtney, N., (2009). Breaking out of our shell: expanding the definition of outreach in academic libraries. In: N. Courtney, ed. *Academic library outreach: beyond the campus walls*. Westport, CT: Libraries Unlimited. pp. 1–6.

Cox, A. and Brewster, L., (2020). Library support for student mental health and well-being in the UK: before and during the COVID-19 pandemic. *Journal of Academic Librarianship*. 46(6), 102256. doi:10.1016/j.acalib.2020.102256

Crawford, J. and Irving, C., (2011). Information literacy in the workplace and the employability agenda. In: G. Walton and A. Pope, eds. *Information literacy: infiltrating the agenda, challenging minds*. Oxford, UK: Chandos. pp. 45–70.

Cribb, G., (2005). Human resource development: impacting on all four perspectives of the Balanced Scorecard. In: *Libraries – a voyage of discovery, 71st IFLA General Conference and Council, August 14–18, Oslo, Norway*. http://archive.ifla.org/IV/ifla71/papers/075e-Cribb.pdf

Crilly, J., Panesar, L. and Suka-Bill, Z., (2020). Co-constructing a liberated/decolonised arts curriculum. *Journal of University Teaching and Learning Practice*. 17(2), 9. https://ro.uow.edu.au/jutlp/vol17/iss2/9

Crowe, K., (2015). Libraries and student success: a campus collaboration with high impact educational practices. In: *Creating sustainable community, ACRL 2015, 25–28 March, Portland,*

OR. Chicago, IL: Association of College and Research Libraries. pp. 443–449. https://www.ala.org/acrl/acrl/conferences/acrl2015/papers

Dakers, H., (1998). Intellectual capital: auditing the people assets. *INSPEL*. 32(4), 234–242. http://forge.fh-potsdam.de/~IFLA/INSPEL/98-4dakh.pdf

Dalton, M., (2013). Developing an evidence-based practice healthcare lens for the SCONUL Seven Pillars of Information Literacy model. *Journal of Information Literacy*. 7(1), 30–43. doi:10.11645/7.1.1813

Desjardins, R., (2003). Determinants of economic and social outcomes from a life-wide learning perspective in Canada. *Education Economics*. 11(1), 11–38. doi:10.1080/09645290210127462

Devlin, B., (1997). Conceptual models for network literacy. *Electronic Library*. 15(5), 363–368. doi:10.1108/eb045582

Dewald, N. H., (1999). Web-based library instruction: what is good pedagogy? *Information Technology and Libraries*. 18(1), 26–31.

Dewi, A. and Manuell, R., (2014). HEPPP to be square: sustainable social inclusion at Monash University Library. In: *17th international FYE conference, 6–9 July, Darwin, Australia*. https://unistars.org/past_papers/papers14/13F.pdf

Dilevko, J. and Grewal, K., (1998). Neutrality and media literacy at the reference desk: a case study. *Journal of Academic Librarianship*. 24(1), 1–32. doi:10.1016/S0099-1333(98)90136-7

Doherty, J. J. and Ketchner, K., (2005). Empowering the intentional learner: a critical theory for information literacy instruction. *Library Philosophy and Practice*. 8, 70. https://digitalcommons.unl.edu/libphilprac/70

Duffy, B., Rose-Wiles, L. M. and Loesch, M. M., (2021). Contemplating library instruction: integrating contemplative practices in a mid-sized academic library. *Journal of Academic Librarianship*. 47(3), 102329. doi:10.1016/j.acalib.2021.102329

Dunne, S., (2009). *Local community engagement: extending the role of the academic library to meet the university's mission*. Consortium of National and University Libraries, Academic and National Library Training Cooperative. http://doras.dcu.ie/20242

Ellenwood, D., (2013). Hip-hop and information literacy: critically incorporating hip-hop in information literacy instruction. In: S. Higgins and L. Gregory, eds. *Information literacy and social justice: radical professional praxis*. Sacramento, CA: Library Juice Press. pp. 163–184.

Farkas, M., (2012). Participatory technologies, pedagogy 2.0 and information literacy. *Library Hi Tech*. 30(1), 82–94. doi:10.1108/07378831211213229

Feerrar, J., (2019). Development of a framework for digital literacy. *Reference Services Review*. 47(2), 91–105. doi:10.1108/RSR-01-2019-0002

Feldmann, L. M., (2014). Academic business librarians' assistance to community entrepreneurs. *Reference Services Review*. 42(1), 108–128. doi:10.1108/RSR-04-2013-0021

Fitzgerald, K., Anderson, L. and Kula, H., (2010). Embedded librarians promote an innovation agenda: University of Toronto libraries and the MaRS discovery district. *Journal of Business & Finance Librarianship*. 15(3–4), 188–196. doi:10.1080/08963568.2010.487689

Folk, A. L., (2019). Reframing information literacy as academic cultural capital: a critical and equity-based foundation for practice, assessment, and scholarship. *College & Research Libraries*. 80(5), 658–673. doi:10.5860/crl.80.5.658

Foster, E., (2018). Cultural competence in library instruction: a reflective practice approach. *portal: Libraries and the Academy*. 18(3), 575–593. doi:10.1353/pla.2018.0034

Frey, S. and Codispoti, M., (2010). Bowling alone in the library: building social capital on campus. In: *2010 Joint Conference of the National Popular Culture and American Culture Associations, 31 March–3 April, St Louis, MO*. http://scholars.indstate.edu/handle/10484/919

Fung, D., (2016). Engaging students with research through a connected curriculum: an innovative institutional approach. *Council on Undergraduate Research Quarterly*. 37(2), 30–35. doi:10.18833/curq/37/2/4

Garofalo, D. A., (2013). *Building communities: social networking for academic libraries*. Oxford, UK: Chandos.

Goldstein, S., (2015a). *A graduate employability lens for the SCONUL Seven Pillars of Information Literacy: incorporating a review of sources on how graduate employability relates to information know-how*. London: Society of College, National and University Libraries. https://www.sconul.ac.uk/publication/graduate-employability-lens-on-the-sconul-seven-pillars

Goldstein, S., (2015b). *Perceptions of the SCONUL Seven Pillars of Information Literacy: a brief review*. London: Society of College, National and University Libraries. https://www.sconul.ac.uk/page/seven-pillars-of-information-literacy

Green, H., (2013). Libraries across land and sea: academic library services on international branch campuses. *College & Research Libraries*. 74(1), 9–23. doi:10.5860/crl-259

Guder, C., (2010). Patrons and pedagogy: a look at the theory of connectivism. *Public Services Quarterly*. 6(1), 36–42. doi:10.1080/15228950903523728

Gwynn, D., Henry, T. and Craft, A. R., (2019). Collection creation as collection management: libraries as publishers and implications for collection development. *Collection Management*. 44(2–4), 206–220. doi:10.1080/01462679.2019.1579012

Hallam, G., Amberyn, T. and Beach, B., (2018). Creating a connected future through information and digital literacy: strategic directions at the University of Queensland Library. *Journal of the Australian Library and Information Association*. 67(1), 42–54. doi:10.1080/24750158.2018.1426365

Hallyburton, A. W., Buchanan, H. E. and Carstens, T. V., (2011). Serving the whole person: popular materials in academic libraries. *Collection Building*. 30(2), 109–112. doi:10.1108/01604951111127498

Hansen, J. S. ed., (2021). Citizen science skilling for library staff, researchers and the public. In: T. Kaarsted and S. Worthington, eds. *Citizen science for libraries – a guide*. The Hague, Netherlands: LIBER Citizen Science Working Group. doi:10.25815/hf0m-2a57

Harrington, E. G., (2019). *Academic libraries and public engagement with science and technology*. Cambridge, MA: Chandos.

Harris, B. R., (2005). "Big picture" pedagogy: the convergence of word and image in information literacy instruction. In: *Currents and convergence, navigating the rivers of change, ACRL 2005, 7–10*

April, Minneapolis, MN. Chicago, IL: Association of College and Research Libraries. pp. 323–329. https://www.ala.org/acrl/conferences/confsandpreconfs/national/05titleindex

Hartman-Caverly, S. and Chisholm, A., (2020). Privacy literacy instruction practices in academic libraries: past, present, and possibilities. *IFLA Journal.* 46(4), 305–327. doi:10.1177/0340035220956804

Havelka, S., (2013). Mobile information literacy: supporting students' research and information needs in a mobile world. *Internet Reference Services Quarterly.* 18(3–4), 189–209. doi:10.1080/10875301.2013.856366

Henrich, K., (2020). Supporting student wellbeing and holistic success: a public services approach. *International Information & Library Review.* 52(3), 235–243. doi:10.1080/10572317.2020.1785171

Heseltine, R., Marsh, S., McKnight, S. and Melling, M., (2009). Super-convergence: SCONUL shared-experience meeting. *SCONUL Focus.* 46, 121–124. https://www.sconul.ac.uk/publication/focus-46

Hettler, B., (1980). Wellness promotion on a university campus. *Family and Community Health.* 3(1), 77–95.

Hicks, A., (2016). Reframing librarians' approaches to international students' information literacy through the lens of new literacy studies. In: S. McNicol, ed. *Critical literacy for information professionals.* London: Facet Publishing. pp. 43–56.

Hicks, A., (2019). Building intercultural teachers: designing information literacy instruction opportunities for increasingly international populations. *Journal of Academic Librarianship.* 45(2), 146–152. doi: 10.1016/j.acalib.2019.02.001

Hinchliffe, L. J. and Wong, M. A., (2010). From services-centered to student-centered: a "wellness wheel" approach to developing the library as an integrative learning commons. *College & Undergraduate Libraries.* 17(2–3), 213–224. doi:10.1080/10691316.2010.490772

Hines, S. G., (2017). Connecting individuals with social services: the academic library's role. *Collaborative Librarianship.* 9(2), 109–116. https://digitalcommons.du.edu/collaborativelibrarianship/vol9/iss2/8

Holden, I. I., (2010). Science literacy and lifelong learning in the classroom: a measure of attitudes among university students. *Journal of Library Administration.* 50(3), 265–282. doi:10.1080/01930821003635002

Hollister, C., (2005). Bringing information literacy to career services. *Reference Services Review.* 33(1), 104–111. doi:10.1108/00907320510581414

Horton, V., (2013). Going "all-in" for deep collaboration. *Collaborative Librarianship.* 5(2), 65–69. doi:10.29087/2013.5.2.01

Hu, C., (1996). Network literacy: new task for librarians on user education. In: *The challenge of change: libraries and economic development*, 62nd IFLA General Conference and Council, 25–31 August, Beijing, China. http://archive.ifla.org/IV/ifla62/62-huch.htm

Huber, M. T. and Hutchings, P., (2004). *Integrative learning: mapping the terrain.* Washington, DC: Association of American Colleges and Universities. http://archive.carnegiefoundation.org/publications/pdfs/elibrary/elibrary_pdf_636.pdf

Hughes, H., (2001). The international-friendly library – customising library services for students from overseas. In: *ALIA 2001 TAFE libraries conference: passion, power, people – TAFE libraries leading the way, 21–23 October, Brisbane, Australia.* https://web.archive.org/web/20160404131427/http://conferences.alia.org.au/tafe2001

Hughes, H., Hall, N., Pozzi, M., Howard, S. and Jaquet, A., (2016). Passport to study: flipped library orientation for international students. *Australian Academic & Research Libraries.* 47(3), 124–142. doi:10.1080/00048623.2016.1225552

Ignat, T., Ayris, P., Labastida i Juan, I., Reilly, S., Dorch, B., Kaarsted, T. and Overgaard, A. K., (2018). Merry work: libraries and citizen science. *Insights.* 31, 35. doi:10.1629/uksg.431

Iivonen, M. and Huotari, M.-L., (2007). The university library's intellectual capital. *Advances in Library Administration and Organization.* 25, 83–96. doi:10.1016/S0732-0671(07)25004-7

Isbell, D. and Hammond, C., (1993). Information literacy competencies: a curricular building block and marketing tool for libraries. *College & Research Libraries News.* 54(6), 325–327. doi:10.5860/crln.54.6.325

Jackson, N., (2008). *The life-wide curriculum concept: a means of developing a more complete educational experience?* Guildford, UK: University of Surrey, Centre for Excellence in Professional Training and Education (SCEPTrE). http://lifewidecurriculum.pbwiki.com/A-more-complete-education

Jackson, N. ed., (2011). *Learning for a complex world: a lifewide concept of learning, education and personal development.* Bloomington, IN: AuthorHouse. https://www.lifewideeducation.uk/learning-for-a-complex-world.html

Jacobs, H. L. M., (2008). Information literacy and reflective pedagogical praxis. *Journal of Academic Librarianship.* 34(3), 256–262. doi:10.1016/j.acalib.2008.03.009

Joseph, K., Guy, J., Wakaruk, A., Sheppard, A. and McNally, M. B., (2020). Know your audience(s): collaborating for copyright education. *International Journal of Open Educational Resources.* 2(1), 80–98. doi:10.18278/ijoer.2.1.6

Kampa, P. and Balzer, F., (2021). Algorithmic literacy in medical students – results of a knowledge test conducted in Germany. *Health Information and Libraries Journal.* 38(3), 224–230. doi:10.1111/hir.12392

Kaplan, R. S. and Norton, D. P., (1992). The balanced scorecard: measures that drive performance. *Harvard Business Review.* 70(1), 71–79.

Kaplan, R. S. and Norton, D. P., (2004). Measuring the strategic readiness of intangible assets. *Harvard Business Review.* 82(2), 52–63.

Keane, E., (2009). Evaluating consumer health information: what fails to harm us makes us smarter. *The Reference Librarian.* 50(2), 178–192. doi:10.1080/02763870902755916

Kearns, K. and Hybl, T. T., (2005). A collaboration between faculty and librarians to develop and assess a science literacy laboratory module. *Science & Technology Libraries.* 25(4), 39–56. doi:10.1300/J122v25n04_04

Kenney, A. R. and Li, X., (2016, July). *Rethinking research libraries in the era of global universities.* Issue brief. New York: Ithaka S+R. doi:10.1866/sr283378

Kirkwood, H. and Evans, K., (2012). Embedded librarianship and virtual environments in entrepreneurship information literacy: a case study. *Journal of Business & Finance Librarianship*. 17(1), 106–116. doi:10.1080/08963568.2011.630583

Klotzbach-Russell, C., Rowley, E. M. and Starry, R., (2022). Librarians in the LaunchPad: building partnerships for entrepreneurial information literacy. *Journal of Business & Finance Librarianship*. 20(1–2), 54–65. doi:10.1080/08963568.2021.1982567

Kostagiolas, P. A. and Asonitis, S., (2009). Intangible assets for academic libraries: definitions, categorization and an exploration of management issues. *Library Management*. 30(6/7), 419–429. doi:10.1108/01435120910982113

Kranich, N., (2001). Libraries create social capital: a unique, if fleeting, opportunity to carve out a new library mission. *Library Journal*. 126(19), 40–41. https://www.libraryjournal.com

Kranich, N., (2010). Academic libraries as hubs for deliberative democracy. *Journal of Public Deliberation*. 6(1), 374. doi:10.16997/jdd.102

Kranich, N., (2019). Academic libraries as civic agents. In: T. J. Shaffer and N. V. Longo, eds. *Creating space for democracy: a primer on dialogue and deliberation in higher education*. Sterling, VA: Stylus. pp. 199–208.

Krygier, J. and Peoples, D. C., (2005). Geographic information literacy and the World Wide Web. In: M. Peterson, ed. *Maps and the internet*. Amsterdam, Netherlands: Elsevier. pp. 17–33.

Kutner, L., (2019). Undergraduate education abroad in community settings: pedagogical opportunities for librarians. In: Y. Luckert and L. I. Carpenter, eds. *The globalized library: American academic libraries and international students, collections, and practices*. Chicago, IL: Association of College and Research Libraries. pp. 299–314. https://scholarworks.uvm.edu/libfacpub/68

Kutner L. and Armstrong, A., (2012). Rethinking information literacy in a globalized world. *Communications in Information Literacy*. 6(1), 25–33. doi:10.15760/comminfolit.2012.6.1.115

Lafrance, H. and Kealey, S. B., (2017). A boutique personal librarian program for transfer students. *Reference Services Review*. 45(2), 332–345. doi:10.1108/RSR-10-2016-0066

Lankshear, C. and Knobel, M., (2000). Mapping postmodern literacies: a preliminary chart. *Journal of Literacy and Technology*. 1(1). http://www.literacyandtechnology.org/volume-1-number-1-fall-2000.html

Lankshear, C. and Knobel, M., (2007). Researching new literacies: Web 2.0 practices and insider perspectives. *E-Learning and Digital Media*. 4(3), 224–240. doi:10.2304/elea.2007.4.3.224

Lantzy, T., (2016). Health literacy education: the impact of synchronous instruction. *Reference Services Review*. 44(2), 100–121. doi:10.1108/RSR-02-2016-0007

Lehto, A., Toivonen, L. and Iivonen, M., (2012). University library premises: the evaluation of customer satisfaction and usage. In: J. Lau, A. M. Tammaro and T. Bothma, eds. *Libraries driving access to knowledge*. Berlin, Germany: De Gruyter Saur. 289–313. doi:10.1515/9783110263121.289

Leong, J. H. T., (2013). Community engagement – building bridges between university and community by academic libraries in the 21st century. *Libri*. 63(3), 220–231. doi:10.1515/libri-2013-0017

Lewis, M., (2010). The University of Sheffield Library Information Commons: a case study. *Journal of Library Administration*. 50(2), 161–178. doi:10.1080/01930820903455040

Li, J., (2012). Serving as an educator: a southern case in embedded librarianship. *Journal of Business & Finance Librarianship*. 17(2), 133–152. doi:10.1080/08963568.2012.661198

Lin-Stephens, S., Kubicki, J. M., Jones, F., Whiting, M. J., Uesi, J. and Bulbert, M. W., (2019). Building student employability through interdisciplinary collaboration: an Australian case study. *College & Undergraduate Libraries*. 26(3), 234–251. doi:10.1080/10691316.2019.1674027

Lindell, A., (2008). *Library support for study abroad*. SPEC Kit 309. Washington, DC: Association of Research Libraries. doi:10.29242/spec.309

Lombard, E., (2018). Gender and leadership in academic libraries. *Journal of Academic Librarianship*. 44(2), 226–230. doi:10.1016/j.acalib.2018.02.003

Loyer, J., (2018). Indigenous information literacy: nêhiyaw kinship enabling self-care in research. In: K. P. Nicholson and M. Seale, eds. *The politics of theory and the practice of critical librarianship*. Sacramento, CA: Library Juice Press. pp. 145–156.

Luckert, Y. and Carpenter, L. I., (2019). Introduction: perspectives on globalization of American libraries. In: Y. Luckert and L. I. Carpenter, eds. *The globalized library: American academic libraries and international students, collections, and practices*. Chicago, IL: Association of College and Research Libraries. pp. vii–xiv.

Lumley, R. M., (2014). A coworking project in the campus library: supporting and modeling entrepreneurial activity in the academic library. *New Review of Academic Librarianship*. 20(1), 49–65. doi:10.1080/13614533.2013.850101

Luther, L., (1989). A review of information services provided to science parks in the United States and England. *Australian Library Journal*. 38(2), 103–114.

MacDonald, A. and Mohanty, S., (2017). Personal librarian program for transfer students: an overview. *Reference Services Review*. 45(2), 346–354. doi:10.1108/RSR-10-2016-007

MacDonald, K., (2010). Entrepreneurship outreach: a new role for the academic business librarian. *Journal of Business & Finance Librarianship*. 15(3–4), 158–160. doi:10.1080/08963568.2010.490767

Mackey, T. P. and Jacobson, T. E., (2011). Reframing information literacy as a metaliteracy. *College & Research Libraries*. 72(1), 62–78. doi:10.5860/crl-76r1

Makula, A., (2019). "Institutional" repositories, redefined: reflecting institutional commitments to community engagement. *Against the Grain*. 31(5), 40–41. https://www.charleston-hub.com/2019/12/v315-institutional-repositories-redefined-reflecting-institutional-commitments-to-community-engagement

Marcum, J. W., (2002). Rethinking information literacy. *Library Quarterly*. 72(1), 1–26. doi:10.1086/603335

Markless, S. and Streatfield, D., (2009). Reconceptualising information literacy for the Web 2.0 environment? In: S. Hatzipanagos and S. Warburton, eds. *Handbook of research on social software and developing community ontologies*. Hershey, PA: Information Science Reference. pp. 316–334. doi:10.4018/978-1-60566-208-4.ch022

Marrall, R. M., (2014). Teaching the digital divide: connecting students to community, knowledge, and service learning. *Library Philosophy and Practice*. 1126. https://digitalcommons.unl.edu/libphilprac/1126

Martin, C. M., Garcia, E. P. and McPhee, M., (2012). Information literacy outreach: building a high school program at California State University Northridge. *Education Libraries*. 35(1–2), 34–47. doi:10.26443/el.v35i1-2.314

Martin, L., (2006). Enabling eLiteracy: providing non-technical support for online learners *ITALICS: Innovation in Teaching and Learning in Information and Computer Sciences*. 5(4), 97–108. doi:10.11120/ital.2006.05040097

Maslow, A. H., (1943). A theory of human motivation. *Psychological Review*. 50(4), 370–396. doi:10.1037/h0054346

Mathews, B., (2014). Librarian as futurist: changing the way libraries think about the future. *portal: Libraries and the Academy*. 14(3), 453–462. doi:10.1353/pla.2014.0019

Mathuews, K. B. and Harper, D. J., (2019). Designing academic library makerspaces: bridging technology and community engagement. In: *Libraries: dialogue for change, 85th IFLA general conference and assembly, 24–30 August, Athens, Greece.* http://library.ifla.org/2478/1/205-mathuews-en.pdf

Mawhinney, T. and Zhao, J. C., (2017). Implementing a peer support program for international students: a case study at McGill University Library. In: S. Arnold-Garza and C. Tomlinson. eds. *Students lead the library: the importance of student contributions to the academic library*. Chicago, IL: Association of College and Research Libraries. pp. 165–185. https://escholarship.mcgill.ca/concern/parent/nk322j46p/file_sets/m326m5663

Mawson, M. and Haworth, A. C., (2018). Supporting the employability agenda in university libraries: a case study from the University of Sheffield. *Information and Learning Science*. 119(1/2), 101–108. doi:10.1108/ILS-04-2017-0027

McBride, M. F., (2012). Reconsidering information literacy in the 21st century: the redesign of an information literacy class. *Journal of Educational Technology Systems*. 40(3), 287–300. doi:10.2190/ET.40.3.e

McBurney, J., Hunt, S. L., Gyendina, M., Brown, S. J., Wiggins, B. and Nackerud, S., (2020). Library research sprints as a tool to engage faculty and promote collaboration. *portal: Libraries and the Academy*. 20(2), 305–338. doi:10.1353/pla.2020.0016

McCrank, L. J., (1992). Academic programs for information literacy: theory and structure. *RQ*. 31(4), 485–498.

McDonald, E., (1985). University/industry partnerships: premonitions for academic libraries. *Journal of Academic Librarianship*. 11(2), 82–87.

McIntosh, M., Mangum, J. and Phillips, M. E., (2017). A model for surfacing hidden collections: the rescuing Texas history mini-grant program at the University of North Texas Libraries. *The Reading Room*. 2(2), 39–59. https://readingroom.lib.buffalo.edu/PDF/vol2-issue2/vol2-issue2.pdf

Meyer, J. and Land, R., (2003, May). *Threshold concepts and troublesome knowledge: linkages to ways of thinking and practising within the disciplines*. Edinburgh, UK: University of Edinburgh, School of Education. http://www.etl.tla.ed.ac.uk//docs/ETLreport4.pdf

Miller, R. K. and Pressley, L., (2015). *Evolution of library liaisons*. SPEC Kit 349. Washington, DC: Association of Research Libraries. doi:10.29242/spec.349

Miller, W. A. and Billings, M., (2012). A university library creates a digital repository for documenting and disseminating community engagement. *Journal of Higher Education Outreach and Engagement*. 16(2), 109–122. https://openjournals.libs.uga.edu/jheoe/article/view/935/934

Moniz, R. J. and Moats, J. eds., (2014). *The personal librarian: enhancing the student experience*. Chicago, IL: ALA Editions.

Moore, E. A., Collins, V. M. and Johnston, L. R., (2020). Institutional repositories for public engagement: creating a common good model for an engaged campus. *Journal of Library Outreach and Engagement*. 1(1), 116–129. doi:10.21900.j.jloe.v1i1.472

Morris, S., Mykytiuk, L. J. and Weiner, S. A., (2014). Archival literacy for history students: identifying faculty expectations of archival research skills. *The American Archivist*. 77(2), 394–424.

Morrison, K. L., (2017). Informed asset-based pedagogy: coming correct, counter-stories from an information literacy classroom. *Library Trends*. 66(2), 176–218. http://hdl.handle.net/2142/101408

Murphy, H. and Tilley, E., (2019). Libraries supporting transition: developing a pre-arrival open educational resource (OER) for taught Master's students. *New Review of Academic Librarianship*. 25(2–4), 271–294. doi:10.1080/13614533.2019.1622580

Murray, A., (2015). Academic libraries and high-impact practices for student retention: library deans' perspectives. *portal: Libraries and the Academy*. 15(3), 471–487. doi:10.1353/pla.2015.0027

Nann, J. B., (2010). Personal librarians: the answer to increasing patron contact may be simpler than we think. *AALL Spectrum*. 14(8), 20–23. https://www.aallnet.org/wp-content/uploads/2017/11/pub_sp1006.pdf

New London Group., (1996). A pedagogy of multiliteracies: designing social futures. *Harvard Educational Review*. 66(1), 60–92.

Nichols, J., Williams, B. F. and Ervin, C., (2020). Students at the center of the studio: service design, studio pedagogy, and peer learning. In: E. Sengupta, P. Blessinger and M. D. Cox, eds. *International perspectives on improving student engagement: advances in library practices in higher education*. Bingley, UK: Emerald. pp. 59–77. doi:10.1108/S2055-364120200000026005

Nicholson, A., (2007). Spatial literacy and information literacy: an evolution of GIS services in libraries. *Association of Canadian Map Libraries and Archives Bulletin*. 129, 3–5. https://openjournals.uwaterloo.ca/index.php/acmla/issue/view/173

Nutefall, J. E. ed., (2016). *Service learning, information literacy, and libraries*. Santa Barbara, CA: Libraries Unlimited.

Nutefall, J. E., Barry, M., Gruber, A. M. and Ivey, O., (2021). Assessing service-learning programs in academic libraries: a rubric in action. *portal: Libraries and the Academy.* 21(1), 9–35. doi:10.1353/pla.2021.0003

O'Bryan, C., (2018). The influence of political capital on academic library leadership. *Library Leadership & Management.* 32(4), 7292. https://journals.tdl.org/llm/index.php/llm/article/view/7292

OECD., (2001). *The well-being of nations: the role of human and social capital.* Paris, France: Organisation for Economic Co-operation and Development, Centre for Educational Research and Innovation.

Orgeron, E., (2001). Integrated academic student support services at Loyola University: the library as a resource clearinghouse. *Journal of Southern Academic and Special Librarianship.* 2(3). https://southernlibrarianship.icaap.org/content/v02n03/orgeron_e01.htm

Peacock, J. A., (2008). Not yours, not mine . . . but ours: integrating learning skills for integrated learning. In: *Dreaming 08, ALIA 2008 biennial conference, 2–5 September, Alice Springs, Australia.* https://eprints.qut.edu.au/14427/1/14427a.pdf

Peacock, R., (2013). My first years as a first-year librarian. In R. Peacock and J. Wurm, eds. *The new academic librarian: essays on changing roles and responsibilities.* Jefferson, NC: McFarland. pp. 27–33.

Piele, L. J., Pryor, J. and Tuckett, H. W., (1986). Teaching microcomputer literacy: new roles for academic librarians. *College & Research Libraries.* 47(4), 374–378. doi:10.5860/crl_47_04_374

Pun, R. and Houlihan, M. A. eds., (2017). *The first-year experience cookbook.* Chicago, IL: Association of College and Research Libraries.

Pun, R. and Kubo, H., (2017). Beyond career collection development: academic libraries collaborating with career center for student success. *Public Services Quarterly.* 13(2), 134–138. doi:10.1080/15228959.2017.1300558

Pun, R., Collard, S. and Parrott, J. eds., (2016). *Bridging worlds: emerging models and practices of U.S. academic libraries around the globe.* Chicago, IL: Association of College and Research Libraries.

Quinn, T. and Leligdon, L., (2014). Executive MBA students' information skills and knowledge: discovering the difference between work and academics. *Journal of Business & Finance Librarianship.* 19(3), 234–255. doi:10.1080/08963568.2014.916540

Radniecki, T. and Klenke, C., (2017). Academic library makerspaces: supporting new literacies and skills. In: *At the helm: leading transformation, ACRL 2017, 22–25 March, Baltimore, MD.* Chicago, IL: Association of College and Research Libraries. pp. 15–22. http://www.ala.org/acrl/conferences/acrl2017/papers

Ramsey, E., (2016). It's not just what you know but who you know: social capital theory and academic library outreach. *College & Undergraduate Libraries.* 23(3), 328–334. doi:10.1080/10691316.2016.1206317

Ramsey, E. and Aagard, M. C., (2018). Academic libraries as active contributors to student wellness. *College & Undergraduate Libraries.* 25(4), 328–334. doi:10.1080/10691316.2018.1517433

Rapchak, M., (2019). That which cannot be named: the absence of race in the Framework for Information Literacy for Higher Education. *Journal of Radical Librarianship*. 5, 173–196. https://www.journal.radicallibrarianship.org/index.php/journal/article/view/33

Rawlings-Sanaei, F., (2017). Educating the global citizen. In: J. Sachs and L. Clark, eds. *Learning through community engagement: vision and practice in higher education*. Singapore: Springer. pp. 65–78. doi:10.1007/978-981-10-0999-0_5

Reading, J., (2016). Providing enhanced information skills support to students from disadvantaged backgrounds: Western Sydney University Library outreach program. *Journal of Academic Librarianship*. 42(6), 694–704. doi:10.1016/j.acalib.2016.08.002

Reedy, K. and Goodfellow, R., (2014). 'You've been frameworked': evaluating an approach to digital and information literacy at the Open University. *Journal of Learning Development in Higher Education*. 7(Special edition). doi:10.47408/jldhe.v0i0.291

Reiter, L., (2015). Financial literacy and the academic library: exploring the peer-to-peer approach. *Journal of Business & Finance Librarianship*. 20(1–2), 54–65. doi:10.1080/08963568.2015.977732

Repanovici, A., Landøy, A. and Koukourakis, M., (2018). Homework with Kahoot in copyright literacy. In: *Alternative facts, fake news, getting to the truth with information: WBLIC 2018, 21–22 June, Bihać, Bosnia and Herzegovina*. Limerick: Ireland: Limerick Institute of Technology. pp. 36–41. https://hdl.handle.net/1956/18035

Resnis, E. and Natale, J., (2017). The ingredients for assessing a personal librarian program for first year students. In: R. Pun and M. A. Houlihan, eds. *The first-year experience cookbook*. Chicago, IL: Association of College and Research Libraries. pp. 144–146.

Ridley, M. and Pawlick-Potts, D., (2021). Algorithmic literacy and the role for libraries. *Information Technology and Libraries*. 40(2). doi:10.6017/ital.v40i2.12963

Robinson, A. and Nelson, E., (2002). Plug-ins for critical media literacy: a collaborative program. *Online*. 26(4), 29–32.

Rockenbach, B. and Fabian, C., (2008). Visual literacy in the age of participation. *Art Documentation*. 26(2), 26–31. doi:10.1086/adx.27.2.27949492

Rourke, L. E., (2020). Then you can start to make it better: how academic libraries are promoting and fostering student wellness. In: S. Holder and A. Lannon, eds. *Student wellness and academic libraries: case studies and activities for promoting health and success*. Chicago, IL: Association of College and Research Libraries. pp. 13–33.

Ruleman, A. B., Horne-Popp, L. and Hallis, R., (2017). Show me the learning, navigating information literacy through multiple life perspectives. In: *At the helm, leading the transformation, ACRL 2017, 22–25 March, Baltimore, MD*. Chicago, IL: Association of College & Research Libraries. pp. 627–636. http://www.ala.org/acrl/conferences/acrl2017/papers

Ryan, M. and Swindells, G., (2018). Democratic practice: libraries and education for citizenship. *portal: Libraries and the Academy*. 18(4), 623–628. doi:10.1353/pla.2018.0036

Saunders, L., (2016). Re-framing information literacy for social justice. In: *Information literacy: key to an inclusive society, ECIL 2016, 10–13 October, Prague, Czech Republic*. Cham, Switzerland: Springer. pp. 56–65. doi:10.1007/978-3-319-52162-6_6

Schlak, T. M., (2015). Social capital and leadership in academic libraries: the broader exchange around 'buy in'. *Library Management*. 36(6), 394–407. doi:10.1108/LM-11-2014-0133

Schlak, T., (2016). Social capital as operative in liaison librarianship: librarian participants' experiences of faculty engagement as academic library liaisons. *Journal of Academic Librarianship*. 42(4), 411–422. doi:10.1016/j.acalib.2016.04.008

Schopfel, J., Roche, J. and Hubert, G., (2015). Co-working and innovation: new concepts for academic libraries and learning centres. *New Library World*. 116(1/2), 67–78. doi:10.1108/NLW-06-2014-0072

SCONUL., (1999). *Information skills in higher education: a SCONUL position paper.* London: Society of College, National and University Libraries. https://www.sconul.ac.uk/sites/default/files/documents/Seven_pillars2.pdf

SCONUL., (2011). *The SCONUL Seven Pillars of Information Literacy: core model for higher education.* London: SCONUL. http://www.sconul.ac.uk/sites/default/files/documents/coremodel.pdf

Secker, J. and Coonan, E. eds., (2013). *Rethinking information literacy: a practical framework for supporting learning.* London: Facet Publishing.

Senior, K., Bent, M., Scopes, M. and Sunuodula, M., (2008). *Library services for international students.* Briefing paper. London: SCONUL. https://www.sconul.ac.uk/publication/library-services-for-international-students

Shapiro, J. J. and Hughes, S. K., (1996). Information literacy as a liberal art? *EDUCOM Review*. 31(2), 31–35. http://educom.edu/web/pubs/pubHomeFrame.html

Sharkey, J. and Brandt, D. S., (2005). Integrating technology literacy and information literacy. In: D. D. Carbonara, ed. *Technology literacy applications in learning environments*. Hershey, PA: Information Science Publishing. pp. 64–74.

Shea, G. and Derry, S., (2019). Academic libraries and autism spectrum disorder: what do we know? *Journal of Academic Librarianship*. 45(4), 326–331. doi:10.1016/j.acalib.2019.04.007

Sheppard, N. and Nephin, E., (2014). Digital literacy in practice. *SCONUL Focus*. 60, 68–71. https://www.sconul.ac.uk/sites/default/files/documents/21_13.pdf

Sheu, F. and Panchyshyn, R. S., (2017). Social introduction to library services for international students: the international student reception at Kent State University Libraries. *Library Review*. 66(3), 1–31. doi:10.1108/LR-08-2016-0072

Shuler, J. A., (1996). Civic librarianship: possible new role for depository libraries in the next century? *Journal of Government Information*. 23(4), 419–425. doi:10.1016/1352-0237(96)00022-6

Shuyler, K. and Chenevey, L., (2018). Fulfilling our potential: libraries supporting civic engagement in Virginia. Virginia Libraries. 63, 1600. doi:10.21061/valib.v63i1.1600

Sidorko, P. E. and Yang, T. T., (2011). Knowledge exchange and community engagement: an academic library perspective. *Library Management*. 32(6–7), 385–397. doi:10.1108/01435121111158538

Skoyles, A., Bullock, N. and Neville, K., (2019). Developing employability skills workshops for students' Higher Education Achievement Reports. *New Review of Academic Librarianship*. 25(2–4), 190–217. doi:10.1080/13614533.2019.1622139

Solomon, L., (2013). *The librarian's nitty-gritty guide to social media.* Chicago, IL: ALA Editions.

Sreenivasulu, V., (1998). Computer and information literacy: challenges for the modern information professional at the advent of the XXI century. *Online & CD-ROM Review.* 22(6), 395–397. doi:10.1108/eb024695

Stark, M. R., (2011). Information in place: integrating sustainability into information literacy instruction. *Electronic Green Journal.* 32. https://escholarship.org/uc/item/1fz2w70p

Stephenson, E. and Caravello, P. S., (2007). Incorporating data literacy into undergraduate information literacy programs in the social sciences: a pilot project. *Reference Services Review.* 35(4), 525–540. doi:10.1108/00907320710838354

Stevens, C. and Campbell, P., (2006). Collaborating to connect global citizenship, information literacy, and lifelong learning in the global studies classroom. *Reference Services Review.* 34(4), 536–556. doi: 10.1108/00907320610716431

Stewart, J., (2005). Breaking down barriers to information: the HE library's role in widening participation. *Education Libraries Journal.* 48(2), 5–9.

Stonebraker, I., Maxwell, C., Garcia, K. and Jerrit, J., (2017), Realizing critical business information literacy: opportunities, definitions, and best practices. *Journal of Business & Finance Librarianship.* 22(2), 135–148. doi:10.1080/08963568.2017.1288519

Stover, M., Jefferson, C. and Santos, I., (2019). Innovation and creativity: a new facet of the traditional mission for academic libraries. In: J. Crum and S. S. Hines, eds. *Supporting entrepreneurship and innovation.* Bingley, UK: Emerald. pp. 135–151. doi:10.1108/S0732-067120190000040006

Street, B., (1993). Introduction: the new literacy studies. In: B. Street, ed. *Cross-cultural approaches to literacy.* Cambridge, UK: Cambridge University Press. pp. 1–21.

Swanson, T. A., (2004). A radical step: implementing a critical information literacy model. *portal: Libraries and the Academy.* 4(2), 259–273. doi:10.1353/pla.2004.0038

Swanson, T. A., (2005). Applying a critical pedagogical perspective to information literacy standards. *Community & Junior College Libraries.* 12(4), 65–77. doi:10.1300/J107v12n04_08

Swartz, P. S., Carlisle B. A. and Uyeki E. C., (2007). Libraries and student affairs: partners for student success. *Reference Services Review.* 35(1), 109–122. doi:10.1108/00907320710729409

Sweet, C. A., (2013). Information literacy and service-learning: creating powerful synergies. In: L. Gregory and S. Higgins, eds. *Information literacy and social justice: radical professional praxis.* Sacramento, CA: Library Juice Press. pp. 247–273. https://digitalcommons.iwu.edu/ames_scholarship/91

Terrile, V. C., (2021). Academic libraries supporting students experiencing homelessness and housing and basic needs insecurity. In: J. C. Skinner and M. Gross, eds. *Underserved patrons in university libraries: assisting students facing trauma, abuse, and discrimination.* Santa Barbara, CA: Libraries Unlimited. pp. 123–136.

Todorinova, L., (2018). A mixed-method study of undergraduate and first year librarian positions in academic libraries in the United States. *Journal of Academic Librarianship.* 44(2), 207–215. doi:10.1016/j.acalib.2018.02.005

Toner, J., (2019). The role of the university library in supporting international students: a survey of practices across UK universities. *Journal of Library Administration*. 59(7), 812–829. doi:10.1080/01930826.2019.1652045

Town, S., (2015). Implementing the value scorecard. *Performance Measurement and Metrics*. 16(3), 234–251. doi:10.1108/PMM-10-2015-0033

Town, S., (2018). The value scorecard. *Information and Learning Science*. 119(1/2), 25–38. doi:10.1108/ILS-10-2017-0098

Tyner, K., (1998). *Literacy in a digital world: teaching and learning in the age of information*. Mahwah, NJ: Erlbaum.

Tyrer, G., Ives, J. and Corke, C., (2013). Employability skills, the student path, and the role of the academic library and partners. *New Review of Academic Librarianship*. 19(2), 178–189. doi:10.1080/13614533.2013.787538

Vautier, L., (2014). Universal design: what is it and why does it matter? In: *Connect and thrive (Pou whakairo), LIANZA conference 2014, 12–15 October, Auckland, New Zealand*. https://lianza.org.nz/wp-content/uploads/2019/06/Vautier_L_Universal_Design.pdf

Wallace, M. K., Trkay, G., Peery, K. M. and Chivers, M., (2017). Making maker literacies: integrating academic library makerspaces into the undergraduate curriculum. *ISAM 2017, 24–27 September, Cleveland, OH*. 61. http://hdl.handle.net/10106/27017

Walsh, A., (2012). Mobile information literacy: a preliminary outline of information behaviour in a mobile environment. *Journal of Information Literacy*. 6(2), 56–69. doi:10.11645/6.2.1696

Walter, S. and Goetsch, L., (2009). *Public engagement*. SPEC Kit 312. Washington, DC: Association of Research Libraries. doi:10.29242/spec.312

Walton, G., (2018). Supporting student wellbeing in the university library: a core service or a distraction? *New Review of Academic Librarianship*. 24(2), 121–123. doi:10.1080/13614533.2017.1418240

Wang, L., (2007). Sociocultural learning theories and information literacy teaching activities in higher education. *Reference & User Services Quarterly*. 47(2), 149–158. doi:10.5860/rusq.47n2.149

Ward, D., (2006). Revisioning information literacy for lifelong meaning. *Journal of Academic Librarianship*. 32(4), 396–402. doi:10.1016/j.acalib.2006.03.006

Warnken, P., (2004). The impact of technology on information literacy education in libraries. *Journal of Academic Librarianship*. 30(2), 151–156. doi:10.1016/j.acalib.2004.01.013

Weaver, M. ed., (2008). *Transformative learning support models in higher education: educating the whole student*. London: Facet Publishing.

Weaver, M., (2013). Student journey work: a review of academic library contributions to student transition and success. *New Review of Academic Librarianship*. 19(2), 101–124. doi:10.1080/13614533.2013.800754

Whitehurst, A., (2010). Information literacy and global readiness: library involvement can make a world of difference. *Behavioral & Social Sciences Librarian*. 29(3), 207–232. doi:10.1080/01639269.2010

Whitworth, A., (2014) *Radical information literacy: reclaiming the political heart of the IL movement*. Oxford, UK: Chandos.

Wiggins, G. P. and McTighe, J., (2005). *Understanding by design*. 2nd ed. Alexandria, VA: Association for Supervision and Curriculum Development.

Wilkinson, L., (2011). Bridging the gaps: teaching transliteracy. In: *11th brick and click libraries, 4 November, Maryville, MO*. Northwest Missouri State University. pp. 27–35. https://files.eric.ed.gov/fulltext/ED526899.pdf

Wissinger, C. L., (2017). Privacy literacy: from theory to practice. *Communications in Information Literacy*. 11(2), 378–389. doi:10.15760/comminfolit.2017.11.2.9

Witek, D. and Grettano, T., (2014). Teaching metaliteracy: a new paradigm in action. *Reference Services Review*. 42(2), 188–208. doi:10.1108/RSR-07-2013-0035

Witt, S., Kutner, L. and Cooper, L., (2015). Mapping academic library contributions to campus internationalization. *College & Research Libraries*. 76(5), 587–608. doi:10.5860/crl.76.5.587

Wood, E. H., (1988). Teaching computer literacy: helping patrons to help themselves. *Medical Reference Services Quarterly*. 7(3), 45–57. doi:10.1300/J115v07n03_04

Woodard, B. S., (2003). Technology and the constructivist learning environment: implications for teaching information literacy skills. *Research Strategies*. 19(3–4), 181–192. doi:10.1016/j.resstr.2005.01.001

Yates, F., (2014). Beyond library space and place: creating a culture of community engagement through library partnerships. *Indiana Libraries*. 33(2), 53–57. https://journals.iupui.edu/index.php/IndianaLibraries/article/view/16424

Zaugg, H. and Warr, M. C., (2018). Integrating a creativity, innovation, and design studio within an academic library. *Library Management*. 39(3/4), 172–187. doi:10.1108/LM-09-2017-0091

Zhong, Y., (2012). Universal design for learning (UDL) in library instruction. *College & Undergraduate Libraries*. 19(1), 33–45. doi:10.1080/10691316.2012.652549

6

Forecasting a Future for Academic Libraries: Engagement, Community Building and Organisational Development

Tim Schlak

. . . academic libraries need to continue to adapt their roles and develop stronger relationships across the university in order to maintain and promote their relevancy to all stakeholders. Embedded roles in research and teaching, and an embedded existence through collaboration and outreach will strengthen the academic library's presence within its parent institution.

(Delaney & Bates 2015, p. 30)

Introduction

This chapter brings together several compelling yet disparate areas of scholarly focus in the library and information science (LIS) literature and research into *organisational development* and maturity to argue that library engagement, social networks and relationship and *community building* are functions of social and intellectual capital and are considered critical concerns for libraries in the 2020s. The underlying premise is a theoretical argument that the social future of academic libraries depends on a form of organisational development within academic libraries both at the individual and group level that prioritises the social agency and reach of the library as it faces an approaching transition point that requires a new contextualisation of its value proposition. For this transition to be met and overcome, organisations of all stripes must seek congruence between internal and external conditions for optimal viability. In this regard, social capital serves as a uniquely useful framework in which to conceptualise the work academic libraries do.

The type of socially driven professional behaviour and organisational outcome that I am arguing for would be a natural expression of an organisation at a high level of development and growth that, like a *learning organisation*, would be capable of transforming itself. It would do so in service to an evolving mission and values as well as external circumstances that demand responses that at times stretch the organisation past comfortable thresholds and organisational boundaries. One of the few non-monetary coins of the realm in higher education is *engagement*, which is usually parsed as *student engagement* and encompasses a wide but well-defined set of activities, behaviours and outcomes that are agreed as being foundational to student learning and development. Zepke (2018) supports a holistic, inclusive understanding of student engagement and, although he resists formal definition of the concept, his summary description can serve as a working definition: 'student engagement is a complex construct used to identify what students do, think and feel when learning and how teachers can improve that doing, thinking, and feeling in instructional settings' (Zepke 2018, p. 433).

Academic libraries have long been seen as playing an important but passive role in information provision through resources and services that meet a set of static student needs around coursework, research and learning (Kuh & Gonyea 2003). These engagement behaviours are well understood and frequently measured outside of academic libraries at nearly all institutions of learning in the USA and are a popular set of practices in many other countries as well. Yet, within academic libraries the term itself is used frequently in the literature as a buzzword that carries diminished impact outside library circles because of lack of precision and congruence with the way the term is understood (Schlak 2018). Engagement has often been used to describe aspects of a library's enterprise that align with student engagement in various ways. Schlak (2018) found that library literature on student learning and citizenship/service-based learning coincides with the broader dimensions of student engagement as discussed outside the library literature. More nebulous uses of the term describe programmatic, relational/service-focused and library-as-space conceptualisations of student learning that strain to match student engagement as it is understood by university administrators, teaching faculty and non-library staff. The existence of parallel discussions about student engagement is nothing new, as Tight (2020, p. 697) points out that researchers in the field often share their work with a limited group of 'like-minded researchers' but ignore others researching similar questions about student engagement and retention from different perspectives.

Student engagement is introduced in this chapter's framework as a central focus that, along with faculty collaboration/partnership (Atkinson 2018), can be understood as an organisational outcome of high-functioning learning organisations that are central in playing an information gap-spanning role in the lives of learners, researchers and instructors. Intellectual capital provides a complementary lens that situates the academic library's **intangible assets** such as networks of productivity, relational and social capital and capacity to harness the correct knowledge resources in questions of organisational development, which remains a concern in the LIS and practitioner literature. The stages of organisational life as a research focus outside libraries has been revived since the turn of the 21st century, with emphasis on critical (and often crisis-driven) moments in the life of the organisation where it must stretch and grow in order to survive. The impetus behind the *social future of academic libraries* that this volume advances is driven by a tacit assumption that the value proposition that academic libraries currently offer may not be a stable or safe way of justifying why we remain in the business we are in as higher education enters periods of unparalleled and unknown challenges (Grawe 2018).

Engagement and collaboration

Intellectual capital and social capital are practical frameworks that help library professionals to understand that librarianship is a set of activities and behaviours that encompass more than the mere tangible assets that comprise our services and resources. In an increasingly competitive and enrolment-driven environment (Conley 2019), academic libraries of all stripes are seeking ways of making their value and return on investment clearer to their stakeholders and reporting bodies (Murray & Ireland 2016). The LIS literature is well established with articles and treatises on the value of engaging students (Schlak 2018; Douglass & Mack 2015; Mayer & Bowles-Terry 2013; Snavely 2012; Kuh & Gonyea 2003) and collaborating with faculty on teaching and research projects (Yu et al. 2019; Chung 2010; Bakar 2009; Bennett & Gilbert 2009; Doskatsch 2003; Kotter 1999; Chu 1997; Dilmore 1996), and a number of valuable anecdotal reports have been published that continue to inspire library staff across the globe about how to refine services to heighten impact on retention (Soria, Fransen & Nackerud 2017; Murray, Ireland & Hackathorn 2016; Haddow & Joseph 2010).

The question that remains largely unanswered in much of this research has to do with the long-term ends to which we should be engaging and collaborating with students and faculty. Typically, shifting faculty needs and the demand to rationalise our existence are proffered as justification, but this chapter and the larger volume in which it appears argue that this line of reasoning lacks the holistic response that would reposition not just the librarian's work but the library as an organisation much more forcefully in the *social enterprise* that modern academic institutions of higher learning are becoming. The relevance of intellectual and social capital becomes apparent in a tightening fiscal environment for many institutions worldwide as academic libraries in some contexts, such as the USA, have seen their support fall over previous decades (Kolowich 2012).

Where academic libraries might aspire to reorganise themselves as dynamic social entities that are deeply networked into the research and learning productivity cycles of their campuses, the output of these emerging organisations will need to achieve closer alignment: with *student engagement* as understood by those outside the library's walls; and through forms of collaboration that continually reshape the organisation from within. The fundamental capacities that academic library practitioners must develop in this scenario relate to social networks and social capital, while the broader capacities that the organisation must embrace are learning and a form of *deep collaboration* that challenges static organisational boundaries. These skills and capabilities are the tools for building an engagement and collaboration culture around library services and resources that aligns with the bottom line of our institutions: a robust student engagement that positively impacts on enrolment, retention and a shared understanding that libraries not only participate in mission setting but also help to drive and stretch the organisation's sense of identity and purpose around that mission.

To move in this direction requires academic libraries and their leadership to consider the role that organisational development plays and how libraries might currently be constituted and structured for growth towards greater organisational maturity. What possibilities are inherent in frameworks that explain why academic libraries are in business and what organisational characteristics align with those reasons? And what developing social functions and operations must libraries evolve and grow into in order to take on more substantive work around an engagement and collaboration that would advance the library towards greater organisational learning?

As the type of student engagement that is argued for here exceeds the preferred usage in the academic library discourse (Schlak 2018), the deeper type of collaboration that is sought by liaison and embedded librarianship typically begins with faculty and results in meaningful, engaging contact with students (Schlak 2016). The field of collaboration in academic libraries is vast and rich and includes many more dimensions than student engagement. In a summary of the library literature on collaboration, Atkinson (2018, pp. 12–26) identified a broad range of domains of collaboration, including: general participatory approaches to library services, internal library collaboration (e.g., strategic planning), collaboration with faculty on research and teaching, collaboration with support departments, convergence of IT and library services, collaboration with students (e.g., student workers), subject/liaison librarian collaborations, embedded librarianship, information literacy instruction, research support, learning spaces collaborations, consortial collaborations (local, regional, national and international), shared procurement, shared storage and community collaborations.

Atkinson (2018, p. 11) provides one of the best summaries of collaboration by academic libraries; his explication of the concept recognises that collaboration in academic libraries is increasingly referred to as 'deeper collaboration' and involves partnerships across traditional professional boundaries with the goal of providing better value and to improve the student experience (Melling & Weaver 2012). Numerous case studies exist that look at how libraries are shifting to new internal stewardship models of resource sharing and collection building to purchase, store and provide access to materials (Hale 2016). There are also many examples of external collaborations involving project management and user engagement (Mallon & Bernstein 2015). Horton (2013, p. 66) confirms the trend towards librarians describing such ventures as 'deep collaboration' and also provides a definition of the concept: 'Deep Collaboration is two or more people or organizations contributing substantial levels of personal or organizational commitment, including shared authority, joint responsibility, and robust resources allocation, to achieve a common or mutually-beneficial goal.'

The potential territory for academic library collaboration is evidently vast and involves both internal and external partners, far and near. The number of articles on collaborative working that indicate the need to reconsider models of partnership and collaboration is telling and is taken here as assumption of broad agreement that this is a central portion of the collaborative future to which academic libraries are gravitating. Given that collaboration and partnership stretch at organisational seams and require radical changes in the way we work (Neal 2011), the development of collaboration cultures and organisational development theory converge where academic libraries seek to exceed their traditional boundaries.

Organisational development

A large literature exists that maps organisational growth patterns to stages of a business's development. This work was initially framed in the 1970s and 1980s (White & Wooten 1983; Churchill & Lewis 1983; Adizes 1979; Greiner 1972; Mueller 1972) through organismic metaphors with analogies to sequential stages that correspond to stages in an organism's lifecycle such as conception/creativity (Greiner 1972). From its humble beginnings, organisational development has focused, like those 'problems of puberty and aging', on crises and moments of evolution when the firm must confront an external (or internal) challenge such that it will either 'recognize, confront, and cope with a paramount critical concern – or it may suffer crippling . . . damage' (Lippitt & Schmidt 1967, p. 104). Later analysis of the lifecycle model came to criticise its homogeneous approach to organisations as overly simplistic and prone to reducing subtle transformations to predictable and deterministic patterns (Phelps, Adams & Bessant 2007, p. 2). This subsequent reconsideration permits a broader perspective whereby other organisation types can be included, including non-profit organisations (Simon 2001). Commonalities between the corporate and non-profit stages are common and, despite subsequent criticism, the organismic approach's stages continue to inform the organisational stages set forth even today. These often include a progression through:

1 conceiving of a business or service proposition;
2 investing in the organisation through structural and financial commitments;
3 incorporating the business around a set of products or services and sustaining growth around the initial proposition;
4 experimenting in order to review and renew the founding model by subjecting it to alternative solutions that exceed its current capacity;
5 some form of renewal that loops back into step 3 above, an organisational culmination in either decline or termination (Torbert et al. 2004; Simon 2001).

These sources advocate for an '[e]volutionary model of a corporation from founding to growth to maturity' in order to stipulate 'the organizational structure, leadership style, and strategy that support each stage of growth' (Kurian 2013, p. 219). Schein (2010) argues that organisations operate in an organic and, as time goes by, social fashion, and along the way create identifiable cultures that support their work. As these models gain in sophistication, they increasingly point to key transition moments (Nicholls-Nixon 2005) in the life-course of an organisation that are not some pre-set sequence. Rather, organisations evolve through periods of stability and instability caused by conditions that are the basis for managerial responses and practices (Phan, Baird & Blair 2014). Rooke and Torbert (1998) were early adopters of this trend and tie in a leader's own maturity along the adult stages of ego development (Cook-Greuter 2013; Kegan & Lahey 2009) to *organisational transformation* in order to argue that leadership is a critical component in ensuring that organisations make wise, strategic and transformational decisions that create a more effective organisation that is more informed about its surrounding environment than prior. In their context, leaders make themselves vulnerable to transformation so that members of the organisation can in turn do so; it is their collective transformations that together create the conditions in which the organisation itself can transform into a more evolved, capable version of itself.

This transformation lies at the heart of Senge's influential 1990 work on *learning organisations*, which bring workers together to pool their collective capacities to create results they are passionate about and that can trigger a virtuous cycle of creative responses to emerging challenges. A group's level of response can be differentiated along three factors, as the classic theory of single, double and triple loop learning elucidates:

- *Single-loop learning* 'permits the organization [. . .] to achieve its present objectives' (Argyris & Schön 1978, p. 2, quoted by Romme & Witteloostuijn 1999, p. 440) and can be summarised as knowing what the right things to do are.
- *Double-loop learning* occurs when 'error is detected and corrected in ways that involve the modification of an organization's underlying norms, policies and objectives' (Argyris and Schön 1978, p. 3) and is expressed simply as knowing how to do the right things.
- *Triple-loop learning* is manifested through 'collective mindfulness', which Romme and Witteloostuijn (1999, p. 440) indicate occurs when 'members discover how they and their predecessors have facilitated or inhibited learning, and produce new structures and strategies for learning'. This form of organisational learning is characterised as knowing how to decide what is right in any given context and moment.

Applied to academic libraries, these types of learning can be used to describe organisational performance at a high level. In such an analysis, single-loop learning would enable routine services such as technical services to function. Double-loop learning would arise infrequently, but most often during strategic planning efforts. Creating a heightened sense of ongoing awareness so that increasing numbers within the organisation see the fuller scope and impact as well as the integrity of their actions (Torbert et al. 2004, p. 55) would be a first step in moving into the realm of triple-loop learning. It would also be a highly appropriate response when an academic library faces a transformational opportunity that requires rethinking the enterprise. In fairness to academic libraries, most organisations regularly function at the level of single-loop learning, with occasional ventures into double-loop learning and with triple-loop learning seen from those organisations committed to changing their paradigm in response to a significant threat or opportunity. The most effective organisations make use of all three feedback loops in order to increase the legitimacy and effectiveness of their reach. A number of organisations, however, 'very often halt along the path to becoming learning organizations when they reach what could be transformational opportunities and challenges. Instead of transforming, they defend their current culture and structure and become rigid, lose their identity in a merger, or go out of business' (Torbert et al. 2004, p. 130).

Torbert et al.'s (2004) explanation of organisational stasis is a succinct generic restatement of the proposition advanced in this larger volume: that traditional academic libraries and their digital ecospheres are approaching an inflection point where the traditional configuration of services, resources and personnel may no longer be sufficiently compelling as a value proposition to the senior administrative stakeholders in our institutions who face a competing torrent of pressing priorities. Indeed, academic libraries' budgets in the main have not been deemed compelling priorities for budget increases; in the USA, 61% of library budgets remained flat for a period of five years and 19% saw their budgets decline (ACRL 2017). Presidents, boards of trustees and chief academic officers' eyes are on fast-moving shifts in the world of work as automation and artificial intelligence promise a radical revolution in the way students learn and how they work after graduation. And this shift that the world is undergoing heavily emphasises a form of student engagement that will stretch not just academic libraries beyond their organisational boundaries but the institutions themselves: 'But what will separate the top talent from everyone else in the workplace of tomorrow will be a flexible and growth mindset that recognizes learning never ends. The ability to communicate, work in teams, solve problems on the fly, and adapt to change are more important than ever before' (Selingo 2017, p. 4). Marcus (2019) continues: '[c]olleges and universities that fail to adapt risk joining the average of 11 per year that the bond-rating Moody's says have shut down in the last three years'.

This chapter poses no explicit solutions to these problems. Rather, it seeks to frame the problem itself in terms of organisational capacity and response, as well as in the framework of social capital. Organisational development as a formal effort focused on organisation-wide effectiveness through planned interventions arose in the LIS literature as a brief fad that began in the late 1990s (Schwartz 1997; Worrell 1995), lasted less than a decade in intensity and had particular focus on the academic library as a learning organisation. Fowler wrote in 1997 (p. 2): 'Confronted with this task [of responding to information technology and change], academic librarians struggle to understand the dimensions of the change and to find the means to accomplish it.' The advice then (and now) was for the academic library to create organisational conditions where it is 'continually preparing itself for the future by modifying its behavior, based upon knowledge it creates, acquires, or transfers through contact with its environment' (Fowler 1997, p. 3).

The topic continued to proliferate with introductory articles on the subject (Hawthorne 2004; Arabito 2004; Giesecke & McNeil 2004; Russell & Stephens 2004; Auster & Chan

2003). It has continued with the occasional work or case study appearing on the need for leadership development and leadership throughout the organisation (Al-Harrasi 2014; Crawley-Low 2013; Gilstrap 2007; Kassim 2007), on organisational change management (Holloway 2004; Limwichitr & Broady-Preston 2015; McGuidan 2012; Russell 2008), as well as on its relationship to information literacy (Hallam, Hiskens & Ong 2015). One of the primary shared findings among many of these studies is that implementing organisational change is difficult in academic libraries and that it requires that both library leadership and the broader organisation deeply engage with the concept in order to transform the library system. The general consensus remains the same as it did at the turn of the century: academic libraries would stand to benefit enormously with greater efforts towards becoming learning organisations.

One hypothesis for why the potential of the learning organisation concept still lies largely untapped is that academic libraries have incorporated a set of services and resources over the centuries that have an enduring presence even as libraries respond to technological and societal changes. Academic libraries have been very successful in translating historical responsibilities and values into modern digital terms and frameworks that remain relevant, thanks in no small part to the continued commodification of information behind paywalls. The value that academic libraries have continued to represent around this information has remained the same: the guide on the side who arranges the information into a seamless platform and can provide timely assistance as needed. In this light, embedded librarianship and the latest evolution of liaison models (Brown et al. 2017) represent true forms of experimentation that have moved our organisations forward and represent great potential as we seek to leverage the social assets that we already possess (and that represent significant proportions of our budgets in the form of library personnel salaries and wages). They are also ideal examples of academic libraries embracing aspects of the learning organisation concept where, when their learning is used to drive further change, 'people are continually learning how to learn together' (Senge 1990, p. 3).

Torbert et al.'s (2004, pp. 128–129) model of organisational maturity, presented thus far as consistent with classic stages of organisational development, continues where other models end, to include the learning organisation paradigm. The location most stable businesses find themselves in and that would characterise successful academic libraries (measured by the standards of the day) is systematic productivity, where attention is focused on procedures that accomplish the predefined task attended by structures and roles that are taken for granted, and the viability of the service or product is used as the dominant criterion of success. Beyond this stage, he describes two stages that are critical for this analysis: *social network* and *collaborative inquiry* (Torbert et al. 2004, p. 126). Until these stages, organisations have been playing by conventional rules and within traditional boundaries where the mission is known and the primary challenge is achieving congruence between structures and strategies that meet end-users' needs. As organisations evolve towards learning organisations, their members and leaders are motivated by the dawning recognition that the 'organizing mission is actually a mystery that requires the practice of

[. . .] continual researching and reformulating [. . .] if members' actions are to be truly guided by the mission' (Torbert et al. 2004, p. 150). Torbert et al. (2004, pp. 93, 150) term this a 'post-conventional' approach that recognises the absolute fluidity of human meaning-making and the relativity of human organisation, and that leads to the eventual recognition that 'it is not only the changing external environment that creates new problems for the organization, but its own way of operating'.

If one were to venture a guess as to why academic libraries have not succeeded in creating a landscape of learning organisations (Limwichitr & Broady-Preston 2015), one supposition would be that the conventional logic that persists in libraries is that the organisation's boundaries are useful for prescribing user behaviours, needs and expectations that confine and direct user needs to a defined resource ecosphere that we control. The backdrop to this struggle to assert our relevance is that we at times insist on this mission even while we grapple with existential threats like Google, declining institutional support and shifting user perspectives on libraries, as this is a long-standing way of creating congruence between mission and outcomes. The alternative would be to collectively inquire (as organisations and as a field) into alternative ways and modes of being, but this may take a significant shock to the system in the form of an otherwise insurmountable crisis and implies a collective agency that would have to be developed. This would require not only a transformation in 'the structure of an objectionable social entity, but also to transform the consciousness of many of its members' (Torbert et al. 2004, p. 152), an outcome that would first and foremost apply to leadership, but also to rank-and-file library staff members who seek to create the organisation for which they desire to work. The ask of those who demonstrate leadership in this fashion requires not only 'generating improvements in organizational outcomes, but also continual improvement in leadership awareness and practice, so that each leader's performance truly embodies the vision and strategy associated with the improved outcomes' (Torbert et al. 2004, p. 166).

In the context of academic libraries, organisational development has many implications for more significant consideration of social capital as organisational outcomes that are becoming increasingly relevant to library leaders as they seek to expand their impact.

Implications for intellectual and social capital

Social capital is an ideal expression of the type and direction of organisational development that academic libraries will need to undergo if they are to evolve into more dynamic social learning organisations. The emphasis that intellectual capital places on intangible assets not only calls to the forefront peripheral activities, services and resources, it also centralises all practices of librarianship as a unified whole that we can view as being in service to an increasingly social orientation to our work. In this framework, services, resources, personnel, organisational structure, values, organisational (and individual) assumptions, leadership and management, assessment, as well as vision and mission become forms of the organisation's intellectual capital that will support the social evolution that academic libraries will pursue in their path to continued relevance at the heart of the educational and research enterprise. The social transition has been described as the shift from transactional to collaborative approaches to our work (Jeffcoat & Colati 2018, p. 1), a description that aptly captures the overall transition away from an organisational structure of systematic productivity organised around the transactions that comprise contemporary services and resources and that are attended by rather uniform organisational hierarchies. It also describes revising the organisational structure to respond more appropriately to the challenge that a social reorientation brings (Jeffcoat & Colati 2018, p. 3).

As it is precisely engagement and collaboration that are both the input and output of an academic library that is thriving as a learning organisation, engagement and collaboration need to become values that are broadly and consistently understood within the library as well as outside. At the same time, legacy systems, services and resources are to be reviewed in light of their contribution to innovative and virtuous cycles that emerge between librarian, faculty and student. Moreover, 'planned abandonment' (Evangeliste & Furlong 2014, p. x) needs to be given consideration when services no longer pass the social litmus test. A critical need in this process is understanding the academic library's role in preserving the world's information heritage as libraries evolve to become more social.

The argument in this chapter is that the preservation of the information heritage and the social orientation of our work need not be mutually exclusive, but that the information heritage becomes an intellectual asset that is leveraged to create a more social library system that more deeply engages students and faculty in this heritage. Nonetheless, the preservation of and access to the world's heritage is an overwhelming question that must be considered, especially as libraries become more socially dynamic versions of themselves. The need for an open future that preserves our digital and print memory is increasingly seen as acute (Ovenden 2019) and as the result of collaborations at scale (Morris & Hammer 2019) that value the interdependence that characterises academic libraries (Ellis 2019). In a different context, Van de Ven (1986, p. 596) writes: 'the older, larger, and more successful organizations become, the more likely they are to have a large repertoire of structures and systems that discourage innovation'. Library collections demand significant resources for acquisitions, organisation, upkeep and storage while innovations that reposition the library, its staff, spaces, structures and services as socially oriented functions require significant operating and capital funds. And, as this chapter posits, this organisational tension is a primary driver keeping academic libraries in a state of systematic productivity that limits further organisational growth towards becoming learning organisations that can realise the possibilities inherent in a social capital model that embodies and is directed by **trust**/trustworthiness, relationships, mutuality and **reciprocity** (see Chapter 4, Social Capital and Academic Libraries) as primary functions of the library's systems. It is incumbent upon academic libraries, their leadership and their team members to understand the importance of these functions not only from within, but as seen and understood by those with whom they would partner and engage (Schlak 2015).

Features of learning organisations

The classic model of a learning organisation that Senge (1990) realised consists of five disciplines that organisations master:

1 *systems thinking* or observing the entire system, and that unifies the remaining four disciplines;
2 *personal mastery* that individuals aspire to in order to realise the vision;
3 (adapting to new) *mental models* that upset and challenge existing assumptions;
4 a shared vision that inspires others to contribute because they want to;
5 *team learning* through dialogue and listening where assumptions are suspended.

To apply learning organisations to a social future for academic libraries, these five concepts can be translated to the increasingly social nature of academic librarianship. It is not a question of recreating the wheel; the library literature is replete with innovations and successes that do precisely this. Rather, it becomes a question of the whole and degree, as illustrated in the translations and examples below.

1 *Systems thinking* is a holistic approach to observing and analysing the way various parts of an organisation interrelate and work together over time to achieve larger systematic goals. In its outcomes, systems thinking points to patterns of change and interrelationships (Senge 1990) rather than things, as the three types of loop learning reviewed above make clear. In the case of California Polytechnic State University in San Luis Obispo, systems thinking was used to contextualise workplace issues around library instruction in order to probe larger issues dealing with the nature of the organisation's information and knowledge as well as the purpose of its work (Somerville, Schader & Huston 2005). It is the attention to use of feedback in systems thinking that makes it an effective instrument in the change management toolbox.

2 *Personal mastery* is another way of stating that individuals must make themselves vulnerable to transformation. This aspect of the learning organisation has been developed in great detail by Kegan and Lahey (2009), Cook-Greuter (2013) and Torbert et al. (2004), with stages of adult ego development such as the 'socialized mind' or the 'self-authoring mind' (Kegan & Lahey 2009, p. 16). With each development around the spiral of human growth, individuals are capable of handling more and more complexity. In the library context, Cook-Greuter's (2013) and Torbert et al.'s (2004, p. 78) stages of *expert* and *achiever* would describe previous understandings of how librarians and management should function as defined by their own knowledge and ability to manipulate that knowledge and the surrounding conditions to achieve a given end. For example, a bibliographer or acquisitions librarian with deep knowledge of parts of the collection may see their expertise as

absolute and struggle to come to terms with the implications of patron-driven acquisition. Or, for instance, a director may advance project after project that improves or expands existing services and resources, but is driven by the need for accomplishments and achievements. Martin (2015) points out half of the equation when he singles out library leadership as lacking a transformational component that would help library staff and faculty to adjust to new paradigms, but the other half is individual investment on the part of team members in their own learning and practice in light of the increasing complexity that defines the profession. It would be more accurate to state that it is leadership's responsibility to attempt to create a working environment which encourages personal mastery (defined here in social capital terms as scope of network, influence therein and ability to leverage existing assets to further, possibly transformative, ends). Yet all personal transformation is just that, personal.

3   New *mental models* frequently emerge in academic libraries as a field. It is common to hear about a 'culture of assessment' (Farkas, Hinchliffe & Houk 2015) or the 'customer-driven library' (Woodward 2009, p. 8). Each individual's thought process consists of assumptions about the way the world works. When new information disconfirms those assumptions, a change management situation has arisen. In the case of a social future for academic libraries, the dynamism that it implies could conflict with static understandings of the profession that are often part and parcel of the preservation of the world's heritage and the mediating role librarians play in a transactional understanding of academic libraries.

4   A *shared vision* consists of a collectively held belief that change is necessary and that the organisation will find relevance in a digitised and connected world by leveraging services and resources in socially driven ways that are more inclusive of partnerships. For example, the University Library System of the University of Pittsburgh details guidance to libraries undergoing strategic planning to prioritise cultural change in arriving at a new, collectively held strategic vision (Brenner, Kear & Wider 2017) as central steps in moving forward with strategic planning.

5   Alignment (Senge 1990, p. 234) is when a team functions as a whole and no energy is wasted on cross-purposes. *Team learning* involves both discussion and adaptation to dealing with forces that oppose productive dialogue. When organisations function at such a level, they recognise the reality in Block's (2018, p. 55) assessment that 'we can begin to think of our *communities* as nothing more or less than a conversation [. . .] all real change is a shift in narrative'. Team learning as a discipline is a continuous exercise that the University of Maryland helped to pioneer in academic libraries in the late 1990s with their 'continuous organizational development' program (Lowry 2005).

One criticism that could be levied against this argument would be to question *social capital in service to what?* The answer may be somewhat unsatisfying for those with a deep love of problem solving. The response is social capital in service to creating and sustaining communities by facilitating information transfer and resolving knowledge gaps in the lives of researchers, instructors and students. This is the social capital that is generated externally when an organisation becomes a learning organisation that functions through a social capital lens that promotes: a shared vision; a broader social network view where the organisation's social dimensions and intangible assets are considered; new mental models of librarianship as a social endeavour; team learning that aspires to a higher level of alignment and continuous evolution; and personal growth is encouraged and accepted by team members who would take on the relational responsibilities that help libraries to thrive in the future. These could also be said to be a list (perhaps not complete) of the characteristics that will define the social future of academic libraries.

Modelling a future: organisational development and social capital in academic libraries

While the traditional responsibilities and tasks of librarianship give the profession reliable processes that have formed a somewhat uniform international profession, uncertainty attends the changes in store as institutions grapple with financial challenges, demographic changes and global uncertainty. Amid this backdrop of change, stability and certainty are necessary to provide a common understanding of just what it is we will be doing in the future. The logical response is to continue to solve the same problems we have traditionally solved but in a transposed context. This response worked well when libraries were asked to make the print to electronic transition, but it is unclear whether a transfer of similar scale and scope will suffice for the transition that a public is demanding we make as our mission as information mediators in a transactional context is imperilled. What problems might the social future of academic libraries face and what solutions can be sought? Or consider another line of questioning, which is more in alignment with the open spirit of this chapter. Peter Block (2018, p. 33) writes: 'Our love of problems runs deeper than just the joy of complaint, being right, or escape from responsibility. The core belief from which we operate is that an alternative or better future can be accomplished by more problem solving.' Yet a social future for libraries is not so much a set of problems to be solved as it is a set of communities to create, with academic libraries playing a vital role in the creation and continuation of these communities. Block (2018, p. 33) continues: 'The interest we have in problems is so intense that at some point we *take our identity from* those problems. Without them, it seems as though we would not know who we are as a community.'

New methodologies for the creation of communities have emerged that can envision a future that does not necessarily look like the past and that would be a powerful organising rationale in the appropriate context where experimentation around mission is required. *Theory U* has been advanced by Otto Scharmer (2016) as a human-centric method for *community* creation that demonstrates how 'individuals, teams, organizations and large systems can build the essential leadership capacities needed to address the root causes of today's social, environmental, and spiritual challenges' (Presencing Institute 2019). One of the critical insights that drives Theory U is that leaders must become aware of their 'blind spot' (Scharmer 2016, p. 6), or the source of internal conditions from which all of our actions arise. Leaders that seek to move their organisations forward on this journey learn to help their organisations move past their *past patterns* and see with fresh eyes the field in which they are actually working. In letting go of old assumptions, we move down a U-shaped path where leaders (in the broadest sense) make it possible for new sources of inspiration, aspirations and assumptions to arise that can be crystallised in new visions and intentions that bring new models and ways of doing and being into the world. This is a 'different quality of awareness and connection, a different way of being present with one another and with what wants to emerge' that helps us to transcend our struggle to overcome the limiting '*premodern* traditional and *modern* industrial structures [. . .] of thinking and operating' (Scharmer 2016, p. 3). These same structures could be said to be instantiated in our libraries when we assume that the traditional approach to services and resources is a sufficient role for us to play in our learning and research communities.

The beauty of this methodology is that it does not prescribe what a future looks like. Indeed, the social future of academic libraries cannot be described, as it must be lived so that its features can unfold like a community coming into being. The potential that methodologies like this offer is clear and is already being realised by eminent research institutions outside the library context, such as Theory U 'u.labs' like the one that the Swanson School of Engineering at the University of Pittsburgh launched (Jones 2019) (where the author advised on its creation). These efforts focus on '*presencing*' (Scharmer 2016, p. 165), which is a way of showing up as present in the actual present moment by sensing what the surrounding circumstance actually is. In this application, social capital generation through relationship and community building is a way of presencing and coming to appreciate a more accurate position of the actual surrounding world. For example, think of the most powerful moments of organisational life you can recall – perhaps when a consultant helped your organisation to understand what it is actually all about and what it could become – and you will begin to appreciate the power of presencing. The difference is that it is not a consultant driving conversations, but internal team members who are invested in a shared vision and using their own personal mastery to drive their individual and collective transformations.

By tapping into their collective capacity to create the change they seek, individuals and groups in libraries can become a vehicle for a future that wants to emerge through them. That is, the social future that would arrive through such a methodology would be the product of the individual and structural relationships that the academic library chooses for itself and that it brings into being. It does this by directing its intentions, resources and attention to the possibility that the social future it needs will emerge from the connections and networks the library and librarians have intentionally activated and cultivated (Atkinson 2019). This is a learning organisation in the deepest sense in that it relies on its engagement and collaboration to allow the organisation's future structure and function to emerge through dialogue with trusted stakeholders. In this scenario, cycles of mutuality and reciprocity permit the co-creation and co-evolution of the organisation according to both internal and external conditions. In this dance, traditional aspects and questions of libraries and librarianship such as information sharing, collections and services will find new life as their impact is transformed into an increasingly social context in order to meet the emerging needs of researchers, learners and teachers. These cycles would permit the continual recreation of the academic library (Lowry 2005) as it learns from others how to structure and practise its own learning internally as the foundation for further and sustained engagement and collaboration.

Conclusion

Information technology and the exponential proliferation of information have profoundly reshaped the terrain in which academic libraries function and the way their users learn, work and live with information. As colleges and universities continue to evolve in terms of strategic orientation to their markets, their missions and their mission-supporting business practices, academic libraries need to be increasingly social, innovative and bold if they are to furnish compelling value propositions in coming decades. Social orientations to our learning, teaching and research communities are a powerful and essential way of finding new relevance in the very communities that we would serve and create through our networks and relationship-building practices. Leon C. Megginson (1963, p. 4), paraphrasing Charles Darwin, writes: 'it is not the most intellectual of the species that survives; it is not the strongest that survives; but the species that survives is the one that is able best to adapt and adjust to the changing environment in which it finds itself'.

This chapter has argued that future responses to the challenges academic libraries face will increasingly be social in nature and that academic libraries will need to evolve into more mature forms along the organisational development trajectory that better account for network complexity in an ever-shifting environment. The social functions of academic libraries will become paramount as libraries as organisational entities attempt to shift their value proposition to account for the social and networked preferences and needs of their users. One of the primary values of the social academic library of the future will be as a vehicle for learning communities that want to emerge through the kinds of information sharing that the future will demand and that libraries are poised to deliver. Taking an active role in creating these communities through methodologies like Theory U would position libraries at the forefront of knowledge creation in the academy and create and sustain sufficient social capital to ensure an enduring spot in the educational and research enterprise for years to come.

References

ACRL., (2017). *2016 ACRL academic library trends & statistics*. Chicago, IL: Association of College & Research Libraries.

Adizes, I., (1979). Organizational passages – diagnosing and treating lifecycle problems of organizations. *Organizational Dynamics*. 8(1), 3–25. doi: 10.1016/0090-2616(79)90001-9

Al-Harrasi, N., (2014). The application of organizational learning theory to Oman academic library collaboration. *Procedia – Social and Behavioral Sciences*. 147, 86–90. doi:10.1016/j.sbspro.2014.07.119

Arabito, S., (2004). *Academic libraries as learning organizations: a review of the literature.* MSc independent study, Northumbria University. http://eprints.rclis.org/11715/1/academic_libraries_as_LO.pdf

Argyris, C. and Schön, D. A., (1978). *Theory in practice: increasing professional effectiveness.* San Francisco, CA: Jossey-Bass.

Atkinson, J., (2018). Collaboration and academic libraries: an overview and literature review. In: J. Atkinson, ed. *Collaboration and the academic library: internal and external, local and regional, national and internation*al. Kidlington, UK: Chandos. pp. 11–33.

Atkinson, J., (2019). Collaboration by academic libraries: what are the benefits, what are the constraints, and what do you need to do to be successful? *New Review of Academic Librarianship.* 25(1), 1–7. doi:10.1080/13614533.2019.1575016

Auster, E. and Chan, D. C., (2003). The library as a learning organization and the climate for updating in a period of rapidly changing technologies. *Proceedings of the American Society for Information Science and Technology.* 40, 158–164. doi:10.1002/meet.1450400120

Bakar, A. B. A., (2009). Partnership between librarians and faculty at a Malaysian university library: a focus group survey. *Library Philosophy and Practice.* 2009, 280. https://digitalcommons.unl.edu/libphilprac/280

Bennett, O. and Gilbert, K., (2009). Extending liaison collaboration: partnering with faculty in support of a student learning community. *Reference Services Review.* 37(2), 131–142. doi:10.1108/00907320910957170

Block, P., (2018). *Community: the structure of belonging.* 2nd ed. San Francisco, CA: Berrett-Koehler.

Brenner, A. L., Kear, R. and Wider, E., (2017). Reinvigorating strategic planning: an inclusive, collaborative process. *College & Research Libraries News.* 78(1), 28–31. doi:10.5860/crln.78.1.9604

Brown, S., Alvey, E., Danliova, E., Morgan, H. and Thomas, A., (2017). Evolution of research support services at an academic library: specialist knowledge linked by core infrastructure. *New Review of Academic Librarianship.* 24(3–4), 337–348. doi:10.1080/13614533.2018.1473259

Chu, F. T., (1997). Librarian-faculty relations in collection development. *Journal of Academic Librarianship.* 23(1), 15–20. doi:10.1016/S0099-1333(97)90067-7

Chung, H. D., (2010). Relationship building in entrepreneurship liaison work: one business librarian's experience at North Carolina State University. *Journal of Business & Finance Librarianship.* 15(3–4), 161–170. doi:10.1080/08963568.2010.487432

Churchill, N. and Lewis, V., (1983). The five stages of small business growth. *Harvard Business Review.* 61(3), 30–50. https://hbr.org/1983/05/the-five-stages-of-small-business-growth

Conley, B., (2019). The great enrollment crash: students aren't showing up. And it's only going to get worse. *The Chronicle Review.* 66(6), B6. https://www.chronicle.com/article/the-great-enrollment-crash

Cook-Greuter, S., (2013). *Nine levels of increasing embrace in ego development: A full spectrum theory of vertical growth and meaning making*. Rev. ed. [Preprint]. https://pdf4pro.com/view/a-full-spectrum-theory-of-vertical-growth-and-241f71.html

Crawley-Low, J., (2013). The impact of leadership development on the organizational culture of a Canadian academic library. *Evidence Based Library and Information Practice*. 8(4), 60–77. doi:10.18438/B8P593

Delaney, G. and Bates, J., (2015). Envisioning the academic library: a reflection on roles, relevancy and relationships. *New Review of Academic Librarianship*. 21(1), 30–51. doi:10.1080/13614533.2014.911194

Dilmore, D. H., (1996). Librarian/faculty interaction at nine New England colleges. *College & Research Libraries*. 57(3), 274–284. doi:10.5860/crl_57_03_274

Doskatsch, I., (2003). Perceptions and perplexities of the faculty–librarian partnership: an Australian perspective. *Reference Services Review*. 31(2), 111–121. doi:10.1108/00907320310476585

Douglass, K. and Mack, T., (2015). What do you give the undergraduate researcher who has everything? An academic librarian. *Journal of Academic Librarianship*. 41(5), 540–547. doi:10.1016/j.acalib.2015.07.008

Ellis, L., (2019). The future of campus libraries? 'Sticky interdependence'. *The Chronicle of Higher Education*. 66(10), A.42. https://www.chronicle.com/article/the-future-of-campus-libraries-sticky-interdependence

Evangeliste, M. and Furlong, K. eds., (2014). *Letting go of legacy services: library case studies*. Chicago, IL: ALA Editions.

Farkas, M. G., Hinchliffe, L. J. and Houk, A. H., (2015). Bridges and barriers: factors influencing a culture of assessment in academic libraries. *College & Research Libraries*. 76(2), 150–169. doi:10.5860/crl.76.2.150

Fowler, R. K., (1997). *The university library as learning organization for innovation*. PhD thesis, University of Michigan.

Giesecke, J. and McNeil, B., (2004). Transitioning to the learning organization. *Library Trends*. 53(1), 54–67. http://hdl.handle.net/2142/1718

Gilstrap, D. L., (2007). *Librarians and the emerging research library: a case study of complex individual and organizational development*. PhD thesis, University of Oklahoma. https://hdl.handle.net/11244/1274

Grawe, N. D., (2018). *Demographics and the demand for higher education*. Baltimore, MD: Johns Hopkins University Press.

Greiner, L. E., (1972). Evolution and revolution as organizations grow: a company's past has clues for management that are critical to future success. *Harvard Business Review*. 50(4), 37–46. https://hbr.org/1998/05/evolution-and-revolution-as-organizations-grow

Haddow, G. and Joseph, J., (2010). Loans, logins, and lasting the course: academic library use and student retention. *Australian Academic & Research Libraries*. 41(4), 233–244. doi:10.1080/00048623.2010.10721478

Hallam, G., Hiskens, A. and Ong, R., (2015). Conceptualising the learning organisation: creating a maturity framework to develop a shared understanding of the library's role in literacy and learning. *Bibliothek Forschung und Praxis*. 39(1), 61–72. doi:10.1515/bfp-2015-0007

Hale, D. ed., (2016). *Shared collections: collaborative stewardship*. Chicago, IL: ALA Editions.

Hawthorne, P., (2004). Redesigning library human resources: integrating human resources management and organizational development. *Library Trends*. 53(1), 172–186. http://hdl.handle.net/2142/1719

Holloway, K., (2004). The significance of organizational development in academic research libraries. *Library Trends*. 53(1), 5–16. https://hdl.handle.net/2142/1721

Horton, V., (2013). Going "all-in" for deep collaboration. *Collaborative Librarianship*. 5(2), 65–69. doi:10.29087/2013.5.2.01

Jeffcoat, H. and Colati, G., (2018). From transaction to collaboration: scholarly communications design at UConn Library. *Insights*. 31, 17. doi:10.1629/uksg.405

Jones, S., (2019). Pitt's U.lab hub hopes to make the world better. *University Times*. 25 September. https://www.utimes.pitt.edu/news/pitt-s-ulab-hub-hopes

Kassim, N. A., (2007). Team learning in a learning organization: the practices of team learning among university librarians in Malaysia. *Malaysian Journal of Library and Information Sciences*. 12(1), 55–64. https://mjlis.um.edu.my/index.php/MJLIS/article/view/6987

Kegan, R. and Lahey, L. L., (2009). *Immunity to change: how to overcome it and unlock the potential in yourself and your organization*. Boston, MA: Harvard Business Press.

Kolowich, S., (2012). Smaller servings for libraries. *Inside Higher Ed*. 21 February. https://www.insidehighered.com/news/2012/02/21/library-budgets-continue-shrink-relative-university-spending

Kotter, W. R., (1999). Bridging the great divide: improving relations between librarians and classroom faculty. *Journal of Academic Librarianship*. 25(4), 294–303. doi:10.1016/S0099-1333(99)80030-5

Kuh, G. D. and Gonyea, R. M., (2003). The role of the academic library in promoting student engagement in learning. *College & Research Libraries*. 64(4), 256–282. doi:10.5860/crl.64.4.256

Kurian, G. T., (2013). *The AMA dictionary of business and management*. New York: Amacom.

Limwichitr, S. and Broady-Preston, J., (2015). A discussion of problems in implementing organizational cultural change: developing a learning organization in university libraries. *Library Review*. 64(6/7), 480–488. doi:10.1108/LR-10-2014-0116

Lippitt, G. L. and Schmidt, W. H., (1967). Crises in a developing organization. *Harvard Business Review*. 45(6), 102–112. https://hbr.org/1967/11/crises-in-a-developing-organization

Lowry, C. B., (2005). Continuous organizational development – teamwork, learning leadership, and measurement. *portal: Libraries and the Academy*. 5(1), 1–6. doi:10.1353/pla.2005.0010

Mallon, M. and Bernstein, S., (2015). Collaborative learning technologies. *Instructional Technologies Tips and Trends*. (Winter). https://acrl.ala.org/IS/wp-content/uploads/2014/05/winter2015.pdf

Marcus, J., (2019). Radical survival strategies for struggling colleges. *New York Times*. 10 October. https://www.nytimes.com/2019/10/10/education/learning/colleges-survival-strategies.html

Martin, J., (2015). Perceptions of transformational leadership in academic libraries. *Journal of Library Administration*. **56**(3), 266–284. doi:10.1080/01930826.2015.1105069

Mayer, J. and Bowles-Terry, M., (2013). Engagement and assessment in a credit-bearing information literacy course. *Reference Services Review*. **41**(1), 62–79. doi:10.1108/00907321311300884

McGuidan, G. S., (2012). Addressing change in academic libraries: a review of classical organizational theory and implications for academic libraries. *Library Philosophy and Practice*. **2012**, 755. https://digitalcommons.unl.edu/libphilprac/755

Megginson, L. C., (1963). Lessons from Europe for American business. *Southwestern Social Science Quarterly*. **44**(1), 3–13.

Melling, M. and Weaver, M. eds., (2012). *Collaboration in libraries and learning environments*. London: Facet Publishing.

Morris, J. and Hammer, S., (2019). Consortia taking responsibility for their technology ecosystem: cultivating agency with emerging community owned solutions. *Journal of Library Administration*. **59**(1), 74–85. doi:10.1080/01930826.2018.1549411

Mueller, D. C., (1972). A life cycle theory of the firm. *Journal of Industrial Economics*. **20**(3), 199–219. doi:10.2307/2098055

Murray, A., Ireland, A. and Hackathorn, J., (2016). The value of academic libraries: library services as a predictor of student retention. *College & Research Libraries*. **77**(5), 631–642. doi:10.5860/crl.77.5.631

Murray, A. L. and Ireland, A. P., (2016). Communicating library impact on retention: a framework for developing reciprocal value propositions. *Journal of Library Administration*. **57**(3), 311–326. doi:10.1080/01930826.2016.1243425

Neal, J. G., (2011). Advancing from kumbaya to radical collaboration: redefining the future research library. *Journal of Library Administration*. **51**(1), 66–76. doi:10.1080/01930826.2011.531642

Nicholls-Nixon, C. L., (2005). Rapid growth and high performance: the entrepreneur's "impossible dream?" *Academy of Management Executive*. **19**(1), 77–89. doi:10.5465/ame.2005.15841955

Ovenden, R., (2019). Open future: we must fight to preserve digital information. *The Economist*. 21 February. https://www.economist.com/open-future/2019/02/21/we-must-fight-to-preserve-digital-information

Phan, T. N., Baird, K. and Blair, B., (2014). The use and success of activity-based management practices at different organizational life cycle stages. *International Journal of Production Research*. **52**(3), 787–803. doi:10.1080/00207543.2013.839893

Phelps, R., Adams, R. and Bessant, J., (2007). Life cycles of growing organizations: a review with implications for knowledge and learning. *International Journal of Management Reviews*. **9**(1), 1–30. doi:10.1111/j.1468-2370.2007.00200.x

Presencing Institute., (2019). Theory U: leading from the future as it emerges. *Presencing Institute*. https://www.presencing.org/aboutus/theory-u

Romme, A. G. L. and Witteloostuijn, A. van., (1999). Circular organizing and triple loop learning. *Journal of Organizational Change Management*, 12(5), 439–454. doi:10.1108/09534819910289110

Rooke, D. and Torbert, W. R., (1998). Organizational transformation as a function of CEO's developmental stage. *Organizational Development Journal*. 16(1), 11–28.

Russell, K., (2008). Evidence-based practice and organizational development in libraries. *Library Trends*. 56(4), 910–930. http://hdl.handle.net/2142/9499

Russell, K. and Stephens, D. eds., (2004). *Organizational development and leadership. Library Trends*. 53(1), 1–264. https://www.ideals.illinois.edu/bitstream/handle/2142/1031/LT-53-1.pdf

Scharmer, C. O., (2016). *Theory U: leading from the future as it emerges; the social technology of presencing*. 2nd ed. San Francisco, CA: Berrett-Koehler.

Schein, E. H., (2010). *Organizational culture and leadership*. 4th ed. San Francisco, CA: Jossey-Bass.

Schlak, T., (2015). Social capital and leadership in academic libraries: the broader exchange around 'buy-in'. *Library Management*. 36(6/7), 394–407. doi:10.1108/LM-11/2014-0133

Schlak, T., (2016). Social capital as operative in liaison librarianship: librarian participants' experiences of faculty engagement as academic library liaisons. *Journal of Academic Librarianship*. 42(1), 411–422. doi:10.1016/j.acalib.2017.09.005

Schlak, T., (2018). Academic libraries and engagement: a critical contextualization of the library discourse on engagement. *Journal of Academic Librarianship*. 2018, 44(1), 133–139. doi:10.1016/j.acalib.2017.09.005

Schwartz, C. A., (1997). *Restructuring academic libraries: organizational development in the wake of technological change*. Chicago, IL: Association of College and Research Libraries.

Selingo, J. J., (2017). *The future of work and what it means for higher education. Part 1: The changing workplace and the dual threats of automation and a gig economy*. Pleasanton, CA: Workday. https://forms.workday.com/content/dam/web/en-us/documents/reports/future-of-work-part-1.pdf

Senge, P. M., (1990). *The fifth discipline: the art and practice of the learning organization*. New York: Doubleday.

Simon, J. D., (2001). *The five stages of nonprofit organizations: where you are, where you're going, and what to expect when you get there*. Saint Paul, MN: Amherst H. Wilder Foundation.

Snavely, L., (2012). Engaging undergraduates with the academic library. In: L. Snavely, ed. *Student engagement and the academic library*. Santa Barbara, CA: Libraries Unlimited. pp. 1–10.

Somerville, M. M., Schader, B. and Huston, M. E., (2005). Rethinking what we do and how we do it: systems thinking strategies for library leadership. *Australian Academic & Research Libraries*. 36(4), 214–227. doi:10.1080/00048623.2005.10755311

Soria, K. M., Fransen, J. and Nackerud, S., (2017). The impact of academic library resources on undergraduates' degree completion. *College & Research Libraries*. 78(6), 812–823. doi:10.5860/crl.78.6.812

Tight, M., (2020). Student retention and engagement in higher education. *Journal of Further and Higher Education*. 44(5), 689–704. doi:10.1080/0309877X.2019.1576860

Torbert, B. et al., (2004). *Action inquiry: the secret of timely and transforming leadership*. San Francisco, CA: Berrett-Koehler.

Van de Ven, A., (1986). Central problems of the management of innovation. *Management Science*. 32(5), 590–607. doi:10.1287/mnsc.32.5.590

White, L. P. and Wooten, K. C., (1983). Ethical dilemmas in various stages of organizational development. *Academy of Management Review*. 8(4), 690–697. doi:10.2307/258270

Woodward, J., (2009). *Creating the customer-driven academic library*. Chicago, IL: American Library Association.

Worrell, D., (1995). The learning organization: management theory for the information age or new age fad? *Journal of Academic Librarianship*. 21(5), 351–357. doi:10.1016/0099-1333(95)90060-8

Yu, T., Chao-chen, C., Khoo, C., Butdisuwan, S., Ma, L., Sacchanand, C. and Tuamsuk, K., (2019). Faculty–librarian collaborative culture in the universities of Hong Kong, Singapore, Taiwan, and Thailand: a comparative study. *Malaysian Journal of Library & Information Science*. 24(1), 97–121. doi:10.22452/mjlis.vol24no1.6

Zepke, N., (2018). Student engagement in neo-liberal times: what is missing? *Higher Education Research and Development*. 37(2), 433–446. doi:10.1080/07294360.2017.1370440

Part 2
Theory into Practice

7
Knowledge and Networks: Subject Specialists and the Social Library

James Kessenides and Michael Brenes

Introduction

What is the role of the subject specialist in the 21st-century academic library? What value does subject knowledge confer, and how best is such expertise deployed? These questions have been much discussed in academic librarianship, as the emergence of new technologies and services has made the subject expert appear by turns a quaint and dubious creature. Here we propose a distinct approach to this set of issues. As a librarian and an archivist, we offer a joint perspective, starting with the term 'subject specialist' itself, which has come simply to connote a liaison librarian even though subject knowledge is often part of an archivist's training and experience too. The profession tends to locate the subject specialist in a subject-based liaison department, despite the leveraging of subject knowledge by a wide variety of information professionals – liaison librarians, as well as archivists, curators and others – in today's academic library. We therefore offer an expanded view of subject specialty and focus on the similar ways liaison librarians and archivists use subject knowledge. In particular, we situate our discussion within the frame of social capital theory and we suggest channels whereby subject specialists (a) contribute to the teaching, learning and research missions of their home institutions and (b) create social capital *within* the library, or in other words across the academic library's own organisational units.

Our chapter first places subject specialty in historical perspective before then considering some 21st-century job trends and relevant professional literature. Ultimately, we draw on our own experiences in outreach, instruction and collection development in order to try to offer a fresh perspective on subject expertise, and to propose the value of subject knowledge for the social future of academic libraries.

The social location of subject experts in the academic library

Notions of **social capital** and studies seeking to elaborate it have proliferated since the 1990s. Definitions are forthcoming from multiple disciplines, but especially – and sometimes dissonantly – from economics and management, political science and sociology. The *Oxford English Dictionary* (OED 2009) draws on all of these fields when it defines *social capital* as 'the interpersonal networks and common civic values which influence the infrastructure and economy of a particular society; the nature, extent, or value of these'. For our consideration here of social capital in the context of academic libraries, we find the sociological framework to be the salient one. 'The advantage created by a person's location in a structure of relationships', writes Ronald S. Burt (2005, p. 4), 'is known as social capital.' Also useful is the more intricate definition put forward by Pierre Bourdieu: 'Social capital is the sum of the **resources**, actual or virtual, that accrue to an individual or a group by virtue of possessing a durable network of more or less institutionalized relationships of mutual acquaintance and recognition' (Bourdieu & Wacquant 1992, p. 119).

Bourdieu's take reminds us that the benefits of social capital can be channelled collectively – a point to which we will return later. A final perspective worth noting at the outset, put forward by the sociologist James Coleman, is that social capital is intangible because 'it exists in the relations among persons' (as cited by Brown & Lauder 2000, p. 227). Location within a **social network**, particular as well as shared situations and the quality of being both concrete and abstract all frame our approach to social capital.

In the professional literature of library and information science, theories of social capital occupy a fairly new place. As Tim Schlak (2016, p. 412) writes: 'Social capital as a practical and operative concept is an under-researched concept in the literature of academic libraries but presents a useful paradigm for exploring the often amorphous and sometimes invisible nature of the individual relationships that partly constitute a successful liaison program.' Schlak (2016) is particularly interested in examining the relationships between liaison librarians and faculty. Undertaking a series of interviews with academic librarians to understand such factors as **trust** and trustworthiness (see Schlak 2016, p. 414), he concludes that 'the strength of ties and networks may play an increasingly important role … in the viability of the academic library as a vital player in the organizational structure of today's institutions of higher education' (Schlak 2016, p. 420). Likewise, Paul Bracke (2015) addresses the role of liaison librarians within the 'engaged' 21st-century academic library (see Díaz 2017), bringing to his analysis the perspectives of social capital. 'Being able to characterize the roles and placement of librarians within broader academic networks', Bracke (2015, slide 18) stresses, 'complements other approaches to measuring liaison productivity and documenting the relational capital of the library'. Bracke (2015), Schlak (2016) and others focus, then, on the relation of liaison librarians to faculty in articulating this nascent area of study among library and information scientists. Below, we will offer our thoughts on this too, along with proposing some ways of homing in on the social capital that is generated within the library itself by subject experts.

But first we will turn to subject specialty viewed historically. The professionalisation of academic libraries over the course of the 20th century as it came to be centred on the emergence of the Master of Library Science (MLS) credential will be a focus of our narrative.

Librarians, archivists and subject specialty

In the early 21st century, changes in both the research landscape and the research library have prompted many reflections on the role of the subject specialist (see Jaguszewski &

Williams 2013; Kenney 2014; Marcum 2012; Miller & Pressley 2015; Rockenbach et al. 2015). Often these assessments have pointed to new kinds of collaborations, including novel partnerships between subject specialists and functional specialists. We sense such possibilities, too, within the social networks formed and social capital wielded by subject and functional specialists working together. But first we offer a historical perspective from before the emergence of networked technologies in the 1990s–2000s and even before the rise of computerised technologies in the 1960s–1970s. For discussions of subject knowledge among academic librarians have a surprisingly deep history, and taking a look at this history allows us to grasp just how long the social future of academic libraries has been in the making.

Since the late 19th century, the professionalisation of libraries and archives has invited ambiguity and tension between conventional subject expertise, on the one hand, and new forms of expertise needed to run a library, on the other. Over the course of the 20th century, as programs of graduate study gained legitimacy first among librarians and then among archivists, questions about appropriate knowledge, training and skills persisted. Funding from the Carnegie Corporation underwrote the creation in 1926 of the influential Graduate Library School at the University of Chicago, where conventional subject experts were to train students in the new discipline of library science, thus embedding in the very origins of the profession a dialectic of subject-versus-library expertise (Horrocks 1993, p. 504). In the interwar years, a similar dialectic surfaced within the archival profession, even as archivists were often to remain historians by training in the decades ahead. In a report submitted to the then recently formed Society of American Archivists (SAA), historian Samuel Flagg Bemis conveyed condescension toward librarians when he wrote in 1939 (p. 157, emphasis in the original):

> A course in "library science" would be useful, particularly for purposes of cataloguing and for the arrangement of libraries auxiliary to archival practice. But there is a distinct danger in turning over archives to librarians who are not at the same time erudite critical historical scholars. They tend to put the emphasis upon cataloguing and administration, on mechanics rather than archival histology and the sacred *principe de provenance*, to which they are usually oblivious.

Bemis (1939, p. 158) proposed a two-fold hierarchy for the profession in which what he called 'archivists of the first class' would be holders of the doctorate in history. This exclusionary vision was challenged by Margaret Cross Norton, long-serving Illinois State Archivist and president of the SAA from 1943 to 1945. Norton argued that historical training was ancillary to record keeping. In 1940, for example, she declared: 'Archivists today must subordinate their scholarly inclinations to administrative work' (as cited in Jimerson 2001, p. 48). The early outlines of distinguishing subject from functional expertise were, then, clear – for archivists as well as for librarians.

The key point of convergence in the training paths of librarians and archivists in the USA proved to be the legitimation after 1945 of graduate degree programs awarding the

MLS as the requisite credential for entry into both professions. This occurred earlier among librarians (c. 1950s) than among archivists (c. 1970s), but in neither case did it dispatch ongoing questions about the kinds of specialisation needed within libraries and archives. The data collected by Perry D. Morrison for his *The career of the academic librarian* in 1969 indicated continuing tensions between the 'scholarly' and the 'technical' aspects of library training (see, for example, Morrison 1969, p. 35). Surveying three broad groups of library professionals (leaders, managers and non-supervisory personnel), Morrison (1969, p. 36, Table 19) asked his respondents what areas they would prioritise in library science education. The replies here displayed a felt need to balance a variety of library skills with subject knowledge in the disciplines, as the number one answer was 'Practical help in the techniques of reference, circulation, acquisitions, cataloging, etc.', followed as the number two answer by 'General acquaintance with important titles in each of the broad curricular fields – social science, humanities, science, technology' (Morrison 1969, p. 143).

Varied opinions on professional training could likewise be found among archivists in roughly the same time period. Rather than debate (as did librarians) the internal components of library science curricula, archivists tended to pit library science programs against graduate degree programs in history. In 1965, T. R. Schellenberg judged: 'Library schools are the proper places in which to provide archival training' (as cited in Martin 1994, p. 555). In the ensuing years, the MLS did gradually gain traction among archivists, though still almost 15 years later, Nancy E. Peace and Nancy Fisher Chudacoff (1979, p. 458) expressed dissatisfaction that 'archivists have shied away from prescribing whether archives education should take place in history departments or library schools'. The authors then forthrightly offered their own advice: 'We believe that the master of library science (M.L.S.) program, with an increased archives component, can provide the most effective education for archivists and librarians' (Peace & Chudacoff 1979, p. 458). So it was that archivists joined librarians in emphasising the educational prerogatives of the MLS by the late 20th century.

Despite the shared post-war trajectory toward the MLS among both librarians and archivists, the Association of Research Libraries (ARL) proceeded to distinguish librarians as 'subject specialists' from archivists as 'functional specialists'. This provides a final piece of broad historical context for today's discussions of subject expertise. For years after its first regular appearance in the mid-1970s, the ARL Annual Salary Survey defined subject specialists as those 'who most commonly help build collections and offer specialized reference and bibliographic services' (this example taken from Fretwell 1980, p. 6). The Survey left archivists out of its professional categorisations until 1985, when *Archivist* officially appeared as a sub-category of *Functional Specialist* (Fretwell 1986, p. 52, see 'Instructions for Optional Categories'). Since then, subject specialists have remained synonymous with bibliographers and their latter-day successors (i.e., liaison librarians) as new areas of expertise tied to information technologies and computerised data have emerged in what Stanley J. Wilder (2003, pp. 20–23) has termed 'the rise of the functional specialist'.

Wilder (2003, pp. 21–22) noted that the 'most dramatic change' in hiring from 1985 to 2000 was 'the burgeoning number of functional specialists', by which he meant 'non-supervisory positions that require information-technology related expertise'. By the time of Wilder's (2003) analysis, the stage had thus been set for a reconsideration of the role of subject knowledge. Since then attention has often focused on the changing roles of subject specialists and functional specialists in academic libraries, with the role of the traditional subject expert seeming more and more uncertain. One recent report notes:

> Today's library leaders want subject specialists and liaisons to provide strong engagement and valued services. While many libraries have turned once again to hiring PhD's who can bring deep subject expertise to these roles, others are seeing that subject expertise may not be the only, or in some cases most important, ingredient in formulating a valuable liaison program.
>
> (Cooper and Schonfeld 2017, p. 3; cf. Frenkel et al. 2018)

As a backdrop, ARL has introduced new professional categorisations to reflect changing trends. For instance, starting with the 2012–13 Annual Salary Survey, the entire suite of information technology-related positions previously classed under the heading *Functional Specialist* have appeared instead under the new ARL heading *Digital Specialist* (Kyrillidou & Morris 2013, pp. 121–122).

Clearly, the research landscape has changed a good deal since the 1990s – indeed, since the 1940s. The decades-long history whereby the MLS emerged as the professional credential of choice in academic libraries seems to us significant for thinking about social capital theory today. Establishing the MLS credential removed subject expertise to the external networks conventionally associated with the disciplines – networks that can now be approached as a matter of the social capital residing inside the library. All of which leads us to say a few words about how we define 'subject specialist'.

Specialisation is a relative term and the possibility is always present that librarians and archivists will field questions beyond the realm of what they know in a factual sense. We focus, then, on knowledge of the research practices of a discipline, including first-hand familiarity with the research process, as a main defining factor. Such knowledge may often still remain relative; but, whether gained through formal or informal training, it allows liaison librarians and archivists (and others too, such as curators) to bring social capital to the novel constellation of user research needs in the digital age. It is the source of networks formed both within the library and across campus, and it helps to foster the sorts of collaborations coming to be at the forefront of the 21st-century research library. In the final section of this chapter, we put forward some of these ways that subject knowledge can fruitfully be viewed as social and intellectual capital in support of teaching, learning and research, and as a contribution to the organisation and operation of the academic library itself.

From propinquity to intangible assets: reflections on the value of subject expertise

Subject specialists in the 21st-century academic library enjoy many opportunities to engage with partners both within the library and throughout campus. In doing so, they help to generate social capital for the entire organisation, and they deploy intellectual assets perhaps difficult to identify or measure but nonetheless real ('**intangible assets**'). As Bracke (2016, p. 138) notes (referring especially to an earlier article in the *California Management Review*): 'Social network theory provides a framework for understanding the invisible work of relationship building that is critical to the success of new liaison models.' Physical proximity, or **propinquity**, certainly plays a key role in the formation of social networks too (see Kadushin 2012, p. 18), so that a continuum ranging from the observable to the seemingly hidden bases of the social value of subject expertise in the academic library will be outlined here.

Value 1

Subject expertise invites a wide variety of connections and collaborations in outreach and instruction. It aids classroom pedagogy by informing the selection of materials (through disciplinary knowledge) and the choice of search techniques (through methodological familiarity) to be shared with students during an instruction session. Such contributions 'provide shared meaning and representations and are bolstered by shared codes, languages, and narratives' (Schlak 2016, p. 414). While trust may already be present in outreach interactions where a librarian's or archivist's subject knowledge is known, demonstrating subject knowledge in classroom instruction fosters trust in a practical way. And, as Schlak (2016, p. 414) points out: 'Trust and trustworthiness are essential preconditions for the development of social capital.'

The value of subject expertise extends not only to faculty and students, but also to colleagues within the library, as when subject specialists collaborate with functional specialists, including digital humanities (DH) and other digital scholarship support specialists in classroom teaching and project-based research support. Indeed, social capital theory reminds us of the 'strength of **weak ties**' (see Johnson 2015). As summarised by Catherine A. Johnson (2015, para. 4; the original work is that of M. S. Granovetter): 'The advantage of weak ties is that they link people into networks containing new information that they are unable to attain from close ties. Having weak ties in your network, therefore, could be the social capital that gives you an advantage over others.'

In the context of the academic library, subject specialists who might usually work most closely with one another build social capital when collaborating with functional specialists, and what might otherwise appear as independent skillsets together propel an expanded and meaningful set of services for the research university. Put differently, we have an instance of **intellectual capital**, or of the 'intangible capacity to produce, store, curate, and transmit knowledge as well as the capability to operate as a social *collectivity*' (Schlak 2016, p. 414, emphasis added).

Value 2

Subject expertise contributes to the appraisal and acquisition, maintenance and management of a research library's collections. Here we are pointing once more to the intangible assets offered by subject specialists, as when the latter assess and anticipate the research value of library materials for current and future researchers. While professional literature exists regarding the assessment of liaison librarians (see Mack & White 2014), there is less discussion to date of intangible assets. On some level, this reflects the as yet relatively nascent consideration of intangible assets in library science research in the US context (see Corrall 2014). However, Sheila Corrall (2014, p. 22) has noted:

> One specific theme in the academic and practitioner discussion of evaluation methodologies is a resurgence of interest in examining the intangible assets (IAs) of library and information services (LIS), especially to prove the worth of library and information workers (an area of investment that is particularly vulnerable as a result of the global economic downturn [of 2008]). Several commentators propose that assessment of library value in the knowledge economy should include consideration of intangible (knowledge-based) assets to give a fuller picture of value for stakeholders.

We agree, and suggest that the role of subject knowledge in collection development – whether general or special collections – represents such an intangible asset. This holds especially true at a time of increasing interest in text mining and other novel uses of materials at scale among humanists and humanistic social scientists. Input from archivists on, say, the selection of archival materials for *digitisation*, or from liaison librarians on the appropriate historical newspaper data sets for computerised analysis by researchers, lends the academic library more value. Here, then, we once again observe a relationship between subject specialists and functional specialists that is both fluid and collaborative in contributing to the academic research mission.

Value 3

Subject knowledge remains an important ingredient in the provision of the distinctly digital, networked services that are defining the 21st-century academic library. We have hinted at such services above (e.g., collaborations around DH course and project support), but these examples only begin to indicate the whole range of current research needs. Reviewing a number of widely cited reports on the future of the liaison librarian model, Bracke (2016, p. 137) reiterates that such writings consistently discussed 'the need, not only for transformed subject specialists, but also for new types of functional specialists in teaching, scholarly communication, research data management, and so forth'.

The contributions of subject specialists here derive from their knowledge of the research process – the concepts and methods of a discipline, the evidentiary expectations of that same discipline and, by extension, the kinds of questions to be asked when addressing new service areas such as scholarly communications and publishing. These contributions result even more from familiarity with research practices (e.g., What sort of evidence is sufficient and persuasive for a claim to be made?) than they do from specific content knowledge (e.g., What happened during World War I?). This holds true for additional new areas of library work like metadata creation (see Corrall 2015, pp. 227–229) – all rich fields for further elaboration of collaborative models of library support that join both subject and functional expertise.

Conclusion

We have stressed the history of subject and functional roles in the academic library because that history helps us to understand the social future of academic libraries more clearly. The current moment is certainly a transitional one. As Corrall (2015, p. 228) puts it: 'The skillset required by contemporary subject liaisons is a continuing subject for debate. In addition to the perennial question of how much subject knowledge is needed for liaison work, and the pedagogical know-how needed to support learning and teaching, the competencies required to provide effective support for research in the current environment have become a major concern.'

Perhaps the role of the subject specialist will remain always in flux, yet we hope to have established the continuing relevance of subject knowledge when viewed in the context of social capital theory, and to have highlighted some of the 'intangible assets and efforts', as Bracke (2016, p. 135) observes, 'that are not well-accounted for in assessment models'. Whether in support of teaching, collections or any of the array of digital services situated within the academic library, subject specialists will be found among archivists as well as liaison librarians, despite the definitional narrowing of 'subject specialist' that occurred mostly in the 1970s and 1980s. Today librarians and archivists with subject knowledge can provide social capital for the networked research environment of the digital age. Challenges will no doubt remain. As Bourdieu (1986, p. 250) commented: 'The reproduction of social capital presupposes an unceasing effort of sociability'. But such is also the promise of the social future of academic libraries.

References

Bemis, S. F., (1939). The training of archivists in the United States. *The American Archivist.* 2(3), 154–161. doi:10.17723/aarc.2.3.r1ht0v6740rp3053

Bourdieu, P., (1986). The forms of capital. In: J. G. Richardson, ed. *Handbook of theory and research for the sociology of education*. New York: Greenwood Press. pp. 241–258.

Bourdieu, P. and Wacquant, L. J. D., (1992). *An invitation to reflexive sociology*. Chicago, IL: University of Chicago Press.

Bracke, P., (2015). Social networks and relational capital in library service assessment. In: *11th Northumbria international conference on performance measurement in libraries and information services, 20–22 July, Edinburgh, UK*. https://www.slideshare.net/paulbracke/social-networks-and-relational-capital-northumbria

Bracke, P., (2016). Social networks and relational capital in library service assessment. *Performance Measurement and Metrics*. 17(2), 134–141. doi:10.1108/PMM-04-2016-0019

Brown, P. and Lauder, H., (2000). Human capital, social capital, and collective intelligence. In: S. Baron, J. Field and T. Schuller, eds. *Social capital: critical perspectives*. New York: Oxford University Press. pp. 226–242.

Burt, R. S., (2005). *Brokerage and closure: an introduction to social capital*. New York: Oxford University Press.

Cooper, D. and Schonfeld, R. C., (2017). *Rethinking liaison programs for the humanities*. New York: Ithaka S+R. doi:10.18665/sr.304124

Corrall, S., (2014). Library service capital: the case for measuring and managing intangible assets. In: S. Faletar Tanacković and B. Bosančić, eds. *Assessing libraries and library users and use: proceedings of the 13th international conference Libraries in the Digital Age (LIDA), 16–20 June, Zadar, Croatia*. pp. 21–32. http://ozk.unizd.hr/lida/files/LIDA_2014_Proceedings.pdf

Corrall, S., (2015). Capturing the contribution of subject librarians: applying strategy maps and balanced scorecards to liaison work. *Library Management*. **36**(3), 223–234. doi:10.1108/LM-09-2014-0101

Díaz, J., (2017). Engaging with engagement: an administrator's perspective. *portal: Libraries and the Academy*. **17**(4), 655–664. doi:10.1353/pla.2017.0038.

Frenkel, A., Moxham, T., Cook, D. B. and Marshall, B., (2018). Moving from subject specialists to a functional model. *Research Library Issues*. **294**, 39–71. doi:10.29242/rli.294.5

Fretwell, G. comp., (1980). *ARL annual salary survey 1978–1979*. Washington, DC: Association of Research Libraries. http://www.libqual.org/documents/admin/2012/ARL_Stats/1978–79ss.pdf

Fretwell, G. comp., (1986). *ARL annual salary survey 1985*. Washington, DC: Association of Research Libraries. http://www.libqual.org/documents/admin/2012/ARL_Stats/1985ss.pdf

Horrocks, N., (1993). Library education: history. In: R. Wedgeworth, ed. *World encyclopedia of library and information services*. Chicago, IL: American Library Association. pp. 503–509.

Jaguszewski, J. M. and Williams, K., (2013). *New roles for new times: transforming liaison roles in research libraries*. Washington, DC: Association of Research Libraries. https://www.arl.org/wp-content/uploads/2015/12/nrnt-liaison-roles-revised.pdf

Jimerson, R. C., (2001). Margaret C. Norton reconsidered. *Archival Issues*. **26**(1), 41–62. http://digital.library.wisc.edu/1793/43741

Johnson, C. E., (2015). Social capital and library information science research: definitional chaos or coherent research enterprise? *Information Research*. **20**(4), 690. http://www.informationr.net/ir/20-4/paper690.html

Kadushin, C., (2012). *Understanding social networks: theories, concepts, and findings*. New York: Oxford University Press.

Kenney, A. R., (2014). *Leveraging the liaison model: from defining 21st century research libraries to implementing 21st century research universities*. New York: Ithaka S+R. https://sr.ithaka.org/wp-content/uploads/2014/03/SR_BriefingPaper_Kenney_20140322.pdf

Kyrillidou, M. and Morris, S. comps., (2013). *ARL annual salary survey 2012–2013*. Washington, DC: Association of Research Libraries. https://publications.arl.org/ARL-Annual-Salary-Survey-2012–2013

Mack, D. C. and White, G. W., (2014). *Assessing liaison librarians: documenting impact for positive change*. Chicago, IL: Association of College and Research Libraries. https://www.cmich.edu/library/Ebooks/9780838987094_liaisons.pdf

Marcum, D. B., (2012). Do librarians need PhDs? *Information Outlook*. **16**(5), 33–35.

Martin, R. S., (1994). The development of professional education for librarians and archivists in the United States: a comparative essay. *The American Archivist*. 57(3), 544–558. doi:10.17723/aarc.57.3.116720kn81j25108

Miller, R. K. and Pressley, L., (2015). *Evolution of library liaison*. SPEC Kit 349. Washington, DC: Association of Research Libraries. doi:10.29242/spec.349

Morrison, P. D., (1969). *The career of the academic librarian: a study of the social origins, education attainments, vocational experience, and personality characteristics of a group of American academic librarians*. Chicago, IL: American Library Association.

OED., (2009). social capital. In: *Oxford English dictionary*. 3rd ed. Oxford: Oxford University Press.

Peace, N. E. and Chudacoff, N. F., (1979). Archivists and librarians: a common mission, a common education. *The American Archivist*. 42(4), 456–462. doi:10.17723/aarc.42.4.t12r201v6g5g1166

Rockenbach, B., Ruttenberg, J., Tancheva, K. and Vine, R., (2015). *Association of Research Libraries/Columbia University/Cornell University/University of Toronto pilot library liaison institute: final report*. Washington, DC: Association of Research Libraries. https://www.arl.org/resources/library-liaison-institute-final-report

Schlak, T., (2016). Social capital as operative in liaison librarianship: librarian participants' experiences of faculty engagement as academic library liaisons. *Journal of Academic Librarianship*. 42(4), 411–422. doi:10.1016/j.acalib.2017.09.005

Wilder, S. J., (2003). *Demographic change in academic librarianship*. Washington, DC: Association of Research Libraries. https://www.arl.org/resources/demographic-change-in-academic-librarianship

8

Conceptualising the Sociocultural Nature of the Development of Information Literacy in Undergraduate Education

Amanda L. Folk

Introduction

With a few exceptions, the social nature of the development of information literacy has remained largely implicit in the library and information science literature. Given the ratio of practitioners to both scholars and practitioner-scholars in academic librarianship, it is not surprising that the literature related to information literacy has mostly focused on pedagogical and practical strategies, with emphasis on brief, one-time instructional interventions (i.e., 'one shots') that still remain ubiquitous in higher education. Relatively recent literature focusing on critical pedagogies in information literacy instruction (see Tewell 2015 for an overview) has highlighted the need to develop students' critical or socio-political consciousness, not just their ability to select keywords and search relevant databases, which can be difficult to do within a single instruction session. Although important to recognise, this narrow focus does not account for the ways in which students' information literacy develops within the broader undergraduate academic landscape in which students' learning is situated, as well as barriers to the development of (critical) information literacy, student learning and student academic success.

Some have acknowledged the importance of the social and cultural contexts in which information literacy is developed. Lloyd (2012) and Tuominen, Savolainen and Talja (2005) have argued that we must consider the epistemic and professional *communities* in which information literacy is negotiated and developed. Within academic librarianship, both Elmborg (2006) and Nicholson (2014) have considered the broader academic culture in which students are developing and being asked to demonstrate their information literacy. Specifically, Elmborg (2006, p. 195) notes that students must be aware of 'the codes used by the *community* and the customs and conventions in play' to successfully demonstrate their information literacy to their faculty or risk being perceived as 'rejects' (ibid., p. 194) in the community. Both the Association of College and Research Libraries (ACRL 2016) and the Chartered Institute of Library and Information Professionals (CILIP 2018) have reconceptualised their articulations of information literacy, focusing on the critical, reflective and analytical ways of thinking about and using information rather than on discrete tasks or skills. This shift has resulted in an acknowledgement and articulation of the codes, customs and conventions related to information literacy within academic culture (Folk 2019); however, academic librarianship still lacks a working framework for conceptualising and exploring the social and cultural aspects of the development of students' information literacy.

In this chapter, which is based on my doctoral research (Folk 2018b), I present a working conceptual framework for exploring the development of undergraduate students' information literacy that draws upon and combines several theoretical and conceptual foundations that account for social interactions and cultural context, including *communities of practice*, **social and cultural capital**, and academic literacies. This conceptual framework was used as a foundation for a phenomenological study that explored the ways in which first-generation college students, a student population that has historically been underserved in American higher education, transitioned into and within the undergraduate academic community. In particular, I examined how students learned the expectations for performance on research assignments, and the accumulation of social capital through interactions with faculty, librarians and other academic support staff was an essential aspect of this exploration. The findings of the study indicate that the accumulation of social capital was critical for these students in learning the expectations for performance, as was the shift from interactions with faculty to the development of relationships as students moved to upper-level coursework in their discipline(s). The findings of the study resulted in a refinement of the conceptual framework, and they present implications and new opportunities for our professional practice, including the role that academic librarians can fulfil in this transition and learning process as discourse mediators.

Developing a working conceptual framework
In this section, I present a working conceptual framework for exploring the ways in which undergraduate students develop their information literacy as they participate in the academic community at their institution of higher education. To build this conceptual framework, I combine information literacy with theories and concepts from education and writing studies. I will first present each of the theories and concepts, and then discuss the ways in which they work together to provide a framework for considering the social and cultural nature of the development of information literacy.

Communities of practice and situated learning
Lave and Wenger's (1991) community of practice concept forms the foundation of the working conceptual framework. The community of practice concept has been fairly popular in librarianship, being used to form communities of practitioners who seek to learn more about a particular topic together (i.e., learning communities). This use of the community of practice concept is primarily rooted in Wenger's (1998) follow-up work. Another use of the original community of practice concept, one that interrogates the power dynamics related to joining a particular community, has been less popular in the profession. This

approach uses the community of practice concept as a heuristic to examine 'the ways in which learning does or does not take place and foregrounds not just success but constraints on learning and full participation in a community's practices' (Lea 2005, p. 188). In other words, the heuristic approach allows one to maintain a critical stance toward the structure, values, expectations and discourse(s) of the community and how those elements can serve to marginalise or alienate novices as they seek membership in a particular community.

In general, the heuristic approach to the community of practice concept provides a basis for exploring the ways in which individuals join and are recognised as members of a community. New members are referred to as *legitimate peripheral participants*. They are legitimate because they have made the decision or commitment to enter that community, and established members, or full participants, have recognised them as novice members of the community. They are peripheral because, as new members, they are still outsiders in terms of the community's culture, values and practices. The progression from legitimate peripheral participant to full participant is tied to situated learning theory, in which peripheral participants learn relevant skills or acquire knowledge about acceptable ways of communicating and behaving as they participate in the community. In situated learning, peripheral participants move towards full participation through a process of acculturation, or the adoption of the community's sociocultural traits and patterns, through active participation in the community (Contu & Willmott 2003).

Social capital

Given the social nature of joining a community, *social capital* (Bourdieu 1986) is helpful in examining the opportunities and barriers to participating fully in the community based on the development of relationships with other legitimate peripheral and full participants. Social capital provides students with information about how to act within or navigate an educational institution based on the community's culture and values, so the accumulation of social capital is powerful for membership within an educational community. Bourdieu's (1986) conceptualisation of social capital is critical of underlying structural and social barriers that encourage inequality between different social classes. Social capital can reinforce **social reproduction** and stratification (i.e., the powerful remain powerful), as the dominant class uses the accumulation of social capital to retain their power and remain dominant. Therefore, the use of social capital in this working conceptual model allows for the examination of the ways in which current and common practices in higher education reproduce persistent equity gaps among student populations who have traditionally been marginalised in higher education.

Cultural capital and habitus

Another important aspect of the heuristic approach to the community of practice concept is the role of culture and an individual's ability to learn the expectations of navigating and participating in that culture. *Cultural capital* (Bourdieu 1986) is 'a set of cultural competencies which a person needs to acquire to participate in a whole range of cultural activities' (Goulding 2008, p. 235). Common examples of cultural capital include an individual's knowledge of fine arts, literature and music, as well as the ways in which one dresses or speaks. One's knowledge of the cultural values and preferences – or the **habitus** – of a particular community can signal belonging or affiliation to the other members of the community. *Habitus* has been defined as a 'set of socialized dispositions, which unconsciously incline people (agents) to "act or react" in certain ways in particular social spaces' (Burke 2012, p. 40). However, cultural values and preferences can remain tacit for new members of a community unless they have accumulated social capital with established members who help the new members to understand the rules of participating and engaging in the community.

Academic literacies

The concept of academic literacies provides the foundation for understanding the *habitus* of the undergraduate academic community of practice. Academic literacies include the academic skills, attitudes and practices (Stierer 2000) that students are expected to demonstrate as they progress from being a first-year student to becoming an upper-level student. Tapp (2015, p. 712) writes that academic literacies are 'embedded in specific academic contexts that include particular ways of constructing meaning, making judgments, and determining what counts as valuable knowledge reflecting tacit beliefs and values'. Because academic literacies validate certain forms of knowledge, critical analysis and knowledge practices, students who have not been exposed to the skills, attitudes and competencies that are valued in the undergraduate academic community, through no fault of their own, are sometimes viewed as 'intellectually inferior' or 'lacking ability' (Burke 2012, p. 193). In other words, a student's ability to internalise, or at least recognise and demonstrate, the cultural values or preferences of the undergraduate academic community are critical to signalling that they belong in that community.

Information literacy

In the working conceptual framework, information literacy is one of the academic literacies that resides within the *habitus* of the undergraduate academic community of practice. For many years, information literacy was conceived as skills or tasks related to the identification of a particular information need and knowing how to effectively and efficiently search for, evaluate and use information (ACRL 2000; SCONUL 1999). However, the conceptualisation of information literacy has shifted to describing the critical, reflective and analytical modes of thinking that are critical to consuming information and creating new knowledge (ACRL 2016; CILIP 2018). For example, ACRL (2016) now defines information literacy as six interrelated threshold concepts. Meyer and Land (2006, p. 14) describe threshold concepts as discursive, asserting that 'specific discourses have developed within disciplines to represent (and simultaneously privilege) particular understanding and ways of seeing and thinking'. Thus, threshold concepts have both social and cultural dimensions.

Research assignments

I argue that research assignments, as discursive artefacts of the values of academic culture, are a type of situated learning within the undergraduate academic community of practice. As a reification of the undergraduate academic community's *habitus*, these assignments require students to become members of a scholarly conversation by reading and synthesising what other scholars, experts or professionals have written in order to make their own argument about a topic. Elmborg (2006, p. 195) articulated a similar conception of activities like research assignments, referring to these kinds of activities as 'literacy events', in which students must know 'the codes used by the community and the customs and conventions in play'. Some students will receive feedback throughout the process of constructing a final product (i.e., a term paper or a presentation), which helps them to develop academic literacies valued and rewarded in the undergraduate academic community. Faculty evaluate students' overall performance related to the valued academic literacies through a final grade, which could signal membership or exclusion within the community.

Summary of the working conceptual framework

When combined, the theoretical and conceptual frames provide a unique way to explore undergraduate students' academic experiences as they transition from first-year students at the periphery to becoming full participants within the undergraduate academic community as they approach completion of their degree. Figure 8.1 provides a visual representation of how I combined these concepts and theories to explore first-generation students' transition into and within the undergraduate academic community of practice, paying particular attention to the role that research assignments might play in these transitions. Students' progression through the academic curriculum is included in this

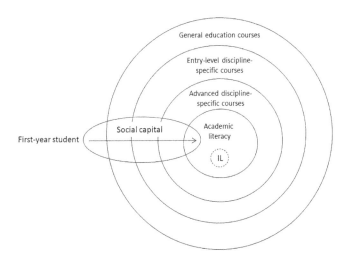

Figure 8.1 *Undergraduate community of practice: working conceptual framework*

working conceptual framework, though it is worth noting that this represents the undergraduate academic experience that is common in the USA, where the academic curriculum often requires students to receive a general education; in addition to focused coursework in their major field(s) of study, students must take a number of courses in broad topical categories that cross a range of disciplines, such as quantitative reasoning, ethical reasoning, arts appreciation, effective communication, diverse and global perspectives and scientific thinking. Academic literacies comprise the community's *habitus*, and students develop these academic literacies as they progress through the academic curriculum and draw upon existing, pre-college social capital and accumulate social capital in their new academic community. Information literacy, a facet of academic literacy, is situated within this core.

As a reification of the community's core values, academic research assignments theoretically require that students demonstrate the accepted dispositions and knowledge practices embodied in the concept of information literacy. The community of practice heuristic helps to frame the expectation that students will develop more sophisticated ways of interacting with and using information within academic research assignments as they move from general education and introductory coursework, such as a college composition course, to more advanced, discipline-specific courses and culminating research experiences in their major field(s) of study. Situated learning and social capital indicate that students must interact with other members of the community of practice, faculty in particular, to demonstrate competencies related to academic literacies, including information literacy, in their academic research assignments. In addition, faculty serve as gatekeepers to the community through the evaluation of performance on these assignments based on both explicit requirements and implicit expectations.

Previous research examining the academic research experiences of undergraduate students has provided only a snapshot of their experiences in developing a line of inquiry and finding, evaluating and using information for academic assignments, or has asked students about their practices more generally rather than connected to a specific assignment. The findings of this previous research have been useful in gaining a general understanding of students' research practices, but they have not demonstrated how students develop their information literacy as they move from being first-year students to joining their major field(s) of study as upper-level students. This working conceptual framework provides a foundation for addressing this gap in the research, as well as providing the opportunity to explore the ways in which academic culture can enable or constrain success for students whose identities have traditionally been marginalised in higher education. The use of the communities of practice concept and social capital enable the exploration of power dynamics related to participation in academic culture; and academic literacies and information literacy serve as an articulation of some of the privileged modes of thinking in academic culture that may remain tacit for many students, particularly students from under-represented and underserved populations.

Application of the working conceptual framework

This working conceptual framework was developed to guide a research study that explored first-generation college students' experiences with academic research assignments throughout college. In the USA, first-generation college students are typically defined as students whose parents have not completed a four-year post-secondary degree (Nunez & Cuccaro-Alamin 1998). In general, first-generation students are less likely to persist after both their first and second years of college than their continuing-generation peers (Engle & Tinto 2008; Ishitani 2006), and are therefore less likely to complete their degree (DeAngelo et al. 2011; Ishitani 2006). This difference in academic outcomes indicates the existence of a persistent social-class equity gap (Stephens, Hamedani & Destin 2014). Although there are many factors that likely contribute to this equity gap, first-generation students may have a steeper curve in learning the rules for engaging with collegiate academic culture, given that their parents have not completed a four-year undergraduate degree (Collier & Morgan 2008; Yee 2016). Furthermore, research indicates that first-generation students may be less likely to interact with faculty and other academic support staff, thus accumulating social capital at a slower rate than students whose parents have attained a four-year post-secondary degree (Yee 2016). Academic culture's rules for engagement that remain tacit for many underserved student populations are sometimes referred to as the 'hidden curriculum'. Despite the ubiquity of research assignments (Head & Eisenberg 2009) and their direct connection to students' academic outcomes (i.e., grades), the contributions of research assignments to the social-class equity gap have not been explored.

For this study, I conducted semi-structured interviews with 30 first-generation students who were in at least their third year of study at two regional campuses of a large research university in the USA. Interviews lasted no more than 75 minutes, and students received a $25 gift card as an appreciation of their time and willingness to share their experiences. The interview protocol aligned with the working conceptual framework described in the previous section. Students were first asked about their experiences of transitioning academically to college. The next two sections of the interview explored how students' experiences with research assignments did or did not change as they became more embedded in collegiate academic culture, asking students to describe one of the first research assignments that they completed in college and the most recent research assignment they had. The interview concluded with questions asking them to reflect on their experiences with research assignments throughout college, as well as asking them what kind of advice they would give to a new first-year student.

Brief overview of the findings

Further details of these findings and implications are available in Folk (2018b, 2021).

Accumulation of social capital

The first-generation students that participated in this study began to accumulate social capital when they first got to college in two ways – using a social approach or an individual approach. The approach that a student used seemed to be related to how successfully they were able to transfer and apply the academic skills and strategies that they had developed in high school to their new collegiate environment. Students who took a social approach to their transition to college knew that it was essential that they initiate conversations with their faculty about expectations for performance, even when initiating those conversations was intimidating or uncomfortable. These students would ask questions during or after class, e-mail their professors and attend office hours, and they viewed these activities as being important to establishing a positive relationship with and reputation among their faculty.

Students who took an individual approach, however, were less likely to reach out to their faculty to learn about or clarify expectations for performance or to establish a relationship or reputation with faculty. These students often struggled in silence, though they occasionally reached out to their peers with questions. Often these students reported being disappointed by the feedback and grades they were receiving on their assignments, because they believed they had put in legitimate effort (Valentine 2001), only to find out that it was not enough. These students began to accumulate social capital in two ways. The first way was through required interactions related to research assignments with faculty or academic support staff (i.e., librarians, writing centre staff). The other was through the transition into their major field(s) of study, as they would have repeated interactions with the same faculty and began to feel more comfortable with them. Despite the eventual accumulation of social capital, these students did not seem to have the same access to higher levels of academic opportunities, such as presenting at conferences, as the students who took a social approach did.

Perceptions of research assignments

Many of the participating students perceived research assignments in their lower-level and general education courses as situated practices, though they did not use that phrase. Students indicated that the research assignments they were required to complete in their first couple of years of college were meant to prepare them for the more complex research assignments that they would be required to complete in their upper-level courses, particularly courses in their major field(s) of study. In addition, all of the students who participated in this study were required to complete a culminating research experience, referred to as a capstone project, prior to degree completion. In general, students saw the capstone experience as an opportunity to synthesise what they had learned through their college experiences and apply that to a project serving as a summative assessment of learning. In other words, the capstone experience validated that these students were becoming or had become full members in the undergraduate academic community of practice.

Despite the fact that research assignments, in general, were viewed as a form of situated learning, students did not provide much evidence that they were developing the critical thinking skills related to information literacy through their experiences with these assignments. Many students seemed to perceive that the emphasis was placed on the final product, such as a research paper or a presentation, rather than the process they used to develop that final product. Students knew that they needed to use high-quality sources in their papers, particularly as they moved into their upper-level courses, but most students reported using a checklist approach to evaluating their sources. Based on the interviews, it did not seem that students spent much time reading their sources or reflecting on how these sources could help to answer their research question(s) or enhance the argument(s) they were making. One exception to this was when students were intrinsically motivated to learn more about a topic that was significant or personal to them (Folk 2018a). Despite critical thinking and information literacy being valued academic literacies in academic culture, students did not perceive that the cultivation of these academic literacies was important for participating and performing well within the undergraduate academic community of practice.

Implications for professional practice

The findings of the study suggest that research assignments are a potential vehicle for students to accumulate social capital as they transition into and within college, particularly within the collegiate academic context. In addition, the findings suggest that students may not be developing and refining their information literacy as they progress through the academic curriculum. Rather, many of them are learning how to perform satisfactorily within undergraduate academic culture. These findings may provide an expanded role for academic librarians and the development of students' information literacy, despite the fact that librarians did not play a prominent role in the experiences that these students shared.

Historically, academic librarians have primarily focused on the development of information literacy in teaching and learning contexts in which they are responsible for taking a lead role in teaching students, such as instruction sessions, research consultations and reference interactions. Though some attention has been paid to the role of librarian as discourse mediator (Simmons 2005) and collaborative librarian–faculty assignment development, these opportunities have remained underexplored. Simmons (2005) positions academic librarians as discourse mediators, helping to facilitate communication between faculty (i.e., experts) and undergraduate students (i.e., novices). Simmons (2005, p. 298) highlights academic librarians' 'unique position that allows mediation between the non-academic discourse of entering undergraduates and the specialized discourse of disciplinary faculty' due to being 'simultaneously insiders and outsiders of the classroom and of the academic disciplines in which [we] specialize'. The findings of this study suggest that this may be an impactful role for librarians, particularly in developing the information literacy of student populations who have traditionally been underserved in higher education, such as first-generation students.

As I have articulated in a previous publication (Folk 2019), the role of discourse mediator may help academic librarians to be integrated into the (re)design of research assignments. Based on the findings of my research, as well as other studies, there are likely several potential benefits for students' learning and success. First, using a strategy like Decoding the Disciplines (Middendorf & Pace 2004; Miller 2018) in combination with *The framework for information literacy for higher education* (ACRL 2016) or the CILIP (2018) *Definition of information literacy* can help faculty to identify and deconstruct some of their tacit expectations for student performance rooted in the internalisation of academic cultural values. This strategy prompts conversations about breaking larger and complex research assignments into smaller assignments in which students are encouraged or required to meet with their faculty or other academic support staff (i.e., librarians or writing tutors) and receive valuable formative feedback before submitting a high-stakes, summative assignment. If librarians target courses that are aimed at lower-level undergraduate students (i.e., first- and second-year students), we may be able to help all students, including those who take an individual approach, to accumulate social capital early in their collegiate experience and begin to build an academic support network that they can rely on through degree completion.

In addition, when academic librarians assume the role of discourse mediator, we can also help faculty with the ways in which they make their expectations for performance on research assignments transparent and accessible to students, particularly those students for whom academic cultural values may remain tacit. One strategy that I have used and recommend (Folk 2019) is Transparency in Learning and Teaching (TILT, Winkelmes et al. 2016). Not only does TILT encourage faculty to identify and articulate the tasks that students will need to do in order to successfully complete an assignment, it also encourages faculty to articulate the purpose of the assignment, both from the faculty member's perspective and the student's perspective. This means that faculty should be taking into account students' learning goals, as well as their career aspirations, interests, identities and lived experiences. In a previously published article based on the findings of this research study (Folk 2018a), I highlighted the importance of an **asset**-based (Ardoin 2018; Martin, Smith & Williams 2018) or identity-conscious (Pendakur 2016) approach to research assignments for the development of students' information literacy. When students' learning goals and passions are explicitly taken into account, their motivation toward, engagement with and investment in their research, including the research process, increases.

While my intention is not to suggest that the 'one-shot' style of information literacy instruction is without value, the findings of this study, combined with existing research, suggest that academic librarians, when we assume the role of discourse mediator, may play an impactful role in helping students to accumulate social capital and develop their information literacy as they transition into and within the undergraduate academic community.

The revised conceptual framework

Figure 8.2 opposite provides a visual representation of how the findings of the study provided a more complex and nuanced understanding of the role of social capital within first-generation students' experiences of transitioning into and within the undergraduate academic community. In the initial conceptual framework, I implicitly defined the social

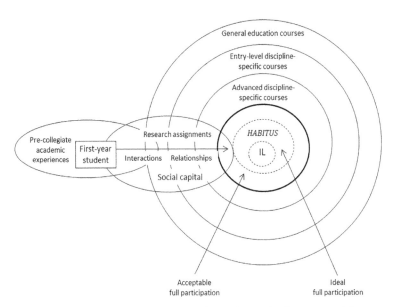

Figure 8.2 *Undergraduate community of practice: revised conceptual framework*

capital that students brought with them from high school to college as positive relationships that they developed with their high school teachers. However, most students reported having developed positive relationships with their high school teachers, and this did not seem to influence students' overall transition experiences. The findings indicate that the 'college knowledge' that students derive from these relationships and their pre-college academic experiences, as well as students' success in transferring and applying that knowledge in the undergraduate academic community, are important to how students approach this initial transition. In the revised framework, students' pre-college academic experiences and accumulated social capital intersect with their entry into the undergraduate academic community, because participants' reflections indicated that students bring these both to bear on their engagement with courses, assignments and faculty early in their collegiate careers.

The findings also provide a more nuanced understanding of the accumulation of social capital within the undergraduate academic community, in that this accumulation may have a relationship with students' approach to interacting and developing relationships with their faculty. Students who successfully transferred and applied the college knowledge they gained in high school were more likely to begin the intentional development of an academic support network. In addition, the findings suggest that the academic curriculum not only serves as a mechanism to introduce students to a community's cultural values, it also is a mechanism by which students develop 'institutionalized relationships of mutual acquaintance' (Bourdieu 1986, p. 248) and accumulate social capital within the undergraduate academic community. Students' entry into their college major(s) seemed to indicate a shift from supportive interactions, which could either be voluntary or required, to the development of relationships with faculty. In addition, research assignments, as sites of situated learning, throughout the academic curriculum, presented opportunities for students to accumulate social capital through voluntary or required supportive interactions with faculty about their academic performance. In the revised diagram, I demonstrate the shift from interactions to relationships with faculty through experiences with research assignments, the accumulation of social capital and movement from lower-level courses to upper-level courses in the college major.

Conclusion

In this chapter, I introduced a working conceptual framework that accounts for the social and cultural nature of the development of undergraduate students' information literacy. In this working conceptual framework, I have situated information literacy within a broader undergraduate academic community of practice and positioned information literacy as a core cultural value of this academic community. The use of critical theories – social capital and cultural capital – highlights the ways that current practices related to information literacy and research assignments may exacerbate the persistent equity gaps experienced by marginalised and traditionally underserved student populations, particularly within higher education in the USA. The findings of the research study present both challenges and opportunities, as well as adding more nuance and complexity to the original conceptual framework.

The challenges include combatting the product-over-process mentality that was evident in many of the students' interviews, as well as moving beyond simply understanding how to adequately or successfully perform in the undergraduate academic context to the development of critical thinking skills. The opportunities include the potential benefit of an asset-based (Ardoin 2018; Martin, Smith & Williams 2018) or identity-conscious (Pendakur 2016) approach to research assignments to the development of students' information literacy and critical thinking skills, especially when coupled with a pedagogical strategy like Decoding the Disciplines (Middendorf & Pace 2004; Miller 2018) to identify and address stumbling blocks to student learning. Despite the contributions of the findings, there are still many areas that are ripe for further exploration. These include an examination of students' experiences with research assignments prior to college and the potential relationship to their collegiate academic transition; the role that the size and nature of the institution, as well as the medium of instructional delivery, plays in students' engagement with research assignments, accumulation of social and cultural capital and development of information literacy; and, finally, the applicability of the working conceptual framework to other student populations who have traditionally been underserved and marginalised in higher education.

References

ACRL., (2000). *Information literacy competency standards for higher education*. Chicago: Association of College & Research Libraries. http://hdl.handle.net/11213/7668

ACRL., (2016). *Framework for information literacy for higher education.* Chicago: Association of College & Research Libraries.
http://www.ala.org/acrl/sites/ala.org.acrl/files/content/issues/infolit/Framework_ILHE.pdf

Ardoin, S., (2018). Helping poor- and working-class students create their own sense of belonging. *New Directions for Student Services*. **162**, 75–86. doi:10.1002/ss.20263

Bourdieu, P., (1986). The forms of capital. In: J. G. Richardson, ed. *Handbook of theory and research for the sociology of education*. New York, NY: Greenwood Press. pp. 241–258.

Burke, P. J., (2012). *The right to higher education: beyond widening participation*. New York: Routledge.

CILIP., (2018). *CILIP definition of information literacy 2018*. London: Chartered Institute of Library and Information Professionals. https://infolit.org.uk/ILdefinitionCILIP2018.pdf

Collier, P. J. and Morgan, D. L., (2008). "Is that paper really due today?": differences in first-generation and traditional college students' understandings of faculty expectations. *Higher Education*. **55**(4), 425–446. doi:10.1007/s10734-007-9065-5

Contu, A. and Willmott, H., (2003). Re-embedding situatedness: the importance of power relations in learning theory. *Organization Science*. **14**(3), 283–296. doi:10.1287/orsc.14.3.283.15167

DeAngelo, L., Franke, R., Hurtado, S., Pryor, J. H. and Tran, S., (2011). *Completing college: assessing graduation rates at four-year institutions*. Los Angeles, CA: University of California, Los Angeles, Higher Education Research Institution.
https://www.heri.ucla.edu/DARCU/CompletingCollege2011.pdf

Elmborg, J., (2006). Critical information literacy: implications for instructional practice. *Journal of Academic Librarianship*. **32**(2), 192–199. doi:10.1016/j.acalib.2005.12.004.

Engle, J. and Tinto, V., (2008). *Moving beyond access: college success for low-income, first-generation students*. Washington, DC: The Pell Institute for the Study of Opportunity in Higher Education. http://www.pellinstitute.org/downloads/publications-Moving_Beyond_Access_2008.pdf

Folk, A. L., (2018a). Drawing on students' funds of knowledge: using identity and lived experience to join the conversation in research assignments. *Journal of Information Literacy*. **12**(2), 44–59. doi:10.11645/12.2.2468

Folk, A. L., (2018b). *Learning the rules of engagement: exploring first-generation students' academic experiences through academic research assignments*. PhD thesis, University of Pittsburgh. http://d-scholarship.pitt.edu/35132

Folk, A. L., (2019). Reframing information literacy as academic cultural capital: a critical and equity-based foundation for practice, assessment, and scholarship. *College & Research Libraries*. **80**(5), 658–673. doi:10.5860/crl.80.5.658

Folk, A. L., (2021). Exploring the development of undergraduate students' information literacy through their experience with research assignments. *College & Research Libraries*. **82**(7), 1035–1055. doi:10.5860/crl.82.7.1035

Goulding, A., (2008). Libraries and cultural capital. *Journal of Librarianship and Information Science*. 40(1), 235–237. doi:10.1177/0961000608096713

Head, A. J. and Eisenberg, M. B., (2009). *Lessons learned: how college students seek information in the digital age*. Seattle, WA: University of Washington, Information School, Project Information Literacy. http://projectinfolit.org/publications

Ishitani, T. T., (2006). Studying attrition and degree completion behavior among first-generation college students in the United States. *Journal of Higher Education*. 77(5), 861–885. doi:10.1080/00221546.2006.11778947

Lave, J. and Wenger, E., (1991). *Situated learning: legitimate peripheral participation*. Cambridge, UK: Cambridge University Press.

Lea, M., (2005). 'Communities of practice' in higher education: useful heuristic or educational model? In: D. Barton and K. Tusting, eds. *Beyond communities of practice: language, power, and social context*. New York: Cambridge University Press. pp. 180–197.

Lloyd, A., (2012). Information literacy as a socially enacted practice: sensitising themes for an emerging perspective of people-in-practice. *Journal of Documentation*. 68(6), 772–783. doi:10.1108/00220411211277037

Martin, G. L., Smith, M. J. and Williams, B. M., (2018). Reframing deficit thinking on social class. *New Directions for Student Services*. 162, 87–93. doi:10.1002/ss.20264

Meyer, J. H. F. and Land, R., (2006). Threshold concepts and troublesome knowledge: an introduction. In: J. H. F. Meyer and R. Land, eds. *Overcoming barriers to student understanding: threshold concepts and troublesome knowledge*. New York: Routledge. pp. 3–18.

Middendorf, J. and Pace, D., (2004). Decoding the disciplines: a model for helping students to learn disciplinary ways of thinking. *New Directions for Higher Education*. 98, 1–12. doi:10.1002/tl.142

Miller, S. D., (2018). Diving deep: reflective questions for identifying tacit disciplinary information literacy knowledge practices, dispositions, and values through the *ACRL Framework for Information Literacy*. *Journal of Academic Librarianship*. 44(3), 412–418. doi:10.1016/j.acalib.2018.02.014

Nicholson, K., (2014). Information literacy as a situated practice in the neoliberal university. In: M. Griffis, H. Julien and L. Given, eds. *Proceedings of the 42nd annual conference of the Canadian Association for Information Science, 28–30 May 2014, St. Catharines, ON, Canada*. https://journals.library.ualberta.ca/ojs.cais-acsi.ca/index.php/cais-asci/article/view/864/778

Nunez, A. M. and Cuccaro-Alamin, S., (1998). *First-generation students: undergraduates whose parents never enrolled in post-secondary education*. (NCES 98-082). Washington, DC: U. S. Department of Education. https://nces.ed.gov/pubs98/98082.pdf

Pendakur, V., (2016). Two distinct paths and a missed opportunity. In: V. Pendakur, ed. *Closing the opportunity gap: identity-conscious strategies for retention and student success*. Sterling, VA: Stylus. pp. 1–9.

SCONUL., (1999). *Information skills in higher education: a SCONUL position paper*. London: Society of College, National and University Libraries. https://www.sconul.ac.uk/sites/default/files/documents/Seven_pillars2.pdf

Simmons, M. H., (2005). Librarians as disciplinary discourse mediators: using genre theory to move toward critical information literacy. *portal: Libraries and the Academy*. 5(3), 297–311. doi:10.1353/pla.2005.0041

Stephens, N. M., Hamedani, M. G. and Destin, M., (2014). Closing the social-class achievement gap: a difference-education intervention improves first-generation students' academic performance and all students' college transition. *Psychological Science*. 25(4), 943–953. doi:10.1177/0956797613518349

Stierer, B., (2000). Schoolteachers as students: academic literacy and the construction of professional knowledge within master's courses in education. In: M. R. Lea and B. Stierer, eds. *Student writing in higher education*. Buckingham, UK: Open University Press. pp. 179–195.

Tapp, J., (2015). Framing the curriculum for participation: a Bersteinian perspective on academic literacies. *Teaching in Higher Education*. 20(7), 711–722. doi:10.1080/13562517.2015.1069266

Tewell, E., (2015). A decade of critical information literacy: a review of the literature. *Communications in Information Literacy*. 9(1), 24–43. doi:10.15760/comminfolit.2015.9.1.174

Tuominen, K., Savolainen, R. and Talja, S., (2005). Information literacy as a sociotechnical practice. *Library Quarterly*. 75(3), 329–345. doi:10.1086/497311

Valentine, B., (2001). The legitimate effort in research papers: student commitment versus faculty expectations. *Journal of Academic Librarianship*. 27(2), 107–115. doi:10.1016/S0099-1333(00)00182-8

Wenger, E., (1998). *Communities of practice: learning, meaning, and identity*. Cambridge, UK: Cambridge University Press.

Winkelmes, M., Bernacki, M., Butler, J., Zochowski, M., Golanics, J. and Weavil, K H., (2016). A teaching intervention that increases underserved college students' success. *Peer Review*. 18(1/2), 31–36. https://www.aacu.org/peerreview/2016/winter-spring/Winkelmes

Yee, A., (2016). The unwritten rules of engagement: social class differences in undergraduates' academic strategies. *Journal of Higher Education*. 87(6), 831–858. doi:10.1080/00221546.2016.11780889

9

Social Network Theory in Emerging Library Learning Spaces and Programs

Alice Rogers, Sara Sweeney Bear and Scott Fralin

Introduction

Since 2013, Virginia Tech has expanded the services provided by the University Libraries to include spaces and programs atypical of an academic library. Such services include the Studios Network, a series of spaces that provide open access to technology and resources for users to explore, and two exhibit programs that curate and display content from courses taught on campus. These initiatives provide support to patrons in ways that are challenging to describe in terms used for more traditional library services. They are outward facing; patrons of the library are able to see and engage with work from around the University by entering into the studio and exhibit spaces, as well as through content made available online. These services are intended to create low barriers of entry for patrons to create and play, and to act as a gateway to other resources and activities available at Virginia Tech.

In this chapter, we will discuss how non-traditional library services can be better understood and their impact more fully measured using **social network analysis**. Based on our experiences managing these programs and spaces, we will describe the connections facilitated by the programs we support and discuss how they differ from more traditional library services in ways that positively affect the Virginia Tech community. Our use of social network analysis focuses on the qualitative elements of our **social networks**: their **reciprocity**, intensity and **multiplexity** (Tichy, Tushman & Fombrun 1979, p. 509). Our goal in outlining these relationships is to demonstrate how their value might be expressed, particularly in comparison with other library services that may serve a greater number of patrons, but not in the same capacity. Data for this effort have been drawn from our experiences as founding managers of our respective programs, as well as public outcomes of our work. Studios and exhibits are relatively new services provided by libraries, and so this chapter will contribute to scholarly literature on how these programs work, as well as how their value can be communicated.

We begin the chapter with a description of the Studios Network and exhibit programs and outline the values and ideas that guided their development, many of which allow for greater collaboration among patrons. We then elaborate on how considering social network theory can demonstrate the importance of such programs, focusing on three examples:

Fusion Studio, the Course Exhibit Initiative and the Active Learning Curation Program. Fusion Studio is a collaborative workspace that provides student groups with a space and resources to pursue and develop projects. The Course Exhibit Initiative supports the creation and display of exhibitions throughout Newman Library that feature course content from a variety of Virginia Tech classes. The Active Learning Curation Program showcases innovative teaching methods that are used in flexible and SCALE-UP learning spaces. Originally developed at North Carolina State University (NCSU 2021), Student-Centered Active Learning Environments with Upside-down Pedagogies are designed to support active learning and facilitate interaction in large classes.

While each of these programs connects people to one another in unique ways, there are a number of commonalities that we will explore, especially the interdisciplinary nature of the connections between people, and how we use the connections we have with one another to provide better support for patrons of these programs.

Our chapter builds on the work done by other library professionals who have used social network theory and analysis featuring social or relationship capital to demonstrate and quantify the value of work in library spaces. Paul Bracke's (2016) work provides a framework for beginning this analysis; his research demonstrated how social network theory highlighted otherwise unseen work done by liaison librarians that was crucial to their success. We use the terminology described by Noel M. Tichy, Michael L. Tushman and Charles Fombrun (1979) to frame this chapter, but there are other similar studies that use alternative terminology. Lluís Anglada's (2007) study of the evolution of different types of relationships in Spanish university libraries categorises the types of relationships by how they are institutionally connected. J. Stephen Town (2015) discusses relationship assessment methods from a number of industries to develop useful areas of focus for documenting and measuring relationships for the value scorecard. We chose our terminology based on what highlighted the nature of the relationships we were seeing in our programs, but these studies indicate how other methods and words can be used to effectively understand library services.

To provide data for this project, we have chosen to conduct a limited number of interviews about our work, in addition to using publicly available data about patrons with whom we have collaborated. The data referenced for our research can be found on the websites for our programs, which also provide more information on the initiatives described in this chapter (Virginia Tech Libraries 2019a; 2019b; 2022a; 2022b).

While we are not directly following any of the methodologies suggested by Tichy, Tushman and Fombrun (1979), several other scholars have used such methods to collect effective and useful data on relationships. Octavia-Luciana Madge's (2018) study of Romanian library directors documented sentiments about the state of collaboration between Romanian institutions. Tim Schlak's (2016) research on the importance of relationship capital for liaison librarians used interviews with open-ended questions to gather data, which provided areas of importance that interested and affected the work of the group as a whole. While our qualitative data is more limited and institution specific, as we assess our effectiveness this is the information most relevant to our needs.

Programs and values
Studios

The University Libraries Studios Network was created to provide low barriers to entry to technologies or experiences that are otherwise cost restrictive or limited to a particular group of people. The studios share many characteristics with *makerspaces*, which a growing number of universities are incorporating into their academic libraries. Makerspaces are open spaces in which patrons can use and explore tools and technology, and institutions that have created such spaces have made unique choices about staffing, technology and departmental affiliations (Barrett et al. 2015). The 3D Design Studio, the first of the Studios Network, was originally conceived as our version of a makerspace. As **resources** and space were scarce, the Library's Learning Environments team decided to instead focus on prototyping and honing individual studios in smaller spaces. Over time, these studios expand and evolve to fit patrons' needs. As of the writing of this chapter, the studios provide access to 3D design, scanning and printing; virtual and augmented reality; media design tools; and space for student teams working on long-term, collaborative projects. We also deliver workshops, consultations and in-class instruction on these topics. In social network analysis terms, the transactional content of these spaces would primarily be categorised as an exchange of services and information.

As we create each studio, the following values guide the selection of services and the design of our service model:

- *People centred*: Users' needs are front and centre;
- *Accessible*: The studios are for everyone; we do not charge for our services, and no previous experience with a skill or technology is required.
- *Hands on*: We emphasise peer-to-peer, informal learning so that, via sharing our expertise, our users can also become experts.
- *Playful*: We allow library patrons to use our services for play as much as for work. We encourage users to prototype and take risks.
- *Community oriented*: We believe creativity is a collective endeavour, and we work to connect our users and build partnerships to support them.
- *Adaptive*: The spaces themselves are prototypes, and we are constantly adapting them to changing needs and technologies.

While these values are built into the services we provide, they are also codified in promotional materials developed to help new users and potential partners understand our work.

The Studios Network thrives on relationship building and the development of **social capital** among university employees and patrons. Each studio is managed by an 'expert' in their service, and all but Fusion are supported by student staff. We hire these student staff based first and foremost on their ability to be welcoming to new users. We can always train them on the specific technologies in the studios, but, to provide a low barrier to entry, it is important that the student staff – as the face of the studios – can create an air of openness and make people feel comfortable trying something new. In Fusion, where there are no student staff, this is accomplished through relationships among members.

Exhibits

The first exhibit created by the Course Exhibit Initiative (CEI) was a collaboration with a Religion in America class in the fall of 2013 where students created final projects designed to be on public display. It was inspired by a one-time project at the Georgia Tech Libraries, *A History of the Mad Housers* (2008), where students built a structure in the Library for their final project rather than write a paper or give a presentation. When Brian Mathews, who was at the Georgia Tech Libraries at the time, became associate dean at the Virginia Tech Libraries, he started a program with Scott Fralin to engage the Virginia Tech community through exhibits in the Library based on the work students were creating in classrooms all over campus. The intentions of the CEI were, and still are, to take student work outside the classroom, to share it with the wider *community* and to create meaningful and serendipitous experiences for patrons of the Virginia Tech Libraries. As the CEI has grown, the scope has widened to include research projects, commemorative month celebratory exhibits and collaborations with non-academic departments.

The idea of showcasing student work through exhibits – while common, expected and enjoyed in the Virginia Tech Libraries now – was radical and risky when the CEI began. Literature on library-based exhibitions is limited, and, in their efforts to reach out to exhibit creators at other institutions, the exhibit creators at the Virginia Tech Libraries discovered that similar programs are uncommon. There was uncertainty as to whether library patrons would enjoy a display featuring work created by their peers, whether patrons would engage with the materials on display or if we could ever find professors willing to participate in creating exhibits. Thankfully, we have enjoyed success in all of these areas, so much so that a new endeavour was created to further our efforts to showcase scholarship on campus.

The Active Learning Curation Program (ALCP) was created as an extension of the CEI, intended to move public exhibits into the New Classroom Building (NCB), constructed in 2016. These exhibits would have a greater focus on sharing teaching techniques and learning practices that were unique to the classrooms in NCB, which feature movable furniture and innovative technologies. The furniture and technology were selected to encourage teaching methods beyond lecturing. Room setups are flexible and allow for quick reconfigurations between classes so professors can teach in a variety of styles, not limited by the classrooms. The classroom technology is set up in a similar way, with screens around the room in addition to central projectors, and connections can be made individually to screens or shared across all of them. This allows instructors and students to present in the room from any location. All of these things are meant to encourage instructors to guide students as they navigate their own learning experiences, rather than imparting information throughout the class.

Learning environments

Both the studios and exhibits programs are housed in the Learning Environments division of the Library, as they facilitate educational experiences within physical spaces. We view the Library as departmentally agnostic, and therefore patrons from across campus have access to all of our services. Additionally, because Virginia Tech is a land grant institution, the University Libraries functions as a public library, and community members who are not associated with the University can access most of our services. As a result, relationships among patrons and employees are complex and multitudinous. Each studio and exhibit program has their own network and sets of clusters they work with and have connections to, but we also all share these connections with each other and other library services. Very often, once a patron gets in the door and is introduced to one library service we find that they have needs for nearly all of them.

Employees of the Learning Environments division within University Libraries track their interactions using an application developed at the Library. We manually enter information about our work, and use this information to provide the American Library Association and the Association of College and Research Libraries with data about how many interactions we have with patrons. Internally, we use this application to track projects and to ensure that users have received services that they expected. It allows us to track the progress of projects, as well as to note when patrons are using multiple library services. While we do not report the details of this data, it helps us to understand our work in relation to the work of our colleagues and see opportunities for defining those connections more clearly. In addition, some of the broader data or information that we collected from public locations have helped to inform the findings of this article.

The Fusion Studio

Fusion, like all of the studios, functions around the idea of increasing the 'adjacent possible' by connecting students to new people, technologies and experiences. The idea of the *adjacent possible* stems from Steven Johnson's 2010 *Wall Street Journal* article, 'The genius of the tinkerer', in which he explains that the more we connect with new people and ideas, the more we increase what we can discover and create. In the Fusion Studio, the role of the studio manager primarily focuses on building relationships or creating a platform for relationships – among individuals in a team, among teams in the studio, and sometimes between teams and external partners. It is built into the very design of the space. Fusion Studio members have swipe access whenever the Library is open – but they cannot book the studio. Instead, Fusion operates as a shared workspace, and the students who use the space must learn to navigate that dynamic. There are only a few workspaces meant for individuals, and there is no way to divide off your own section of the space. To put it in the language of Tichy, Tushman and Fombrun (1979), the studio manager's job is to improve the nature of links within and among clusters in the Fusion network.

We have found that teams often start by expecting to simply receive a service from the studio (space to work, access to resources, etc.) and are pleasantly surprised to find that the main benefit of the space is the relationships they develop with other members. Over the course of the two and a half years that Fusion has been open, the relationships among members of the space have become increasingly meaningful and complex. Late-night conversations become the start of new collaborations – from a simple exchange of critique to more formal contribution to a project. In an interview on 29 November 2018 about using the studio, one student responded: 'I think the main benefit that my project gets from this studio is that we get to see feedback from other groups that are sort of more in tune with giving feedback, they're more critical. [. . .] If you don't engage in that dialogue with other design teams or students, the whole project is depleted.' This student is explaining what many members have found – that they can build intense, reciprocal relationships with their peers that lead to greater learning and success.

Members also reinforce the norms of the space and hold one another accountable to being a responsible member of the community. The studio manager tries to support this behaviour by offering occasional social gatherings and providing virtual communication channels. Likewise, the studio manager's social capital with teams is inherited. A team's tenure in the space can be as short as just a few weeks, and it's rare that it extends beyond a few years, given the lifecycle of student projects and the limited time they're on campus. The studio manager relies on veteran members of the space to encourage new teams to see her as a trusted advisor.

Even beyond the studio manager's work with students, her role in the library relies heavily on building partnerships with others on campus to see how our services can help each other. Bracke (2016) explained that the role of librarians has increasingly come to include building relationships to co-ordinate new work; rather than serving as a guest lecturer, they are developing transactional partnerships to provide learning experiences for students. The relationships the studio manager has formed are generally reciprocal and range in complexity from a formal referral pipeline to partnering in the facilitation of a week-long Maker Camp for middle schoolers, when campers spend the week learning about *design thinking*, 3D design and printing, building 3D forms from cardboard, coding, circuitry and process documentation, and each team then uses their new skills to build something based on a challenge issued at the beginning of the week. Bracke (2016, p. 139) explains that 'One might expect [. . .] that deeper partnerships in teaching and learning might be characterised by increased reciprocity between librarian and faculty, relationships initiated by both parties and an increase in bi-directionality, and an increase in formality of relationships.' In the case of the Fusion Studio, this has proven to be true. As the studio manager partners with others more often to build learning experiences, those partnerships become rooted in a sense of **trust**, and there is more mutuality in the relationship. As a result, the studio manager can more easily refer her students to other services on campus that can help them reach their goals, and those offices also refer students to the Fusion Studio.

All of these complex interactions and the partnerships they generate are important to the success of the space; they are also intangible, hard to capture, and happening all the time in both physical and digital environments. As Corrall (2014) explains, it is becoming increasingly important that we collect data about these '**intangible assets**', and yet traditional systems of data collection and reporting reduce these relationships to hours on our calendars or numbers of departments worked with. This overlooks several aspects of what happens in the Fusion Studio. For instance, the studio manager meets with each team in the studio for about the same time each month. However, the relationship between the studio manager and each team varies significantly. There are always teams that seek her advice more frequently and express a desire to 'give back' via participation in data collection or events that help us improve and promote the space. Using the network properties laid out by Tichy, Tushman and Fombrun (1979), that relationship has greater intensity and reciprocity than others. Information such as this has helped the studio manager hone her interactions with teams to potentially replicate that relationship with others.

The Course Exhibit Initiative

The CEI gives students at Virginia Tech an opportunity to share their work more widely than in the classroom. Traditionally, classrooms act as dense clusters where many transactions take place. However, these clusters can be limited in terms of reach and the strength of connections built there (Tichy, Tushman & Fombrun 1979, p. 509). More often than not, the work students create in college classrooms is seen by their fellow students in the class, the professor teaching the class and no one else. The CEI gives that work a wider audience that includes peers from other majors and departments, visitors from other universities, faculty, staff and the public. We work with these classroom clusters to explore ways in which they might share what they're doing more widely and increase their **weak ties** outside of the relatively small cluster of the classroom. This wider reach of their work opens the students up to the benefits of weak ties such as more expression of affect, exchange of information and exchange of services (Tichy, Tushman & Fombrun 1979, p. 509). The CEI itself also benefits from additional weak ties via other faculty who either see the exhibit or hear about the experience of creating an exhibit through their colleagues.

Since 2013, the CEI has worked with students, faculty, staff and researchers at Virginia Tech to produce over 70 physical exhibit installations. One major network around these exhibits is clustered around departments in our College of Liberal Arts and Human Sciences (CLAHS). Traditionally, departments within CLAHS have very **strong ties** to the Library, since much of their research and work relies heavily on traditional library services such as collections and archival materials. The strength of these ties made them ideal partners for exhibits, due in part to the fact that the interaction is more reciprocal than it would be with a department that relies on the Library far less. The departments in CLAHS use the Library, send their students to the Library and are excited to have the work created in their classes shown in the Library. In addition to CLAHS, the CEI has worked with every academic college on the Virginia Tech campus, several institutes and many non-academic departments to create exhibits and offer other services.

The exhibits take many shapes, including large-scale immersive installations, smaller and simpler displays of student work and gallery-style installations featuring primarily flat works on walls or mobile galleries. As often as possible, interactive elements are built into the exhibit design to encourage those who visit the exhibits to share an opinion, participate in a poll or otherwise leave their own mark on the exhibit. This is an important aspect of the exhibits because it actively engages those who choose to participate and gives them a sense of ownership of the Library and the exhibits. This feeling of ownership and pride is doubly true with the students whose work is featured in the exhibits. During an interview conducted on 11 November 2018 Dillon Cutaiar, a student who has had work featured in multiple exhibits, stated that:

> I've been in school for 15 years and in all that time almost none of the things I've created have been seen by anyone other than me or my teachers. It just gets filed away in a box or tossed out. I'm proud and excited to have my work on display in the library and it is fun when I walk by and remember that something I created is out here for everyone to see.

The feeling this student describes illustrates how well the CEI gives students a transaction found sparingly in the classroom – expression of affect (Tichy, Tushman & Fombrun 1979, p. 509). While there might be lauding from peers in courses focused on creative output, students in a large range of classes receive little to no indication that their work is valued, aside from the grade assigned. Even if the student whose work is on display does not directly witness library patrons expressing how much they like the exhibit and their work, the fact that their work was chosen to be displayed in a public place in a way that is important matters to them.

The CEI often works directly with the faculty members in order to create and curate the exhibit based on their students' work. This usually happens after the beginning of the semester, but in some cases this relationship can begin prior to the teaching of the class, which allows the CEI to have greater input on the assignment or project which will be exhibited. We work closely with the faculty member as the semester goes on to learn more about the class and assignment to make sure the exhibit design is appropriate for the content. In many cases, the CEI is the catalyst for exhibit creation. It is not simply a service that provides a wall onto which students hang their work. We provide context and critique for the faculty and students and act as an objective observer who can help them figure out the best way in which to present their work. This does make for a more difficult and lengthy design process, but, as a result, each exhibit is a bespoke creation tailored to the class and content featured. This intensive design-and-build process often builds a strong tie between the CEI and the faculty member, even if only for the duration of the exhibit design process. While the strong ties might not last forever, the weak ties created are much more persistent.

In addition to the work that the CEI does to bring student work to the public, it also provides a peripheral service to fellow library departments and others on campus. For instance, we might create custom structures for departments that do not have the resources to create them on their own, or help external departments to use public spaces in the Library to communicate with other clusters. The CEI has provided assistance to Virginia Tech *living-learning communities*, internal library departments and other non-academic units on campus. Living-learning communities integrate topics of interest – such as arts, engineering or entrepreneurship – into the programming and community aspects of a residence hall. Products of these collaborations include public art creations and displays, info booths and tables, and co-designed exhibits.

The highlight of the CEI's annual report each year is the list of departments we have collaborated with. The exhibits created, artefacts shown and people who visit the exhibits are important, but the true end-product of the CEI is the connections built with the many varying departments. Since the CEI has been going on for so long, it has transformed from a purely transactional library service to a service of connection – connection between students and their peers, the Library and academic departments, and faculty and other faculty. Over time, the CEI has expanded to creating exhibits with non-academic campus partners, creating exhibits in-house to celebrate commemorative observations and working with campus partners to create public art outreach projects.

The assessment of our exhibits has always been a challenge. The exhibits often do not have distinct entries and exits, ruling out the traditional library metric of gate counts. To achieve an accurate number of visitors to exhibits would require student staff to sit and watch exhibits for hours, counting the people who entered and exited the space, which is not feasible or a good use of students' time. We have also experimented with using computer vision, embedded computers and software developed in-house to help with assessment, but the accuracy was too low and the cost too high. Thus, describing the impact of the exhibits using the language and theory of social network analysis in combination with some qualitative data gathered through strategic observation of exhibits has proven to be the most effective way to communicate their value. A small amount of strategically collected numerical data supplements the information we gather surrounding the number of people who participated in creating the exhibit and the cohort with whom they share their work.

The Active Learning Curation Program

The ALCP's pedagogy-centric focus requires different content than course- or research-based exhibits, where much of the content can be developed from the end-products of a course. Because the learning process and teaching techniques can be challenging for instructors to capture during their classes, this program offers the opportunity to have classes documented for the instructors. The manager of the program typically attends around eight sessions for an in-depth study. This provides her with a good overview of teaching techniques used in the class and an opportunity to see how students adopt practices to learn over the course of the semester. While this process allows for documentation of what learning techniques are happening in the room, interviews provide a more holistic picture of reasonings and meanings behind the actions in the classroom. Interviews are conducted with both students and instructors, typically with around ten questions rooted in observations made during the semester.

The exhibits facilitate different types of community building and connections depending on where they are located. The ALCP consists of almost entirely digital exhibitions, but they exist in two very different spaces. Some manifest as slides that are displayed on screens in public spaces around the NCB. The digital displays serve users of the building, which include students, faculty and staff involved in teaching and learning in similar rooms and spaces to those depicted in the exhibitions. The NCB is designed for instructors and students to be able to see what others are doing in the building; classrooms and casual seating areas have glass walls facing the corridor. Exhibitions developed for the digital displays take this process one step further and provide context for what is being seen by patrons of the classroom building. Some also provide names and course titles as users interact with them. In this way, exhibitions in the NCB can help those working in the space to feel more connected with one another.

Other exhibitions of active learning are presented online. These can include videos, pictures and text from interviews and documentation, as well as creative explorations of the documentation process. We make use of tagging systems embedded in the platforms used to host and publicise these unconventional exhibitions, making them discoverable when users search for things like active learning, pedagogy, higher education and terms specific to disciplines and courses being depicted. In this way, our aim is to foster connections between Virginia Tech's community of instructors and learners and people in other higher education institutions doing similar work. These are much less intense connections than are fostered in other places within the exhibit work because these more rarely lead to direct links between someone featured in an exhibition and another person at a different institution. Our goal is instead to create an awareness of work like this at Virginia Tech, much like the CEI brings awareness within Virginia Tech's community to specific courses taking place on its campus.

The process of collecting information and disseminating it requires more time than some other library services, but it also creates more intense ties between the faculty and students involved. Of the instructors who have participated in the ALCP, half have been involved in other library-based projects in the time since their classes have been documented. While students' involvement beyond the initial project is more challenging to document, the ALCP acts as an introduction to many library services available to students. Interviews are conducted using equipment from the Media Design Studios and throughout the documentation process we recommend services that might be useful to instructors and students: workshops relevant to their course, online resources that support learning and other library workers who may have more information.

In addition to creating more intense connections to the Library, the ALCP facilitates connections between the Library and other administrative departments around campus. The ALCP manager works closely with facilities, Technology-enhanced Learning and

Online Strategies and classroom Audio/Visual services, supporting them in their work when necessary, helping with installation, documentation and statistics surrounding changes they make to the building when appropriate. The ALCP manager also refers users of NCB spaces to these campus groups as appropriate, along with their online resources that support active learning practices in a variety of campus spaces. It should be noted that this program was created in conjunction with the Moss Arts Center at Virginia Tech, and as such the program creates a stronger connection between the two institutional structures. This circumstance has had a number of positive outcomes, including a repository to document the art held by different groups at Virginia Tech.

Conclusion

This chapter has documented how considering social networks when describing outcomes of non-traditional library services can help to express their value to other information professionals, administrators and academic institutions. While numerically some services may seem underutilised, library programs like studios and exhibits can reach a wide variety of students, faculty and community members, and create intense connections between different patrons of these spaces.

While a library's general public space allows for patrons to work and have access to numerous resources, the Fusion Studio allows for a group of motivated students to work together and create a more connected community. Exhibits provide contributors with an opportunity to use their coursework to connect with a wide variety of library patrons and foster interdepartmental relationships as those who participate in exhibitions look to see what fills the space after their content is removed. In addition, those who do not typically find themselves requiring library services can make use of the exhibits programs, and we as library faculty can point them in the direction of other useful services.

As we embarked on this analysis of our services it became clear that each one, though born from very similar values such as accessibility and playfulness, has developed in a way that creates a unique experience for people interacting with the services. Fusion Studio users end up with highly reciprocal interactions with each other and the studio manager. The CEI exists within a vast network of ties that create a network of collaborators and users which is high in multiplexity. And the ALCP takes deep dives with its partners that result in high intensity connections. One thing all three programs have in common is difficulty in considering how we might adapt and use the concepts and language of social network analysis in our current assessment structure. We all found what we learned very useful, and enlightening at times, but it is difficult to take what we have learned in this research and practically apply it to our work.

As we advocate for the value of using these types of data in assessment of traditional library services, they can also be used to support the development of new spaces that are unfamiliar to academic library spaces. Our work has largely been based on information manually collected and analysed, which takes a great deal of time to curate and is not as easily replicated by other institutions. Also, the data is less easily understood by those unfamiliar with our specific circumstances and programs. Finding ways to collect data more efficiently and quickly will be key in using social network analysis to improve our programs in the future, and communicating that data effectively will likely come with that process.

We anticipate that further analysing more quantitative and formal qualitative data will reveal ways in which we can create more clustered and intense social networks. A study that examines how social network concepts have been successfully used in formal assessment outputs could provide guidance on incorporating such analysis into library annual reports. Additionally, the development of a shared vocabulary for libraries to use in assessment would be a boon for the use of this type of analysis. Research that determines other ways to collect information about the connections and relationships developed in library spaces – whether they are traditional, non-traditional or something new altogether – could allow us to more accurately represent our impact on the populations we serve. It is clear to us that through further investigation, social network analysis could have a significant and valuable impact on the way we measure success in library services.

References

Anglada, L. M., (2007). Collaborations and alliances: social intelligence applied to academic libraries. *Library Management*. 28(6/7), 406–415. doi:10.1108/01435120710774530

Barrett, T. et al., (2015). A review of university maker spaces. In: American Society for Engineering Education (ASEE). *ASEE annual conference and exposition, 14–17 June, Seattle, WA*. pp. 26.101.1–26.101.17. doi:10.18260/p.23442

Bracke, P., (2016). Social networks and relational capital in library service assessment. *Performance Measurement and Metrics*. 17(2), 134–141. doi:10.1108/PMM-04-2016-0019

Corrall, S., (2014). Library service capital: the case for measuring and managing intangible assets. In: S. Faletar Tanacković and B. Bosančić, eds. *Assessing libraries and library users and use: proceedings of the 13th international conference Libraries in the Digital Age (LIDA) 16–20 June, Zadar, Croatia*, pp. 21–32. http://ozk.unizd.hr/lida/files/LIDA_2014_Proceedings.pdf

Georgia Tech Library., (2008). *A history of the Mad Housers: celebrating 20 years of Mad Housing*. https://smartech.gatech.edu/handle/1853/20521

Johnson, S., (2010). The genius of the tinkerer. *The Wall Street Journal*. 25 September. https://www.wsj.com/articles/SB10001424052748703989304575503730101860838

Madge, O. L., (2018). Academic libraries in Romania: cooperation and partnerships as seen through the eyes of library directors. *Library Management*. 39(8/9), 625–634. doi:10.1108/LM-10-2017-0103

NCSU., (2021). Frequently asked questions. *SCALE-UP: Student-Centered Active Learning Environment with Upside-down Pedagogies*. https://sites.google.com/view/scale-up/faq

Schlak, T., (2016). Social capital as operative in liaison librarianship: librarian participants' experiences of faculty engagement as academic library liaisons. *Journal of Academic Librarianship*. 42(4), 411–422. doi:10.1016/j.acalib.2016.04.008

Tichy, N. M., Tushman, M. L. and Fombrun, C., (1979). Social network analysis for organizations. *Academy of Management Review.* 4(4), 507–519. doi:10.5465/amr.1979.4498309

Town, J. S., (2015). Measures of relationship capital for the value scorecard. *Library Management.* 36(3), 235–247. doi:10.1108/LM-11-2014-0134

Virginia Tech Libraries., (2019a). *Exhibits* [past exhibit listing]. https://vtechworks.lib.vt.edu/handle/10919/85649

Virginia Tech Libraries., (2019b). *The Studios at Newman Library: what will you create?* [brochure]. https://lib.vt.edu/content/dam/lib_vt_edu/studios/StudiosBrochure.pdf

Virginia Tech Libraries., (2022a). *Exhibits.* https://lib.vt.edu/research-teaching/exhibits.html

Virginia Tech Libraries., (2022b). *Fusion Studio.* https://lib.vt.edu/create-share/fusion-studio.html

10
Advancing Research Data Management: A Social Capital Perspective on Functional Librarianship

Andrea Kosavic and Minglu Wang

Introduction

This chapter investigates librarianship in the area of research data management (RDM) through the lens of **social capital** theory. If social capital theories and concepts have the potential to bring to light the invisible or non-quantifiable value of academic library services (Bracke 2016; Corrall 2015), we postulate that they will lend a generative lens to explore the symbolic, network and normative effects of engagement within the academic library. Using librarian- and archivist-authored RDM literature as a case study, we will explore the dynamic relationships between network structures and the effects of functional librarianship on the social capital of academic libraries.

User studies of scientists and case studies of library RDM programs (Perrier et al. 2017) are common in the literature, but their underlying theoretical frameworks are limited to individual behaviourism (Fecher, Friesike & Hebing 2015), normative and historical institutionalism (Akers et al. 2014; Zenk-Möltgen et al. 2018), 'wicked problem' theory (Cox, Pinfield & Smith 2014) and organisational subculture theory (Cox & Verbaan 2016). Insights about the unique positionality of libraries within the academic community (Gold 2007) and potential leadership opportunities (Flores et al. 2015) have been mentioned but have yet to be clearly theorised to the level of a useful framework for deeper analysis or practical application of RDM research.

A social capital perspective will offer a theoretical framework which contextualises the potential benefits born of functional engagement, including access to information attributed to network positionality and bridging connections, mutual supports found in *communities* with dense ties and group cohesion, and agency for enhancing reputation (Lin et al. 2001). As the presence of social capital can be used as a predictor of healthier institutional, disciplinary and departmental climates, this examination will highlight opportunities for strengthening social capital in libraries. We will also suggest modalities for libraries and related organisations to more consciously transform themselves using identified relationship building strategies.

We provide a review of current RDM literature which summarises the existing theoretical assumptions applied in the research to describe the development of RDM services and solutions in light of existing challenges. This is followed by an introduction of classic symbolic, normative and network views of social capital theory, which are synthesised and applied to our sample during our coding exercise. Several essential themes surface in our axial coding exercise and they are summarised in our results and findings.

Literature review

In her 2007 article, Anna Gold predicted that research data services could lead to an upstream trajectory for library research support at the beginning of the research lifecycle. While the acquisition of necessary data skills and a deeper domain knowledge would be an investment for librarians to acquire, she maintained that acquiring this **human capital** was a worthwhile journey, as libraries are uniquely positioned stakeholders in that they exhibit a *culture* of collaboration across institutional boundaries (Gold 2007, section 2.4). While this early *social capital p*erspective on RDM did not see further exploration, since the 2010s RDM services have seen gradual establishment in many higher education institutions worldwide (Tenopir et al. 2015; Tenopir et al. 2017; Yoon & Schultz 2017; Koltay 2019).

According to a scoping review by Perrier et al. (2017), 301 elements of literature on RDM, including interviews and case studies, have emerged prior to April 2016. In these texts, individual behaviourism and normative institutionalism form the theoretical backbone which underlies most studies focusing on researchers' individual motivations and concerns about data sharing (Perrier et al. 2017, p. 9). When outside pressures are included in these analyses, for example, social policies or cultural norms, they are seen as eventually taking effect on individuals through attitudes, perceived benefits (Fecher, Friesike & Hebing 2015; Kim & Stanton 2016) and capacity for control (Zenk-Möltgen et al. 2018) at the cognitive level.

The reality of RDM appears much more complicated than what can be solved by combining 'carrots and sticks' as suggested by individual behaviourism and normative institutionalism. Instead, as a series of studies (Cox, Pinfield & Smith 2014; Awre et al. 2015) reveal, RDM challenges have met the criteria of a 'wicked' problem, in that it is viewed differently by different stakeholders, constrained by complicated cultural, political and economic factors, has no finite list of solutions and is under great resistance to change (Awre et al. 2015, p. 361). New types of leadership and new modes of addressing the challenges are needed, and, among them, relationship building and collaboration are key (Cox, Pinfield & Smith 2014, p. 13; Awre et al. 2015, p. 368).

A comparison of historical institutionalism approaches has been applied to describe the different pathways for establishing RDM services at variety of institutions (Akers et al. 2014; Bryant, Lavoie & Malpas 2018). In these studies, different institutional **resources** and contexts are compared and analysed and the results suggest that, in spite of their uniqueness, institutions seem to take a similar route to engaging with RDM, involving the following: environmental scan, needs assessment, creation of policy and service institutionalisation on one or more dimensions of the three RDM capacities which include education, expertise and infrastructure. Wicked problem theory and historical institutionalism highlight the multifaceted challenges of RDM and dynamic institutional RDM strategies. What remains absent is how individual researchers, libraries and other stakeholders are socially connected in this global RDM movement.

Another thread of theory (Verbaan & Cox 2014; Cox & Verbaan 2016; Jackson 2018) looks at the research library as an organisation in parallel with other research support units such as information technology (IT), ethics review boards and research administrators. These entities hold either complementary or differing views on RDM and thus could be perceived as partners as well as competitors for libraries when claiming authority over this growing area of research support. Research in this area helps libraries to better co-ordinate with these partners and creates a sense of momentum among libraries by highlighting the risk of missing this opportunity for leadership.

Coates (2014) reminds us that momentum for library leadership in RDM extends beyond a need for libraries to demonstrate their ongoing relevance to the academy. She underscores that advancing RDM is fundamentally about a cultural change and, as she states: 'A change in culture is long overdue' (Coates 2014, p. 599). This cultural change can be characterised by a more open, collaborative and participatory way of enacting science, but is experienced as a slow and complex process (National Academies 2018; Nemer 2018; Guédon et al. 2019). Could libraries be more conscious about our social and human capital and lead the engagement of researchers towards the open science culture envisioned worldwide?

Based on their experiences with researcher and library communities, a group of research fellows of the Council on Library and Information Resources and the Digital Library Federation advocate that libraries should leverage their relationships at different levels both internally and externally to assume a leadership role in fostering a more collaborative RDM landscape for researchers (Flores et al. 2015, p. 83). Due to the uneven development of RDM policies and practices at varying levels, they predict that demands and opportunities for library support at these different levels will flourish (Flores et al. 2015, pp. 88–90). Here, we see a tacit articulation of a need for social capital theory to analyse libraries based on their special network positionality.

Theories of social capital

To structure our analysis, we examined symbolic, network and normative views of social capital (Angelusz & Tardos 2001, p. 299). This section will briefly introduce these approaches and their key distinguishing elements, from which we have derived the scheme for our content analysis and interpretation.

Symbolic

A symbolic view of social capital carries an association with the work of Pierre Bourdieu. Bourdieu identifies three forms of capital: economic, cultural and social capital, and underscores the fluidity of connection between them (Bourdieu 1986). An individual's volume of social capital can be measured by 'the size of the network of connections he can effectively mobilize and on the volume of the capital (economic, cultural or symbolic) possessed in his own right by each of those to whom he is connected' (Bourdieu 1986, p. 249). Bourdieu's networks are not value neutral, they are class-based, power-laden structures that can shift to maintain particular group membership and exclude the other.

As will be seen with the normative and network approaches, network maintenance is critical for retaining social capital. Bourdieu (1986) advises that material and/or symbolic exchanges are required for maintenance and reinforcement of social capital, although a titular endowment ensures a socially instituted and guaranteed position. In this way, social capital is institutionalised through **expressive acts** between individuals that reinforce a privileged group and can be equated with the maintenance and reproduction of the dominant class.

Our symbolic analysis of the literature considers status, privilege, solidarity, group membership and the reproduction of reputation and inequality.

Normative

The normative view of social capital is often associated with the work of Coleman (1988; 1994) and Putnam (1993; 2000) and can be characterised in terms of social co-operation and norms of **reciprocity** and co-operation, often realised most readily through **network closure**. We see evidence of Durkheim's rational choice theory in that actors build social capital as a by-product while aspiring towards the maximisation of their utility (Häuberer 2011, p. 41).

Coleman (1988, p. S119; 1994, p. 312) identifies several forms of social capital: 'obligations and expectations, which depend on trustworthiness of the social environment, information-flow capability of the social structure, and norms accompanied by sanctions' and authority relations. The individual actor is assumed to have a set of resources that can be contributed to a greater social structure on which a group can draw. Coleman (1988, pp. S105–S108) believes that networks that have closure are especially useful, as they maintain a level of **trust**.

For Putnam (2000, p. 19), as for Coleman, social capital refers to efficiencies enjoyed by way of the norms of reciprocity and trustworthiness that arise from the connections among individuals. Putnam (2000, pp. 22–23) diverges from Coleman by dividing social capital into two main non-interchangeable categories which he terms '**bridging social capital**' and '**bonding social capital**'. Bridging social capital most resembles Coleman's view of social capital, in that it generates broader identities and a need for reciprocity, while bonding social capital acts as a form of 'sociological superglue such as that found in families that runs the risk of excluding the other' (Field 2017, p. 18).

Our coding for normative elements includes evidence of network closure, group obligations, endorsement of behaviours, identity building and social capital as an aid with the acquisition of credentials.

Network

The network approach is often discussed in terms of the work of Nan Lin (2001) and Ronald S. Burt (1992; 2004). They both view social capital in terms of how individuals mobilise resources for personal gain with a nod to the benefits or constraints of an individual's or group's network positionality.

Häuberer (2011, p. 87) explains that in Burt's theory actors can leverage their 'possession of financial, human and social capital generated from their position in the social structure'. The possession of these forms of capital determines an actor's ultimate access to social capital. In contrast to normative views of social capital, Burt (1992 cited in Häuberer 2011, p. 92) argues that social capital can be found in open networks that contain non-redundant connections between contacts called '**structural holes**'. Burt's optimal efficient network is where 'an actor reaches a network through just one contact' (cited in Häuberer 2011, p. 92).

For Lin (2001, p. 54), social capital revolves around the individual actor and their potential for finding and exploiting available resources; it is a given that individuals are ordered hierarchically in society, and that their position affects their ability to form networks with others and the degree of benefit they will obtain from their interaction. Lin (2001, p. 29) defines social capital as 'resources embedded in a social structure that are accessed and/or mobilized in purposive actions'. In general, Lin (2001, p. 48) indicates that preferred partners are those with slightly higher social statuses, as they offer a '**prestige effect**'. In Lin's theory, actors can engage in either expressive or **instrumental actions**. 'Expressive action' is motivated by asserting one's claims to resources and/or sharing sentiments, while 'instrumental action' is motivated by resource gain in the form of economic, political and/or social returns (Lin 2001, p. 75).

Our content analysis considers network elements including non-redundancy of contacts, **bridges** between networks, network positionality and expressive and instrumental action. Having laid out these three theoretical positions on social capital, we'll now proceed with describing our process.

Methodology

From an extensive bibliography of recent library literature discussing RDM services, a sample of 20 texts was assembled to represent RDM services at various levels and among different stakeholders, including published papers, white papers, website descriptions, reports from the field and case studies. This original material was imported into Dedoose software for analysis.

We completed two rounds of coding. For the first round, the corpus was coded deductively against a baseline coding scheme of key social capital concepts. The second round of coding followed a grounded theory approach. An axial coding strategy was employed and excerpts were re-examined to identify key themes that are relevant to the observed phenomena identified during the coding process.

Unlike qualitative studies which directly interview research subjects based on a predesigned instrument, the material we gathered was not written for the purpose of this particular research. We were conscious of this limitation of the evidence with respect to the theoretical social capital aspects we intended to examine. Other limitations of our sample included a narrowing to North American coverage and the potential for bias due to a disciplinary slant, the backgrounds of the authors and the attributes of scholarship intended for library audiences. Nevertheless, these sources offered ample data for examining the dynamics of social capital.

Results and discussion

From a quantitative perspective, the first round of coding offered minimal insights. We worked with a corpus of 20 texts, 12 top-level codes and 105 sub-codes. Coding yielded 304 excerpts with 706 code applications. We noted that code application favoured network characteristics of social capital, with 47% of our assigned codes describing network-related phenomena, 22% describing normative behaviours and 5% speaking to symbolic elements. The codes most often used spoke to network concepts: bridging ties at 5%, expressive action at 5% and network positionality at 4%.

These three most frequently applied codes demonstrated interesting code co-assignments. As an example, the code *expressive action* was found to be co-assigned with *human capital, facilitation of flow of information, instrumental action, network positionality, building self-identity* and *reputation*. This finding is supported by the literature, where Lin (2001, p. 45) explains that expressive actions are actions geared to preserving and maintaining one's resources; actions that are expressive in nature often take the form of broadcasting one's position in a network; however, the outcome remains 'primarily expressive: acknowledging ego's property rights or sharing ego's sentiment'.

For the code *bridging ties*, we saw frequent code co-assignment with *partnership, network position, instrumental action, expressive action* and *heterophily*. Here we see a reference to Putnam's view, which, while primarily normative in classification, does offer a network element. For Putnam, bridging social capital brings together people from diverse backgrounds, which is better for linkage to external **assets** and for information diffusion (Field 2017, p. 18). The co-assignment with **heterophily** is also to be expected, as 'heterophilous interaction' refers to an exchange of resources between actors with dissimilar resources, which is anticipated in the context of a bridging tie (Lin, 2001, p. 47).

For the code *network position*, frequent code co-assignment was found with *offset lack of other forms of capital, group expectations and obligations* and *network closure as exclusion*. This is an interesting code co-assignment, as it suggests a relationship between the inherent benefits of normative structures and how they can offset challenges of lower network positionality. We will discuss below examples of how libraries form normative structures at higher administrative levels, which help to better establish libraries as a partner, thus opening up opportunities that would be much more difficult to access without the establishment of normative expectations.

While the first round of coding offered minimal insights, the second round yielded several themes more relevant to an exploration of RDM in the library context. These themes examine and interrogate points of intersection between different theoretical views of social capital and are further explored below.

Symbolic positioning

A symbolic analysis in the area of faculty–librarian relations necessitates a discussion of **cultural capital.** Bourdieu (1986, p. 248) writes that 'academic qualification … institutes an essential difference between the officially recognized, guaranteed competence and simple cultural capital, which is constantly required to prove itself'. From a symbolic perspective, with the understanding that the degree requirements for American Library Association accreditation for professional librarians reside at the Master's level (ACRL 2018), there is potential that a disparity of cultural capital exists between librarians and faculty by way of elevated base requirements for faculty credentialling.

This disparity may also extend to a librarian's rank and status in the academy, where the availability of tenure to librarians in the academy is variable. As an example, Gillman's research of 664 doctorate-holding librarians shows that only 37% hold tenure-track status (Gillman 2008). We see in the literature, however, that equivalence in rank and status is not a panacea for symbolic positionality. Librarians with a Master of Library Science degree who have faculty status still face symbolic obstacles: 'The fact that faculty status can be given to an individual holding only a master's degree may also invite resentment from other faculty members holding PhDs, some authors have noted' (Silva et al. 2017, p. 430).

We observe limited articulation of inequality between faculty and librarians in our study. Poole and Garwood (2018, p. 814) speak to faculty misconceptions that libraries 'don't hire the type of person who … has the technical knowledge' to advance digital humanities work. They also surface in their literature review that librarians may struggle from a timidity born of an 'academic inferiority complex' (Vandegrift & Varner, 2013, p. 76). Dearborn (2018, p. 35) adds that the field of archivy also faces challenges with inclusion: 'While data management is certainly a space where archivists belong, it does not mean the sense of belongingness comes easily.'

As libraries are forming connections with researchers (Witt 2012; Akers et al. 2014; Ippoliti et al. 2018), schools and departments (Hiom et al. 2015), interactions run the risk of the library being perceived as a service provider, where librarians are not seen as equal research partners in the relationship. Claibourn (2015) describes a case where a library's RDM effort and leadership on campus surfaced feelings of territoriality. This was overcome by leveraging the pre-existing research identity of the new RDM librarian: 'Bringing in an academic with existing ties to the internal community proved vital. My prior experience helped to lessen some faculty's sense of the Library as "the other" and to enhance the Library's credibility among several key departments' (Claibourn 2015, p. 102).

Symbolic resistance to the role of libraries in the field of RDM, however, is not the general case. Our sample includes successful outcomes where librarians are principal investigators on research projects and substantially contribute to scholarly production: 'the involvement of librarians has ranged from helping to create a plan from scratch to reviewing plans, writing letters of support for grant proposals, and being named on grants as co-principal investigators and senior personnel' (Witt 2012, p. 181).

Regardless of perceived symbolic positioning, libraries, prior to engaging in broader campus outreach, tend to mobilise their own functional and subject liaison units or librarians and connect with or form working groups, training programs or support teams (Witt 2012; Akers et al. 2014; Ippoliti et al. 2018). Connections with IT services also help to bolster an initial RDM offering as the relationship between the library and IT is described as **homophilous relationship** and complementary: libraries offer data preservation and curation expertise, and IT departments offer data storage, security and potentially HPC (high performance computing) capacity, which promotes a reciprocity of referrals based on specific needs (Witt 2012). One might surmise from these actions that libraries are electing to bolster other forms of capital to offset a potential perceived lack of **symbolic capital**, but we are unable to assert this from our sample.

Bridging and bonding: leveraging and addressing low network density

An examination of our sample shows that libraries and their services suffer from a lack of understanding and visibility to their potential user groups. Surkis et al. (2017, p. 186) note 'a widespread lack of awareness of many available library services', while Poole and Garwood (2018, p. 813) describe an assumption about the range of library expertise: 'I really don't think if I went into the library I would have learned from someone who's a staff member [...] how to use MongoDB.' Whether these assumptions are born of a lack of interaction: 'It could be just that there's a lack of communication between my field and the librarians, so I may not know what they can do for me' (Poole & Garwood 2018, p. 817), or not being understood, it underscores the necessity for libraries to leverage their capacity for network building.

Our sample shows that the liaison model is a helpful tool for establishing bridging (low-density) ties across the institution. It also underscores the challenges of disseminating information: 'the importance of individual contacts within schools and faculties cannot be underestimated [sic]; they have been fundamental in establishing workshops and promoting the event amongst researchers' (Hiom et al. 2015, p. 479); 'departments with the highest attendance ... indicat[ed] that direct outreach to a user community is highly effective . . . The uptick in registrations with each new means of outreach indicated that there was no sole means of reaching the entire medical center community' (Surkis et al. 2017, p. 189).

The above quote by Surkis et al. (2017) suggests that the density of networks between and among faculty and across departments/schools can be characterised as low, and that there is a lack of bonding (high-density) connections between them. Scholars tend to find connection and belonging within their discipline or subdiscipline and are often a challenge to reach with any measure of reliability via institutional channels. The library liaison strategy directly addresses this challenge by building bridges to disparate networks and user communities, often one scholar at a time. This allows for personal channels by which to broadcast information to the campus community. In this way, liaisons have the capacity to bridge structural holes in the organisation.

Acting as a *bridge* between networks over a structural hole is a powerful position from a social capital perspective and affords four levels of **brokerage**: (1) an ability to communicate between networks, (2) the facility to share best practices with both groups, (3) the skill of drawing analogies between ostensibly different groups to translate and share beliefs or practices of utility and (4) the ability to synthesise new beliefs or behaviours that combine elements from both groups (Burt 2004, p. 355).

We observe that libraries make use of all four levels of brokerage internally as a result of the intersection of liaison with functional models. When librarians with RDM, metadata and subject domain expertise work with each other, they bring together information from their individual brokerage positions to the table. This is a powerful mechanism which allows for the synthesis of effective new services/programs in the libraries.

Libraries do not rely exclusively on low-density bridging strategies. We see in our sample many attempts to combat the challenge of outreach to disparate networks by building network density and functional groups on many levels. These can be seen internally within the library, such as described by Akers et al. (2014, p. 181) where library research data services 'permeate throughout the entire library culture'. We also see the model of embedding librarians into research groups, which establishes a sense of normativity with respect to librarians having a key role in advancing RDM services. As described by Clement et al. (2017, p. 110), 'The planned makeup of the institutional teams, each consisting of a faculty principal investigator, two student researchers, a librarian, and an educational technologist or IT support person, was a deliberate attempt to bring together stakeholders with diverse perspectives and complementary skill sets.'

Further to these examples, we note the forming of partnerships as a key strategy to increase institutional awareness of library expertise. Frequently mentioned partnerships include the forging of relationships with IT and sponsored research departments as mentioned by Clement et al. (2017). Other partnerships include national consortia working on a 'process for identifying data curators, expertise and activities . . . as part of a broader "network-building" initiative' (Moon et al. 2019, p. 1). Partnerships are also significant from a normative perspective, as is noted by Hiom et al. (2015, pp. 488–489), where the success of embedding into faculty projects is determined by the ability to 'align our educational programs with current disciplinary cultures and norms, as well as with local practices and needs' (Carlson et al. 2013, p. 207).

Leveraging network positioning

Whether it is at the level of the dean/library director or via established groups, forming connections with administrative entities is pivotal to the success of establishing libraries as key partners and leaders for RDM at the institutional level (Akers et al. 2014; Hiom et al. 2015; Ippoliti et al. 2018). It is notable that many of the outreach and partnership efforts in our sample are initially spearheaded by the dean/library director. This has theoretical significance from both a symbolic and network view of social capital.

From a symbolic perspective, Bourdieu theorises that an action may yield different returns 'according to the extent to which one is able to mobilize by proxy the capital of a group' (Bourdieu 1980, cited in Field 2017, p. 5). Functioning at an administrative level, a dean/library director has the symbolic authority and status to speak on behalf of the resources of their unit, which provides a more powerful and potentially more convincing voice at the table.

From a network perspective, a dean/library director functions at a higher level of network positionality within the institution and serves as an intermediary between library academic and professional staff and university administration. The notion of the *intermediary* is significant in social capital theory. An 'intermediary, with its embedded and commanded resources, projects better social credentials, so that its willingness to serve as an intermediary assures or elevates ego's credentials' (Lin 2001, p. 61). The **prestige hypothesis** (Laumann 1966) is also significant here, as it indicates that: 'preferred partners for interactions are those occupying slightly higher social statuses … The implication is that such interaction is expected to enhance the prestige of the less advantaged actors' (Lin 2001, p. 48).

Hence, examining a dean/library director's expressive action on behalf of the library elevates the credentials and the status of library activity in a particular area.

Normativity and the effectiveness of groups

Social capital is theorised by Putnam (1993, cited in Field 2017, p. 16) to have normative effects as it 'contributes to collective action by increasing the potential costs to defectors; fostering robust norms of reciprocity; facilitating flows of information, including information on actors' reputations; embodying the successes of past attempts of collaboration; and acting as a template for future cooperation'.

These effects are predicated on the formation of **social networks**, and in particular groups, which give rise to norms from which trust and reciprocity may arise (Field 2017, p. 18). Trustworthiness is not automatic and will more likely develop when social structures are closed, or relationships exist among all actors, as obligations and expectations can be raised and sanctioned effectively (Coleman 1988, p. S107; Häuberer 2011, p. 43).

Examples of normativity abound in the library profession and are particularly visible in planning documents that outline norms for group engagement. As an example, Atwood et al. (2017) share a breakdown of planning committee roles, offering a roadmap for others in the field to establish their own *communities of practice*. The norms introduced within the article can be interpreted as a social contract of sorts, laying out expectations for terms of engagement.

The Research Data Alliance (RDA 2018) similarly offers an expression of normative expectations established by a group. Nurnberger (2018, p. 27) speaks to the norms established by the RDA which are coalesced under the concept of *'radical collaboration'*:

Lacking the strategic oversight of TAB [Technical Advisory Board] or a similar group that is focused on inclusion, balance, and processes enabling representation, participants in an institutional setting must be self-conscious in considering with whom they are sharing a collaboration, who else should be involved, and how they will establish an environment that normalizes the behavioral expectations required for radical collaboration.

The forming of groups to effectively deliver RDM services within and beyond the institution is prevalent in our sample. In some cases, authors characterise directly the normative benefits of group membership: 'by investing in approaches to train and educate the research data management community in transparent, open, and welcoming ways, archivists and allies can frame the act of making good practices as an easy choice that contributes to a common, sustainable good' (Soyka 2018, p. 51). In others, we see a tacit reference to normativity in the formalisation of networked resources that are committed to sustainability and mentorship: 'And the human sustainability is fostered through the active mentoring and expertise transfer between the Senior Technical Consultant and the Data Management Consultants and the close collaboration between the DMS [data management services] and DC [Data Conservancy] teams' (Shen & Varvel 2013, p. 555).

These examples illustrate a recognition of the library community with respect to the effectiveness of group creation and the inherent nature of social capital as a structural asset that emerges out of networks of relations with individuals or collectives with the character of a public good (Häuberer 2011, p. 145).

Durability of ties

There is agreement among theorists that social capital is subject to diminishing without an actor's investment in its regular renewal. This section reflects on the durability of network structures in use by libraries.

Networks emerging from grant-funded projects require considerable investment from a limited number of participants and institutions. Librarians involved in these projects form dense ties due to the intensity of interactions required to successfully meet their mandates. For example, the Data Information Literacy project was focused on RDM training for graduate students (Carlson et al. 2013) and the Data Curation Network remains focused on data curation (Johnston 2018). While they have clear project goals, these networks are less durable, as they are vulnerable to sustainability challenges due to fixed terms of funding. Project-based networks would do well to invest in forming and renewing connections with related actors and communities to maximise the success of expressive action and ensure that outputs produced are communicated as valuable resources for the broader *community*.

Event-based regional RDM networks, particularly those anchored by rotating regional host institutions, hold the potential for greater network longevity (Atwood et al. 2017). While the conference and roundtable formats of these events tend to offer bridging opportunities, these connections are with librarians in close proximity who are encouraged to share practical experiences and learn from each other through mechanisms of discussion, lightning talks and workshops. Events of this nature evoke Bourdieu's (1986, p. 248) definition of social capital where these meetings help to create 'a durable network of more or less institutionalized relationships of mutual acquaintance and recognition – or in other words, membership in a group'.

The Canadian Portage Network, prior to joining the Digital Research Alliance of Canada (the Alliance), actively cultivated network durability. The network offered no shortage of opportunities for the community to join working and 'expert' groups and members worked closely and intensively within the active projects (Moon et al. 2019). These working groups enabled the constant renewing of ties within the community and offered opportunity to broadcast ongoing successes to keep the project front of mind. Portage also invested in renewing external connections by consciously building relationships with national partners. As both a close community of RDM experts in academic libraries and a formal and active national organisational co-ordinated structure, Portage embraced the opportunity to leverage library successes to secure their involvement as critical players within the future RDM landscape. The success and sustainability of Portage and its merger with the Alliance to integrate advanced research computing and research software can likely be attributed to its ability to renew and build meaningful relationships with other RDM stakeholders at institutional, national and international levels.

Conclusion

In this chapter we have investigated library involvement in RDM through a social capital lens with a focus on how libraries build and leverage social capital to advance their work. The concepts and theories discussed helped us to look at library interactions with the academic community beyond the lens of individual behaviourism and normative institutionalism. We found that researchers and RDM stakeholders are social entities connected dynamically on symbolic, normative and network dimensions and that libraries demonstrate a tacit understanding of how to leverage social capital.

Symbolic capital was often created and expressed through partnerships that multiply symbolic weight and value, and was utilised by deans/library directors who leveraged their network positionality to bridge structural holes in the institution and to connect personnel with contacts at higher levels. Consciously integrating normative elements of reciprocity, trust and clarity of obligations and expectations into governance and policy at all levels effectively leveraged the affordances of network closure. Functional and subject liaison models, particularly in partnership, created bridging ties over structural holes and performed expressive action to maintain network positionality and awareness.

At best, the strategies identified in this chapter refer to the RDM literature in aggregate, which brings a variety of successes to light but does not associate winning strategies with the differing resources libraries may have at their disposal. It is also not possible to tell why the libraries in our sample chose particular courses of action and how they reasoned between choices. A suggestion for future research would be to identify groupings of libraries based on perceived levels of social capital, and to examine methods in light of these different conditions to help decide between approaches. Should this research come to pass, creating a guidance document in the style of *Starting the conversation: university-wide research data management policy* (Erway, 2013) would help libraries with formulating successful strategies that best reflect their respective climates.

As an international cultural movement, RDM requires the full social and cultural engagement of researchers and related stakeholders to evolve social and technical infrastructure. As academic libraries continue to actively create new forms of social capital in partnership with a broad base of collaborators, an emphasis on professional education in the field to build an understanding of social capital for both students and practitioners would make available a useful theoretical frame of reference for strategy and practice. As academic libraries and the higher education sector seek innovative solutions for ever expanding challenges within a context of growing fiscal constraint, the social capital perspective is a framework that can help practitioners and leaders to recognise and critically evaluate their social positioning and assets, as well as strategically develop, leverage and deploy their resources.

References

ACRL., (2018). Statement on the terminal professional degree for academic librarians. Chicago, IL: *Association of College & Research Libraries*.
http://www.ala.org/acrl/standards/statementterminal

Akers, K. G., Sferdean, F. C., Nicholls, N. H. and Green, J. A., (2014). Building support for research data management: biographies of eight research universities. *International Journal of Digital Curation*. 9(2), 171–191. doi:10.2218/ijdc.v9i2.327

Angelusz, R. and Tardos, R., (2001). Change and stability in social network resources: the case of Hungary under transformation. In: N. Lin, K. Cook and R. S. Burt, eds. *Social capital: theory and research*. New York: Aldine de Gruyter. pp. 297–323.

Atwood, T. P., Condon, P. B., Goldman, J., Hohenstein, T., Mills, C. and Painter, Z. W., (2017). Grassroots professional development via the New England Research Data Management Roundtables. *Journal of eScience Librarianship*. 6(2), e1111.

Awre, C. et al., (2015). Research data management as a "wicked problem". *Library Review*. 64(4/5), 356–371. doi:10.1108/LR-04-2015-0043

Bourdieu, P., (1986). The forms of capital. In: J. G. Richardson, ed. *Handbook of theory and research for the sociology of education*. New York: Greenwood. pp. 241–258.

Bracke, P., (2016). Social networks and relational capital in library service assessment. *Performance Measurement and Metrics*. 17(2), 134–141. doi:10.1108/PMM-04-2016-0019

Bryant, R., Lavoie, B. and Malpas, C., (2018). *Sourcing and scaling university RDM service: the realities of research data management, Part 4*. Dublin, OH: OCLC Research. doi:10.25333/C3QW7M

Burt, R. S., (1992). *Structural holes: the social structure of competition*. Cambridge, MA: Harvard University Press.

Burt, R. S., (2004). Structural holes and good ideas. *American Journal of Sociology*. 110(2), 349–399. doi:10.1086/421787

Carlson, J., Johnston, L., Westra, B. and Nichols, M., (2013). Developing an approach for data management education: a report from the Data Information Literacy Project. *International Journal of Digital Curation*. 8(1), 204–217. doi:10.2218/ijdc.v8i1.254

Claibourn, M. P., (2015). Bigger on the inside: building Research Data Services at the University of Virginia. *Insights*. 28(2), 100–106. doi:10.1629/uksg.239

Clement, R., Blau, A., Abbaspour, P. and Gandour-Rood, E., (2017). Team-based data management instruction at small liberal arts colleges. *IFLA Journal*. 43(1), 105–118. https://www.ifla.org/files/assets/hq/publications/ifla-journal/ifla-journal-43-1_2017.pdf

Coates, H., (2014). Ensuring research integrity. *College & Research Libraries News*. 75(11), 598–601. doi:10.5860/crln.75.11.9224

Coleman, J. S., (1988). Social capital in the creation of human capital. *American Journal of Sociology*. 94(Supplement), S95–S120. doi:10.1086/228943

Coleman, J. S., (1994). Social capital. In: J. S. Coleman, *Foundations of social theory*. Cambridge, MA: Belknap Press. pp. 300–331.

Corrall, S., (2015). Capturing the contribution of subject librarians: applying strategy maps and balanced scorecards to liaison work. *Library Management*. 36(3), 223–234. doi:10.1108/LM-09-2014-0101

Cox, A. M. and Verbaan, E., (2016). How academic librarians, IT staff, and research administrators perceive and relate to research. *Library & Information Science Research*. 38(4), 319–326. doi:10.1016/j.lisr.2016.11.004

Cox, A. M., Pinfield, S. and Smith, J., (2014). Moving a brick building: UK libraries coping with research data management as a 'wicked' problem. *Journal of Librarianship and Information Science*. 48(1), 3–17. doi:10.1177/0961000614533717

Dearborn, C., (2018). Archives and data management: the Purdue story. *Research Library Issues*. 296, 33–36. doi:10.29242/rli.296.4

Erway, R., (2013). *Starting the conversation: university-wide research data management policy*. Dublin, OH: OCLC Research. https://www.oclc.org/content/dam/research/publications/library/2013/2013-08.pdf

Fecher, B., Friesike, S. and Hebing, M., (2015). What drives academic data sharing? *PLoS ONE*. 10(2), e0118053. doi:10.1371/journal.pone.0118053

Field, J., (2017). *Social capital*. 3rd ed. Abingdon, UK: Routledge.

Flores, J. R., Brodeur, J. J., Daniels, M. G., Nicholls, N. and Turnator, E., (2015). Libraries and the research data management landscape. In: J. C. Maclachlan, E. A. Waraksa and C. Williford, eds. *The process of discovery: the CLIR Postdoctoral Fellowship Program and the future of the academy*. Washington, DC: Council on Library and Information Resources. pp. 82–102. https://clir.wordpress.clir.org/wp-content/uploads/sites/6/RDM.pdf

Gillman, T., (2008). Academic librarians and rank. *The Chronicle of Higher Education*. 4 January. https://www.chronicle.com/article/Academic-LibrariansRank/45926

Gold, A., (2007). Cyberinfrastructure, data, and libraries, part 2: Libraries and the data challenge: roles and actions for libraries. *D-Lib Magazine*. 13(9/10). doi:10.1045/july20september-gold-pt2

Guédon, J.-C. et al., (2019). *Future of scholarly publishing and scholarly communication: report of the Expert Group to the European Commission*. Brussels, Belgium: European Commission, Directorate-General for Research and Innovation. doi:10.2777/836532

Häuberer, J., (2011). *Social capital theory: towards a methodological foundation*. Wiesbaden, Germany: VS Research. doi:10.1007/978-3-531-92646-9

Hiom, D., Fripp, D., Gray, S., Snow, K. and Steer, D., (2015). Research data management at the University of Bristol: charting a course from project to service. *Program*. 49(4), 475–493. doi:10.1108/PROG-02-2015-0019

Ippoliti, C., Koshoffer, A. E., Julian, R., Vandegrift, M., Soper, D. and Meridien, S., (2018). Scaling research data management services along the maturity spectrum: three institutional perspectives. *LIS Scholarship Archive*. doi:10.31229/osf.io/wz8fn

Jackson, B., (2018). The changing research data landscape and the experiences of ethics review board chairs: implications for library practice and partnerships. *Journal of Academic Librarianship*. 44(5), 603–612. doi:10.1016/J.ACALIB.2018.07.001

Johnston, L., (2018). Barriers to collaboration: lessons learned from the Data Curation Network. *Research Library Issues*. 296, 37–43. doi:10.29242/rli.296.5

Kim, Y. and Stanton, J. M., (2016). Institutional and individual factors affecting scientists' data-sharing behaviors: a multilevel analysis. *Journal of the Association for Information Science and Technology*. 67(4), 776–799. doi:10.1002/asi.23424

Koltay, T., (2019). Accepted and emerging roles of academic libraries in supporting research 2.0. *Journal of Academic Librarianship*. 45(2), 75–80. doi:10.1016/J.ACALIB.2019.01.001

Laumann, E. O., (1966). *Prestige and association in an urban community*. Indianapolis, IN: Bobbs-Merrill.

Lin, N., (2001). *Social capital: a theory of social structure and action*. Cambridge, UK: Cambridge University Press.

Lin, N., Cook, K. S. and Burt, R. S. eds., (2001). *Social capital: theory and research*. Hawthorne, NY: Aldine de Gruyter.

Moon, J., Wilkinson, S., Morin, J. and Wilson, L., (2019). *Portage progress report: for the period of January–March 2019*. Ottawa, Canada: Portage Network. doi:10.5281/zenodo.4597493

National Academies of Sciences Engineering, and Medicine., (2018). *Open science by design: realizing a vision for 21st century research*. Washington, DC: The National Academies Press. doi:10.17226/25116

Nemer, M., (2018). *Annual report of the Chief Science Advisor*. Ottawa, Canada: Office of the Chief Science Advisor. https://www.ic.gc.ca/eic/site/063.nsf/eng/h_97756.html

Nurnberger, A., (2018). The radical collaboration of RDA and what it means for developing institutional data management services. *Research Library Issues*. 296, 23–32. doi:10.29242/rli.296.3

Perrier, L. et al., (2017). Research data management in academic institutions: a scoping review. *PLoS ONE*. 12(5), e0178261. doi:10.1371/journal.pone.0178261

Poole, A. H. and Garwood, D. A., (2018). "Natural allies": librarians, archivists, and big data in international digital humanities project work. *Journal of Documentation*. 74(4), 804–826. doi:10.1108/JD-10-2017-0137

Putnam, R. D., (1993). *Making democracy work: civic traditions in modern Italy*. Princeton, NJ: Princeton University Press.

Putnam, R. D., (2000). *Bowling alone: the collapse and revival of American community*. New York: Simon & Schuster.

RDA., (2018). The value of the Research Data Alliance to libraries. *Research Data Alliance*. https://rd-alliance.org/get-involved/value-research-data-alliance-libraries

Shen, Y. and Varvel, V. E., (2013). Developing data management services at the Johns Hopkins University. *Journal of Academic Librarianship*. 39(6), 552–557. doi:10.1016/j.acalib.2013.06.002

Silva, E., Galbraith, Q. and Groesbeck, M., (2017). Academic librarians' changing perceptions of faculty status and tenure. *College & Research Libraries*. 78(4), 428–441. doi:10.5860/crl.78.4.428

Soyka, H., (2018). Seeking sustainability and inclusivity with transparent practices for research data management. *Research Library Issues*. 296, 49–52. doi:10.29242/rli.296.7

Surkis, A., LaPolla, F. W. Z., Contaxis, N. and Read, B., (2017). Data day to day: building a community of expertise to address data skills gaps in an academic medical center. *Journal of the Medical Library Association*. 105(2), 185–191. doi:10.5195/JMLA.2017.35

Tenopir, C. et al., (2015). Research data services in academic libraries: data intensive roles for the future? *Journal of eScience Librarianship*. 4(2), e1085. doi:10.7191/jeslib.2015.1085

Tenopir, C. et al., (2017). Research data services in European academic research libraries. *LIBER Quarterly*. 27(1), 23–44. doi:10.18352/lq.10180

Vandegrift, M. and Varner, S., (2013). Evolving in common: creating mutually supportive relationships between libraries and the digital humanities. *Journal of Library Administration*. 53(1), 67–78. doi:10.1080/01930826.2013.756699

Verbaan, E. and Cox, A. M., (2014). Occupational sub-cultures, jurisdictional struggle and third space: theorising professional service responses to research data management. *The Journal of Academic Librarianship*. 40(3–4), 211–219. doi: 10.1016/j.acalib.2014.02.008

Witt, M., (2012). Co-designing, co-developing, and co-implementing an institutional data repository service. *Journal of Library Administration*. 52(2), 172–188. doi:10.1080/01930826.2012.655607

Yoon, A. and Schultz, T., (2017). Research data management services in academic libraries in the US: a content analysis of libraries' websites. *College & Research Libraries*. 78(7), 920–933. doi:10.5860/crl.78.7.920

Zenk-Möltgen, W., Akdeniz, E., Katsanidou, A., Naßhoven, V., and Balaban, E., (2018). Factors influencing the data sharing behavior of researchers in sociology and political science. *Journal of Documentation*. 74(5), 1053–1073. doi:10.1108/JD-09-2017-0126

11

Relational Capital and Turnover in Liaison Roles in Academic Libraries

Alice Kalinowski

Introduction

Many academic libraries are emphasising building relationships with their campus and *communities*. While this goal is achieved using a variety of strategies, many libraries use liaison staffing models designed to build relationships with assigned groups on campus (Jaguszewski & Williams 2013). Despite the prevalence of relational and externally facing staffing models, the intersection of liaison relationships and staff turnover has not yet been explored. As libraries consider, implement and modify staffing models and liaison responsibilities, developing a framework for understanding the organisational risks and benefits of relationship-based liaison roles is pertinent. (The term liaison will be used as shorthand to encompass all library staff roles with an emphasis on building relationships with stakeholders. This could include subject and functional specialists, librarians and all other library staff.)

Social capital theory can be used as a theoretical framework to examine the effect of liaison turnover on academic libraries. Liaison work has already been explored within the context of social capital theory and relational assets. The emphasis has been on how it informs liaison outreach efforts (Ramsey 2016; Schlak 2016) and suggestions to incorporate relational assets into assessment practices (Bracke 2016). While social capital theory has been used frequently in management and marketing research on boundary-spanning employees and what happens when those employees move into other roles (Bendapudi & Leone 2002; Park & Shaw 2013), it has not been applied to turnover in library liaison roles.

This chapter will begin with an overview of social capital theory (emphasising relational assets) in academic librarianship, management and marketing research. It will then discuss social capital-oriented turnover research focused on boundary-spanning employees in these three fields. The findings of these various areas of research will be synthesised to inform the ways academic libraries can think about, design and implement their liaison programs from a new perspective.

Social capital theory

While definitions of *social capital* vary, one often used is 'The sum of the actual and potential

resources embedded within, available through, and derived from the network of relationships possessed by an individual or social unit' (Nahapiet & Ghoshal 1998, p. 243). In this definition, social capital has three separate but interrelated dimensions: structural, relational and cognitive, with relational assets being those 'created and leveraged through relationships' (Nahapiet & Ghoshal 1998, p. 244).

Social capital theory has been applied to a variety of domains, but as it relates to organisations it falls within the broader **resource-based view** (RBV) of an organisation. This view believes that the social capital of the employees is what allows organisations to gain a competitive advantage in the knowledge economy (Grant 1991). Notably, social capital can be an asset in both intra- and inter-firm relationships and can be held by a person or organisation (Van Wijk, Janse & Lyles 2008). The focus of this chapter will be on discussing how libraries can ensure that the social capital their liaisons create remains with the library in the event of turnover.

Social capital theory in library research

Discussions of social capital theory and liaison librarianship are couched in terms of the relational focus in academic libraries. In their report on the changing roles of liaisons, Jaguszewski and Williams (2013, p. 4) write that 'Building strong relationships with faculty and other campus professionals ... are necessary building blocks to librarians' success'. As a result, some have called for **relational capital** to be included in assessment metrics (Town & Kyrillidou 2013; Corrall 2014) as a way to understand the 'invisible work of relationship building that is critical to the success of new liaison models' (Bracke 2016, p. 138). This theme of using social capital to demonstrate library value to campus administrators is likely partially in response to limited budgets and the current assessment- and metrics-focused climate, but is a challenge due to its intangible nature (Koenig 1997; Town 2015; Kostagiolas & Asonitis 2011; Bracke 2016). Some have suggested using a 'value scorecard' that includes a relational capital dimension (Town & Kyrillidou 2013). Others focus on demonstrating how the library's intellectual and relational capital have contributed to the campus's own **intellectual capital**, such as research outputs and teaching (Koenig 1997; Iivonen & Huotari 2007; Frey & Codispoti 2010).

Social capital scholarship in academic libraries is not limited to discussions of demonstrating library value. For instance, some have used it to frame investigations on best practices in building relationships with faculty (Schlak 2016; Díaz & Mandernach 2017) or to look at how library outreach and programs are ways to *operationalise* social capital (Young & Rossmann 2015; Ramsey 2016). Others note the strategic importance of relationship building for new services around scholarly communications and data use (Town 2015; Lučić & Jagman 2019) and how a relational focus is creating new models for liaison programs (Eldridge et al. 2016; Church-Duran 2017). Even though Douglas and Gadsby (2019) did not directly refer to social capital theory, they focused on how relationships and relational-cultural theory are a way to understand how instruction co-ordinators get things done within their own libraries.

Social capital theory in management and marketing research

While social capital has been extensively applied in various ways in the business literature, this section will summarise those that are most relevant and applicable to liaison roles in libraries. In particular, it will focus on social capital as applied to inter-firm relationships.

Most relevant to this chapter are studies that focus on the social capital gained from relationships between two organisations and the employees who act as boundary spanners. Boundary-spanning roles as defined by Aldrich and Herker (1977, pp. 218–221) consist of two types of functions: 'information processing', including the selection, transmission and interpretation of information coming into the organisation; and 'external representation' of the organisation to external groups in roles involving resource acquisition, political legitimacy and organisational image. Liaison librarians can certainly can be thought of as boundary spanners (Corrall 2010).

In their role as information processors, boundary spanners perform a strategic role in the organisation by filtering and passing along relevant information that can be used to spur innovation and other change (Aldrich & Herker 1977). The relational and network ties these employees have provide organisations with access to resources, or '"who you know" affects "what you know"' (Nahapiet & Ghoshal 1998, p. 252). In other words, the social capital developed in these inter-firm relationships facilitates knowledge sharing that creates intellectual capital that can be used by firms to innovate in the form of new and improved services and products (Athanassopoulou 2006; Madhavaram & Hunt 2017; Tsai & Ghoshal 1998; Rottman 2008). This in itself can increase performance (such as by increased sales due to better products), but can also create value through new industry connections (Athanassopoulou 2006) and expanding market opportunities (Palmatier, Dant & Grewal 2007).

The concept of social capital and boundary-spanning employees in the management literature is supplemented by that of social capital and relational marketing in the marketing literature. Relational marketing is a concept introduced by Berry in 1983 that is about 'attracting, maintaining, and … enhancing customer relationships' (Shih-Tse Wang 2014, p. 318). Many studies have looked at the positive impacts of the relationship between a selling firm and a customer firm, particularly as embodied in boundary-spanning employees such as sales representatives (Palmatier, Dant & Grewal 2007; Athanassopoulou 2006; Huang et al. 2013). These benefits include increased performance, often measured by sales or customer satisfaction (Lahiri & Kedia 2011; Huang et al. 2013; Korschun 2015). Despite the almost overwhelmingly positive take on social capital in the literature, at least one study found that if buyer–supplier relationships are taken to the extreme, buyer firms' performance can decrease, likely because they are not able to make objective decisions (Villena, Revilla & Choi 2011).

Because one of the key ways that boundary-spanning relationships add value is through the intellectual capital they generate, many have tried to understand what factors facilitate or precede knowledge sharing. Researchers generally agree that strong relational ties, commitment, **trust** and co-operation are all key to knowledge sharing both within firms and between firms (Morgan & Hunt 1994; Widén-Wulff & Ginman 2004; Van Wijk, Janse & Lyles 2008; Aurier & N'Goala 2010). Additionally, the older the relationship, the stronger it tends to be (Kumar Scheer & Steenkamp 1995; Palmatier et al. 2006), and the more the boundary-spanning employee identifies with the other organisation, the more collaborative their relationship is (Korschun 2015).

In summary, it is widely accepted that boundary-spanning employees have valuable intellectual and social capital derived from their relationships. What happens when a boundary-spanning employee leaves?

Turnover and social capital theory

There is little literature on turnover in academic libraries, and what does exist focuses on why people leave organisations (Fyn et al. 2019; Antúnez 2018). The most relevant existing study explored how employees' knowledge is captured (or not) when they leave (Agarwal & Islam 2015). This mirrors the arc of the larger body of research on turnover in organisational behaviour, which is still largely focused on why people leave (Rubenstein et al. 2017). However, turnover research is increasingly investigating why people stay and the effect of collective turnover on organisations from a **human capital** perspective (Hom et al 2017).

The management literature has focused on how to understand and prevent the causes of turnover, the effect of turnover on organisational performance and, relatedly, the effect of turnover on customer experience. Turnover has been found to increase when there is a mismatch between employee and firm expectations or beliefs of good service (Schneider & Bowen 1985), when employees are advising those whom they do not have to work with (Soltis et al. 2013), when employees' organisational attachment is weakened (such as through the departure of a valued leader) (Shapiro et al. 2016) and when employees experience emotional exhaustion (Shih-Tse Wang 2014). Turnover can be decreased when employees have feelings of social support (Soltis et al. 2013), strong organisational attachment (Shapiro et al. 2016), lower emotional exhaustion (Shih-Tse Wang 2014) and are adequately onboarded and socialised (Hom et al. 2017).

Staw's (1980) landmark article on employee turnover challenged researchers and organisations to understand what impact turnover has on the organisation. The management literature shows that voluntary turnover negatively affects organisational performance despite there being some benefits to turnover, such as gaining new perspectives (Park & Shaw 2013; Holtom & Burch 2016). Some have attributed this to the loss of human and intellectual capital (Nahapiet & Ghoshal 1998), because employees have to spend more time transferring and acquiring knowledge rather than using knowledge to create value for the firm (Kacmar et al. 2006). Alternatively, it could be due to how voluntary turnover severs inter-firm relationships and the trust and loyalty that had been cultivated among boundary spanners (Holtom & Burch 2016).

Turnover also negatively impacts customer satisfaction (Park & Shaw 2013), which itself can affect organisational performance (Kacmar et al. 2006). This is partially because of a loss of the relational capital (such as knowledge of clients' preferences and needs), human capital (specific job task knowledge) (Ployhart, Van Iddekinge & Mackenzie 2011; Holtom & Burch 2016) and social capital (to get things done efficiently based on the knowledge gained within the firm) (Kacmar et al. 2006).

While there are many benefits to boundary-spanning relationships, there can also be specific risks in regard to employee turnover. Looking through the lens of relational marketing, sometimes a boundary-spanning employee can generate more relational capital or loyalty for themselves than for the organisation, making the firm vulnerable to clients following the employee to a competitor (Bendapudi & Leone 2002; Palmatier, Scheer & Steenkamp 2007). This poses a challenging management question about how to balance the desire to maximise the social capital employees generate from their relationships with clients, while also ensuring that the customer can differentiate between the products or services the firm is providing and the employee who is doing or delivering the work (Bendapudi & Leone 2002). While the danger of faculty following a liaison to a new organisation does not exist in academia in the same way that it can in some industries, there is still a risk that faculty will no longer work with the library as closely as they did with an employee they had developed a relationship with.

Discussion and implications

The literature indicates that when relationships with external groups are of key importance to an organisation, care should be taken to manage turnover so as to minimise the risk to the organisation. As many academic librarians have developed staffing and service models built on relational capital, one could argue that administrators should pay more attention to turnover. One particularly helpful way of framing the outcome of turnover was suggested by Vafeas (2015) and includes three core contexts that will be explored further:

1   how explicit client-specific knowledge is within the service firm;
2   how relationally connected the client is to the service firm; and
3   how the service firm manages the turnover process.

How explicit is department-specific knowledge within the library?

One of the key benefits of boundary-spanning employees is the knowledge they can generate; however, this can provide value to the firm only if it is shared within the organisation and leveraged to make 'market-driven' strategic decisions (Tsai & Ghoshal 1998; Palmatier, Dant & Grewal 2007). This is especially important as customer needs and relationships become more complex and cannot be sufficiently met by one person alone (Bachrach, Mullins & Rapp 2017). The importance and challenges of intra-organisational knowledge sharing exist in many academic libraries that are creating teams to provide more services than can be achieved by one liaison and/or are hiring functional specialists to provide deeper levels of expertise on areas like data management and digital scholarship (Hoodless & Pinfield 2018).

In this regard, many studies have investigated what leads people to share knowledge within their organisations. In addition to fostering a culture of trust and commitment, some practices that can support intra-firm knowledge sharing include formal orientation and socialisation programs, incorporating knowledge sharing in performance reviews and providing technology that supports the existing knowledge-sharing culture (Cabrera & Cabrera 2005). Overall, having a knowledge-sharing and collaborative culture can also help to foster the exchange of the more ambiguous and challenging information (Van Wijk, Janse & Lyles 2008). However, the mitigating factors for *knowledge transfer* within organisations are complex and are still not fully understood (Inkpen & Tsang 2005).

In May 2019, the author attended a workshop on fostering collaboration at the Stanford Graduate School of Business. At the workshop, Professor Francis Flynn led a 'Reciprocity Ring' exercise where participants wrote a request for help (such as a personal request for travel recommendations or a professional request for help in negotiating with a vendor) on a yellow sticky note, which was read aloud and placed on a board in a circle. Once all the notes were on the board, participants indicated on a blue sticky note how they could help fulfil a request. One takeaway from the exercise was that the majority of requests were fulfilled through the secondary networks and connections of the participants, demonstrating the value of relational capital. Additionally, Flynn said that in organisations that value knowledge and unique skillsets (such as in academia), participants make more personal requests than they do professional ones. In this way, an **organisational culture** that prizes unique intelligence and skills can inhibit or prevent the asking for and giving of help. It is likely that this same phenomenon exists within academic libraries. This could be compounded in some organisations if liaisons are seen to be in competition with one another over funding or services to support their assigned groups on campus, which, according to Hoodless and Pinfield (2018), can lead to advocating for the interests of one group rather than the strategic priorities of the entire library.

Knowledge management

Knowledge management is one way to mitigate negative aspects of turnover, particularly when capturing department- or client-specific knowledge. This can be accomplished throughout the liaisons' time at the library, from *onboarding* to *offboarding* and everything in between. For instance, while many academic libraries have formal onboarding programs to introduce new employees to their organisation, fewer focus on internal socialisation with library staff (Graybill et al. 2013), let alone with external groups on campus. This socialisation is important, as it can help to build new employees' social capital within the organisation (Cabrera & Cabrera 2005) that in turn fosters relationships that can facilitate knowledge sharing.

While a boundary-spanning liaison is working, documenting the intangible information they accrue about their assigned departments in reference and instruction tracking or ticketing systems or customer relationship management software is one way to externalise or make explicit social capital. These types of documentation systems can be an invaluable resource to incoming liaisons because of how much intangible knowledge they contain. However, there has been some resistance to these systems, particularly around applying business language to libraries, such as 'selling' the library or 'spying' on faculty behaviour (Barr & Tucker 2018). While there is room to debate the best way to frame and talk about liaison roles, adopting some systems commonly used in the business world would be one way to support the strategic importance that liaison relationships have in many academic libraries by ensuring that knowledge about key patrons is not confined to one liaison.

While knowledge management is often understood to be increasingly important as library work becomes more knowledge-based, knowledge management practices are not consistently implemented (Daland 2016; Nazim & Mukherjee 2016; Koloniari & Fassoulis 2017). The only known study to connect library turnover and knowledge management is by Agarwal and Islam (2015), who surveyed academic libraries about their knowledge management practices when employees were leaving positions and determined that most organisations were not adequately addressing the issue. Investing in increasing knowledge management practices within academic libraries would help existing staff to leverage each other's social capital with library patrons, as well as aiding in the turnover process.

How relationally connected is the department to the library?

Research on customer loyalty shows that part of a customer's loyalty to an organisation rests in a boundary-spanning employee, and so the relationship between the customer and organisation can be jeopardised if that employee leaves their position (Bendapudi & Leone 2002; Kumar & Yakhlef 2016; Palmatier, Scheer & Steenkamp 2007). As a way to mitigate this risk, some suggest reducing the reliance on one person to manage that relationship, such as by utilising shadowing and teams (Rottman 2008; Vafeas 2015), rotations (Palmatier, Scheer & Steenkamp 2007; Vafeas 2015) and providing multiple points of contact (Holtom & Burch 2016). However, these strategies need to be undertaken with care so as not to undermine the value created by boundary-spanning relationships (Palmatier, Scheer & Steenkamp 2007).

The team models many academic libraries are using can be viewed as a potential way to mitigate the risks of liaison turnover, because patrons' relationships do not rest in one liaison. Additionally, documentation systems and other knowledge-sharing mechanisms not only transfer knowledge from an outgoing to an incoming liaison, but also allow knowledge to be shared in real time within the library. This not only helps each liaison to be more effective in their own job but also allows the library to avoid looking uninformed or disorganised when multiple liaisons are working with a single patron.

Keeping various library staff involved and informed with patron interactions can sometimes be challenging, particularly in libraries with very loosely organised liaison programs. Therefore, libraries could create best practices around how this communication should be managed internally. For instance, as there is more of an emphasis on **_translational research_** in sciences, more faculty and students in science, medical and engineering schools are asking business-related questions around market research.

However, there are often no mechanisms in place to share these interdisciplinary questions and interactions between the individual libraries or liaisons who work with these different patron groups. In this case, medical school patrons might be asking these questions to the business librarian directly, and if that information is not shared back to the medical librarians, they may not realise this is an area of interest for their patrons.

In addition to utilising teams of liaisons, another way to mitigate liaison turnover is to emphasise the value of the library in addition to that of the liaison. This could include having staff wear branded attire or emphasise the expertise of others in the organisation (Bendapudi & Leone 2002). One way to aid this is to provide training and support on how to communicate with faculty and other patrons in a way that is designed to improve the liaison's social capital as well as the library's. There are many resources showing how liaisons can effectively communicate with patrons (one example is Bales, Lefkowitz & Tsang 2017), but providing some additional language that can be used by liaisons to promote or advocate for the knowledge and skills of their colleagues might be helpful. Ultimately, the goal is to leverage the personal relationships that liaisons have to the point that they provide value to the library while also mitigating the risk of the liaison leaving and taking that relational capital with them.

How does the library manage the turnover process?

In addition to capturing patron-specific knowledge and ensuring that 'customer' loyalty is held with the organisation as well as a boundary-spanning employee, another way to mitigate the risk of employee turnover is to clearly communicate the turnover process and strategy (Bendapudi & Leone 2002; Rottman 2008; Vafeas 2015; Kumar & Yakhlef 2016). In particular, increasing transparency with patrons about how the transition will be handled and how the knowledge of their relationship and needs would be 'codified' can increase trust and loyalty (Bendapudi & Leone, 2002; Kumar & Yakhlef 2016).

Beyond Agarwal and Islam (2015), little else is written about how libraries are managing knowledge transfer when a liaison changes roles. Therefore, it is important for libraries to develop a turnover or offboarding process with a focus on making sure that it is aiding the knowledge-transfer process and being clearly communicated with the key patrons. This could start with an announcement from the outgoing liaison to provide an introduction to their replacement (or whoever will be filling in until a replacement is hired). To help retain the relational capital that the liaison generated, they can affirm the expertise of the replacement and other library staff, as well as personally contact key faculty and staff whom the liaison has worked with to inform them that all the relevant materials are being passed on to the replacement. Assuming that there will be an interim period between the departure of the liaison and the hiring of a replacement, having the interim liaison keep the department up to date on the recruiting and hiring process (which can take many months in academia) is important.

Another option is to involve patrons in the recruitment process for the replacement, as a way to increase buy-in with the new boundary-spanning employee (Vafeas 2015). This could be accomplished by having the candidate meet with faculty for lunch, inviting them to attend the interviewee's presentation or including a faculty member on the search committee. Then, once a new liaison is hired, the interim contact or another liaison who has worked closely with the department or specific individuals can help with the introductions. This clear communication with patrons about the knowledge management practices and turnover strategy is a way of increasing loyalty and relational ties to the library.

While developing robust turnover programs that maximise the transfer of social capital from the outgoing liaison to the incoming liaison can take time and other resources, the time and effort spent developing and implementing them can be important in supporting the strategic goals of the library if they depend on relationships with others on campus.

Conclusion

This chapter has provided an overview of some key themes within social capital theory in the workplace from three disciplines: academic libraries, management and marketing. In particular, it has looked at how business research has used social capital theory as a way of understanding the effect of boundary-spanning employee turnover on an organisation's performance and relationship with customers, in efforts to apply this to academic libraries.

In summary, academic libraries have been placing increasing emphasis on the relational and social capital employees develop with various people and groups on campus. While this intellectual capital is increasingly recognised and starting to be considered in terms of library value and assessment practices, no attention has been paid to what happens to the relational and social capital when liaisons change positions. Academic libraries can start to explore this area theoretically and empirically by drawing on the insights gained from decades of research in the management and marketing literature. Additionally, library management and human resources staff can create processes and procedures around the turnover process to help mitigate some of the issues that surround that, as well as working to develop or foster a culture that encourages knowledge sharing.

It would be beneficial for libraries to gain a better understanding of how the relational capital that boundary-spanning liaisons generate can be used to strategically support the library and its performance on campus. In particular, coming up with best practices around managing those boundary-spanning relationships, specifically in times of turnover, to help improve the library's return on investment in those relationships would be useful.

References

Agarwal, N. K. and Islam, Md. A., (2015). Knowledge retention and transfer: how libraries manage employees leaving and joining. *VINE*. 45(2), 150–171. doi:10.1108/VINE-06-2014-0042

Aldrich, H. E. and Herker, D., (1977). Boundary spanning roles and organization structure. *Academy of Management Review*. 2(2), 217–230. doi:10.5465/amr.1977.4409044

Antúnez, M. Y., (2018). Perspectives in hiring academic librarians with frequent job changes. *Journal of Library Administration*. 58(3), 205–229. doi:10.1080/01930826.2018.1436747

Athanassopoulou, P., (2006). Determining relationship quality in the development of business-to-business financial services. *Journal of Business-to-Business Marketing*. 13(1), 87–120. doi:10.1300/J033v13n01_03

Aurier, P. and N'Goala, G., (2010). The differing and mediating roles of trust and relationship commitment in service relationship maintenance and development. *Journal of the Academy of Marketing Science*. 38(3), 303–325. doi:10.1007/s11747-009-0163-z

Bachrach, D. G., Mullins, R. R. and Rapp, A. A., (2017). Intangible sales team resources: investing in team social capital and transactive memory for market-driven behaviors, norms, and performance. *Industrial Marketing Management*. 62, 88–99. doi:10/1016/j.inmarran.2016.08.001

Bales, J. G., Lefkowitz, M. and Tsang, M., (2017). Talking so faculty will listen, listening so faculty will talk: engagement strategies for library liaisons [ARL panel presentation and workshop]. In: *American Library Association annual conference, 22–27 June, Chicago, IL*. https://www.arl.org/resources/reimagining-the-library-liaison

Barr, P. and Tucker, A., (2018). Beyond saints, spies and salespeople: new analogies for library liaison programmes. *In the Library with the Lead Pipe*. 19 September. http://www.inthelibrarywiththeleadpipe.org/2018/beyond-saints-spies-and-salespeople

Bendapudi, N. and Leone, R. P., (2002). Managing business-to-business customer relationships following key contact employee turnover in a vendor firm. *Journal of Marketing*. 66(2), 83–101. doi:10.1509/jmkg.66.2.83.18476

Bracke, P., (2016). Social networks and relational capital in library service assessment. *Performance Measurement and Metrics*. 17(2), 134–141. doi:10.1108/PMM-04-2016-0019

Cabrera, E. F. and Cabrera, A., (2005). Fostering knowledge sharing through people management practices. *International Journal of Human Resource Management*. 16(5), 720–735. doi:10.1080/09585190500083020

Church-Duran, J., (2017). Distinctive roles: engagement, innovation, and the liaison model. *portal: Libraries and the academy*. 17(2), 257–271. doi:10.1353/pla.2017.0015

Corrall, S., (2010). Educating the academic librarian as a blended professional: a review and case study. *Library Management*. 31(8/9), 567–593. doi:10.1108/01435121011093360

Corrall, S., (2014). Library service capital: the case for measuring and managing intangible assets. In: S. Faletar Tanacković and B. Bosančić, eds. *Assessing libraries and library users and use: proceedings of the 13th international conference Libraries in the Digital Age (LIDA), 16–20 June, Zadar, Croatia*. pp. 21–32. http://ozk.unizd.hr/lida/files/LIDA_2014_Proceedings.pdf

Daland, H., (2016). Managing knowledge in academic libraries: are we? should we? *LIBER Quarterly*. 26(1), 28–41. doi:10.18352/lq.10154

Díaz, J. O. and Mandernach, M. A., (2017). Relationship building one step at a time: case studies of successful faculty–librarian partnerships. *portal: Libraries and the Academy*. 17(2), 273–282. doi:10.1353/pla.2017.0016

Douglas, V. A. and Gadsby, J., (2019). All carrots, no sticks: relational practice and library instruction coordination. *In the Library with the Lead Pipe*. 10 July.

http://www.inthelibrarywiththeleadpipe.org/2019/all-carrots-no-sticks-relational-practice-and-library-instruction-coordination

Eldridge, J., Fraser, K., Simmonds, T. and Smyth, N., (2016). Strategic engagement: new models of relationship management for academic librarians. *New Review of Academic Librarianship.* 22(2/3), 160–175. doi:10.1080/13614533.2016.1193033

Frey, S. and Codispoti, M., (2010). Bowling alone in the library: building social capital on campus. In: *2010 joint conference of the National Popular Culture and American Culture Associations, 31 March–3 April, St Louis, MO.* http://scholars.indstate.edu/handle/10484/919

Fyn, A., Heady, C., Foster-Kaufman, A. and Hosier, A., (2019). Why we leave: exploring academic librarian turnover and retention strategies. In: *Recasting the narrative: ACRL 2019, 10–13 April, Cleveland, OH, USA.* Chicago, IL: Association of College and Research Libraries. pp. 139–148. http://www.ala.org/acrl/conferences/acrl2019/papers

Grant, R. M., (1991). The resource-based theory of competitive advantage: implications for strategy formulation. *California Management Review.* 33(3), 14–35. doi:10.2307/41166664

Graybill, J. O., Hudson Carpenter, M. T., Offord, J., Piorun, M. and Shaffer, G., (2013). Employee onboarding: identification of best practices in ACRL libraries. *Library Management.* 34(3), 200–218. doi:10.1108/01435121311310897

Holtom, B. C. and Burch, T. C., (2016). A model of turnover-based disruption in customer services. *Human Resource Management Review.* 26(1), 25–36. doi:10.1016/J.HRMR.2015.09.004l

Hom, P. W., Lee, T. W., Shaw, J. D. and Hausknecht, J. P., (2017). One hundred years of employee turnover theory and research. *Journal of Applied Psychology.* 102(3), 530–545. doi:10.1037/ap10000103

Hoodless, C. and Pinfield, S., (2018). Subject vs. functional: should subject librarians be replaced by functional specialists in academic libraries? *Journal of Librarianship and Information Science.* 50(4), 345–360. doi:10.1177/0961000616653647

Huang, Y., Luo, Y., Liu, Y. and Yang, Q., (2013). An investigation of interpersonal ties in interorganizational exchanges in emerging markets: a boundary-spanning perspective. *Journal of Management.* 42(6), 1557–1587. doi:10.1177/0149206313511115

Iivonen, M. and Huotari, M.-L., (2007). The university library's intellectual capital. *Advances in Library Administration and Organization.* 25, 83–96. doi:10.1016/S0732-0671(07)25004-7

Inkpen, A. C. and Tsang, E. W., (2005). Social capital, networks, and knowledge transfer. *Academy of Management Review.* 30(1), 146–165. doi:10.5465/amr.2005.15281445

Jaguszewski, J. M. and Williams, K., (2013). *New roles for new times: transforming liaison roles in research libraries.* Washington, DC: Association of Research Libraries. https://www.arl.org/wp-content/uploads/2015/12/nrnt-liaison-roles-revised.pdf

Kacmar, K. M., Andrews, M. C., Van Rooy, D. L., Steilberg, R. C. and Cerrone, S., (2006). Sure everyone can be replaced … but at what cost? Turnover as a predictor of unit-level performance. *Academy of Management Journal.* 49(1), 133–144. doi:10.5465/amj.2006.20785670

Koenig, M. E. D., (1997). Intellectual capital and how to leverage it. *The Bottom Line*. **10**(3), 112–118. doi:10.1108/08880459710175368

Koloniari, M. and Fassoulis, K., (2017). Knowledge management perceptions in academic libraries. *Journal of Academic Librarianship*. **43**(2), 135–142. doi:10.1016/j.acalib.2016.11.006

Korschun, D., (2015). Boundary-spanning employees and relationships with external stakeholders: a social identity approach. *Academy of Management Review*. **40**(4), 611–629. doi:10.5465/amr.2012.0398

Kostagiolas, P. A. and Asonitis, S., (2011). Managing intellectual capital in libraries and information services. *Advances in Librarianship*. **33**, 31–50. doi:10.1108/S0065-2830(2011)0000033005

Kumar, N. and Yakhlef, A., (2016). Managing business-to-business relationships under conditions of employee attrition: a transparency approach. *Industrial Marketing Management*. **56**, 143–155. doi:10.1016/j.indmarman.2016.01.002

Kumar, N., Scheer, L. K. and Steenkamp, J.-B. E. M., (1995). The effects of perceived interdependence on dealer attitudes. *Journal of Marketing Research*. **32**(3), 348–356. doi:10.1177/002224379503200309

Lahiri, S. and Kedia, B. L., (2011). Determining quality of business-to-business relationships: a study of Indian IT-enabled service providers. *European Management Journal*. **29**(1), 11–24. doi:10/1016/j.emj.2010.08.003

Lučić, A. and Jagman, H., (2019). From survey to social network: building new services through connections. In: *Recasting the narrative: ACRL 2019, 10–13 April, Cleveland, OH, USA*. Chicago, IL: Association of College and Research Libraries. pp. 338–347. http://www.ala.org/acrl/conferences/acrl2019/papers

Madhavaram, S. and Hunt, S. D., (2017). Customizing business-to-business (B2B) professional services: the role of intellectual capital and internal social capital. *Journal of Business Research*. **74**, 38–46. doi:10.1016/j.jbusres.2017.01.007

Morgan, R. M. and Hunt, S. D., (1994). The commitment-trust theory of relationship marketing. *Journal of Marketing*. **58**(3), 20–38. doi:10.1177/002224299405800302

Nahapiet, J. and Ghoshal, S., (1998). Social capital, intellectual capital, and the organizational advantage. *Academy of Management Review*. **23**(2), 242–266. doi:10.5465/amr.1998.533225

Nazim, M. and Mukherjee, B., (2016). Knowledge management tools for libraries. In: M. Nazim and B. Mukherjee, eds. *Knowledge management in libraries: concepts, tools and approaches*. Cambridge, MA: Chandos. pp. 115–148.

Palmatier, R. W., Dant, R. P. and Grewal, D., (2007). A comparative longitudinal analysis of theoretical perspectives of interorganizational relationship performance. *Journal of Marketing*. **71**(4), 172–194. doi:10.1509/jmkg.71.4.172

Palmatier, R. W., Scheer, L. K. and Steenkamp, J.-B. E. M., (2007). Customer loyalty to whom? Managing the benefits and risks of salesperson-owned loyalty. *Journal of Marketing Research*. **44**(2), 185–199. doi:10.1509/jmkr.44.2.185

Palmatier, R. W., Dant, R. P., Grewal, D. and Evans, K. R., (2006). Factors influencing the effectiveness of relationship marketing: a meta-analysis. *Journal of Marketing*. 70(4), 136–153. doi:10.1509/jmkg.70.4.136

Park, T-Y. and Shaw, J. D., (2013). Turnover rates and organizational performance: a meta-analysis. *Journal of Applied Psychology*. 98(2), 268–309. doi:10.1037/a0030723

Ployhart, R. E., Van Iddekinge, C. H. and Mackenzie, W. I., (2011). Acquiring and developing human capital in service contexts: the interconnectedness of human capital resources. *Academy of Management Journal*. 54(2), 352–368. doi:10.5465/amj.2011.60263097

Ramsey, E., (2016). It's not just what you know but who you know: social capital theory and academic library outreach. *College & Undergraduate Libraries*. 23(3), 328–334. doi:10.1080/10691316.2016.1206317

Rottman, J. W., (2008). Successful knowledge transfer within offshore supplier networks: a case study exploring social capital in strategic alliances. *Journal of Information Technology*. 23(1), 31–43. doi:10.1057/palgrave.jit.2000127

Rubenstein, A. L., Eberly, M. B., Lee, T. W. and Mitchell, T. R., (2017). Surveying the forest: a meta-analysis, moderator investigation, and future-oriented discussion of the antecedents of voluntary employee turnover. *Personnel Psychology*. 71(1), 23–65. doi:10.1111/peps.12226

Schlak, T., (2016). Social capital as operative in liaison librarianship: librarian participants' experiences of faculty engagement as academic library liaisons. *Journal of Academic Librarianship*. 42(1), 411–422. doi:10.1016/j.acalib.2017.09.005

Schneider, B. and Bowen, D. E., (1985). Employee and customer perceptions of service in banks: replication and extension. *Journal of Applied Psychology*. 70(3), 423–433. doi:10.1037/0021-9010.70.3.423.

Shapiro, D. L., Hom, P., Shen, W. and Agarwal, R., (2016). How do leader departures affect subordinates' organizational attachment? A 360-degree relational perspective. *Academy of Management Review*. 41(3), 479–502. doi:10.5465/amr.2014.0233

Shih-Tse Wang, E., (2014). The effects of relationship bonds on emotional exhaustion and turnover intentions in frontline employees. *Journal of Services Marketing*. 28(4), 319–330. doi:10.1108/JSM-11-2012-0217

Soltis, S. M., Agneessens, F., Sasovova, Z. and Labianca, G. (J.), (2013). A social network perspective on turnover intentions: the role of distributive justice and social support. *Human Resource Management*. 52(4), 561–584. doi:10.1002/hrm.21542

Staw, B. M., (1980). The consequences of turnover. *Journal of Occupational Behaviour*. 1(4), 253–273.

Town, J. S., (2015). Measures of relationship capital for the value scorecard. *Library Management*. 36(3), 235–247. doi:10.1108/LM-11-2014-0134

Town, J. S. and Kyrillidou, M., (2013). Developing a values scorecard. *Performance Measurement and Metrics*. 14(1), 7–16. doi:10.1108/14678041311316095

Tsai, W. and Ghoshal, S., (1998). Social capital and value creation: the role of intrafirm networks. *Academy of Management Journal*. 41(4), 464–276. doi:10.5465/257085

Vafeas, M., (2015). Account manager turnover and the influence of context: an exploratory study. *Journal of Business & Industrial Marketing*. 30(1), 72–82. doi:10.1108/JBIM-04-2012-0064

Van Wijk, R., Janse, J. J. P. and Lyles, M. A., (2008). Inter- and intra-organizational knowledge transfer: a meta-analytic review and assessment of its antecedents and consequences. *Journal of Management Studies*. 45(4), 830–853. doi:10.1111/j.1467-6486.2008.00771.x

Villena, V. H., Revilla, E. and Choi, T. Y., (2011). The dark side of buyer-supplier relationships: a social capital perspective. *Journal of Operations Management*. 29(6), 561–576. doi:10.1016/j.jom.2010.09.001

Widén-Wulff, G. and Ginman, M., (2004). Explaining knowledge sharing in organizations through the dimensions of social capital. *Journal of Information Science*. 30(5), 448–458. doi:10.1177/0165551504046997

Young, S. W. H. and Rossmann, D., (2015). Building library community through social media. *Information Technology and Libraries*. 34(1), 20–37. doi:10.6017/ital.v34i1.5625

12
Beyond Individual Relationships: Programmatic Approaches to Outreach and Engagement at UC Santa Barbara Library

Rebecca L. Metzger

Introduction

Since the mid-2000s, there has been a proliferation of new academic library positions devoted to outreach, engagement and student success. Libraries are recognising the imperative to position themselves as outward-facing organisations whose purpose is to contribute to the success of their faculty, students and staff. In order to stay competitive for **resources**, administrators realise that they must be able to demonstrate the library's value to the larger college or university mission and strategic goals. The problem is that many of these new outreach and engagement librarian positions have been introduced in an ad hoc manner, without touching the library organisational structure or examining its mission, vision or values. By charging lone librarians to lead outreach and engagement initiatives, academic libraries have prioritised individual relationship building over program development.

In 2009, the University of California Santa Barbara (UCSB) created a position for an Assistant/Associate University Librarian (AUL) for Outreach & Academic Services (later Outreach & Academic Collaboration). By placing outreach at a senior management level, the library signalled a commitment to managing and improving both its external relationships and image. Hired into the position in 2012, I was given staff, budget and the authority to implement events, outreach, communications and partnership programs that advance the library's visibility and impact.

In this chapter, I introduce some of the programmatic approaches implemented at the UCSB Library to build the division of Outreach & Academic Collaboration. I argue that a leadership role dedicated to outreach is essential in harnessing previously invisible relational work toward new and strategic engagement models. Administrators should commit to defining program goals and performance competencies for outreach and engagement work, and invest in them in order to develop and sustain the relationships that support the reputation of the library. Having recently been tasked with overseeing the UCSB Library's subject liaison program, I then look ahead to imagine how an understanding of **relational capital** can shape public services more broadly in academic libraries.

Relational capital and invisible work

The business concept of **intellectual capital** – sometimes called intellectual or **intangible assets** – has only relatively recently been explored in the library literature (Kostagiolas & Asonitis 2009; Corrall & Sriborisutsakul 2010). Intellectual capital captures the aspects of a library that go beyond its financial investments in collections, spaces and services, to include the more invisible investments in people, processes, knowledge and technologies (Corrall & Sriborisutsakul 2010; Town & Kyrillidou 2013). Relational capital is a type of intellectual capital that encompasses the external relationships developed by an organisation, whether with vendors, customers, partners, stakeholders or professional networks (Corrall & Sriborisutsakul 2010; Corrall 2014). It is closely related to the concept of **human capital**, or 'the knowledge, skills, competencies, and creativity that each person who works in a firm or organization has' (Kostagiolas & Asonitis 2009, p. 421). Town and Kyrillidou (2013, p. 12) have argued that libraries have become 'fundamentally relationship organisations'. Libraries spend a large portion of their budgets on human capital, relying on their staff to create and sustain relationships that contribute to the overall success and reputation of the organisation, and yet they don't have good methods for measuring the value of that investment (Kostagiolas & Asonitis 2009; Town 2014; Town 2015; Bracke 2016). In fact, the invisibility of some librarian relational work has contributed to the fragility of positions when libraries have been faced with the need to downsize or redeploy staff (Town 2015).

Marxist and feminist ideas around immaterial labour have been used to explore the cognitive and affective work that librarians are engaged in (Sloniowski 2016; Douglas & Gadsby 2017). As universities increasingly focus on metrics, many librarians perceive that their roles are undervalued, relegated to a support or service function rather than more centrally situated as part of knowledge production (Sloniowski 2016). In particular, the relational and care work that is expected of many academic librarians, and especially of women, to be successful in their jobs – such as teaching, mentoring, co-ordinating, advocacy and collaboration – is not measured as output and is, therefore, rendered invisible (Sloniowski 2016; Douglas & Gadsby 2017). Libraries inherently value relational work, but we rarely build it into our value systems, whether through our mission statements, strategic planning documents, annual reports, or performance evaluations. 'The failure of library assessment models to account for the relational value of librarian activities is problematic in justifying and incentivizing new strategic activities and understanding the importance of libraries' relationships with users and other stakeholders' (Bracke 2016, p. 135). In order to elevate relational work, it needs to be named and integrated into the outputs that libraries measure.

Subject librarians and the turn toward engagement

The most obvious category of academic library staffing through which to explore concepts of relational capital is subject librarianship. Subject librarians, or liaison librarians, are typically assigned as a first point of contact to work with academic departments and programs on campus, promote library services and provide research and instructional support. Domain and subject expertise is only one factor of liaison librarian success; relationship building, which takes time, is a contributing factor in the library's overall image as a trusted partner (Bracke 2016; Schlak 2016). Relational or **social capital** 'provides a useful paradigm for exploring the often amorphous and sometimes invisible nature of the individual relationships that partly constitute a successful liaison program' (Schlak 2016, p. 412). Yet many liaison programs lack the organisation and administrative oversight that would provide a co-ordinated and consistent approach to managing the relationships that are central to this work (Miller & Pressley 2015).

Only relatively recently have libraries and the literature attempted to characterise the cognitive and affective ('soft') skills that subject librarians deploy in their roles. In two small-scale studies, strong relationships between subject librarians and faculty were shown to be the result of planning, patience, networking, bilateral communication, **trust**, shared interests and goals, sincerity, flexibility, responsiveness and **reciprocity** (Schlak 2016; Díaz & Mandernach 2017). Since 2009, libraries at the University of Minnesota, Ohio State University and Massachusetts Institute of Technology, among others, have taken the lead in creating local standardised responsibilities, competencies and best practices for their subject librarians (Williams 2009; Ohio State University Libraries 2012; Horowitz, Crummett & Gabridge 2016). For example, the Ohio State University's (2012) *A framework for the engaged librarian* introduces engagement as one of five core areas of subject librarianship.

Engagement marks a turn away from academic libraries as primarily collections-centric and service-oriented towards the new user-centric role of partner or collaborator (Williams 2009; Gibson & Dixon 2011). The engagement model seeks to position the library's mission more broadly within the context of its larger home institution. Competencies of the engaged librarian at the Ohio State University Libraries include effective communication, partnership development, new service development, problem solving and advocacy (Ohio State University Libraries 2012). Interviews with Association of Research Libraries (ARL) library administrators conducted in 2013 cited these as important skills for the engaged librarian: 'capacity to cultivate trusted relationships with faculty and others, the ability to engage and thrive in the messy and ambiguous, aptitude for *systems thinking* ... and skills including political savvy, analytical and problem-solving skills, program development, conflict fluency, civility, and strong leadership' (Jaguszewski & Williams 2013, p. 14).

Despite the admirable goals of the engagement model, in most cases individual subject librarians are neither hired nor trained for the necessary soft skills, nor are they organisationally positioned to advance the strategic priorities of the library or the university. While a subject librarian may, through their relationships, develop a deep awareness of the needs of several departments and faculty members, those needs may be less than fully understood in the context of wider disciplinary needs or the potential for collaborative solutions with broader effects. A key finding from the ARL 2015 Pilot Library Liaison

Institute report was that 'librarians tend to be unable to see or imagine the impact of their work in the context of solving larger institutional problems' (Rockenbach et al. 2015, p. 21). Many subject librarians direct their own work; our libraries fail them and our users by not creating the structures that can empower them to move beyond transactional service offerings to scalable and potentially transformational ones (Miller & Pressley 2015; Schlak 2015; Bracke 2016).

Outreach librarianship: lofty but vague expectations

Academic outreach librarianship is relatively new, so the literature is scant and multiple definitions of the role abound. While subject librarians usually liaise exclusively with academic departments and serve faculty as their main target audience, outreach librarians connect with multiple groups, including students, parents, alumni, staff and community members. Results from a 2018 SPEC Kit survey on Outreach and Engagement indicate that outreach librarians at ARL institutions are responsible for engaging with constituents on campus and beyond, designing and implementing events, building partnerships and new initiatives, leading tours and orientation programming, and marketing library services (LeMire et al. 2018).

Competencies for the outreach librarian are completely undeveloped in the literature; this is an area ripe for exploration. One would expect such competencies to heavily emphasise relational work, as outreach librarians by definition create **social networks** to accomplish their jobs. Qualifications listed in outreach librarian job advertisements posted in the late 2010s point toward someone with strong skills in, among other things: communication, collaboration, marketing, instruction, planning, emotional intelligence, *community engagement*, navigating culturally diverse environments, user engagement and program development and assessment. Much is expected of outreach librarians, but there are little to no standard training or best practices for this type of role. Furthermore, outreach is often just a portion of someone's job on top of other public services duties, or there is only one librarian tasked with all things outreach.

The Outreach and Engagement SPEC Kit survey revealed that very few academic libraries take a programmatic approach to outreach, as signified by the setting of definitions and goals, as well as the allocation of staffing and budgets for outreach activities (LeMire et al. 2018). Without clear goals or success measures, outreach librarians are often left on their own to determine which activities to initiate, or are put in the position of being reactive to ad hoc requests and opportunities that arise.

Strategic positioning and library leadership

The literature on social or relational capital as exercised by library leaders is sparse and this is another area that deserves deeper scholarly inquiry. The literature that does exist tends to explore the role of library administrators internally in managing staff development programs, relational networks among staff, organisational climate and change projects (Town 2014; Schlak 2015). The Library Leadership and Management Association

(LLAMA) published a set of competencies for library leaders (LLAMA 2016) that introduces relationship building as a subsidiary skill under the heading of 'collaboration and partnerships'. Included in the competencies are other cognitive and affective skills that could contribute to engagement and external relational work, such as: communication skills, emotional intelligence, problem solving and marketing and advocacy.

Library leaders should play an essential role in staying abreast of institutional challenges and priorities, communicating those back to librarians and staff, and resourcing and directing work toward high-impact activities. The kinds of initiatives that serve to position the library strategically within the institution – such as partnering to establish new library spaces and services like learning commons and digital scholarship centres – all involve significant funding and leadership to launch (Cox 2018). The administrator's role in leading change in support of the engagement model is to 'realign the tools and human capital they have at their disposal' (Díaz 2017, p. 656). I believe that the 'engaged library' requires library leaders to create and sustain their own relational capital with key leaders across campus, position their employees appropriately within the organisation to effect change, hire and train librarians for the engagement competencies that we expect them to perform and assess the invisible work that we value, such as relationship building.

The 2012 job posting for my position was unique, setting the stage for a leader to take strategic and programmatic approaches to library outreach:

> Reporting to the University Librarian, the AUL provides administrative and programmatic leadership that shapes and guides the communications, promotion, strategic collaborative relationships, and events advancing the library's visibility and impact across a dynamic community of faculty and student scholars. The AUL is a critical member of the library's leadership and development teams, working closely within the organization and with other campus colleagues to reinforce the critical importance of the library through a comprehensive marketing and advocacy program.

In my first weeks on the job, my boss arranged introductory meetings for me with deans across campus. Not only was this her way of providing me with *starter capital*, but it also indicated to her colleagues that the Library takes seriously its collaborative role with colleges, departments and offices across campus.

UCSB Library
Events and exhibitions
In the seven years since my appointment, I have led the UCSB Library in building several components of the Outreach & Academic Collaboration Division, including a robust events and exhibitions program with a dedicated staff, budget and goals. An Events & Exhibitions Librarian is responsible for defining, creating and implementing an events and exhibitions program that showcases the richness of scholarly and creative work at UCSB, and that connects researchers, instructors, students, librarians and audiences from multiple

disciplines in our central campus location to learn, collaborate and engage with ideas. A Programming & Events Assistant has been added to the staffing portfolio for this program.

Before the program was established, individual librarians or staff would initiate and execute events and exhibitions with no oversight. This situation usually resulted in details falling through the cracks, as no one was paying attention to policies, procedures and best practices. Approaching events and exhibitions in an ad hoc manner puts last-minute pressure on staff who have not been informed in advance about a responsibility they might have, such as technology support, *digitisation* and printing services or rearrangement of spaces and furniture. More importantly, novice organisers may view the audience as an afterthought, designing a program without input or intent. The Events & Exhibitions Librarian centrally manages a significant budget, but to access that budget anyone in the Library who wants to organise an event or exhibition must work through them to explore questions around goals, target audiences and success measures.

The driving objective for the UCSB Library's Events & Exhibitions program is to collaborate with faculty and students to integrate programming with the curriculum. A prime example of this is UCSB Reads, a program led by the Library that brings the campus community together to discuss significant issues of our time through reading and engaging with a common book. Under the management of the Events & Exhibitions Librarian, the number of students assigned the UCSB Reads common book as required reading in a course has tripled since we started recording these numbers in 2012. In 2019, 33 courses from 10 different academic departments listed the book on their syllabi, reaching a total of 2,100 students. Additionally, 44% of the 400-person audience at the culminating author talk were students who were assigned extra credit to attend. The work involved in this faculty buy-in requires careful analysis of the course catalogue and departmental websites, partnering with subject librarians, developing a toolkit for faculty involvement and collaborating directly with faculty. Additionally, the Library's UCSB Reads programming across campus is co-sponsored or co-organised with academic departments, student organisations and others like UCSB's performing arts, film and multicultural centres. These partnerships are fostered, in part, by involving representatives from these organisations on the book selection committee.

Another example, the Pacific Views: Library Speaker Series, provides an opportunity for UCSB faculty and graduate students from diverse disciplines to speak about their current research, publications or creative work (the talks are held in the UCSB Library's eighth-floor Pacific View Room, with stunning panoramic views of the ocean and mountains). In preparing for the launch of the series, our Events & Exhibitions Librarian conducted a needs assessment, reaching out and meeting with faculty from across campus to discover how the Library can differentiate and add value to what is already happening in their home departments, such as research colloquia or symposia. Needs assessments are an essential part of program development. From the beginning, faculty and graduate students have embraced the opportunity to find broader audiences for their work, and the

Library collaborates closely with them to ensure that their talks are shaped for mixed audiences that include students, faculty, staff and community members.

Events and exhibitions are an important way that members of the campus and community interact with the Library. At the UCSB Library, the number of people we reach through events, exhibitions and outreach rivals the number we reach through our instruction program. Events and exhibitions showcase library collections and expertise, act as a gateway to other library services, establish the Library as a platform for knowledge creation and distribution, and attract friends and donors. In measuring the success of the program each year, we look not only at attendance numbers but at new partnerships and relationships that have been cultivated, with the goal of increasing both the number and diversity of partners.

Student success

In 2015, the UCSB Library transformed its Outreach Librarian position into a new role called Student Success Librarian. The purpose was to align the Library's outreach efforts with the mission of the University and to focus our efforts in support of students' academic success. While UCSB had no campus-wide first-year experience or student success centre at the time, the Library hoped to effectively position itself to be a part of evolving conversations and initiatives in these areas. Additionally, in 2015 the University was designated a Hispanic Serving Institution, meaning that at least 25% of the student population is Hispanic. The Student Success Librarian's job is to investigate challenges particular to students, especially first-years and those in traditionally underserved populations, and propose library programs to help them develop as early scholars and, ultimately, thrive as members of the UCSB research community. Defining specific goals for the Student Success program enabled us to stop doing some outreach activities that had less obvious ties to academic success, such as hosting flu shots or game nights in the Library. The Student Success Librarian has increased the Library's interactions, in particular, with the Educational Opportunity Program, Undocumented Student Services and the Undergraduate Research and Creative Activities office.

The Student Success Librarian is responsible for organising annual meetings with student leaders from Associated Students (undergraduate student government/students' union) and the Graduate Student Association, quarterly student drop-in forums with the University Librarian and a Graduating Students Exit Survey. Results from the annual Graduating Students Exit Survey are shared with deans throughout the University to inform them about students' usage of the Library and the services they value. All of these platforms provide the Library with important feedback about student priorities and concerns and, more importantly, the role the Library plays in their learning.

One of the UCSB Library's strategic directions is to serve as a forum for students and faculty to share their work and knowledge. Toward this end, the Student Success Librarian co-ordinates the Library's participation in a monthly Graduate Lunch & Learn series and Grad Slam and Undergraduate Slam contests (competitions designed to showcase student research). Recently, the program launched a new Library Award for Undergraduate Research to recognise students who produce a scholarly or creative work that makes expert and sophisticated use of library collections, resources and services. To support students involved in all these activities, the Library designed a Presentation Practice Room where students can rehearse, refine and record their oral and multimedia presentations.

Assessment strategies for the Student Success program have evolved over the years, aided by pioneering literature exploring multiple methods for measuring outreach work that go beyond counting attendance numbers (Farrell & Mastel 2016). Surveys for our events and outreach activities seek to explore more information about our audiences and the success of our marketing and program design, asking: 'Have you been to the UCSB Library before?', 'Have you attended a UCSB Library program before?' and 'Did you learn something today?'

Communications and marketing

Some of the literature posits that what many libraries mean by outreach is really marketing, if marketing is understood as building relationships with users in order to design, deliver and improve valued services (Dempsey 2009; Ford 2009; Singh 2017). The Communications & Marketing Manager at the UCSB Library is responsible for directing a strategic communications plan that incorporates all aspects of library messaging, including publications, public relations, advertising and content for digital signage, social media and the web. They oversee a Graphic Designer as well as occasional freelance writers, video producers and web developers, and work in close collaboration with a Web Services Librarian. It is particularly important for libraries to place the communications role as high up in the organisation as possible, as there are brand management and crisis communications functions that this person may be called upon to perform. The UCSB Library's Communications & Marketing Manager advises administration on the potential public reception of decisions and 'listens' to what is said about the Library on social channels and in campus and other publications.

Marketing today is no longer just about delivering superior services, but also unique experiences (Singh 2017). Like engagement, marketing is very much about putting the customer or user at the core of the organisation. Understanding and segmenting our users is an essential role of the UCSB Library Communications & Marketing Manager. The same messages cannot be replicated for faculty, graduate students, undergraduate students and community members, but must be authentically and strategically customised for distinct audiences. One of those audiences is student library assistants. In 2018 the UCSB Library's Communications & Marketing Manager launched a dedicated online Slack channel where student assistants who work in different departments throughout the Library can gather and communicate. The hope for the virtual space is to foster a greater sense of *community* among library student assistants as well as a greater sense of belonging with the Library.

Using data from our e-newsletter platform, website and social media channels helps us to understand our audiences and the kind of content they desire, and informs improvements to our communications messages and delivery. For example, by analysing data, the Communications & Marketing Manager was able to learn that content about the UCSB Reads *common book program* is particularly popular. In response, we launched a 'Sneak Peek' campaign that gives the public an inside view into the selection and planning process that takes place over the entire year leading up to the public portion of the program. The campaign includes social media as well as traditional broadcast elements, such as radio interviews.

Like outreach and subject liaison work, effective communications – especially social media – is all about relationships. Successful social media strategy involves not just pushing out library stories, but partnering to amplify them through likes, follows, retweets and hashtags. Social media actually offers an ideal opportunity to start to measure library relationships, with its built-in insights for tracking interactions. These quantitative indices might be interestingly adapted as measures of relationships that occur with the Library outside of social media, whether in digital or physical environments.

Partnerships

During my tenure, the UCSB Library has invited two partner organisations to operate out of the main library building: the Transfer Student Center and the Center for Innovative Teaching, Research, and Learning. As on many other campuses, there is high demand and competition for space at UCSB, and we are approached often by groups who believe the Library might have extra space for their program or centre. From the beginning, the Library strived for co-operation or collaboration with these centres, rather than mere co-location (Bodolay et al. 2016). Library administration was involved in shaping the founding vision for these two new centres in partnership with the Division of Undergraduate Education. We developed memorandums of understanding (MOUs) to define the Library's relationship with each centre, which cover everything from the Library's role in governance (librarians sit on the advisory boards) to the logistics of who is responsible for technology and custodial support in the physical spaces. The Library develops and delivers joint instruction sessions and workshops with both of the centres, customised for their target audiences. An e-mail listserv was established to foster communication with and between all the UCSB Library's building partners (we also house a café that is run by campus dining services, a police satellite station for the University of California Police Department and an adaptive technology centre that is the result of a partnership with the Disabled Students Program).

Other partnerships range in scale and scope. On campus, the Library has partnered with academic departments and research centres to share the cost of subscriptions to library databases, specialised web platforms and data collections. We have partnered with Associated Students to deploy hand sanitisers and phone-charging stations throughout the Library. A new partnership with a locally based open access monograph publisher is testing the ground for an economically sustainable, no-fees press in the Library. These kinds of projects may have their seed in personal relationships but cannot be realised without committing resources from across the Library. All of the partnerships require

MOUs outlining roles and responsibilities, which only the University Librarian or designate can sign. As authors from Massachusetts Institute of Technology assert in an article re-envisioning their subject liaison program: 'Most substantive partnerships require cross-unit support from the library, and liaisons who are poised to engage this way will need an efficient and widely agreed on process to identify, vet, commit to, and support … partnerships' (Peterson & Finnie 2018, pp. 26–27). Relationships can serve as an important gateway to program and service development, but require administrative support, institutional resources and internal collaboration in order to progress.

Looking ahead for UCSB Library subject librarians

My approach as AUL for Outreach & Academic Collaboration was an outside-in approach of bringing marketing principles from my previous career as a public relations and marketing professional into the UCSB Library. I was able to work with dedicated staff to define strategic goals around outreach programs that mapped to library and university goals, direct budgets toward those goals and measure outcomes in alignment with those goals. Still, the outreach division remained small and, initially, did not intersect with the traditional public services side of the Library. Now that my role has evolved to encompass leadership of reference, instruction, access services and subject librarians, I am working from the inside out to take a more programmatic and engagement-oriented approach in all these areas.

In the next phase, the UCSB Library is organising its subject librarians into a dedicated Research & Engagement Department that brings together aspects of our liaison model with the former Outreach & Academic Collaboration Division. As the AUL overseeing this new department, I want the burden for developing and maintaining relationships to be situated as much as possible in teams. Other academic libraries have moved in the direction of reorganising their subject librarian programs around user groups, disciplines or functions. The University of Guelph was one of the first to restructure their subject librarians into teams: 'The new model signalled a move from "individual-to-individual" to "program-to-client group" activity. Instead of relying on liaison librarians to push library services through their personal campus networks, programs were developed and targeted at specific user groups' (D'Elia & Horne 2018, p. 11).

To start at UCSB, we are grouping librarians from across the Library and functional areas (Data Curation, Collection Strategies, Research & Engagement, Teaching & Learning, etc.) into disciplinary teams to share information about engagements with faculty, serve as back-up for each other in supporting them and identify opportunities for cross-departmental service offerings. Given that we need to redistribute subject librarian assignments in support of our reorganisation, the next step will be to identify techniques for success in taking on new liaison roles and transferring relationships or developing new ones. These techniques will form the basis for a toolkit that can aid subject librarians moving into and out of the role in the future, and for setting annual qualitative and quantitative targets to evaluate the program. Some libraries like the University of Miami and University of California, Riverside have initiated structured 'Faculty Conversation' projects as one technique that new liaisons can use in relationship building and to elicit areas of deeper understanding about faculty challenges (UC Riverside Library 2019).

We will be investigating the adoption of customer relationship management software to document interactions with users that can serve to ease transitions between individual library employees, uncover opportunities for deeper connections with the Library and contribute to assessment efforts. At the UCSB Library we have just begun to record librarian engagements that take place off the reference desk, and this is presenting an important data point in informing the redistribution of subject librarian assignments. Team-based liaison approaches can also emphasise relationship development with key stakeholders such as department chairs, rather than just with individual faculty members in response to stated library needs (Eldridge et al. 2016). In order to broaden the perspective of subject librarians at UCSB, we will be inviting key leaders from across campus (e.g., Advising, Registrar, Admissions, Office of Research) to speak about their current priorities and challenges. Finally, we will be looking at how the Communications & Marketing program can support our subject librarians in their efforts to communicate strategically and effectively with faculty, using existing tools that we have like e-newsletter software to deliver measurements of liaison engagement.

As early as 2009, Emily Ford provocatively argued in 'Outreach is (un)dead' that separate outreach positions and departments should be 'killed' as we strive to integrate outreach goals and activities more fully into our libraries. Inspired by Ford's (2009) suggestion, we are eliminating the Student Success Librarian position in favour of distributing the responsibility among librarians. New statements of duties and responsibilities for subject librarians include a section dedicated to their involvement in the Student Success program: 'Shares responsibility … for the design and delivery of orientations, workshops, and outreach activities that introduce students to the library's services, resources, and spaces, often in collaboration with other student support units on campus. Customizes engagement for distinct and diverse populations.'

A new Diversity & Engagement Assistant position has been added to support the Student Success program and the new shared model.

Conclusion

There have been admirable efforts since the second decade of the 21st century to introduce strategic thinking and assessment methodologies into outreach work, as demonstrated by the programming coming out of professional networks devoted to outreach and marketing. Much of this work has not yet been incorporated into the literature, and more could be explored around defining standard competencies for outreach librarians, developing outcomes for successful relationship building and applying social capital concepts to additional categories of library professionals beyond subject librarians. The literature on subject librarianship is more mature and a few libraries have taken lead roles in advancing programmatic approaches to liaison work that recognise and value relational and other soft skills.

At the UCSB Library, I was granted the unique opportunity to lead an outreach program that was valued enough by the University Librarian to situate at a high level in the organisation, and I was able to develop strategic relationships in part because of my position. With dedicated staffing and budget, I created co-ordinated planning approaches to programs in events and exhibitions, student success, communications and marketing, and partnerships. In my newly expanded role over public services and subject liaisons, I will be exploring the potential of using intellectual capital perspectives to recognise competencies and best practices for outreach and engagement work at both the director and librarian level. In particular, I envision working with the librarians in my division to describe, evaluate and improve the relational and other soft skills that contribute to the Library's strategic directions.

Academic libraries rely on outreach librarians and subject liaisons to build relationships with key campus and community constituents in the delivery of quality service and the pursuit of a visible and trusted brand, but individual relationships are inherently subjective and tenuous. As academic libraries move toward engagement models that privilege people over collections, they may be even more inclined to emphasise the importance of relationships. However, individual relational work is largely invisible to library leaders in the day-to-day functioning of their organisations and is often not defined or measured as part of program or performance evaluation cycles. This places a burden on librarians to invest in time-consuming cognitive and affective work that continues to be undervalued. Library leaders need to move beyond prioritising individual relational work, to create programmatic approaches to outreach and engagement that can deliver consistent and scalable services. In order to leverage relationships toward organisational success and sustain them over the long term, relationships should be strategic, team based, documented and assessed.

References

Bodolay, R., Frye, S., Kruse, C. and Luke, D., (2016). Moving from co-location to cooperation to collaboration: redefining a library's role within the university. In: B. Doherty, ed. *Space and organizational considerations in academic library partnerships and collaborations*. Hershey, PA: IGI Global. pp. 230–254.

Bracke, P., (2016). Social networks and relational capital in library service assessment. *Performance Measurement and Metrics*. 17(2). 134–141. doi:10.1108/PMM-04-2016-0019

Corrall, S., (2014). Library service capital: the case for measuring and managing intangible assets. In: S. Faletar Tanacković and B. Bosančić, eds. *Assessing libraries and library users and use: proceedings of the 13th international conference Libraries in the Digital Age (LIDA), 16–20 June, Zadar, Croatia*. pp. 21–32. http://ozk.unizd.hr/lida/files/LIDA_2014_Proceedings.pdf

Corrall, S. and Sriborisutsakul, S., (2010). Evaluating intellectual assets in university libraries: a multi-site case study from Thailand. *Journal of Information and Knowledge Management*. 9(3), 277–290. doi:10.1142/S021964921000267X

Cox, J., (2018). Positioning the academic library within the institution: a literature review: *New Review of Academic Librarianship*. 24(3–4), 217–241. doi:10.1080/13614533.2018.1466342

D'Elia, M. J. and Horne, D., (2018). Leaving liaison behind: reflections on the last decade. *Research Library Issues*. **294**, 8–15. doi:10.29242/rli.294.2

Dempsey, K., (2009). *The accidental library marketer*. Medford, NJ: Information Today.

Díaz, J., (2017). Engaging with engagement: an administrator's perspective. *portal: Libraries and the Academy*. **17**(4), 655–664. doi:10.1353/pla.2017.0038

Díaz, J. O. and Mandernach, M. A., (2017). Relationship building one step at a time: case studies of successful faculty-librarian partnerships. *portal: Libraries and the Academy*. **17**(2), 273–282. doi:10.1353/pla.2017.0016

Douglas, V. A. and Gadsby, J., (2017). Gendered labor and library instruction coordinators: the undervaluing of feminized work. In: *At the helm: leading transformation; ACRL 2017, 22–25 March, Baltimore, MD*. Chicago, IL: Association of College and Research Libraries. pp. 266–274. http://www.ala.org/acrl/conferences/acrl2017papers

Eldridge, J., Fraser, K., Simmonds, T. and Smyth, N., (2016). Strategic engagement: new models of relationship management for academic librarians. *New Review of Academic Librarianship*. **22**(2–3), 160–175. doi:10.1080/13614533.2016.1193033

Farrell, S. L. and Mastel, K., (2016). Considering outreach assessment: strategies, sample scenarios, and a call to action. *In the Library with the Lead Pipe*. 4 May. http://www.inthelibrarywiththeleadpipe.org/2016/considering-outreach-assessment-strategies-sample-scenarios-and-a-call-to-action

Ford, E., (2009). Outreach is (un)dead. *In the Library with the Lead Pipe*. 2 September. http://www.inthelibrarywiththeleadpipe.org/2009/outreach-is-undead

Gibson, C. and Dixon, C., (2011). New metrics for academic library engagement. In: *Declaration of interdependence: ACRL 2011, 30 March–2 April, Philadelphia, PA*. Chicago, IL: Association of College and Research Libraries. pp. 340–351. http://www.ala.org/acrl/conferences/confsandpreconfs/national/acrl2011papers

Horowitz, L., Crummett, C. and Gabridge, T., (2016). Measuring impact of liaison–faculty relationships: a multi-factor assessment framework. In: *Proceedings of the 2016 library assessment conference: building effective, sustainable, practical assessment, 31 October– 2 November, Arlington, VA*. pp. 195–207. http://old.libraryassessment.org/bm~doc/37-horowitz-2016.pdf

Jaguszewski, J. M. and Williams, K., (2013). *New roles for new times: transforming liaison roles in research libraries*. Washington, DC: Association of Research Libraries. https://www.arl.org/wp-content/uploads/2015/12/nrnt-liaison-roles-revised.pdf

Kostagiolas, P. A. and Asonitis, S., (2009). Intangible assets for academic libraries: definitions, categorization, and an exploration of management issues. *Library Management*. **30**(6/7), 419–429. doi:10.1108/01435120910982113

LeMire, S., Graves, S. J., Farrell, S. L. and Mastel, K. L., (2018). *Outreach and engagement*. SPEC Kit 361. Washington, DC: Association of Research Libraries. doi:10.29242/spec.361

LLAMA., (2016). Leadership and management competencies: foundational competencies for library leaders and managers. Chicago, IL: Library Leadership & Management Association. http://www.ala.org/llama/leadership-and-management-competencies

Miller, R. K. and Pressley, L., (2015). *Evolution of library liaisons.* SPEC Kit 349. Washington, DC: Association of Research Libraries. doi:10.29242/spec.349

Ohio State University Libraries., (2012). *A framework for the engaged librarian: building on our strengths.* Columbus, OH. The Ohio State University Libraries. https://cgs.illinois.edu/files/2016/05/Engaged_Librarian_FrameworkPDF.pdf

Peterson, K. and Finnie, E., (2018). MIT libraries liaison program: a paradigm shift. *Research Library Issues.* 294, 16–30. doi:10.29242/rli.294.3

Rockenbach, B., Ruttenberg, J., Tancheva, K. and Vine, R., (2015). *Association of Research Libraries/Columbia University/Cornell University/University of Toronto pilot library liaison institute: final report.* Washington, DC: Association of Research Libraries. https://www.arl.org/publications-resources/3803-library-liaison-institute-final-report

Schlak, T., (2015). Social capital and leadership in academic libraries: the broader exchange around 'buy-in'. *Library Management.* 36(6/7), 394–407. doi:10.1108/LM-11/2014-0133

Schlak, T., (2016). Social capital as operative in liaison librarianship: librarian participants' experiences of faculty engagement as academic library liaisons. *Journal of Academic Librarianship.* 42(1), 411–422. doi:10.1016/j.acalib.2017.09.005

Singh, R., (2017). Marketing competency for information professionals: the role of marketing education in library and information science education programs. *Marketing Libraries Journal.* 1(1), 60–83. http://journal.marketinglibraries.org/MLJv1i1–60–83.html

Sloniowski, L., (2016). Affective labor, resistance, and the academic librarian. *Library Trends.* 64(4), 645–666. http://hdl.handle.net/2142/94934

Town, S., (2014). The value of people: a review and framework for human capital assessment in academic and research libraries. *Performance Measurement and Metrics.* 15(1/2), 67–80. doi:10.1108/PMM-05-2014-0019

Town, J. S., (2015). Measures of relationship capital for the value scorecard. *Library Management.* 36(3), 235–247. doi:10.1108/LM-11-2014-0134

Town, J. S. and Kyrillidou, M., (2013). Developing a values scorecard. *Performance Measurement and Metrics.* 14(1), 7–16. doi:10.1108/14678041311316095

UC Riverside Library., (2019). Conversation starters: innovation through engagement. *News.* 7 May. https://library.ucr.edu/about/news/conversation-starters-innovation-through-engagement

Williams, K., (2009). Framework for articulating new library roles. *Research Library Issues.* 265, 3–8. doi:10.29242/rli.265.2

13
The Role of Academic Libraries in Developing Social Capital by Promoting Quality Reading in Local Communities

Matthew Kelly

Introduction

This chapter focuses upon a problem with public libraries that only an academic library can fix. This problem originates in a view of public library collection development as simply a response to user demand. Where this becomes the prevailing wisdom, as it has in the United Kingdom (UK) and Australia, the result is often that quality materials, such as publications by university presses, are shunned by selectors. For readers who would ordinarily choose this material the remedies to such a state of affairs are few and far between. One remedy is for the disenfranchised reader of quality materials to use the services of an academic library. While this is certainly an option for readers who live close to an academic library, and in much of the developed world it seems that academic libraries do open their doors to these community borrowers, questions arise as to why the academic library should take on the responsibility for catering to these community borrowers.

What has occurred in our conception of the public library that quality materials are, largely, no longer acquired? In this chapter, a sociology-of-knowledge perspective is used to look for explanations of this phenomenon, but more so to provide a way forward based on the understanding that in many cases 'the horse has bolted' with regard to public library collection quality and what remains is to model a new social future for public–academic library partnership that can bring fluidity to citizens' conceptions of what 'my library' means in order to ensure that important works are available to all, and not only the select few.

The explanation that seems to best fit the problem is that public librarians take this course in support of an ideological commitment to reading. Within their professional context, reading *any material* is preferable to a potential user not reading. In terms of the social practice, what seems clear here is how public librarians have appropriated 'routines and interpretations' relating to democratic access to resources and have reinterpreted and reinvented routines as a form of knowledge that they 'feed back into the field of action' – discourses on reading and civic participation, epistemology and the like (Reichertz 2013, p. 4). It is important to not mistake the argument made here as one linked to traditional literary questions of quality or even of scientific truth. What is sought is an understanding of how public librarians can hold – and hold deeply – the dichotomous view that they are serving users best when they refrain from guiding their reading at all.

Advocated here is a means by which unhelpful polemics that locate materials selection in class-based narratives might be transcended (but not forgotten). I take the view that strong advocates for public libraries as ineluctably focused on quality materials (for example, Usherwood 2007) need to be better understood by practitioner communities. Critiques of Usherwood (and his ilk), such as that made by Pateman and Williment (2013) in their 'community-led model', which also, laudably, focuses on delivering quality materials for *all users*, have too little to say, I believe, on deeper questions of truth and associated epistemic concerns relating to collections. Shared concerns for quality materials can, it is hoped, provide an opportunity for us to question just how deep this sense of incommensurability in (public library) selection really does run. I believe a further synergy is due for development that can help to reconcile these views and that it cannot be achieved without considering the social role of the academic library in ***communities*** as part of broader strategies for the sector.

In order to better understand how it is that public libraries have established a less than fulsome relationship with *the knowledge concept* it is helpful to approach the problem from outside the limited perspective that librarianship can offer. Reichertz's (2013) explication of a hermeneutic sociology of knowledge is a helpful starting point to explain the problem of knowledge that librarians seem to so often miss in managing information. Through an extended focus on engaging with this problem as a sociological one, and through engaging with practitioners and the historical narrative of librarianship, it becomes possible to purposively reflect on what responsibilities academic libraries might have for citizen readers left without resources by a circulation-focused public library model.

In this chapter a range of factors that underpin why communities should consider new library models that are better able to contribute to the development of **social capital** are discussed. These include how greater equity can be fostered in delivering quality reading materials and working with cultures of reading that are substantially more complex than is often assumed. I then look to how integrated models of the public and academic library can offer the opportunity to deliver to communities whole-of-life solutions to their information needs and how this helps to maximise the growth of social and cultural capital. Finally, I seek to articulate how the development of a shared future for communities – and all of their libraries – can help users not only to gain, but to maintain, access to knowledge.

Background

Across the world, academic libraries take diverse approaches to how they open up their collection to the communities in which they are situated. The traditional separation of town and gown has become a kind of 'done deal' for scholars and residents, with accommodations on both sides being made to promote mutually fruitful relationships (Rusk & Cummings 2011). Progress has also been made in many jurisdictions since the

1990s, which provides for borrowing rights to be assigned for readers who are not a part of the formal scholarly community.

Academic libraries are able to provide **resources** that many, if not most, public libraries have chosen not to hold. With their central role in facilitating information access to the profitable education sector, academic libraries operate as well-funded critical infrastructure. While there may be disputes of various hues at the local level as to how this plays out, in comparison to public libraries, whose role in society shifts and pitches according to whichever political mission it is called upon to fulfil, academic libraries have a stable vision of meeting the needs of students and researchers on which to base their practice. The perspective argued for here is that they do not operate in the same competitive environment for resources that public libraries in many countries do (being assessed against infrastructure or welfare needs). Academic libraries are at the centre of university life; if they are turned off, the university returns to a primitive state.

With the nearly unique ability to *develop* a collection (to be able to choose to collect most of what is or has been published on a certain subject) academic libraries offer the communities in which they operate a vast contrast with the public library in terms of subject coverage and epistemic stance. While patrons may not ever really consider 'epistemic stance' they do see significantly greater numbers of books shelved, under almost all topics, and they perceive a different approach to knowledge. Academic libraries are less likely to be encumbered by the managerial concerns of shelf space. They are certainly not encumbered by the political requirement to provide similar levels of resources to fiction literature as they do to domain knowledge.

In a very general sense, academic libraries have been keen to reach out to communities, in line with their broader mission of attracting students to their educational programs, since the late 20th century, offering adult entry as a substitute for matriculation, as well as *bridging programs* and tertiary preparation courses to help ensure progress within degree studies for those students who did not complete high school. Providing library borrowing rights to community members has accompanied these types of open access programs.

New library models that develop social capital using existing resources
All users deserve quality reading materials

Undue focus on place as the primary constituent for what libraries can offer in the development of social capital tends to devalue how we assess what materials are held and how these can support core collections worth engaging with. Vårheim (2014) outlines the quest for universality as accepting that public libraries do meet the needs of some societal groups better than others; as a result, coming to terms with how libraries' internal cultural competencies play out (that is, what causes selectors to choose to overlook certain reading groups) involves grasping the nettle to find why better divisions of resource budgets are not made. Where libraries do identify reading groups that they have overlooked, introducing programs that remedy the problem seems to begin to redress the usage issues

(Vårheim 2014). Lilley and Usherwood (2000, p. 22) make clear how 'it is possible to meet both the needs of the community, and the wants of the individual customer, if library managers communicate with both to create a positive image, and a realistic perception, of what the service is about'. Russell and Huang (2009, p. 74) take a similarly pragmatic approach that asks libraries to partner even at the level of the simple invitation 'by inviting [other libraries' staff] to tour their libraries and to learn what is available ... they can pass this information on to others they work with' and then to users. Crawford (2009, p. 59) makes clear how 'libraries must serve users – but all users (or as many segments as possible), not just today's primary users. There's a difference between being user-oriented and pandering, and it's a difference librarians should understand.'

Complex cultures of reading

As Alsop (2007, p. 584) notes, 'while the concept of a canon may have disappeared from most English departments, there are lingering effects in terms of our ongoing attempts to create a collection that reflects the best of the literary world'. Collections framed with quality in mind can almost never be considered by public libraries, and some form of collaborative arrangement with a neighbouring academic library offers a chance to enhance service. Chelin (2015, p. 110) discusses the importance of 'access to specialised stock' in her study of public–academic co-operation in the UK. The desire for access to materials held only in academic libraries, while it is hard to disentangle from aspirations for educational achievement, should not be treated in the same way. In her study of marginalised female students in early 20th-century America, Jarvis (2003, p. 273) points to how 'attitudes to reading were shaped by a complex interplay of desire and aspiration, consumption and identity/identification'.

While unmet demand for resources to meet recreational reading is more likely to be reported in terms of academic libraries ignoring this area, this may be due to the greater prevalence of academic librarians publishing research rather than the problem being at its most acute in that setting. It is worth referring to in order to understand what priorities academic libraries might be allocating to students' reading, as these will have ramifications for communities as well. Research from Dwyer (2000) and Salter and Brook (2007) points to gaps in fiction holdings as indicative of a lack of commitment to promoting reading (the quite reasonable assumption being that college attendance equates to participation in a reading culture). While several researchers highlight how university students in America are keen for popular reading materials to be made available (Hallyburton, Buchanan & Carstens 2011; Van Fleet 2003; Sanders 2009; Dewan 2010), other commentators focus on the need to arrest the decline in reading culture among adults generally in the USA (Rathe & Blankenship 2006). Bosman, Glover and Prince (2008, p. 1) point to how 'the academic library is a natural setting in which to combat this trend'. Mueller et al. (2017), in their research case study, identify how a recreational reading collection might stagnate. Sited in a browsing collection focused on academic uses of the works, it was not given any sort of prominence for other readers to find or notice it.

For Sheldrick Ross (1999), the information encounter in the context of reading for pleasure has transformative qualities for most readers, at least some of the time. Where readers may recognise resemblances to their own life in a text, these connections may be difficult to explain to others, their 'discernibility' remaining personal or ineffable (see also, Vakkari 1991). Sheldrick Ross's (1999, p. 75) research revealed how we should remain open to the 'contextualizing stories' that accompany transformative literature and the ways that new 'perspectives' and 'possibilities' arise for the person within this experiential locus. This is supported by Jarvis's (2001, p. 261) research that affirms the way reading is used to 'examine issues that concern them as members of families and cultural groups', that it needs to be seen as 'a hermeneutic rather than a technical act' and that this is an 'interpretive and intertextual process, shaped by the reader's expectations and experiences and by the social contexts in which it takes place'. That we are dealing with a lifelong process of development and learning and integration leads toward the view that we should take this process to be primarily an ontological one (Jarvis 2001, p. 262). While pressures on academic libraries associated with space and storage capacities are often cited (Van den Hoogen & Fleuren-Hunter 2017) as reasons to hive off responsibility for developing a leisure reading collection in the academic library to the public library, such views seem both narrow in intention and self-defeating in practice. Nothing seems further from the mission of the academic librarian than to allow a culture of aliteracy to take root (Salter & Brook 2007).

Promoting reading culture

The potential for joint partnership between public and academic libraries has been emphasised by Elliott (2009). One solution to the declining reading culture among college students, in her view, is for public libraries to promote their strengths within academic environments. Elliott (2007) has also promoted the expansion of the readers' advisory role beyond the public library setting and into academic libraries. The expansion of readers' advisory into non-fiction work is a significant step forward (Trott 2008, p. 134) in aligning users and collections that can meet their needs. Nicholson (2012, p. 186) advocates for leisure reading collections as a means to contribute to academic success more broadly, but also for their place in aiding transition to the academic library and 'revitalization of the culture of reading on postsecondary campuses'. Mahaffy (2009, p. 163) points to one of the problems with the decline of reading culture being that 'academic libraries often see the role of encouraging pleasure reading as one belonging to public libraries'.

Academic institutions can help to embed 'the place of reading in the lives of the public' and part of the metaphorical payoff is that future students are more likely to have an 'aptitude for learning' once they attend university (Mahaffy 2009, p. 172). Massis (2017) also makes the case for joint-use models between academic and public libraries as means by which 'sustained growth for the academic library' can occur. Using the example of how Nova Southeastern University incorporated services for Broward County Public Library, Massis (2017) describes how academic library planning and partnership initiatives can benefit local communities by providing access to significant collections.

Lyons and Parrott (2015, p. 22) note that libraries must begin to take note of their role in steering readers toward 'higher level reading'. Collaborative relationships between various types of libraries are crucial in seeing this occur. It is no longer the case that the *community development* role that public libraries once had all the responsibility for can be maintained. There are not only economic reasons that preclude public libraries from taking a sole leadership role; there are cultural reasons as well (Rusk & Cummings 2011), associated with how we teach adult learners.

Mani (2017, p. 67) describes transformative aspects of the 'bibliographic imagination', where readers move beyond that which is easily supplied by local creative production and they require more of what only the 'worldly dimension' can supply; as they join 'the reading nation' they find themselves searching beyond the parochial confines of language and culture. Where, unsurprisingly, we see public libraries failing readers such as these, with narrow parameters for selection and evaluation methods that mostly lack bibliometric data, it is harder to accept that many academic libraries also must constantly resort to interlibrary loan because selectors are fearful of purchasing important and popular works (Conklin & Moreton 2015). The inability to connect quality recreational reading to research would seem to plague all but the best academic libraries – those that have never been subjected to unreasonable dichotomies of choice and where solicitude, regarding collections, extends beyond a single decade.

Walker (2018) argues strongly for the intellectual space that opens up when popular materials are included in collection development mandates. Her approach is one of the few that explicitly define the need for collection development librarians to understand the need to collect broadly around academic disciplines (see also, Borgman 2003). Gunnels, Green and Butler (2012, p. 93) are also attuned to the importance of the collection and specifically argue that where formal mergers of libraries take place the success of such a project will be 'dependent on the ongoing coordination and creation of an expanded and more comprehensive collection'.

Integrated library models to better engage with communities of readers

Rather than allow readers without options to become aliterate, a preferable approach is to transform *community engagement*. At the heart of the matter is the need to commit to the means by which 'librarians can become visible, more engaged, and integrated into the community as "social capital partners"' (Baba & Abrizah 2018, p. 103). This includes, but is not limited to, the reinvigoration of readers advisory (Crowley 2015).

Problems associated with instrumentalist views of libraries were voiced at the beginning of the digital age. Two decades ago, Dwyer (2000, p. 61) identified how 'encouragement of independent reading and the culture of the book have declined in academic libraries'. Vander Broek and Rodgers (2015, p. 132) present a model of academic and public library partnership which offers the university the chance to 'better understand how we can connect our teaching and research missions with the interests and needs of the broader community in which we are situated'. Institutions that partner, such as the University of Michigan and Ann Arbor District Library have done, may start with common approaches to collections but end up with the additional benefit of a 'strong relationship where ideas and opportunities can be shared and acted upon in ways that best respond to community interest and activities' (Vander Broek & Rodgers 2015, p. 135). It would seem that further research on such partnerships can help to reveal just how far the solidarity formed between practitioners, with broad commitment to expanding reading at various levels, actually does help to promote dynamic flows between academic and leisure reading collections. Progressive arrangements such as these in Michigan (and those reported by Chelin (2015) in the UK), offer the promise of creating levels of understanding between practitioners that allow for discovery and invention of new and better ways to bring readers to information.

Bush (1945) quite rightly observed that the human mind does not work as a serial problem–solution stop–go mechanism. Rather, 'it operates by association. With one item in its grasp, it snaps instantly to the next that is suggested by the association of thought' (Bush 1945, p. 106), and this is the challenge in searching for knowledge organisation systems that are able to act in social and semantic ways (Weller 2010) and that can assist public library users to transition to the resource complexity available in the academic library. How is it possible to provide links in a public library catalogue that would allow gaps in subject or topic representation to be filled by references to a partner university library? While technically it may be quite straightforward, what are the filters (assuming such are required) necessary to make the search results productive and meaningful to the user? This notion of a heuretic-type inquiry, linked to discovery and invention, is championed by Ulmer (1994) and offers promising directions in terms of how catalogues oriented to the non-academic reader with broad horizons might be developed in the future.

Growing social capital with integrated libraries

It is important to articulate why change is necessary and that debate occurs on level ground if we want to see social or **intellectual capital** (IC) growth understood by communities and prioritised by decision makers. Dumay and Garanina (2013, p. 21) describe how there is a need for 'a longitudinal focus of how IC is utilised to navigate the knowledge created by countries, cities and communities and advocates how knowledge can be widely developed thus switching from a managerial to an eco-system focus'. Universities should be uniquely qualified to provide guidance on such approaches, given their comparatively less bureaucratic and comparatively more cosmopolitan character. Regardless of how explanation of a shift in information provision (from clique to community, perhaps) is explained to governments and funders, a shift in accessibility would bode well for users as members of communities and academies, as well as for librarians for whom the social mission of information mediation and literacy is broadened (Hsieh & Runner 2005).

While measures for how the growth of IC might be fostered by changes of the sort highlighted here are not simple formulations, making the case that innovation grows reliably from improved access to information is not so difficult. One place to start may be with the library professionals themselves and research into how collaboration works at the local level. As Bischoff, Vladova and Jeschke (2011, p. 339) make clear, 'innovative capability does not just depend on the knowledge and potential of individuals, but specifically on their interdisciplinary and interactive thinking and action', with innovation finding its driving force in how 'knowledge resource networks' form through 'the effect of synergy in the relationship of separate individuals'.

Bueno, Salmador and Rodríguez (2004) provide a way to better contextualise any perceived difficulty in measuring the value for integrated libraries. They argue that within the broader framework of the knowledge economy 'social intangibles become essential resources in order to achieve distinctive competencies' (Bueno, Salmador & Rodríguez 2004, p. 556); these are linked to an improved model of social-corporate governance. When it is possible to view 'social capital as **relational capital**' (that is, there is freedom from the limitations that the regular measures of **business capital** impose), we begin to measure *how we all act as social agents* putting 'knowledge into action', for the benefit of stakeholders. Ideally, this creates a wellspring of consensus that allows greater understanding to develop between synergistically oriented organisations and public administration funding bodies that ought to be accompanied by greater commitment to co-operative (or consortial) relations in negotiations with key supplier groups. The measurement of social intangibles (and its incorporation into broader decision matrices) provides 'the encouragement of scientific development; regional economic development; and environmental protection' (Bueno, Salmador & Rodríguez 2004, p. 556). This aligns well with Ingham's (2017, p. 44) notion of putting 'people at the centre of creating value' and, through this, seeing how we can improve the agility of our libraries to use their considerable **organisational capital** 'to do what is most useful rather than just what is in the process' (Ingham 2017, p. 42).

Cultural capital, shared futures and access to knowledge

Arguments are regularly made that access to advanced reading materials reflects a desire to subsidise a small group of disenfranchised readers and that resources are better invested in active stimulus measures (educational programs). The tenor of such arguments tends to decry the elitist nature of the argument for quality reading materials and to unfairly contrast it with popular taste and the genres and formats that might be seen to satisfy demand in these areas. Kingston (2001) argues, within the context of the sociology of education, that such dichotomies are false ones that mistake how we should understand the effect of the **cultural capital** concept. Cultural capital both is desirable and has a univocal expression as normative nurturing practice; it does not have a class-based character, and any attempt to locate it within the exclusionary practices of a social group (such as a class) is misguided. These nurturing practices are 'educationally consequential because they directly stimulate intellectual development and engagement, not because socially biased gatekeepers accord them value' (Kingston 2001, p. 97). Working with the idea that 'participation stimulates ... curiosity, perseverance, sense of mastery, and imagination', Kingston (2001, p. 98) argues that such traits 'are valued by all social groups, and are not arbitrary cultural resources' and are 'no less worthwhile because of some presumed class linkage, nor are they incompatible with the maintenance of many vital subcultural differences'.

At best, readers only ever have free access to a small fraction of available materials, even within their spheres of interest. Technological innovation has opened vast information resources to academics, but what is the cost of leasing information? Putnam (1995) has questioned how we can maintain levels of social capital in proportion to our desire for democratic civil society norms when we continue to be affected by a relentless privatisation of our lives by technology. Such questions remain apposite a quarter of a century later in the context of how we choose to add materials to our publicly accessible libraries. The benefits of an entirely digital academic library experience ought not to be uncritically assumed to be ubiquitous; many problems may arise with the funding of access-only collections that have no residual value except for the limited group who has used them within the licence period. Where arguments are made that digital access is the panacea to all problems of provision of advanced non-fiction materials – and such arguments do have real merit in a fully digitised infosphere – they often overlook the problem of how most commercially produced non-fiction materials are not freely accessible.

Kitcher (2011) offers something of a remedy in a vision of a well-ordered science which can be productively deployed to meet consequential ends that lead to the provision of widely available materials of recognised importance. Where Kitcher (2011, p. 104) aims to deal with 'the different ways in which public knowledge fails to fulfil the much-needed function of supplying information people can use to pursue their legitimate goals', he self-declaredly looks to grounding epistemic equality among interested persons in a society. This contrasts with a more common, less democratic, approach that is the division of epistemic labour that sees all areas of knowledge as 'partitioned' and 'divided into non-overlapping sets' (Kitcher 2011, p. 105). He provides the starting point in terms of how innumerable topics might be made manageable; through shared social life we have a 'a common stock of information' that cannot be appropriated entirely by experts. This is not a vision of Plato's *Kallipolis*. Kitcher (2011, p. 109) entreats us to defend and buttress a 'functional system of public knowledge' that aids citizens' pursuit of legitimate goals. Well-ordered science does not have an Archimedean point from which to set legitimate areas for inquiry; it has, like its humanistic counterpart, many points from which new truths can be variously honed. As Vrana (2010, p. 31) notes, 'there seems to be agreement among public libraries about the importance of public libraries for the presentation of scientific discoveries to the general population', and it is with this goodwill that we should move forward with better programs to use our libraries as hubs for promoting science and culture.

Where resistance to opening academic collections to non-scholars arises in the form of arguments relating to deficit models of understanding ('they won't get it'), libraries need to be prepared to outline alternative constructions. While people will adapt to, and inculcate, new forms of discourse in a range of ways and the engagement with the academic collection may only be occasional, libraries do have the choice to look to the 'funds of knowledge' new patrons bring with them, 'their social networks, and the social and economic exchange relations that such networks facilitate' (Rios-Aguilar et al. 2011, p. 165). Just as this principle is helpful in mediating the uncertainty of economically disadvantaged patrons, the principle applies to other disadvantaged reading groups as well. With a range of educational traditions pointing to the andragogic benefits, it seems fitting that academic libraries have some reasonable engagement with how 'competence and knowledge embedded in the life experiences' (Rios-Aguilar et al. 2011, p. 164) might provide ample girdering for those who have identified their information needs as being substantially within an academic library setting.

While there is substantive commitment to the need to accept the idea that if 'public libraries are to build social capital then they need to make themselves more accessible to new user groups within the community' (Ferguson 2012, p. 31), and promoting culture and skills development through outreach or recommendation (Miller 2014), it is harder to see where libraries are making the connection with collections. Metheny's (2017) discussion on law libraries and social capital provides a counterpoint to (albeit important) discussions of place in social capital development (see also Evjen & Audunson 2009 and Jochumsen, Hvenegaard Rasmussen & Skot Hansen 2012 for discussions on receptiveness to change from users).

Svendsen's (2013) study of branch libraries in rural Denmark provides an unambiguous way to look at social capital creation. He posits institutional social capital as a third type, beyond Putnam's 'bonding' and 'bridging' forms, that develops from public library activity (Svendsen 2013, p. 52). Bonding social capital can link any of us to a limited group with a shared identity. Bridging social capital moves beyond narrow identities to find commonalities between otherwise disparate groups. The specific values Putnam assigns to bonding social capital are 'reciprocity and solidarity', while bridging social capital helps with 'linkages to external assets and for information diffusion' (Putnam 2000, p. 22). Putnam (2000, p. 363) argues that while we usually need both forms to address a given civic problem, it is the bridging form of social capital which is most in need (and the hardest to create) in our searches to solve intractable problems.

Svendsen (2013, p. 53) makes the case for how we can look to more than the social capital generated with individual readers and individual libraries; a 'meso-level analysis' offers the benefit of revealing 'highly beneficial institutional social capital' within the arc of effect of the initiative in question. Public libraries, in his view, are restricted from energising social capital by their very unique roles and cannot be relied upon to 'build up "full-scale" social capital without effective partnerships in the local area' (Svendsen 2013, p. 53). Vårheim (2014) points to the ability of well-functioning libraries to inspire ever-increasing levels of generalised trust in users, with trust being, in his view, a building block of the creation of social capital. While growing trust of this sort is often seen in the context of marginalised populations, there is every reason to see any group whose information needs are unaddressed as worthy of improved services.

Conclusion

Those who believe that the public library has a greater obligation to provide a source of inspiration to communities of readers than current minimalist models undertake to do can continue to make their case to decision makers on library boards and to municipal representatives. Similarly, arguments can be made within the profession that something profoundly dystopian has occurred when the public library models all users as being served by either fiction collections or popular non-fiction with little enduring quality. While it is acknowledged that, internationally, a wide variance in how this model is enacted in individual libraries does occur, the tendency is for usage and use criteria to be so strongly embraced as the only convention in title selection that little remains for a non-fiction collection to educate and enlighten.

Arguing against the people's choice in a liberal and democratic society is always a losing battle. As a result, if the verdict of communities is that they do not want academic books in their libraries, then this should be acknowledged. The taxes that support the resources are the fruits of *their* labour. Librarians with a social conscience will continue to seek ways to link (what is at present) the minority of readers who seek quality materials with them. As outlined here, the only option it seems, at present, is to facilitate access to an academic library for these readers. Significant but, it would seem, underappreciated work is occurring on how we can build new models of the library for diverse reading communities. These libraries are ripe for being built on the model that readers deserve to read what they want but also that a joint infrastructure, municipal and educational, has much to offer readers in maintaining lifelong access to important collections of knowledge. Joint infrastructure is as much about the knowledge that public librarians have of maintaining reading cultures as it is of academic librarians' familiarity with domain knowledge.

Attracting readers and developing an informed and erudite civil society does not come easily (or cheaply). When so much of our time is spent on tasks for sustaining the necessities of life within a capitalist economy, it is unsurprising that serious scientific and cultural inquiry is reserved for the privileged few. Academic and public librarians are asked to be patient with the development of social capital through the dissemination of *the idea of possibility* in books. With commitment, there will be room for science and culture in all our lives, and librarians will be able to be proud, again, of our roles in contributing to the quality of life of the many, rather than just the few.

References

Alsop, J., (2007). Bridget Jones meets Mr. Darcy: challenges of contemporary fiction. *Journal of Academic Librarianship*. 33(5), 581–585. doi:10.1016/j.acalib.2007.05.004

Baba, Z. and Abrizah, A., (2018). Transformation strategies in community engagement: selected initiatives by Malaysian libraries. *IFLA Journal*. 44(2), 90–105.
https://www.ifla.org/files/assets/hq/publications/ifla-journal/ifla-journal-44-2_2018.pdf

Bischoff, S., Vladova, G. and Jeschke, S., (2011). Measuring intellectual capital. In: S. Jeschke, L. Isenhardt, F. Hees and S. Trantow S., eds. *Enabling innovation: innovative capability – German and international views*. Heidelberg, Germany: Springer. pp. 337–347.

Borgman, C., (2003). The invisible library: paradox of the global information infrastructure. *Library Trends*. 51(4), 652–674. http://hdl.handle.net/2142/8487

Bosman, R., Glover, J. and Prince, M., (2008). Growing adult readers: promoting leisure reading in academic libraries. *Urban Library Journal*. 15(1), 46–58. https://academicworks.cuny.edu/ulj/vol15/iss1/5

Bueno, E., Salmador, P. M. and Rodríguez, O., (2004). The role of social capital in today's economy: empirical evidence and proposal of a new model of intellectual capital. *Journal of Intellectual Capital*. 5(4), 556–574. doi:10.1108/14691930410567013

Bush, V., (1945). As we may think. *The Atlantic*. (July), 101–108. https://www.theatlantic.com/magazine/archive/1945/07/as-we-may-think/303881

Chelin, J., (2015). Open doors: library cross-sector co-operation in Bristol, UK. *Interlending & Document Supply*. 43(2), 110–118. doi:10.1108/ILDS-02-2015-0006

Conklin, J. and Moreton, E., (2015). Blurred lines: tying recreational reading to research in an academic library. In: *Creating sustainable community: ACRL 2015, 25–28 March, Portland, OR*. Chicago, IL: Association of College and Research Libraries. pp. 72–77. https://www.ala.org/acrl/acrl/conferences/acrl2015/papers

Crawford, W., (2009). Futurism and libraries. *Online*. 33(2), 58–60.

Crowley, B., (2015). Readers' advisory: differing mental models and the futures of libraries, librarians, and readers' advisory. *Reference & User Services Quarterly*. 55(2), 91–96. doi:10.5860/rusq.55n2.91

Dewan, P., (2010). Why your academic library needs a popular reading collection now more than ever. *College & Undergraduate Libraries*. 17(1), 44–64. doi:10.1080/10691310903584775

Dumay, J. and Garanina, T., (2013). Intellectual capital research: a critical examination of the third stage. *Journal of Intellectual Capital*. 14(1), 10–25. doi: 10.1108/14691931311288995

Dwyer, J., (2000). Books are for use? *The Acquisitions Librarian*. 13(25), 61–79. doi:10.1300/J101v13n25_06

Elliott, J., (2007). Academic libraries and extracurricular reading promotion. *Reference & User Services Quarterly*. 46(3), 34–43. doi:10.5860/rusq.46n3.34

Elliott, J., (2009). Barriers to extracurricular reading promotion in academic libraries. *Reference & User Services Quarterly*. 48(4), 340–346. doi:10.5860/rusq.48n4.340

Evjen, S. and Audunson, R., (2009). The complex library: do the public's attitudes represent a barrier to institutional change in public libraries? *New Library World*. 110(3/4), 161–174. doi:10.1108/03074800910941356

Ferguson, S., (2012). Are public libraries developers of social capital? A review of their contribution and attempts to demonstrate it. *Australian Library Journal*. 61(1), 22–33. doi:10.1080/00049670.2012.10722299

Gunnels, C. B., Green, S. E. and Butler, P. M., (2012). *Joint libraries: models that work*. Chicago, IL: American Library Association.

Hallyburton, A., Buchanan, H. and Carstens, T., (2011). Serving the whole person: popular materials in academic libraries. *Collection Building*. 30(2), 109–112. doi:10.1108/01604951111127498

Hsieh, C. and Runner, R., (2005). Textbooks, leisure reading, and the academic library. *Library Collections, Acquisitions, and Technical Services*. 29(2), 192–204. doi:10.1080/14649055.2005.10766051

Ingham, J., (2017). *The social organization: developing employee connections and relationships for improved business performance.* London: Kogan Page.

Jarvis, C., (2003). Desirable reading: the relationship between women students' lives and their reading practices. *Adult Education Quarterly*. 53(4), 261–276. doi:10.1177/0741713603254029

Jochumsen, H., Hvenegaard Rasmussen, C. and Skot Hansen, D., (2012). The four spaces – a new model for the public library. *New Library World*. 113(11/12), 586–597. doi:10.1108/03074801211282948

Kingston, P., (2001). The unfulfilled promise of cultural capital theory. *Sociology of Education*. 74(Extra issue), 88–99. doi:10.2307/26 73255

Kitcher, P., (2011). Public knowledge and its discontents. *Theory and Research in Education*. 9(2), 103–124. doi:10.1177/147787851140 9618

Lilley, E. and Usherwood, B., (2000). Wanting it all: the relationship between expectations and the public's perceptions of public library services. *Library Management*. 21(1), 13–24. doi:10.1108/01435120010305591

Lyons, R. and Parrott, D., (2015). Caution: adult reading ahead! Steering teens toward higher level reading (and living) with Alex Award winners. *Young Adult Library Services*. 13(4), 22–24. http://yalsa.ala.org/blog/yals/yals-archive

Mahaffy, M., (2009). In support of reading: reading outreach programs at academic libraries. *Public Services Quarterly*. 5(3), 163–173. doi:10.1080/15228950902904267

Mani, B. V., (2017). *Recoding world literature: libraries, print culture, and Germany's pact with books.* New York: Fordham University Press.

Massis, B., (2017). The academic library in 2020. In: D. Baker and W. Evans, eds. *The end of wisdom? The future of libraries in a digital age*. Cambridge, MA: Chandos. pp. 105–111.

Metheny, R., (2017). Improving lives by building social capital: a new way to frame the work of law libraries. *Law Library Journal*. 109(4), 631–648.

Miller, J., (2014). A comparative study of public libraries in Edinburgh and Copenhagen and their potential for social capital creation. *Libri*. 64(4), 316–326. doi:10.1515/libri-2014-0025

Mueller, K., Hanson, M., Martinez, M. and Meyer, L., (2017). Patron preferences: recreational reading in an academic library. *Journal of Academic Librarianship*. 43(1), 72–81. doi:10.1016/j.acalib.2016.08.019

Nicholson, H., (2012). How to be engaging: recreational reading and readers' advisory in the academic library. *Public Services Quarterly*. 8(2), 178–186. doi:10.1080/15228959.2012.675286

Pateman, J. and Williment, K., (2013). *Developing community-led public libraries: evidence from the UK and Canada*. Farnham, UK: Ashgate.

Putnam, R. D., (1995). Bowling alone: America's declining social capital. *Journal of Democracy*. 6, 65–78. doi:10.1007/978-1-349-62397-6_12

Putnam, R. D., (2000). *Bowling alone: the collapse and revival of American community*. New York: Simon and Schuster.

Rathe, B. and Blankenship, L., (2006). Recreational reading collections in academic libraries. *Collection Management*. 30(2), 73–85. doi:10.1300/J105v30n02_06

Reichertz, J., (2013). Hermeneutic sociology of knowledge. *Arbor*. 189(761), 1–8. doi:10.3989/arbor.2013.761n3004

Rios-Aguilar, C., Kiyama, J., Gravitt, M. and Moll, L., (2011). Funds of knowledge for the poor and forms of capital for the rich? A capital approach to examining funds of knowledge. *Theory and Research in Education*. 9(2), 163–184. doi:10.1177/1477878511409776

Rusk, M. and Cummings, E., (2011). Libraries and the local economy: partnerships for economic growth. *Community & Junior College Libraries*. 17(2), 53–61. doi:10.1080/02763915.2011.591708

Russell, S. E. and Huang, J., (2009). Libraries' role in equalizing access to information. *Library Management*. 30(1/2), 69–76. doi:10.1108/01435120910927538

Salter, A. and Brook, J., (2007). Are we becoming an aliterate society? The demand for recreational reading among undergraduates at two universities. *College & Undergraduate Libraries*. 14(3), 27–43. doi:10.1300/J106v 14n03_02

Sanders, M., (2009). Popular reading collections in public university libraries: a survey of three southeastern states. *Public Services Quarterly*. 5(3), 174–183. doi:10.1080/15228950902976083

Sheldrick Ross, C., (1999). Finding without seeking: the information encounter in the context of reading for pleasure. *Information Processing & Management*. 35(6), 783–799. doi:10.1016/S0306-4573(99)00026-6

Svendsen, G., (2013). Public libraries as breeding grounds for bonding, bridging and institutional social capital: the case of branch libraries in rural Denmark. *Sociologia Ruralis*. 53(1), 52–73. doi:10.1111/soru.12002

Trott, B., (2008). Building on a firm foundation: readers' advisory over the next twenty-five years. *Reference & User Services Quarterly*. 48(2), 132–135. doi:10.5860/rusq.48n2.132

Ulmer, G., (1994). *Heuretics: the logic of invention*. Baltimore, MD: Johns Hopkins University Press.

Usherwood, B., (2007). *Equity and excellence in the public library: why ignorance is not our heritage*. Aldershot, UK: Ashgate.

Vakkari, P., (1991). Social structure, book reading and the function of public libraries: effects of selectivity of social structure on the quality and quantity of book reading and the use of public libraries. In P. Kaegbein, B. Luckham and V. Stelmach, eds. *Studies on research in reading and libraries: approaches and results from several countries*. Munich: KG Saur. pp. 259–282.

Van den Hoogen, S. and Fleuren-Hunter, K., (2017). At your leisure pilot project: providing leisure reading materials to a university community through an academic and public library initiative. *Partnership: The Canadian Journal of Library and Information Practice and Research*. 12(1). doi:10.21083/partnership.v12i1.3919

Vander Broek, J. and Rodgers, E., (2015). Better together: responsive community programming at the U-M Library. *Journal of Library Administration*. 55(2), 131–141. doi:10.1080/01930826.2014.995558

Van Fleet, C., (2003). Popular fiction collections in academic and public libraries. *The Acquisitions Librarian*. 15(29), 63–85. doi:10.1300/J101v15n29_07

Vårheim, A., (2014). Trust and the role of the public library in the integration of refugees: the case of a northern Norwegian city. *Journal of Librarianship and Information Science*. 46(1), 62–69. doi:10.1177/096100061 4523636.

Vrana, R., (2010). Public libraries and popularisation of science. *New Library World*. 111(1/2), 26–35. doi:10.1108/03074801011015667

Walker, L., (2018). Women in Horror Month stalks the academic library: highlighting genre and popular culture collections. *Technical Services Quarterly*. 35(3), 246–256. doi:10.1080/07317131.2018.14568 43

Weller, K., (2010). *Knowledge representation in the social semantic web*. Berlin, Germany: De Gruyter Saur.

14
Social Capital in Academic Libraries: A Model for Successful Fundraising

Kathryn Dilworth

Introduction

The social future of libraries needs funding, and libraries need to fundraise. At a time when libraries struggle to connect their value to important stakeholders, fundraising is a vehicle for developing strong relationships built upon understanding and appreciation. Cases for giving are cases for relevance. The donor cultivation process includes the development and exchange of **social capital** between an individual and a fundraiser. Social capital is both the **social network** that evolves through an individual's connections and the tangible outcomes of those connections. Connections between donors and the library engage individuals with the mission. A donation to the library is an expression of perceived value.

The Social Capital Fundraising Model is not new, but, as of this moment, it has a name. The model is already utilised across the non-profit sector, whether practitioners realise it or not. Building connections and relationships is fundamental to fundraising. The point of this chapter and the reason for the new name is to explain why social capital fundraising works and argue that its core element (social capital) be better understood and leveraged intentionally. By implementing a fundraising strategy that is designed to support and expand the social capital of others, fundraising activity will be more efficient and have better outcomes (King 2004). The social capital that the library, itself, builds through this informed practice will support and expand the impact of fundraising.

There is never enough funding, and often the exciting projects are the ones that get put on the back burner so as to meet the cost of basic **resources**. Philanthropic funding is an important and often transformative mechanism for not only filling in the gaps in funding but supporting the most exciting ideas, innovations and initiatives. These are funds that come from private sources, from individuals and philanthropic organisations. Unfortunately, recent studies on fundraising in the academic library reveal that while needs and expectations for raising private funds have gone up since the turn of the century, the resources acquired to fundraise have remained the same (Keith, Salem & Cumiskey 2018). This chapter makes a case for more support and encourages academic library leaders that the effort to get more support is worth it. To that end, it will integrate philanthropy research on giving with academic libraries, provide some helpful information about fundraising in higher education and talk about the benefits of fundraising for the library that go beyond the dollars.

The Social Capital Fundraising Model builds stronger and more meaningful connections with individuals who are in a position to give to the library, and it increases the reputation and value of the library. Finally, because so little scholarship exists on fundraising for the academic library, this chapter adds to this literature. It also brings the academic library into philanthropy literature, which is an area of tremendous growth in the 21st century. My intent is that this chapter will serve as evidence for higher education development programs to invest more in academic library fundraising, recognising it as a viable case for giving for higher education donors. I also hope that it encourages library leaders, staff and faculty to embrace fundraising. In order to fulfil the promise of the social future of libraries, the library must turn outward, beyond the campus and its users, and engage with individuals and entities that can be partners in that future.

There are many academic libraries that enjoy successful fundraising. There are more, however, that struggle (Keith, Salem & Cumiskey 2018). During two years of conducting a study with a colleague on the changing practice of fundraising in academic libraries, I heard of the many challenges that fundraisers face to successfully navigate the process and meet expectations and needs for funding. I have had calls from deans who are frustrated that central development will hardly listen to their claim that the library is a viable fundraising unit. Many libraries lack fundraising support at all. Through the discussion of a fundraising model built upon social capital, I will describe this fundraising process, provide some insight into the fundraiser's experience and demonstrate how fundraising in this way not only brings in funds but creates a culture of philanthropy.

The challenges for fundraising in academic libraries

Central development units across higher education routinely assign prospective donors to the colleges from which they took their degree. This practice is the fundamental barrier to successful fundraising in the academic library. In fact, the phrase 'no natural constituents' is in virtually every publication about fundraising in the academic library, including my own (Dilworth & Henzl 2016). The alumni model is an efficient way to organise a very big job. Many universities have hundreds of thousands of living alumni, and grouping them in this way helps to organise a lot of individuals and anticipate what they may like to support. In addition to presenting a fundraising challenge for all campus units that get left out in this model, this practice makes it less likely for alumni to hear about other interesting things to support at the university.

A 2015 study of 20 years of giving to a university revealed that providing donors with the opportunity to give across campus increased their likelihood of making a major gift to the university, increased the amount they gave compared to those who gave only to a single unit and reduced the likelihood that their giving would go down in difficult economic times (Khodakarami, Petersen & Venkatesan 2015). When prospective donors never hear from the library, they do not know about opportunities to support it, which is a lost opportunity for the donor and the institution. The scoped communication to donors managed and cultivated solely by their academic college makes it difficult for the library to communicate its value broadly. Thus, prospective donors lack knowledge about how the library supports learning and research at the institution. In the traditional higher education fundraising model, when the library fundraiser does have the opportunity to engage alumni, they have the additional challenge of what one fundraiser described as 'education before cultivation'. Gaining access to potential donors is a crucial step in successful fundraising. There are many creative ways that fundraisers in academic libraries navigate this challenge. That issue will be discussed at greater length in a larger project on this topic, but this chapter is about how to take advantage of opportunities libraries do have and how to grow and strengthen that engagement.

It might come as a surprise to learn that fundraising for higher education occurs mostly with donors who are not alumni. Of the total fundraising to support education in the USA last year, 70% of it went to institutions of higher learning. However, only 26% of those funds came from alumni (White 2018). Another reality is that academic units have thousands of alumni who are not managed by fundraisers and available for the library to cultivate. Even the large development units in big research institutions lack the capacity to reach even a fraction of their constituency. Libraries can also collaborate with academic units on proposals for their graduates. In a sense, libraries do have 'alumni' in the form of retired and former faculty, staff and student workers who already know the value of the library.

Individuals who are already in the library need to be aware that it functions in part due to private giving and that there are many opportunities for people to support the funding needs of the library. This includes individuals on both sides of the service scenario. Faculty and staff need to be resourced with information and comfort in order to communicate this information. Cultivation through student and faculty is a long game, but beginning the process in that engagement is crucial to future success. The best time to help users understand how philanthropy functions in the library is yesterday. And, as we will discuss next, individuals are very open to hearing about giving back to the library when they are benefiting from it. Also, by involving faculty and staff in the fundraising process, they can help to identify prospective donors whom they engage with already through their user service.

Library service builds social capital for the library user. Resources and services from the library provide the user with benefits that, much like **financial capital**, can be spent, invested, given away and shared in order to enhance the life of the individual and others in their network. These benefits include information, knowledge, spaces to study and gather. I once received a gift from an alumnus because he was grateful for being able to sleep at the 24/7 library on campus during a year when he had terrible room-mates. The fundraising model based on cultivating alumni is not going to change in higher education, because it works so well for the academic units. But if the library embraces and mobilises the model for fundraising grounded in building the social capital of others, it can achieve strong, sustained success as well. Relationship-building strategies that build social capital for donors and prospective donors connect the library to them as well as their networks.

The larger the network and the stronger the connections within that network to the library, the more the library's social capital will also grow (Strauss 2010). A library with strong social capital has a greater likelihood of receiving philanthropic support.

What is social capital?

Social capital is really having a moment. A Google analytics search for the term suggests that it hardly existed before 1990, but since then it has exploded in both academic and *public scholarship* and across disciplines (Google Books 2013). Much of the credit goes to Robert Putnam, whose best-selling book, *Bowling Alone*, confirmed the fears of many working in the non-profit sector: individual engagement with groups and associations is waning. When he pointed this out to the world in 2000, the non-profit sector scrambled to respond. Scholars started looking at how social capital influenced behaviour. In the field of philanthropy, this included charitable giving. It became clear in this research that social capital and giving have strong ties.

The evolution of the definition of social capital resembles the process of building social capital. It starts with the network and builds in complexity. Early scholarship defines social capital as simply the networks that allow for certain actions by individuals in the structure (Coleman 1988). This held firm until Fukuyama's (1999) work a decade later claimed that the norms that develop on these networks were what defined social capital. Putnam (2000) was developing his theory at the same time and ended up differentiating between two kinds of connections in the network, described as **bridging and bonding social capital.** The bonded connections were between similar kinds of people. These held up well to external forces, but also put individuals at risk for clannish ideologies. Bridged connections are those made between people who have differences. These are not as strong as bonds, but they bring diverse ideas, perspectives and cultural norms into the network. Another scholar whose addition to the definition is important for this discussion suggests that the benefits that result from high social capital are also a fundamental part of its definition (Portes 1998).

The benefits are an important piece for the field of philanthropy, where research had already shown that the benefits of volunteering and giving are strong motivators for giving. In a study that first identified the most common motivation for giving, Schervish and Havens (1997) demonstrated that self-serving motivations were actually greater than altruistic ones. They were not suggesting that donors give for selfish reasons, necessarily, but that they are more motivated when giving is not just a cost but, instead, provides a benefit. Before we get stuck on the term 'benefit', consider Simmons (1991, pp. 10, 16), who pointed out that acts taken in the service of others are still something to admire even when 'subtle self-rewards' might have encouraged them to do so.

The academic library has many benefits to offer donors. Information, knowledge, friendship, an opportunity to meet others with affinity for the library, or simply a good feeling for doing something good are examples. However, in interviews with library fundraisers discussing social capital, it became apparent that the term benefit has strongly negative connotations. This model is not meant to encourage benefits that undermine the mission of the library. Thankfully, higher education fundraising has developed ethics of practice through professional associations and these can be a guide for defining the parameters of ethical benefits (CASE 2019). In her book on the ethics of fundraising, philosopher Marilyn Fischer (2000) examines and sets standards for decision making on all matters of practice from relationships with donors to organisational mission and **trust**.

Part of the challenge to agree on a definition of the term social capital is due to its broad application. For this discussion, I define it in two parts: the first is the network created by bonding and bridging connections. The second is the benefits that come from those connections. Brown and Ferris (2007, p. 86) explain the impact of social capital on philanthropy in terms of the 'norms of trust and **reciprocity** that facilitate collective action'. An individual can increase and decrease his or her social capital, spend it, save it or use it to build the social capital of others. For example, having connections with others who are well regarded and have a positive reputation can increase the social capital of an individual who is connected to them, simply due to a perceived value. Not surprisingly, donating money to organisations that help others can increase an individual's social capital (Putnam 2000). Organisations can also build their social capital through activities that support their mission, including fundraising (King 2004). Fundraising is particularly meaningful for building organisational social capital because it is a way to connect to individuals who have positive reputations, which is one of the most meaningful kinds of social connection for building social capital (Strauss 2010). For the academic library, intentionally leveraging social capital with its network is a strategy to expand its reach and build the kinds of connections that support giving.

Impact of social capital on fundraising

Social capital matters in fundraising because individuals with high social capital have been shown to donate more than others (Brown & Ferris 2007). Therefore, donors who are already giving are the best prospects for future giving. Another study finds that reputation and peer recognition are the 'social consequences' of giving and actually encourage more giving (Bekkers & Wiepking 2011, p. 936). Supporting the social capital of a donor by stewarding their giving makes it much more likely that they will give again. Rather than spend the majority of time discovering new donors, the academic library is better off providing meaningful engagement with individuals who are already giving something, even if it is their time (Wang & Graddy 2008). This is also why staff and faculty are so valuable to the fundraising effort, because they are often the ones who engage with potential donors first. A meaningful engagement is a strong foundation for giving in the future.

In a study by Kearns et al. (2014), the researchers interviewed non-profit leaders to determine the kind of funding most often preferred. They overwhelmingly reported that they prefer gifts that motivate more giving. More giving can come in the form of a donor whose giving becomes larger or repetitive, a new donor who gives because of the example of an individual in their social network or a foundation that renews grants because of the positive impact of previous funding. In each of these examples there is an exchange in social capital. Fundraising training in donor relations and stewardship describes the value of a positive giving experience as part of a process in the donor continuum. Though the term social capital is not used in this description, they acknowledge the phenomenon that if donors experience a meaningful engagement following their gift the likelihood is very high that they will stay engaged. There are also strong measurements that show that the cost of finding a donor is much more than properly stewarding one you already have (McGrath 1997). Fundraisers want to cultivate lifelong donors. Brown and Ferris (2007, p. 90) determined that the 'network-based social capital' is a key indicator for a donor's likelihood to give. This evidence is strong support for a strategy to connect the library with the social networks of current donors and contribute to the social capital of prospective donors, because their robust social networks are made up of individuals who are likely to participate in philanthropy.

Beyond this idea that individuals with strong social capital are likely connected with individuals who give, a study on how social capital relates to fundraising discovered that having an individual who asks for donations on a social network is also a powerful motivator to give. The authors explain: 'Both having a giver and an asker in one's social network increase the likelihood that one participates in charitable giving' (Herzog & Yang 2018, p. 390). This explains the common question posed to fundraisers in training seminars: 'What is the main reason that people do not give?' The answer: 'They have not been asked.' The academic library is in a strong position to successfully fundraise by creating and leveraging social capital. There are many entry points to potential donors. Special and discipline-specific collections are entry points to connect to someone's social network through a specific interest. Initiatives can connect to prospective donors whose values and interests align. Cases for giving around open access, scholarly publishing, digital scholarship, information literacy, informed learning, equal access to information and the application of emerging technologies to teaching and learning are all entry points for connection. There are potential donors far beyond the institution who have great passions for the examples above and many more. Giving to the library can be mutually beneficial when library resources and services align with the personal passions of individuals with robust social networks and high social capital.

The social capital phenomenon in the fundraising process requires a highly skilled fundraising practice. That includes at the very least a professional fundraising staff, a long-term fundraising strategy and a strong narrative about the value of the library. This kind of investment is costly, and it requires a team of professionals with diverse skills. Professional practice is not the same as transactional giving, and transactional giving does not strongly impact on social capital. Professional practice includes fundraising that offers individuals an opportunity to do something meaningful for the library and the individual. Hank Rosso, the founding director at the Fund Raising School at Indiana University describes fundraising as 'the gentle art of teaching the joy of giving' (Lilly Family School of Philanthropy 2019). Research on giving shows that everyone involved in fundraising can benefit from the positive experience of contributing to a meaningful mission (Anik et al. 2009). In the USA, over half of households give to philanthropic organisations. The average amount given is over $2,500 per household, with $900 being the median amount. As individuals get older, the percentage of households goes up. By age 65, nearly 75% of households give (Ottoni-Wilhelm et al. 2017). This is a remarkable reality and a robust indicator that the library has strong opportunities to enjoy successful donor engagement and fundraising. The mission of libraries to support teaching, learning and research is a very attractive philanthropic priority for a wide range of individuals and philanthropic organisations.

In order to fully leverage the Social Capital Fundraising Model, the library needs a fundraising team. Social capital is not built simply because there is a connection. That connection has to be developed in such a way that trust forms and reciprocal benefits are created (Putnam 2000). Doing this requires more than one person. Unfortunately, surveys reveal that if an academic library has fundraising staff at all, it is usually only a single individual (Keith, Salem & Cumiskey 2018). Some libraries share one fundraiser with other units, but many do not have one at all. In a survey to show change over a 25-year period, Dilworth and Heyns (2020) discovered that while fundraising needs had increased, the investment in fundraising in the form of staff had remained very much the same. One fundraiser for the library is simply not enough to facilitate a social capital model for fundraising, or any other fundraising model, frankly. The four stages of fundraising detailed below require time, skill and talent that a single person cannot possibly provide. Each stage requires unique skills.

The following is a shortened version of *The Eight Step Major Gift Management Cycle* taught at the Fund Raising School at the Lilly Family School of Philanthropy at Indiana University:

- *Identification* – This stage includes research and evaluation of prospective donors who have the inclination and wealth capacity to make a major gift. From this research comes the creation of a list of prospective donors. This stage is typically the first time a fundraiser engages with a prospect. Professionals required for this stage are the fundraiser, prospect researcher, data manager and support staff to assist with visits, travel and reporting.
- *Cultivation* – This stage is when cases for giving to the library are developed with library leadership, faculty and staff to define and prioritise needs and opportunities for philanthropic support. It is when giving opportunities are discussed with prospective donors to determine the appropriate focus and amount and to build interest. It is when relationship building occurs. Professionals required for this stage are the fundraiser, library dean in some cases or faculty, communications staff for building collateral around opportunities to give and staff to support travel and reporting.

- *Solicitation* – This is 'the ask'. It can take years to get to this stage. Proposals are written and those who will make the solicitation plan and rehearse. The fundraiser will be at this important meeting, and often the library dean. Other professionals required for this stage are gift services staff, who book the gift in the institution's financial system. Often managers in central development are crucial for collaboration and oversight to ensure that proposals meet the institution's policies and best practice.
- *Stewardship* – This stage includes US federal government Internal Revenue Service processes for reporting a gift. The donor is acknowledged during this phase and provided with tax documentation. Often, visits with the fundraiser continue in order to maintain the relationship and prep them for the next cultivation phase. University-wide events, access to key leaders and strategic volunteer opportunities help to maintain and grow the relationship. Professionals needed in this stage include the fundraiser, dean, strategic staff and faculty and central development leadership to assist with important tasks like building a new strategy for the next cultivation cycle, annual financial reporting for endowments from finance specialists and data management.

Robert Putnam's (2000) definition of social capital as a network that provides benefits is particularly poignant when thinking about the process of engaging a donor, building a relationship with them, asking them for support, walking them through the process of making a gift and maintaining a long-term relationship with them. He identified two types of social capital: bonding and bridging. He theorised that *bonding* is the kind of social capital that forms between similar people or groups (Putnam 2000). A family is a good example of this, as well as a religious community. Those who share bonding connections share similarities, and these bonds are extremely strong. An example of a bonding connection for library fundraising is a retired library faculty member setting funds aside in a bequest to benefit student workers. The social capital created between the library faculty member and the library is based on a similar passion for academic libraries and strong affection for the one where he or she enjoyed a meaningful career.

The other kind of connection is *bridging* capital. These are the bonds across difference. They are easily broken, unfortunately, because they are made between people who do not share similarities (Putnam 2000). However, they are valuable because they support diversity and give voice to more ideologies and ideas. A bridging bond is a graduate whose bond is with their department but who has come to appreciate the fact that making a gift to library resources is a valuable way to support his or her department. This connection is not strong like the first example, but it is a valuable gift and an opportunity for the library to become a part of a very different social network than the one they shared with the library faculty member.

The words bonding and bridging are also commonly used in fundraising. Fundraisers talk about bridging people to a mission or a particular case for giving. A prospective donor can become bonded to the fundraiser, others engaged in the process and the organisation itself through fundraising. These bonds are built by engaging the interests and philanthropic goals of the prospective donor with the organisation. The bonds are held together through trust and authentic relationships between the donor, individuals in the library and the library itself. Bonds are made stronger between the library and the donor when the donor can see the impact of their gift. The process of fundraising is a mechanism that can transform a bridging connection into a bonding one. With skilful fundraising practice, an interest in a giving opportunity can grow into a passion for the library and its mission. Many who have been a part of this transformation can attest to the phenomenon. It may be one explanation for the reason why giving motivates more and increased giving. It also is a warning that, as with any connection, if the fundraising process breaks down, the bridge and the bond can be lost.

This new model of building social capital to support fundraising for the library begins with a recognition and acknowledgment that the library's social capital enables fundraising. Fundraising will not, in fact, happen without it. Social capital built through fundraising not only facilitates giving to the library but also creates a cycle of giving. Each engagement connects the social capital of the library to others, and in turn this connects the library to their network. Building the social capital of the library happens with intention. A simple way to begin is by investing time and attention in the donors who are already bonded to the library. If they already love the library, they are more likely to consider further support. Even if an existing donor lacks a strong personal social network, the story of that donor and that connection can attract more donors.

Another priority should be discovering the nature of the library's social capital. Who is already a part of the library's social network? How can this network be leveraged to support fundraising? An example is a research collection that is unique, popular, trendy or relevant to current social or political activities. There may be no researchers in a position to financially support this collection, but who are they writing for? Who is their audience? Who already supports the kinds of research that utilises this collection? Thinking more broadly in this way with social capital as a driver for strategies can identify potential donors never considered before. The library also can make progress in building their social capital and networks by helping donors and prospective donors to build theirs. Even those who do not know what social capital is want to do this. This takes strategic engagement that brings people together in meaningful ways where they can bridge and bond.

Fundraising requires investment. It takes a lot of time, collaboration and information to identify and cultivate donors. This process needs to be successful in order to ensure the future of academic libraries. That means more than simply survival. The activities connected to fundraising must also be mastered in order to ensure the innovation of the future. Connecting to social networks and realising the mutual benefits that come from those connections improves the overall success of the library. This model of engagement can positively impact on service, collaborations and the reputation of the library and those connected with it. It can be expensive, but a collective effort has the capacity to achieve high social capital for the library across the full range of efforts and initiatives. However, a single fundraiser is not going to have any more success doing this for fundraising than a single information professional trying to push through a new, complex initiative.

Fundraiser turnover in higher education is extremely high. A survey of over 1,000 fundraisers in North America by *The Chronicle of Philanthropy* revealed that half the fundraisers surveyed intended to leave their current position in under two years (Joslyn 2019, p. 8). Some of the reasons included high pressure to succeed, a lack of appreciation and not enough help to do their job (Joslyn 2019, pp. 9, 10). Fundraisers do not want to be in a situation where they cannot be successful. This is a role in which assessment is entirely quantitative. If a fundraiser cannot meet and exceed fundraising goals, then he or she will not stay. However, 93% of the fundraisers surveyed said they could not work for an organisation if they did not believe in their cause (Joslyn 2019, p. 11). With a mission-driven passion for their professional work, it makes sense that, of those who leave, they most often cite a feeling of betrayal when an organisation makes it impossible for them to succeed (Joslyn 2019, p. 10).

Culture of philanthropy in the library

The work of building social capital begins on the inside by building a culture of philanthropy. This is achieved by treating employees as if they are potential donors. Cultivating a positive environment for library faculty and staff, anticipating their needs, connecting them to potential colleagues and friends in the organisation and cultivating their passion for their work are examples of ways to create connections that are meaningful and mutually beneficial. A culture of philanthropy sets a tone for compassionate, professional treatment of faculty and staff towards each other. Thinking of users as potential donors positively influences service. The benefits to the library take the form of commitment to mission, long and valuable service and maybe one day even giving.

Fundraisers in the academic library are often new to this environment and need to develop an understanding of how the library contributes to the success of the institution. They should therefore be embraced and taught about the library. The fundraiser's lack of awareness about the library reflects the condition they face with potential donors. The faster they get up to speed on what a modern academic library does, the sooner they can develop cases for giving which they can present to potential donors. Another important way to create a culture of philanthropy in the library is by engaging faculty and staff with the fundraising process. For giving opportunities that support research or teaching, faculty can be part of the cultivation process by joining donor meetings to talk about their work and its impact on student success, for example. All faculty and staff can be a part of helping fundraisers to demonstrate the impact of giving to existing donors through their participation in events and the effort to make donors feel they are part of the library. Individuals give to organisations because they want to do something good, help to solve problems or contribute to something exciting. It is often crucial for them to get to know the ones who are facilitating all the good things that the fundraiser is telling them about.

Bridging and bonding someone from the outside to the mission of the library is powerful. And, of course, landing major gifts can be transformative. Inviting and including library faculty and staff to be a part of this process will bond them to the mission as well, expand their social network and positively impact on their social capital.

Conclusion

One of the goals of this chapter was to encourage and empower the library to take a new approach to fundraising. The alumni model is not going to ever go away in higher education, and many decades of library fundraising have proven that it is not effective for the library. The other goal was to demonstrate what the new approach requires to be successful. The Social Capital Fundraising Model can begin with the existing staff, but it cannot reach its true potential with a single fundraiser. This model is, in fact, intended to provide evidence that more resources for fundraising are required and will pay off. Poor fundraising performance in the library is not about a lack of compelling opportunities for giving; it is about a lack of resources.

In regard to social capital, success breeds more success. Activities related to fundraising build the social capital of the library, even though every engagement will not result in a gift. A long-term strategy to build the social capital of the library will result in successful fundraising. The future of the library will be leveraged on social capital built across all relationships. Donors can play a big part in this future by helping the library to achieve dreams and goals that expand the capacity to facilitate the mission of the library.

References

Anik, L., Aknin, L. B., Norton, M. I. and Dunn, E. W., (2009). *Feeling good about giving: the benefits (and costs) of self-interested charitable behavior.* Harvard Business School Marketing Unit Working Paper 10-012. doi:10.2139/ssrn.1444831

Bekkers, R. and Wiepking, P., (2011). A literature review of empirical studies of philanthropy: eight mechanisms that drive charitable giving. *Nonprofit and Voluntary Sector Quarterly.* 40(5), 924–973. doi:10.1177/0899764010380927

Brown, E. and Ferris, J. M., (2007). Social capital and philanthropy: an analysis of the impact of social capital on individual giving and volunteering. *Nonprofit and Voluntary Sector Quarterly.* 36(1), 85–99. doi:10.1177/0899764006293178

CASE., (2019). *Ethics resources.* Washington, DC: Council for the Advancement and Support of Education. https://www.case.org/resources/ethics-resources

Coleman, J. S., (1988). Social capital in the creation of human capital. *American Journal of Sociology.* 94(Supplement), S95–S120. doi:10.1016/j.socec.2007.06.014

Dilworth, K. and Henzl, L. S., (2016). *Successful fundraising for the academic library: philanthropy in higher education.* Cambridge, MA: Chandos.

Dilworth, K. and Heyns, E. P., (2020). Fundraising in academic libraries: looking back and defining new questions. *Journal of Academic Librarianship.* 46(5), 102192. doi:10.1016/j.acalib.2020.10219

Fischer, M., (2000). *Ethical decision making in fund raising.* New York: John Wiley.

Fukuyama, F., (1999). Social capital and civil society. In: *International Monetary Fund conference on second generation reforms, 8–9 November, Washington, DC.*
http://www.imf.org/external/pubs/ft/seminar/1999/reforms/fukuyama.htmi

Google Books (2013). Ngram Viewer. *Google Books.* https://books.google.com/ngrams

Herzog, P. S. and Yang, S., (2018). Social networks and charitable giving: trusting, doing, asking and alter primacy. *Nonprofit and Voluntary Sector Quarterly.* 47(2), 376–394.
doi:0.1177/0899764017746021

Joslyn, H., (2019). Moving on: why fundraisers leave, and how to keep them. *The Chronicle of Philanthropy.* 31(10), 8–16.

Kearns, K. P., Bell, D., Deem, B. and McShane, L., (2014). How nonprofit leaders evaluate funding sources: an exploratory study of nonprofit leaders. *Nonprofit and Voluntary Sector Quarterly.* 43(1), 121–143. doi: 10.1177/0899764012458038

Keith, B. W., Salem Jr., J. A. and Cumiskey, K., (2018). *Library development.* SPEC Kit 359. Washington, DC: Association of Research Libraries. doi:10.29242/spec.359

Khodakarami, F., Petersen, J. A. and Venkatesan, R., (2015). Developing donor relationships: the role of the breadth of giving. *Journal of Marketing.* 79(4), 77–93. doi:10.1509/jm.14.0351

King, N. K. (2004). Social capital and nonprofit leaders. *Nonprofit Management and Leadership.* 14(4), 471–486. doi:10.1002/nml.48

Lilly Family School of Philanthropy., (2019). *About the Fund Raising School.* Indianapolis, IN: Indiana University, Lilly Family School of Philanthropy.
https://philanthropy.iupui.edu/professional-development/fundraisingschool/index.html

McGrath, S., (1997). Giving donors good reason to give again. *Journal of Nonprofit and Voluntary Sector Marketing.* 2(2), 125–135. doi:10.1002/nvsm.6090020204

Ottoni-Wilhelm, M., Pasic, A., Rooney, P. M., Osili, U. O., Bergdoll, J., Han, X. and Gondola, T., (2017). *Overview of overall giving: based on data collected in 2015 about giving in 2014.* 1–16. The 2015 Philanthropy Panel Study. Indianapolis, IN: Indiana University–Purdue University Indianapolis.
http://generosityforlife.org/wp-content/uploads/2017/10/Overall-Giving-10.5.17-jb-CJC.pdf

Portes, A., (1998). Social capital: its origins and applications in modern sociology. *Annual Review of Sociology.* 24, 1–24. doi:10.1146/annurev.soc.24.1.1

Putnam, R. D., (2000). *Bowling alone: the collapse and revival of American community.* New York: Simon & Schuster.

Schervish, P. G. and Havens, J. J., (1997). Social participation and charitable giving: a multivariate analysis. *Voluntas.* 8(3), 235–260. doi:10.1007/BF02354199

Simmons, R. G., (1991). Presidential address on altruism and sociology. *The Sociological Quarterly.* 32(1), 1–22. doi:10.1111/j.1533-8525.1991.tb00342.x

Strauss, J. R., (2010). Capitalizing on the value in relationships: a social capital-based model for non-profit public relationships. *PRism.* 7(2).
https://www.prismjournal.org/uploads/1/2/5/6/125661607/v7-no2-c3.pdf

Wang, L. and Graddy, E., (2008). Social capital, volunteering, and charitable giving. *Voluntas*. 19(1), 23–42. doi:10.1007/s11266-008-9055-y

White, A. E., (2018). Giving USA 2018: implications for higher ed. *JGA Blog*. 20 July. http://info.jgacounsel.com/blog/giving-usa-2018-implications-for-higher-ed

15
Design as an Accelerator of Social Capital in Academic Libraries

Andrew Dillon

Introduction

Since the 2002 National Academies report entitled *Preparing for the revolution* (National Research Council 2002), there has been general acceptance that the technological infrastructure supporting scholarly research and teaching practices would induce disruption of traditional academic library operations. Since then, the increasing computational power, diffusion of networks and adoption of digital tools and resources have resulted in significant shifts in user behaviour, but it is less clear that academic libraries and their staffs have been instrumental rather than reactive to these changes.

The evolving global information infrastructure has been accompanied by a growth in design communities who create and share software resources in order to customise tools and tailor solutions for specific use contexts (see, for example, resource sites such as OpenSource.com). An activist bent in many such **communities** reflects a challenging of the status quo and belief that our information world should not be pre-packaged or controlled by a few, but must enable groups or organisations to tailor technical elements of their environment for local considerations. Further, there is evidence that technology-mediated research practices in some areas are reliant on dedicated software that is produced by team members in real time and which borrows heavily from and reuses parts of other tools (*see*, for example, Howison & Bullard 2015). In such an environment, co-working practices can result in better infrastructures for specific users and tasks while forming strong community ties that increase **social capital**. This ecology of mutual design and use covers many different scenarios, but as an approach to technical work it offers a model for organisational design that I believe has significant potential in scholarly environments.

In Dillon (2008) I argued that design approaches to academic library service delivery offered a stronger way of aligning the library and its staff with the core mission of the university. The argument for a design studio framing is outlined further in this chapter. However, I extend the argument for this approach through a consideration of social capital theory as a guiding orientation in which to situate the activities and methods of *design thinking*. In the following sections I outline how design thinking offers a framing approach to service provision that can place academic libraries into better mission alignment with major stakeholder concerns and activities related to data management, learning support and research practices. Such an approach directly focuses attention on the structural, relational and cognitive dimensions of social capital as **intellectual capital**, outlined by such authors as Nahapiet and Ghoshal (1998) among others, and provides a practical approach to rethinking the role and activities of academic libraries in the coming decades. Through a strong commitment to designing for user experiences, both the practical and credentialing concerns of professional education are considered.

The existential challenge for academic libraries

The Council on Library and Information Resources (CLIR 2008) report *No brief candle: reconceiving research libraries for the 21st century*, presented a case for transforming academic libraries for survival in the coming decades. The report suggested that, with increasing numbers of faculty and host universities questioning the role and value of the traditional library on campus, the existence of an academic library, particularly as a physical space, may be challenged. In response, it argued that a new type of library professional, operating differently than before and untethered to the typical accredited graduate degree, might be required. Further, the report suggested that collections and their managers might be embedded in distributed locations to add value to broader stakeholders in the university. In so saying, the report also asked (but stopped short of answering) if the purpose of the research library might shift to incorporate new responsibilities in the near future.

The challenges raised in that CLIR report are echoed broadly in the literature on academic librarianship. We continually read of ongoing reviews and university task forces set up to chart the future of their library system in an age of digital disruption and decreasing financial support. The Association of College and Research Libraries (ACRL Research Planning and Review Committee 2018) listed among the top challenges facing academic libraries in 2018 the need for greater project management skills, the move into analytics and discovery processes, handling the acquisition and management of new media datasets and repositories, open access initiatives and the continuing issue of dealing with legacy collections. Taking a longer perspective than the calendar year, Storer (2014) predicted that the number one challenge for academic librarians in the coming century will be making services engaging to researchers and students. According to Storer (2014, Section 1), 'you have to fully absorb the needs and wants of students and researchers so you can make a substantial and engaging difference in their work moving forward'.

However, such emphasis might not actually be shifting attitudes within the academic library profession. Saunders (2015) content-analysed strategic plans of 63 academic libraries, revealing continual concerns with physical space challenges, collections, collaboration and support for learning. Related emphasis, but at a slightly lower level, concerned staffing, training, data services and budgets. In fact, so traditional are many of these listed concerns that Saunders suggested academic libraries were actually planning not strategically but reactively, likely missing the opportunity to lead or advance their institutional homes in a significant manner. As she reported, the emphasis in too many plans was on familiar issues related to space or staff resources, with too little attention paid to data services, student success or mobile environments. In sum, she concluded that moving libraries out of their traditional comfort zones was important for the future, 'and in fact, these new areas could represent a leadership opportunity for academic libraries' (Saunders 2015, p. 290).

To lead as Saunders (2015) advocates requires a significant mind-shift among the academic library community and a move from firefighting and trend-jumping to rethinking the organisational mission and service provision of academic libraries in a changing environment. The argument is not particularly new, but the steps to follow are neither agreed nor obvious. Storer (2014) might have thought this was the challenge of the century, but a real concern is that taking so long to adjust might be too long for many of our institutions. One approach that I believe holds genuine potential now lies in the adoption and nurturing of design-oriented practices, and their potential not just to help address challenges in the information landscape but to build relationships and partnerships across campus that enhance social capital for academic librarians.

Design thinking as problem solving

The term *'design thinking'* is employed widely in contemporary discussions of innovation, management, product design and problem solving. Since the term is now so generally invoked, there is no fixed definition that satisfies all uses, but most parties would accept a representation of design thinking as a problem-solving process based on the active exploration of solutions to problems, with an emphasis on idea generation, questioning of assumptions, prototyping and testing possible solutions continually in the search for improvements or innovations that work for people (see, for example, the literature collated by the Interaction Design Foundation at www.interaction-design.org/literature/topics/design-thinking). In general ways that seem to bear little relation to actual practice, design thinking has popularly been characterised as the opposite of or quite distinct from scientific thinking, which is then characterised as logical, linear and rule bound, though most evidence of scientific research and discovery suggests that such a polarised distinction fails to represent either design or science accurately (Lawson 2005; Chalmers 2013).

Johansson-Sköldberg, Woodilla and Çetinkaya (2013) distinguish five scholarly uses of design or, as they also refer to it, 'designerly' thinking in the literature. In their review, the term 'design thinking' is employed in reference to:

1 the creation of artefacts
2 a reflexive practice
3 a problem-solving activity
4 a way of reasoning/making sense of things
5 the creation of meaning.

There is considerable overlap among these uses, as well as points of distinction, but for present purposes it is appropriate to consider each use as varyingly relevant to the challenge of building social capital for academic libraries. Rather than select one or two as key, I prefer to think of each view of design thinking as having a place in the cycle of activities involved in the creation of new solutions in all domains, from making sense of the world to delivering on artefacts through practice and problem solving.

My reading of the design literature over the years suggests a possible distillation of these various uses into some key ideas which I will emphasise in this chapter. First, there is a shared recognition that problems do not always lend themselves to logical analysis and deduction. Rather, thorny or challenging problems are best thought through by exploring options, considering partial solutions and iterating through cycles of testing and redesign. These steps can often lead to recasting of the problem space, while the testing of partial solutions can help to reveal the true user needs that remain blurred when only observing or interviewing people in the established contexts. While there is much promotional baggage attached to the label now in the business and popular medias, if considered as a process, there is in fact a very close mapping of design thinking to the user-centred design approaches long advocated by those in the human–computer interaction/user experience (UX) communities (see, for example, Ritter, Baxter & Churchill 2014).

The steps and methods advanced by the design thinking and user-centred design communities tend to use slightly different terms, but in general the overlap among them is sufficiently close for us to use a generic form that serves most advocates' goals, as outlined in the following steps:

- *empathy* – an effort to learn about the users for whom you're designing and their context of use in the real world;
- *definition* – a phase of establishing user needs, clarifying the problem;
- *ideation* – generating ideas for potential or innovative solutions;
- *prototyping* – developing these possible solutions and new ways of working;
- *testing* – trying out the ideas on real users and gaining feedback.

While listed here as a sequence, the emphasis throughout is on multiple iterations, taking ideas, testing them out and using the insights gained through these tests to revisit the definition and ideation stages, often repeatedly, always grounded in the responses and reactions, thoughts and inputs of the users and stakeholders for whom one is designing. To practise such user-centred design thinking requires a significant early effort in exploring the practices, tasks and workflows of people whom we hope to support through a new or revised product or service. Only by truly understanding their requirements and the obstacles or challenges they face in their working worlds can we hope to offer improvements or solutions.

Of course, users either are often unaware of the possibilities that new technologies can deliver, or they cannot provide plausible or reliable alternatives when asked what they need. However, the goal of true user-centred design is to spend time in the users' world exploring how their practices might be improved and how this might be accomplished without undue cost (financial or cognitive). This part of the process is key, and where design thinking moves beyond the typical surveying of user needs or provision of learning resources that require users to adjust or be trained to the system. The aim is to be open to potentially radical change in accordance with opportunities of the work context so as to deliver clear and sometimes significant improvements to key stakeholders. Designers often report that imagined solutions emerge only after significant back-and-forth with people, following deep immersion in working environments, and after initial proposals are considered and rejected in tests.

This empathising with users in order to establish requirements for a new design of product or service is necessarily time consuming. Indeed, as a process, user involvement must be continuous, and the design team must be willing to dismiss otherwise appealing design solutions, even after investing time in their development, if user testing suggests the solution is not appropriate or satisfactory. We have decades of evidence in the user-centred design world that both hearing what users really want and applying these insights to resulting designs is not an algorithmic process but a knowledge-intensive one that requires strong listening, observational and problem-solving skills. Further, we know that the testing phase, the point at which many assume a near-finished design will have its final kinks worked out, is often the most informative one in generating the true user requirements, since it is one of the first times users really get to try out a new approach, not just talk about one in the abstract or consider it in low-fidelity form. Thus, the process must be agile, iterative and continually based on inputs from the very people we are trying to serve.

The popularity of design thinking as a method and philosophy has co-occurred with a major shift in the global infrastructure of information. In particular, the explosion of the development and deployment of new digital tools places emphasis on participatory movements for design, rapid prototyping, automatic data collection and a networked environment that changes radically the physical and geographic restrictions on access to information. This much we know and have recognised for years. The challenge is exploiting these shifts to deliver an information infrastructure that truly adds value for people now and into the future.

It is encouraging that design thinking approaches are gaining traction in the LIS domain and an emerging literature addresses the need to consider library services and products through this lens (see, for example, Clarke & Bell 2018, or Meier & Miller 2016). However, much of the work, in keeping with the general tenor of much in the design thinking literature, is rather general, leaning towards advocacy (see, for example, Fosmire 2016). This is important, but it seems that there are too few practitioners listening; and, once they listen, it will be important to provide the skills and methods necessary to deliver on this shift, as I shall discuss later when considering the education of new professionals.

Without underestimating the commercial interests that govern the decision making and budgeting in higher education generally, I believe we are at a moment where academic libraries should usefully and honestly question many of their existing practices so as to explore potential futures through an ongoing effort built on the leveraging of new technologies and design thinking methods. I am not suggesting that every challenge faced by academic libraries can be solved by following this approach, but the essence of user-centred design methods can reshape the thinking about what a modern academic library might deliver in terms of services and products. Further, the process of engagement required by design thinking will offer commensurate benefits to the library, due to its direct involvement of community members across the university. It is this aspect that brings social capital into consideration and offers a way of guiding future planning for long-term success that is more solidly guided by theoretical insight than is usually considered important or even necessary by design thinkers.

Social capital as a lens on the academic context of design thinking

Social capital theory has been criticised for being overly generalised, difficult to define and lacking predictive power (see, for example, Poder 2011). Part of the challenge with social capital as a concept is its multidimensional nature. Full treatments of the theory place emphasis on the network of relationships that exist across groups and organisations, the norms of social action within the context of study and the types of actors involved, rendering generalisation difficult. There is also considerable disagreement concerning the level at which social capital can be thought to exist, with some considering it possibly an individual variable while others posit that it makes sense only at the collective or organisational level.

In advocating for design as an enabler and trying to situate this within a broader organisational understanding, I adopt Nahapiet and Ghoshal's (1998) identification of social capital as structural, cognitive and relational. The structural relies on the network of people and **resources** that may exist in a given context, which for present purposes is the university and its socio-technical world. Cognitive aspects of social capital relate to the understanding network members share of this space, particularly its purpose and operational characteristics, while **relational capital** is best conceived of as the values and beliefs that members have, which give rise to **trust** within the network. Clearly, these forms are interrelated, but in an ideal context we aim to raise social capital levels through improving the connections, resources, mutual understanding and trust among network members. Research confirms the positive correlation among aspects, but the distinctions matter, since it is their interconnectedness and mutual reinforcement which help to identify and operationalise the social capital construct in a given context.

Lin (2001) emphasises the importance of action in enabling social capital and I consider this to be the bridge between design thinking and raising social capital within academic libraries. He argues that actors in a network engage in action either to protect their social capital or to increase it. Important to this distinction in the present context is the view of a protectionist strategy entailing actions which focus on rights and legitimacy, and that a protection bias in many individuals and organisations often reveals a greater motivation to avoid loss of resources than to increase capital. Typical maintaining actions are **expressive**, the creation of messages about purpose, mission or proprietary rights. It is perhaps this type of action that we see too often in academic libraries with the emphasis on explaining what services are offered or offering classes in using the existing resources in an effort to encourage greater uptake. Such a protectionist approach might be useful when libraries are threatened but offers little long-term prospect for growth.

Action to increase capital is, according to Lin's (2001) theory, purposive, and involves **instrumental** efforts to engage and cause reactions and responses in other network members. In particular, rather than just engaging in an effort to increase one's resources, the ideal of action for social capital growth is to create interactions that, according to Lin (2001, p. 46), enhance each network member's opportunities to 'access and use one another's resources for their own purposes'. This is crucial. What we are ideally seeking is a process of engagement that benefits each stakeholder's capital, a mutually beneficial scenario whereby action leads to collective improvement in conditions. This is a strong selling point in most university environments.

A further distinction is made by Lin (2001) between **homophilous** and **heterophilous interactions**, which refers to the types of relationships that can exist between actors within a network. In the former, each actor is considered to possess similar or comparable resources, while in the latter case there are clear inequalities. Social capital theory suggests that *homophilous* interactions involve lower effort on the part of actors, but can offer a return only when both parties are engaged in maintaining the status quo. To engage in action to increase capital, the highest yield will come from seeking heterophilous interactions, but these are necessarily high-effort activities for the lesser-resourced actors.

To situate academic libraries in this context, one can reasonably view the academic environment as a network of *heterophilous* actors (within which there are layers of homophilous stakeholders). Within this environment, the library is typically challenged resource-wise, and traditionally has emphasised protectionist action to limit the negative effects of budget reductions, escalating costs, space challenges and technological upheaval. This type of action is considered low effort when engaging with similarly resourced groups (there are always some traditional supporters of libraries among the university membership, but these are likely not the best resourced), but it is high effort for low return when engaging better-resourced (heterophilous) actors in the academy. Viewed through this lens, such action is familiar, but even with great effort is unlikely to yield significant tangible return. According to social capital theory as espoused by Lin (2001), the only significant yield that a library can expect in the university context will require purposive interaction with the better-resourced units, or, in the language of social capital theory, where they act intentionally with heterophilous actors in their network. This is where I see the greatest opportunity for applying the philosophy and methods of user-centred design thinking.

Of course, to initiate such relationships requires a tremendous effort at building trust between partners. In social capital theory, trust is a central concept that is considered to grow within a *community* as co-operative interactions become routinised and anticipated. Trust is an enabler; partners who share it are more likely to engage together on joint projects or to allow another to change existing practices. The challenge is initiating such relationships. While there is generally a high level of trust within universities for the common-good mission of libraries, by seeking more heterophilous relationships the leadership within academic libraries will need to build out from existing trust networks and enable their best staff to connect with the necessary partners. This is more than just facilitating introductions and opening doors; it requires investment in resources (time, people, facilities and technologies) that will perhaps be challenging and may not lead immediately to obvious successes. In leadership terms it will require a retelling of the story about what the academic library does, how it does it and what the pay-off will be. This is a very different narrative to the type of mission statement Saunders (2015) reported as common to most academic libraries.

Design thinking as a generator of social capital

It is not my intention to provide a guide to applying design thinking in library contexts in this chapter, but we can consider key aspects of the process which offer some insights into how its application might help to raise the social capital of the academic library. By engaging in a design thinking approach, actors within the library need to empathise deeply with the better-resourced sectors of the academy for whom they can provide a service. This process must involve immersing staff or representatives in the working world of such actors. It is not enough to survey faculty or students to determine what they like or want from their libraries; instead, members of the library design team must take it upon themselves to become intimately familiar with the practices, needs, goals and tasks of key stakeholders in their routine academic work. Surveying is too passive and overly reliant on the false belief that people are able to articulate easily what they need. There is an extensive research literature that challenges this assumption and suggests that users are rarely able to state, in advance and to a survey or interview prompt, what new products or services would be best for them (see, for example, Holtzblatt & Beyer 2017). Task-force inputs that invite general opinions or statements of how to improve services might serve protectionist goals (and maintain homophilous relationships), but are often too disconnected from real user activities to offer solutions that matter for people and thereby improve social capital.

In particular, it is vital that a design team working in an academic library context get out of the library and into the spaces where the processes critical to the institution's mission are enacted, namely the research and instructional front lines. In the spirit of engaging heterophilous agents, this must mean seeking out the groups who are not predisposed to using the library heavily and identifying those who are tackling problems where non-traditional research infrastructures are emerging and where actors are challenged by massive data, dynamic open source software and idiosyncratic tools and methods that are being shaped through use. Rather than just assuming that the library will serve a data repository function, it is important to explore what else a skilled information design team might enable and deliver for such user groups. (In my experience, many libraries claim this function, but then place restrictions on faculty use that significantly limit uptake.) The purpose of design thinking is first to ask such questions of a function or service and attempt to engage relevant actors in generating insights that lead to testable, prototype solutions.

Reduced to its essentials, the overarching goal of applying design thinking in this context is to forge new relationships based on problem solving. Unpacking this of course opens up more complicated questions of the skills required, the resources involved and the challenges, technical and social, that are entailed in engaging with external groups on thorny problems. However, if the goal is to position the academic library within the university as a core provider of information solutions, then the task at hand must be to meet the key users where they live, so to speak. In a very real sense, this is an inversion of the library as sacred space model which invites faculty and students inside and continues to insist on the library as an important physical location for faculty and students at the centre of campus with a large (and largely unused) collection and maybe a coffee shop as a token commitment to modernity. In a distributed information environment, there is real work to be conducted at the interface of researchers and their data, in the offices and laboratories of academic units and in the classrooms and networks where instruction is delivered. But more than location, the work involves situating librarians (or whatever such professionals will be called) in the real-life working practices of those they seek to support, delivering services more than spaces.

Coupled with the embedding of designers across the university, there must be a radical rethinking of attitude. Librarians are quick to claim user-centredness as an abiding philosophy, but a plethora of recent publications emphasising a greater need for user-centredness likely indicates that the claim has not always been enacted in practice (see, for example, Benedetti 2017 and Connaway & Hood 2016). Too often libraries operate in a rule-bound, fixed-policy manner that serves to limit rather than enhance users' real opportunities to explore, discover and exploit the information infrastructure of the university. Design without true user-centredness offers little chance for enhancing social capital. Instead, there must be an organisation-wide commitment to understanding and serving users at all times. Clearly, this does not mean that the user is always right but it does mean that the user has privileged access to their own needs and preferences, and any design intended to support them must seek to establish these in a meaningful way to advance the kinds of high-value services libraries can provide. Without this attitude change, growth of the library's social capital is unlikely to occur.

Implications for education

A significant challenge to implementing a design-oriented approach within academic libraries is the skillset required. Without even addressing the market challenges in an era where the job opportunities for designers far outstrip the supply of new talent, there exists a serious problem in the education of library professionals who seek employment in college and research libraries. Accredited graduate degrees are still required for too many positions, often for no good pedagogical reason, and while the growth of large online programs is increasing the supply of credentialed graduates, it is not obvious to me that these types of graduates are what is required. This is a difficult topic for many, given the history, sense of identity and somewhat protectionist ideology that runs through accreditation, but in my experience there is almost no serious discussion (with notable exceptions such as Clarke & Bell 2018) at a national, never mind international, level about educational quality or how to deliver the education of information professionals who are prepared to lead user-centred design efforts in a non-traditional environment.

It is important to note that an education in the design methods I advocate here is not equivalent to coding or programming; it is a focus on understanding people, observing them and engaging with them in a mutual exploration of options and alternatives to current practices. This skillset involves any number of soft skills and social science knowledge that are likely more important and difficult to acquire than technical or programming capabilities. Such skills are not alien to librarians but must be cultivated and applied if the social capital benefits are to be realised.

In an earlier work (Dillon 2008) I proposed a shift to a more studio-based form of education for library professionals to take students out of talking-head classrooms into active learning experiences involving product and service design. With the exception of a few programs, I believe we have made far too little progress on this front. Examinations of curricular offerings across programs might encourage one to believe that user-centredness is generally present in Master's degrees, but too few graduate schools in our field really provide the sort of learning and hands-on design experiences that will prepare new professionals for the challenges involved in the kind of work outlined here. Again, there are exceptions and grounds for optimism in some of the curricular initiatives at top iSchools (see, for example, the new design methods sequence required at Pittsburgh, or the emphasis on UX across the curriculum at Texas and Michigan), but I believe the profession risks limiting the long-term prospects of generations of new graduates if educational practices and accreditation standards don't change, if only because those with the design thinking skills we require will have far better prospects for careers in other sectors.

Conclusion

This chapter has explored a particular way of addressing what might be considered an existential challenge for academic libraries. It proposes moving from a 'collections and locations'-based view of service to one that pushes designerly thinking as a means of creating and enabling meaningful and continuous information solutions in context. Applied across the university, design thinking methods have the potential to increase the social capital of academic libraries, particularly where design thinking is used to address challenges in working practices for better-resourced actors, by enhancing structural, cognitive and relational connections in the network.

To engage in this type of new library practice requires the formation of design teams well prepared in methods of user-centred problem solving, and familiar with a social capital theory for framing purposive action in an organisational context. Such preparation is not typically provided by traditionally accredited programs; consequently it is important for leadership to agitate for and provide opportunities for appropriate change in education or even hiring practices. This is no time for protectionist stances.

Conceiving the future through a social capital perspective serves to push libraries to align themselves with the critical mission of their home institutions and to emphasise local solutions where necessary. This involves a certain degree of risk and a willingness to move outside the comfort zone of protectionist action, but the returns are likely to have greater benefit than any alternative course.

References

ACRL Research Planning and Review Committee., (2018). 2018 top trends in academic libraries: a review of the trends and issues affecting academic libraries in higher education. *College & Research Libraries News*. 79(6), 286–293, 300. doi:10.5860/crln.79.6.286

Benedetti, A., (2017). Promoting library services with user-centered language. *portal: Libraries and the Academy*. 17(2), 217–234. doi:10.1353/pla.2017.0013

Connaway, L. and Hood, E., (2016). *Integrating the library in the life of the user: an annotated bibliography of practical ideas*. Dublin, OH: OCLC Research. http://www.oclc.org/content/dam/research/publications/2015/oclcresearch-library-in-life-of-user.pdf

Chalmers, A., (2013). *What is this thing called science?* 4th ed. St. Lucia, Australia: University of Queensland Press.

Clarke, R. I. and Bell, S., (2018). Transitioning from the MLS to the MLD: integrating design thinking and philosophy into library and information science education. In: J. Percell, L. C. Sarin, P. T. Jaeger and J. C. Bertot, eds. *Re-envisioning the MLS: perspectives on the future of library and information science education*. Bingley, UK: Emerald. pp. 195–214. doi:10.1108/S0065-28302018000044A018

CLIR., (2008). *No brief candle: reconceiving research libraries for the 21st century*. Washington, DC: Council on Library and Information Resources. https://www.clir.org/wp-content/uploads/sites/6/pub142.pdf

Dillon, A., (2008). Accelerating learning and discovery: refining the role of academic librarians. In: *No brief candle: reconceiving research libraries for the 21st century*. Washington, DC: Council on Library and Information Resources. pp. 51–57. https://www.clir.org/pubs/reports/pub142/dillon

Fosmire, M., (2016). What can design thinking do for libraries? *Issues in Science and Technology Librarianship*. 83. doi:10.5062/F4SN06ZT

Holtzblatt, K. and Beyer, H., (2017). *Contextual design: design for life*. 2nd ed. New York: Morgan Kaufmann.

Howison, J. and Bullard, J., (2015). Software in the scientific literature: problems with seeing, finding, and using software mentioned in the biology literature. *Journal of the Association for Information Science and Technology. 67(9), 2137–2155.* doi:10.1002/asi.23538

Johansson-Sköldberg, U., Woodilla, J. and Çetinkaya, M., (2013). Design thinking: past, present and possible futures. *Creativity and Innovation Management.* 22(2), 121–146. doi:10.1111/caim.12023.

Lawson, B., (2005). *How designers think: the design process demystified.* 4th ed. Oxford: Architectural Press.

Lin, N., (2001). *Social capital: a theory of social structure and action.* Cambridge, UK: Cambridge University Press.

Meier, J. J. and Miller, R. K., (2016). Turning the revolution into an evolution: the case for design thinking and rapid prototyping in libraries. *College & Research Libraries News.* 77(6), 283–286. doi:10.5860/crln.77.6.9506

Nahapiet, J. and Ghoshal, S., (1998). Social capital, intellectual capital and the organizational advantage. *The Academy of Management Review.* 23(2), 242–266. doi:10.2307/259373

National Research Council., (2002). *Preparing for the revolution: information technology and the future of the research university.* Washington, DC: The National Academies Press. doi:10.17226/10545

Poder, T. G., (2011). What is really social capital? A critical review. *American Sociologist.* 42(4), 341–367. doi:10.1007/s12108-011-9136-z

Ritter, F., Baxter, G. and Churchill, E., (2014). *Foundations for designing user-centered systems: what system designers need to know about people.* London: Springer.

Saunders, L., (2015). Academic libraries' strategic plans: top trends and underrecognized areas. *Journal of Academic Librarianship.* 41(3), 285–291. doi:10.1016/j.acalib.2015.03.011

Storer, R., (2014). Top 10 challenges for academic libraries in the 21st century. *SirsiDynex Blog.* 25 September. https://web.archive.org/web/20141201102208/http://www.sirsidynix.com/blog/2014/09/25/top-10-challenges-for-academic-libraries-in-the-21st-century

Conclusion: Into the Social Future

Paul J. Bracke

Introduction

Since the 1990s, libraries have been grappling with significant and accelerating changes, resulting in new strategies for serving their communities. The relationship between library and community has always been central to the value and impact of libraries, but the nature of the relationship between library and user need has changed dramatically. As we consider the ways in which digital information technologies, changing practices within higher education and broader societal movements impact upon the roles of information in everyday life, we observe how academic libraries have been developing and evolving strategies for library work centred on deepening engagement with users, with other units at their institutions and with other libraries. This model of increasing engagement and even interdependence has many implications for future libraries.

While there has been frequent discussion of the ubiquitous nature of the library of the future, such discussion has often focused on instrumental understandings of this concept. For example, with the use of digital technologies, library collections and services will be available at the user's point of need, regardless of spatial, temporal or other barriers to physical access. They may even be integrated into digital learning platforms or other online environments where library users work. While these aspects of future libraries are certainly important, these are not the only ways in which libraries are becoming ubiquitous or hold value for their users and communities. The social trajectory of academic libraries, as described by the contributions in this book, is one in which libraries are deeply embedded within the social networks of their user communities through which they co-construct services, resources and value with their users.

This emergent model of practice places the social assets of the library – its people, expertise and relationships – on equal footing with the information resources, spaces and services they provide. This is a significant shift for libraries, but the trends impacting on libraries are also impacting on society at large. Theoretical frameworks developed from the late 20th century to the present to describe and explain social and organisational changes, such as those covering social and intellectual capital and social networks, provide a conceptual framework for the future trajectory of academic libraries. As the arguments presented throughout this book demonstrate, the applicability of these frameworks is not strictly academic. They are also useful in the development of further innovations in libraries, for developing responses to the ongoing technological and social disruptions that challenge libraries and in assessing and articulating the effectiveness and impact of library contributions to the educational and scholarly life of their institutions.

The social reconfiguration of the academic library

As described in the Introduction, foremost among the trends facing academic libraries is the social nature of the response libraries are making to the evolving relationship between information need and information service in a world of ubiquitous information access and shifting notions of authority. In this environment, it is a challenge for the academic library to continue to be positioned as an authoritative provider of information resources and services. The view of the library as a collection of assets (e.g., collections, spaces, etc.) developed and managed by librarians and associated staff is being expanded to take into consideration the roles of the interaction between the library and its users in co-creating the information services that meet the needs of the community. Furthermore, shifts to neoliberal and corporatised models of higher education are leading to funding models contingent upon demonstrated value and alignment with market-oriented organisational behaviours.

Accordingly, libraries now envision themselves as dynamic actors within institutions of higher education that rely not only on their material assets but also upon intellectual capital and social networks to fulfil their mission and contribute to the success of their parent institutions. This social turn of the library into an engagement-centred paradigm represents a shift in philosophical orientation that requires libraries to think strategically at every level about their relation to their communities. From the increasing internal emphasis on organisational development and repositioning as learning organisations to the reconfiguration of services and partnerships, libraries are increasingly intentional about their social reconfiguration. The chapters in this book provide theoretically informed on-the-ground strategies currently being employed for designing and implementing the emergent social library. They present a view of reconfigured academic libraries designed to leverage their social, intellectual and human capital as well as their tangible assets through social networks at multiple levels – internally, at the campus level and with external partners – to provide authoritative services in an environment in which the value of academic libraries is under constant negotiation rather than an assumption. This shift is described in several ways throughout this work.

First, the social turn in libraries requires the adoption and development of new approaches to leading and developing the organisation, as well as evolutionary and even revolutionary shifts in existing roles, structures and practices. In Chapter 15 Dillon's discussion of design thinking 'as a means of creating and enabling meaningful and continuous information solutions in context', for example, suggests an intellectual framework for maintaining library relevance through the application of user-centred approaches and for developing social capital. This includes the possibility of strengthened connections to well-resourced actors on campus. This is an approach that leverages the social and intellectual capital within libraries, that does so by connecting academic libraries more integrally to campus social networks and that aligns with the increasingly entrepreneurial bent of many universities.

Second, active participation in socially oriented thinking about libraries suggests intentionality about the roles undertaken by librarians and how they intersect with academic networks. This is illustrated by this volume's chapters contributing to the ongoing debate on the nature of subject and functional expertise in libraries. In Chapter 7 Kessenides and Brenes explored the value of intellectual capital in the form of subject expertise within the contemporary academic library. They argued that subject-based library expertise provides the social capital necessary to develop distinctive, networked research environments in a digital age. On the other side, in Chapter 10 Kosavic and Wang described the relationship-building strategies that can emerge in the development of functional services, in this case research data management (RDM). They described, in aggregate, how libraries have been able to take advantage of the network positionality of library directors and liaisons to bridge structural holes in an institution, for example. While they acknowledge that it is not always clear why particular approaches work at institutions, they do suggest that future work could be done to provide guidance on social capital-informed approaches to RDM. This suggestion connects to Dillon's advocacy for design approaches to service development and, in the case of RDM, is one that holds promise for the co-creation of transformed global social and technical infrastructure.

Third, social and cultural approaches are not only applicable to the development of academic libraries as research environments, but also in developing critical approaches to their teaching mission. By using theoretical constructs such as social and cultural capital, in Chapter 8 Folk situated information literacy within a broader academic cultural context than that of libraries. This allows for a more nuanced view of the challenges in developing effective approaches to information literacy instruction, overcoming common obstacles to developing information literacy and critical thinking skills, and addressing persistent equity gaps. This approach also holds promise for future research into important issues such as the role of information literacy instruction in the accumulation of social and cultural capital among students.

Fourth, fulfilling the promise of these emerging roles requires evolved thinking about managing programs in support of the outreach services and collaboration needed to build and leverage social capital in the evolution of academic libraries. In Chapter 12 Metzger presented a case study of administrative strategies that enable relationship development and engagement work, particularly in outlining the intersections between strategic thinking, employee development and assessment. The definition of clear programmatic outcomes can be used for competency development, in turn allowing the library to invest in the intellectual capital of its employees in support of engagement work. Specifically, strategies for recognising skills related to relational capital which are strategically aligned and assessed reinforce the importance of relationship development. The social turn in libraries does not merely require strategic repositioning in the library to maximise the intangible assets of a library, but calls for active investment in their development.

Fifth, social capital can be a lens that is used to evaluate the health of libraries as organisations. Kalinowski's Chapter 11 used social capital perspectives from library and information science, management and marketing to examine the impact of liaison librarian turnover on academic library performance. As relational, social and intellectual capital are increasingly valued as assets of the academic library, the departure of the individuals who have developed or hold such capital can have a significant impact on the library. It was proposed that social capital theory can help library management and human resources staff to create processes and procedures around the turnover process and cultural practices within the organisation to help mitigate the impact of employee departures.

Finally, the social turn in libraries can be viewed as repositioning the library within the political economy of corporatised higher education. In an environment in which academic units and libraries are increasingly expected to engage in market or market-like behaviours, alignment of the library with external sources of funding is critical. Dillon's chapter suggested one method in which this occurs – the development of social capital and networks linking libraries to better-resourced partners on their campuses. RDM services, as described by Kosavic and Wang, are one example of this, with libraries developing services that are useful in meeting the mission of the library, but that also connect them to researchers with external grant funding. Dilworth's Chapter 14 presented a different mode of leveraging social capital in service of resource development for academic libraries. In this case, social capital is developed and leveraged to promote philanthropic support of libraries. In her Social Capital Fundraising Model, a long-term strategy to develop the social capital of the library with external partners was put forth as a pathway to successful fundraising and the alignment of the academic library with the material resources needed to achieve goals within a resource-constrained environment.

The social turn and the post-pandemic academic library

One of the challenges in compiling books such as this one is the possibility of new developments in the environment that have a major impact in the present and significant implications for our collective future. The social landscape, globally, changed significantly as this book was being developed. From 2020 to the time of writing this conclusion in 2022, the world has been experiencing a global pandemic and a reckoning around racial injustice and inequity. Both have demanded immediate response and raised important questions for the future at a societal level. The theoretical framing and practical approaches explored in this book will be even more important, moving forward, than we could have imagined when writing the proposal for this book.

The COVID-19 pandemic has caused incredible disruptions to every aspect of life worldwide. Academic libraries were not, of course, immune to its impacts. They have faced significant challenges during the pandemic: shutdowns that prevented physical access to many libraries, the rapid transition to exclusively online instruction experienced at many bricks-and-mortar universities, the challenges of managing library services in a pandemic environment and an increasingly remote workforce. Almost every aspect of academic libraries changed in some manner. The economic conditions under which academic libraries operate have also been challenging, with college and university finances stressed by enrolment challenges, loss of revenue from in-person operations that could not function as normal and, for some, the expenses of managing campuses during a pandemic in a manner that was consistent with public health guidance. This has led many libraries to operate under conditions of financial austerity, with cuts to collections and operating budgets, hiring freezes and staffing reductions. These material conditions will have enduring impact on libraries. Additionally, these factors have complicated the social pivot occurring in academic libraries and left several open questions for libraries as they emerge from the pandemic. These are all questions that the theoretical approaches outlined in this book will be helpful in addressing.

First, how will the pandemic have impacted on relationship-building activities for academic libraries? Academic libraries have been developing services, programs and partnerships for decades that bring them into closer collaboration and relationship with their user communities. This, of course, requires significant communication and opportunities to interact and collaborate with campus constituents. During the two-plus years since the pandemic's outbreak, however, some libraries have found themselves in a place where these interactions have been difficult to sustain. Some libraries, even those with established course-integrated information literacy programs, have found that opportunities for instruction have declined during the pandemic. With increased remote working and teaching, librarians, faculty and other collaborators may not be together on campus as much, and opportunities for interaction, such as seminars, may not be offered as frequently or at all. While e-mail and video-conferencing are viable communications tools, they do not necessarily offer the affordances for informal interaction that can be useful in building networks and developing social capital. While the trajectory of activities described throughout this book will likely continue, academic libraries may find themselves in a place where they are navigating the pivot to a 21st-century social organisation in an environment of changed post-pandemic social norms and modalities of work. The strategies for building social, relational and intellectual capital outlined by this volume's authors will prove useful in navigating this environment.

Second, the 'Great Resignation' has become a worldwide phenomenon in the wake of COVID-19, with many countries seeing mass resignations across economic sectors. Potential contributing factors include: shifting personal priorities, long-term job dissatisfaction, concern over personal safety during a pandemic and a desire for greater flexibility or remote working arrangements. Reductions in staffing levels and difficulties in filling vacancies pose challenges for academic libraries. On the one hand, competing demands and obligations may place constraints on the ability of librarians to engage in the sorts of activities described in earlier chapters in a time of limited staffing. At a more fundamental level, the Great Resignation highlights the need for academic libraries to focus on organisational health. Even before the pandemic, issues with organisational climate in libraries were well known. Kendrick's (2017) work on low-morale libraries highlights the experience of library employees with workplace abuse, the mental and physical health impacts of low-morale and impacts on career trajectories. These are all important issues, regardless of the specific circumstances of today, and they also disproportionately impact on library workers from marginalised backgrounds (Kendrick and Damasco 2019). In the context of the Great Resignation, addressing the climate of libraries is more important than ever. The theoretical frameworks presented in this book are applicable not only in thinking about the relationships between libraries and their users, but also in considering the relationships and cultures within academic libraries. As Kalinowski indicates in her chapter on liaison librarian turnover, social capital can improve organisational practices aimed at reducing turnover and mitigate its impacts.

At the same time as COVID-19, a reckoning on racial issues has spread worldwide. While libraries and institutions of higher education have long been concerned with issues of equity, diversity and inclusion, the murder of George Floyd and Black Lives Matter movements have served as a catalyst to heighten awareness, reflection and action about what institutions have, and have not, done to address systems of oppression, racism and injustice. This is a reckoning that has occurred globally, impacted on organisations of every sort and led to some academic libraries considering what actions and commitments they can take towards the end of advancing equity, diversity and inclusion, and in some cases transform themselves into anti-racist organisations. One notable example, the University of North Carolina Libraries' Reckoning Initiative Framework (UNC 2021), outlines the following actions:

1. Studying the past to understand what role the University Libraries has played and continues to play in upholding systems of oppression, exclusion, and inequity
2. Eradicating inequity and increasing equity throughout all library systems and services
3. Instilling antiracism practices, policies, and procedures into all library work
4. Engaging and partnering with communities that have been erased, dehumanized, silenced, or marginalized in the University Libraries or by the University Libraries
5. Making the University Libraries a more inclusive environment where both staff and library users can be their true and authentic selves
6. Prioritizing accessibility
7. Increasing the diversity of the library staff
8. Providing appropriate resources to incentivize and reward antiracist work
9. Prioritizing programs and events that promote, center, and highlight marginalized groups
10. Offering education and training to help employees become more aware of injustice, inequity, unconscious bias, and other barriers to diversity and inclusion
11. Being an engaged and active voice for racial equity, inclusion, and antiracism work on campus, in the community, and in our professional organizations.

These steps all require the reconfiguration of social networks within the library and between the library and campus; the development of social capital that supports the inclusive practices internally and in external engagement; and new forms of intellectual capital to support these shifts. Taken as an exemplar of an approach that many libraries are considering, they are clear ways in which these actions may be both informed by and understood through social theories described throughout this book. They have numerous implications for libraries and challenge them to consider the ways in which libraries can support equity and inclusion internally, and the ways in which they support the success of all students and members of their campus communities. As we consider the ways in which academic libraries are seeking to innovate, and to adapt to a post-pandemic environment, social theory can inform libraries' continued growth in a manner that invites all.

References

Kendrick, K. D., (2017). The low morale experience of academic librarians: a phenomenological study. *Journal of Library Administration*. 57(8), 846–878. doi:10.1080/01930826.2017.1368325

Kendrick, K. D. and Damasco, I. T., (2019). Low morale in ethnic and racial minority academic librarians: an experiential study. *Library Trends*. 68(2), 174–212.

UNC., (2021). University Libraries' reckoning initiative framework. Chapel Hill, NC: University of North Carolina University Libraries. https://library.unc.edu/reckoning/framework

Index